LIFE IN REVERSE

LIFE IN REVERSE

Tales of a Very Stable Narcissist

RON WESTRAY

FIRST HILL BOOKS
An imprint of Wimbledon Publishing Company Limited (WPC)

This edition first published in UK and USA 2021
by FIRST HILL BOOKS
75–76 Blackfriars Road, London SE1 8HA, UK
or PO Box 9779, London SW19 7ZG, UK
and
244 Madison Ave #116, New York, NY 10016, USA

British Library Cataloguing-in-Publication Data
A catalogue record for this book is available from the British Library.

Library of Congress Control Number: 2021944169

ISBN-13: 978-1-83998-039-8 (Hbk)
ISBN-10: 1-83998-039-7 (Hbk)

Cover image: Ginger Westray

This title is also available as an e-book.

This book is dedicated to the living memory of my mother and father:
Virginia Ann Bush Westray and Ronald Kenneth Westray, Sr.

Contents

Preface

I am a middle-aged man, in the middle of manhood. To a degree, I aim to explore the nature of conversation between an intelligent African American man and *women*. Admittedly, I'm not sure how much of this I have accomplished so far. My narcissistic tendencies are countered by an awkward, downright passive aggressiveness. This book is not about money. It's about not letting things just slip away. I may not be able to control life and death. But I *can* control this account of my life and times. I'm not coming from an egotistic place (more than some, less than others). Or perhaps I am? Ultimately, this book is also about an ability, the ability to communicate on different levels at different times (or all at once). I say *an* ability because it's not always in force; sometimes, I run a one-track thing. My actual passions are the glory of this work and not *uniqueness*.

As the title suggests, the book proceeds backwards chronologically, with each chapter representing a year in my life—sometimes meaning when the words were written, sometimes the events covered—though there are departures and exceptions and liberties taken. It is also a tribute to my mother's writing and free-verse poetry. My father's death is documented towards the end, as is my grandfather Joe Westray's luminary associations as a local jazz legend on the Pittsburgh scene. This work also involves interpolating ordinary conversation from sources such as texting and emails. Even emojis are intact. In some instances, I am using the conversation to shed light on the fallibility of human relations; and, within reason, the length of conversations *is* meant to be overbearing—in order to suggest the opening of an even larger conversation. The correspondences cover different decades and the different emotional states of different women at different ages—and my own emotional states.

I'm not trying to come off as a Don Juan. I would rather be viewed as a traveling man who has, for the most part, enjoyed the companionship and friendship of, and even marriage to, select women of different styles, over time. I am grateful for the experiences of those relationships; and this book is not a comparison of those interactions. At times, the conversations border on the mundane, but I hope they can be appreciated in the sense of reading someone else's love letters—with comparisons and relevance to the reader's own relationships.

The profundity of the writing may (or may not) contract (or expand) within, and without, your perception; however, when you think you know, look out! It has taken three decades to write, compile and finish dumping my early manuscripts into the digital realm. I could've finished sooner, but I made sure to have a little fun along the way. The idea of burning the candle at both ends pales in comparison with the wideness of the wheel that I have chosen to (and had to) turn (more than some, less than others). Within these turns, I afforded myself more time to create.

As to the length of my text conversations with my sister V., at the beginning of the book, it covers the essence of our relationship and the love we share as siblings (countered with her comparable absence in most of the writing).

Being raised by a family of women, doted on as "baby boy" and growing up in close quarters with my sister, I was taught by my mother to respect women and their privacy. Because of this, and other beliefs, I have decided to use only the initials of the women I am in dialogue with.

My third wife was also my first wife. Her name is L. We are all fragile; so, rather than purport this memoir as profound, I would prefer it be regarded as common. Finally, and as compared to the itinerary, I have not expended too much energy on women abroad. Most of my time and efforts have involved African American women. As for now, I am in my prime, and I AM.

★ ★ ★

Now this is not the end. It is not even the beginning of the end.
But it is, perhaps, the end of the beginning.

—*Winston Churchill*

Acknowledgments

People that have been particularly helpful as I developed this book include Carl Wilson (for his initial editing), Joe DiStephano (for putting me in contact with *Anthem*), Gregory Clark (for his writing suggestions and advice), Robert Sterling Beckwith (for his inspiring sarcasm, intellect and dogged resilience) and David Lidov (for his intellectual support and advice). Furthermore, the entire team at Anthem Press has given me the needed confidence to complete this arduous task; and thank you to the selected reviewers for their encouraging critiques. I would also like to thank my family, my friends and my associates for their love and support—before, during and after the evolution, and production, of this book.

Introduction

Of course it defeats the purpose to confuse the readers. However, the book was never prepared in the linear sense. It began as the journal of a college kid c. 1990, slowly expanding, over time, into an active, year-based compilation of poems, essays and interpolations (texts/emails) amid "active" writing.

On analysis, there are a *myriad* of themes imbedded in the work: Perhaps that *is* the theme? I also decided, along the way, that I wanted the reader to experience the feeling of a movie that starts in the present and proceeds backwards (*Forrest Gump* comes to mind). I always enjoyed that effect with movies; so, I set out to achieve this in reading/writing. This "technique" also has a mathematical underpinning to its justification: as a modern composer of music, "retrograde" processes are a huge part of compositional history and have added depth and complexity to the process; moreover, I am heavily influenced by these practices. Also, from a sequel point of view, and though *backwards*, it could (conceptually) allow for the addition of continued autobiographical content going *forward: a stroboscopic effect*! This "reverse" idea also emanates from my personal plight: I often remark that "I do everything backwards" (e.g., I only learn the "hard way"). For instance, my last two children were born post divorce! So, the title corroborates a (sort of) metaphor of my life→the structure of the book supports the title→and the subtitle supports the nature of the main character. My mother, who knew me best, preempted (and predicted) the title of the book in her original postcard (the cover art for the book) upon which she scripted these words: "Reverse is a state … of being."

This is a book about a jazz musician—and the place of the artist/musician in his society/in the jazz world and how the artist/musician navigates the challenges he faces—also my own artistic lineage, from my mother and grandmother to my father and grandfather; but it is not a book about jazz. The book is also about love; sex and marriage and family; and the pull of artistic practice that takes the musician away from this life at home.

This is a story of surviving the deaths of my father and grandfather at an early age; of being raised in a tight-knit situation with my older sibling sister and by a widowed mom who survived my father by 42 years, without remarrying. I see my audience as a general audience—readers that like biographies and higher-level writing (including the "jazz" reader). The book (memoir/epic journal) *can* also be viewed as a book about everything and nothing (at the same time). A large part of the book contains disparate correspondences much like a journal. Hence, a certain disjunction between the narratives could be expected; but the central character binds *all* of the topics together.

This book is about *conflicts*, *resolutions* and *extremes*, and, as mentioned earlier, it proceeds backwards. The character is operating above and below morality (as well as passivity and aggression, reason vs. reaction, etc.). Writing spans from academia, to poetry and existential essays, to cursing bouts, marriages, divorces, sabbaticals, residencies, incarceration and so on.

The anti-marginalization/stereotyping of the (average) African American male is an important part of the subliminal intent in this work—not only as it relates to racism but also in relation to career marginalization: for example, it's important to me that my contemporaries realize that my (intellectual) goals (though invisible) are high. I would like readers to walk away with the idea that any African American *man* (or musician) *could be* experiencing life (and love) through more than the stereotyped lens that has been assigned us—an intellectual lens (if you will), among other lenses—and that he or she can appreciate the idea of an individual that has worked hard in their profession—and consider the nature of the (methodical) approach required to have captured *some* of the experiences that form such a reality—in time, on time.

Ultimately, it's a story about a man surviving these, and other, ubiquities (as generally described in the writing), carrying forth his legacies and establishing his own: Surviving, and enjoying, existential-actuality.

Chapters 51/50

For the first time in a while, I heard the incessant hum of the I-20—the interstate just a "field's length" from my bedroom, in the same neighborhood I grew up in, the same block. Overnight, as the blue horn blew more than necessary, the roar of the intra-freight train awakened me. As I turned over in my bed, again, it made me sad to think, to know, that good things, and bad things, shall return. There it goes again—the sound of commerce—the echo of a semi-truck tire bursting forth like gunfire as the driver desperately makes his payload roll. And there goes the freight train again—just now—tooting its own horn like "We got this!" And out in the garage, serenity is eroding at a rapid pace.

Harangue II

Now that we are meeting our spouses and kids, again, for the first time, let's talk.

The first sign of devolution was the food and toilet tissue dilemma. With regard to annual resolutions, this could have been viewed as a time to conserve, eat less, do more, and far less toilet tissue would have been needed.

Second, I can no longer view prerecorded shows; kissing on camera already looks weird; and how did the idea of the filmed love scene (porn notwithstanding) come to subjugate the human imagination?

Third, stationing on the sofa, catching up on complete seasons of a cancelled show after the Peloton membership has waned, is not the answer; and enough of this fake obsession with observing a "performance of the vicissitudes of existence" on stage and screen—all while the vacillated upon (e.g., the transient) get zero respect in real life.

Last, good nutrition, being fit and rest will not only help today, it will help us in the future; and inside of wise choices, let us also proceed based on our best thinking, not our worst fears. The expansion rate of the universe is accelerating. Vamoose!

Harangue

Nobody could *just play*. Everyone comes out with an umbilical cord, knowing nothing. Even Nostradamus—he absorbed many absolutes in order to become. But myth is easier for people to digest. It's like sugar and salt: you know it's not healthy, but you prefer the taste to the truth. The artist is also guilty of leaning back when the work is done, and the cameras show up, and describing how their feelings had to do with the production. Yeah, right, I assure you they weren't thinking about feelings when choosing the right sounds and harmonies; they were within the craft. It's how art is done. The products of art evoke feelings, but feelings do not create art. In order to draw a straight line, Picasso's deeper truths will not suffice. Jackson Pollock did not know what he would get; but he had technique. Rewarding the skill of the artist, technique feeds the soul of the purveyor. We all want to be perceived a certain way (but that's not necessarily the truth). Amid a myriad of possibilities, people only appreciate what they (choose to) understand.

Expression, along with commercialization and materialization, will continue to do battle with logic and rationale, and no matter the circumstance, homo sapiens will find a way to divide an issue.

For instance, during the current crisis (in relationship to masking and vaccination) the idea of "following" quickly becomes an issue of "liberty," but no one dares question freedom of expression. Sometimes, anti-expertise and anti-intellectual sentiment have to be checked by the presence of experts. It's similar to the idea of blues emoting (expressing) versus jazz improvisation (following). Tethered to this idea is the falsehood that blues expression is awarded only to the experienced—the Robert Johnson decision, the Jimi Hendrix question, the Billie Holiday saga and so on. I wish to debunk the romantic notion that these artists sound the way they do (Bob Dylan, etc.) because they are consciously channeling real life through their instruments—that Billie sounds the way she does because she was abused and so on. While this may be good for commercial spin, it does a disservice to the integrity of the artist's talent (not circumstance) and how it might have developed without said hardships. Having assimilated Bessie Smith, Ma Rainey, Lil Hardin and many more, it *is* possible that Holiday would still use the same vibrato and hang her head to one side, saying yes, at the end of a phrase. She understood the blues as a dialect. This is why she sang as she did.

B. B. King would still play a single line (with no chords) and shake his head in a mad frenzy when the notes "go" up high. "Blue" is not earned by camping out at "the crossroads" and waiting on the devil to pay you a visit—or the balance in your checking account—much less, savings (pun). Placing a heavy vibrato in the right spot, on the right note, is not a mere feeling. It's what you do—there. When Lester Young holds his head to the side and looks sad, that's not why he is killing it on the blues. Aside from growing up in a whole family of astute multi-instrumentalists, you will find the same implications in the phrasing of his predecessors. Lester does not sound "fine and mellow" because he was mistreated in the Army: *My sergeant just called me "boy"—let me play a phrase to express that.* Perhaps he was a fine and mellow person (I believe his siblings would have attested to that). Marlon Brando, for instance, wasn't great because he was eccentric. He was eccentric because he was great; Ellington, the same.

It's the same reason you think Billie was singing the blues based on her life story. That is a fairy tale that has been presented to you for purchase. Ask Billie, and she would probably say, "Honey Chile, I'm not all that sad, right now. That's just the way Satchmo used to sing it."

And let's not forget that the blues is not just an idea about being sad. Louis Armstrong already debunked that ideology—as did Albert Murray in his book *Stomping the Blues.*

The understanding of the history informs every choice, each nuance. It's not coming from "them." It is the sound of music—the choices we have learned, as in life. Moving on, did you know that history has ultimately revealed that Mozart was not such an exceptional child? He, like many, made a decision to become; and he practiced his wig off. It's the same for Bird (ask Jo Jones). John, clearly, was not "Coltrane" yet (except on his Army badge). They are great because they practiced being great—sounding great. Miles was the son of a doctor, and he could play the blues. The blues is a theory, too. It can be assimilated absent negative life experiences. Exactly how experienced is that eight-year-old prodigy on the morning show playing Muddy Waters blues transcriptions? That kid has learned the language of a craft—the function of a language. This debunks the idea that you have to "live it." In fact, it would take you far longer to try and live the blues into your art form than it would for you to do your homework and learn the actual language of the blues. Ben Webster is not expressing visceral sensations in his tone quality. Save the romance for Netflix. Clapton is not playing the way he does because he grew up in the dirty south. He can play Robert Johnson because he practiced his ass off—memorizing language, blues and otherwise. And the idea that Robert Johnson received his talent from the devil is just another way of undermining his singular achievement. It's easy to be inspired, but it's hard to get started. It's hard to accept that visible talent is preceded by invisible toil. It's easy to assume cabin boredom, but it's hard to subdue a fever. Just as you cannot imagine something that doesn't exist, you cannot hear something that is not (already) there.

Unfortunately, it comes down to rights. It's the same reason people are protesting. The machine has told them that they deserve what they want—that they deserve to be, buy, do, think what they want in the name of freedom (oh yeah, and commerce). You have the liberty to focus on the fact that you have rights—as opposed to the suggestions of science. You can, also, choose to ignore

Holiday's (actual) talent in favor of a romanticized notion. Real achievement takes hard work and sacrifice; so don't confuse fame with greatness. Greatness, *style*, means staying the course. There was no "10,000-hour rule" when I came along, thank goodness. We practiced one million hours without even knowing it. Talent is a production item, not an endowment.

It's not meant for everyone to be great; but ironically, the sacrifices that are required are eerily similar to those that are being imposed on us all at this time. To those in opposition to silence, patience, self-control, reflection, courage, dignity, reverence for mankind, logic and the natural sciences, welcome to the world of the disciplined. But if you work hard enough, long enough, learning and doing that which inspires, you will be soulful.

REALITY: Perceptions are different from person to person; our individual, multiple explications of signs and symbols render us, at the least, unable to describe things within a shared philosophy; at most—unlikely to. Hence, what you call "reality" represents a singular perspective; even physical properties are hardly more than "signs" to be interpreted. Thus, actuality, too, is a mere prospect.

BOREDOM: To "claim" boredom is to say that you don't care about something. It is to say that "That which needs to be done may cause physical, perhaps, 'emotional' discomfort." After all, life is all about comfort, right? And you already work hard enough, right? To profess that you are bored is to say that "I don't 'feel like' sweeping"; "I don't 'feel like' going to the gym"; "I don't 'feel like' taking the car to get its oil changed"; "I don't 'feel like' pulling those weeds." And that feel-like (feel-good) part, that's your brain on comfort. Though we tend to hold others accountable for our woes and worries, most problems are internal—other problems are (materially) external; and yet, amid a myriad of human explanations for our (various) stations (in life), (self) realizations (and delusions) manifest as embitterment and condemnation of others (and ourselves). Then, the "blame-game" converts (downward) into a selfishness that pervades and contaminates our lives and our collective (human) "mind" (not to be compared to the functions of the (human) brain). The truth is that "true" happiness comes by means of solving life's problems; but the atypical "doer" can only be described in relationship (and in response) to the group (the bored).

QUERY: Because we humans know that we are here, and that we have come to dominate the entire planet, we also know that we will not remain here indefinitely. To sustain the expectation that those of us living presently (or later) would universally, voluntarily, as a single species, be smart enough in their own time, to limit the use of their own resources, is futile. A person that is not afraid to live is also not afraid to die; consequently, the fear of dying is the fear of life; because without death, life has no meaning. Perhaps, the sooner we accept mortality, the lesser the industrial resources we will waste attempting to bolster humanity, materially; and more becomes possible?

SPIRIT: The complexity of the human experience is amazing; the transmogrification from childhood to adulthood is magical. Religion generates Spirit, Science corroborates Energy and betwixt these (opposing) beliefs resides Magisteria—equalizing the authority of both. Words (and ideas) are substituted for the true reflections of the psyche; for, the growth of the "essential" being can only be quantified by deeds.

DESTINY: As modern society barrels its way toward dystopia, I am reminded that you can only "feel" things if you are living—that life is (possibly) designed to be painful, confusing, disappointing and depressing. Without fail, "want" (continually) equals lack; and expectation (always) leads to disappointment. The battle (of wanting and expecting—and the concurrent struggle to make this a way of life) must be acknowledged. However, physical, emotional and monetary strifes are comparably small "prices" to pay to retain a pulse; because just being alive is great!

FUTURE MEMORY: Amid the actuality of social angst and physical distance, perhaps we can fully understand and appreciate the virtue of the previous prevailing idea of "YOLO" (you only live once). As we learn and accept that this idea has more to do with internal, not external factors, where do we go from here? Some have suggested that we return to normal as soon as possible—that is to say, back to the signifying, chest bumping, choreographed-for-television world. How did that work out for us?

Presently, "YOLO" has more to do with saying NO than saying yes; and the incontrovertible fact of "only living once" should never have been reduced to the prospect of mere fun, games and vacations.

FUTURE MEMORY II: Within the dawn of a new paradigm, we might accept the idea that congregational factors may never be the same. Artificial intelligence (via technology) could soon dominate educational, industrial and domestic landscapes.

FUTURE MEMORY III: There seems to be a debate between those who still long for the ostensible awesomeness of the pre-COVID world—wherein false imperatives and real impertinences prepared us for nothing ahead—and those who are in awe of the switch to relevant innovation, renewed awareness and the verisimilitude of it all.

FUTURE MEMORY IV: Never before in American history has the economic window closed for so many at once. As the spigot of death and despair fully opens upon the previously disenfranchised, we might consider the fact that integration was manifested as mere compliance.

As majorities discuss the statistics with feigned amazement (as if the underlying social-political conditions suddenly appeared along with the pandemic), may we never again pretend-to-forget the fact that economic disparity and marginalization correlate directly to *health*. And you know this, man!

FUTURE MEMORY V: To profess the hope that people will have a new appreciation for the things we can no longer do is a dupe. It is to say that we should return to some of the same useless patterns that rendered us ill prepared. Conversely, I hope that we will continue to appreciate many of the things that we are having to do.

FUTURE HAPPINESS: Clearly, scientists could only dream of emissions-free data. So, before we start 1950s car-hopping and idle time at drive-in movies, let us consider that the planet has given us a one-time pass to clean the air. The most dangerous part about our desire to return to normal life is infection; but the most destructive and devastating aspect will be an incremental return to the same carbon footprint as in the past.

★ ★ ★

I hate that I love you.
In the storm, in the mist of everything, look how beautiful the rainbow is.
Look high and look low; look at the rainbow go.
And as the rainbow has no purpose when times are good, I don't love you as I should.
For, when times are good, loving you seems to get in my way.
In fact, I hate that I love you.

As with all things that were already vulnerable prior to COVID, my relationship with L. has, once again, ended (a zero-sum game).

★ ★ ★

8/14/20:

Hi, L.

I prefer Ron, not Ronald. You only use that when I'm in trouble. Thanks for this, and thanks for finally admitting to your role in this historical dilemma of ours. Due to a hack, I haven't had access to this email since May, until last night. So, I also read your letter from mid-July. It sounded just like the other letters in which you went back through everything that has negatively transpired in the relationship. You can't get over it—perhaps even from 1999. And as you stated, you couldn't regain your passion, which led to the laxness about returning my texts and calls, effectively turning me off, too.

Furthermore, who would not want their family with them during the quarantine? I recall bickering over the fact that you wanted me to come to you all. I do not recall you ever saying, "We want to come to you." I would have welcomed my family with open arms. That was never the conversation. So, lose the fib about me rejecting you all during Covid (btw: that sounds nothing like me). You may say we had a misunderstanding about that, instead, or you may continue to build your own narrative (just as you did about me "moving on")—neither of which is accurate, but all of which suits your innocent-bystander narrative. Now I realize that you were actually pouting and punishing me for your false concept of me rejecting you all during the quarantine. When have I ever rejected my family? You need to reassess that idea/conversation. I certainly will not be embracing that as a matter of fact, nor will your premise haunt me, because it's not true.

Overall, it's all been "the pits" with you for as long as I can remember; I honestly can't remember a sustained good time with you from any era. I wish I could. I want to be able to. And for the record, I have never told any woman that I want to control her outright (or whatever you said). And as for the guy that you described could have "controlled" you with his sweetness, I'm more than certain that I have been that guy, too. Be for real. You can't be molded by any guy—remember that? That is your quote. And that's too bad, 'cause I do like to, at least, feel that way—knowing that women do what they want to do, including rationing such titles or not. I'm not just learning that. Congratulations! You did it, L.! I have never felt that I *had* you, and that has nothing to do with proximity, per se. It's all been too hard for as long as I can recall, and for what? What have I, actually, gotten from our exchange that you did not get? Don't say the children. I never got what I needed or wanted, emotionally, before the children or after.

You have been a hard case the entire time, and for what? You need to ask yourself why you could never let go and let a real man have you. Trust issues about me, you say? Well, that's the "chicken vs. egg" concept. Perhaps if I had ever gotten any real feelings from you, I would have been inspired to be yours fully. Instead, for as long as I can remember you have been "rationing" your devotion (and sex) to me, as if I should be grateful. I guess that's how your older sisters taught you to treat a man that *really* wants you: make him suffer. I'm just guessing. I'm not angry, but I won't be at peace with the situation for some time. Maybe we will resurface as some kind of real friends—something we have never, ever been. Take Care. Westray—Out!

8/8/20:

Ronald,

I am sitting here thinking about the discord we are experiencing. I realized that I have never really been able to say things to you. I have always felt that in my attempts to speak to you, tell you my feelings, I have always been shot down. In my attempts to ask you questions or explain to you my misunderstandings or simply my perspectives on what you might be saying, I have always been shot down. Perhaps that was because of the way I expressed them. Perhaps you sensed my fear or apprehension in saying them to you, and you went in on me, almost as if I were wrong for asking or objecting to your views.

I hate confrontation. I hate trying to explain myself and in doing so, it never comes out right. It seemingly, always makes it worse. How I wished you knew me, how I felt, so that I didn't have to explain myself. This has always been my challenge with you. We have never been able to communicate or simply talk to each other in a safe space, semi judgment-free. So much has been marred by ineffective communication, compounded by resentment and hurt. We have caused each other so much hurt and disappointment.

For the record, I have never disregarded your efforts to show me love. I have heard you and have considered everything you have expressed to me in intent and actions. Many things I have agreed with and understood. Many, I had trouble accepting because they didn't resonate with me. I still had questions. Either way, so much was never resolved, new things entered the picture, and at the core, we or I didn't communicate these things. We were never on the same page.

I have had a lot of time to think, pray, and deal with myself, lately. I hate the way I feel. I hurt because of the way that things have transpired. I apologize for being a part of your hurt.

Whether you say it or not, you are hurt. We are both hurting. This is not the way we planned it. We did not foresee that after March we would be here. Both of us were too stubborn and proud to submit to the other, to say I love you and I miss you. Love is not proud. Yet, pride won. Pride, with a myriad of other feelings, won over. And so, this is what it is. Here we are, again.

I will be at peace with you. At the core of all of this anger is deep-seated hurt and disappointment and love for each other. Our roots are too deep! The love is too deep! We have disappointed each other in that we have not said or given in to the other because we felt that the other wasn't giving enough or equal. Yet, we both believe we have given everything.

Ronald, so much time has passed. I am not angry. I am heartbroken. Again, I never imagined this. I just did not understand your refusal of our "quarantining" together. I was relying on your creativity to help with the girls during this time and to be with me. I felt rejected. I felt you were being selfish and made other plans for your time. After a while, I simply felt I was being played. I tried to express this in the first phone call, then in a letter. Eventually, I believed I made the decision that you wanted anyway.

We are both two, beautiful people. We have three beautiful children together. I am not angry with you. I honestly cannot imagine a life without speaking to you, hearing your voice.

My love for you is beyond my control. At this time though, I need us to resolve to be at peace with each other. I hope we can agree on this.

Love,

L.

7/12/20:

Wow! Who knew that after all of our attempts from January until now, that we would be in this place. After all of the attempts to reconcile and move forward, that we would not be speaking, not expressing any forms of love that we did in March, before this pandemic. But this is what has been proven, the effects of this pandemic.We have been forced to deal with those things that have not been dealt with. And to that effect, I am tired of feeling and dealing in the manner in which we have been trying to cope and exist.

I can't express enough that I am writing this letter in love. I am writing it because I need to be able to tell you how I have been feeling for some time. And I promise you I am not writing it for a response. I am not writing it to pass judgment. I felt that when I was speaking to you on the phone you were not hearing me. I wanted sympathy, empathy of the fact that I was hurting about quarantining with the girls, when I wanted to do this jointly. I thought that this time was such an opportune time to be together as a family, considering the fact that we had discussed moving to Canada. I thought and hoped that you would have seen it the same. I didn't understand that if we were coming from one home straight to where you were, that it would be a problem.

When you declined, resentment set in, especially since you never voiced any hope or insistence that we get there soon. I felt as if you did not want to see us, me.

Again, I am writing this, expressing this, because I have been hurting for a long time. I can't help reiterating my sentiments of what I felt when you said you wanted to marry again. I believed with all my heart that you were ready for who I was as a person, a woman, the mother of your children, someone who has always been in love with you. I believed that you knew me.That you respected who I was spiritually, and where I wanted to remain. I believed that you were privy to the things that I felt about past hurts in the relationship as it related to other women. Finally, I believed that we were going to grow together and raise our girls. I believed that we were a more mature, better version of who we were 10 years ago.

I know that you don't like to hear me say this, but it is how I feel. I did not know that your marijuana dependency had increased. I did not know or anticipate your expectations for me to provide for you sexual experiences that you had with other partners. I honestly was caught off guard. And I can honestly say that had I known, I would have held off on moving forward with marriage.

But then again, I was so excited by the fact that you wanted to do this again that I did not ask any questions or look for anything that would make me question my decision and resolve to be with you. I have not been able to quite shake you off.

It's interesting to me that you say that you have always wanted this relationship more than I did. Perhaps that was true in our initial dating stages of the 90s. But since our vows from the first marriage, my heart has always been faithful to you. It has affected and determined all of my relationships that came thereafter. I always had a problem with trusting you, after finding out about your infidelity. This second time around, you renewed my trust in you by your simple action of remarrying. I believed again, that you knew me, you knew that I trusted you. I believed that you would not hurt me in that way again.

I couldn't believe the arguments that ensued after we married the second time. It was crazy! And I always walked away hurt and confused. I always looked at the fact that I took off of work and flew to Toronto to be with you, to show you that I wanted our marriage to work. I was determined to show you that I understood that we were apart physically, by distance, but I wanted you to know that I was invested in you and our marriage. I would always be greeted by the comment that you felt uncomfortable with me. You could not feel my energy. You never had anyone else complain to you about your smoke. But I looked at the fact that I had been working all week, traveled to be with you, and perhaps was a little tired when I got there, but was happy to be with you. I just simply wanted to be where you were. I felt like you never considered that I might be feeling some things too. And then came the arguments. Then came the calling out of my name, accompanied by so many acts of lovelessness. And every time I left, I asked myself what had I gotten myself into? I would say to myself that I did not deserve this. I would question how long I could sustain it. And then

I would say or remember that you lost your mom and that I did not want to feel like I abandoned you. And so I stayed and hoped that things would get better.

Eventually, you stopped calling me out of my name. Although, I could never understand how you could be with a person that you felt so strongly about calling her out of her name! That is not to say that you have never done things to me to make me beyond angry. And yet, I could never fathom calling you anything as despicable or deplorable as what you truly thought of me. The most harm came when you told me that you had been with women that had given you more than you could take or imagine! I would wonder why you wanted to marry me if you had all those things available to you. The whole dynamic changed and has never been regained.

I was so intent on proving to you that I loved you and was willing to do whatever you asked. I wanted you to know that I was all in for making you happy and letting you know that you were all I wanted. I suffered all forms of degradation, berating, your invasion of my personal space to make me feel fear of you? I don't know. I guess what you were going for was domination? Crazy! Never heard a man tell me that he wanted to dominate me. Yet if he were smart and wanted to dominate me, he would have showered me with so much love, not to be confused with sex, although that would've worked as well.

He would've showered me with genuine affection and never tried to compare me with something he had in his past. He would have valued the opportunity that he chose in asking me to marry him, by putting me above all others.

Again, Ronald, I am writing this to you because I need to express to you my personal truth. I could never say it to you. I know you would never receive it. Communication has always been flawed. And again, I am not expressing this because I want a response.

Actually, I do not want a response. I don't want to continue in a spiral of exchanges out of hurt or anger. I don't want a tit for tat in terms of what the other has provided or given or whatever. I just have to say what I've been feeling because I have never said it. You are and will always be an integral part of my life. You are my history. You are all I have ever known. And so I needed you to know this. I don't know how to heal and I am sure you have your hurts and grievances too. I know that you know that I love you. And I know that if you are honest, you have always been able to say that I loved and was still in love with you.

Anyway, I am sitting here in my car on a beautiful Sunday. I pray for you and for me every day. I pray that we would be able to heal. I pray for love and peace in our lives. The word for today said to wait on the Lord. I am and have been waiting for the Lord to give me directions and insight into our relationship. I trust and hope that you are praying for the same. And to that end, I trust your guidance in deciding what we do moving forward. I do ask that if you choose to respond, you express yourself in compassion for how I express my truth. I do love you. Always have.

Your wife,

L.

⋆ ⋆ ⋆

January 2020: Around this time I was in a preliminary conversation with GC regarding setting music to Kenneth Burke's music manuscripts; due to COVID, it never panned out.

GC: Ron, the Burkes called last night, and the brothers are comfortable with giving us access to the music diaries.

ME: Wow this is great!

GC: Ron, I put a set of photos of Burke's music notations in a file on Google Drive. It all seemed too big for text message. Take care, G

ME: Hey. OK thank you. Until soon. I'm driving along. About 30 miles out from home.

GC: Good news.

⋆ ⋆ ⋆

ME: Hey. Can you resend the Burke scores? I goofed up … Never mind, found it!

GC: Good.

ME: A preliminary idea would be to compose a jazz/modern suite based on his complete score archive, accompanied by his voice, a la narration.

GC: Those are just a sampling. There are a lot more notebooks. When and if you want to proceed, I'll connect you with his sons, who are his literary executors and hold the rights. They may have voice recordings. There is also a large archive in the Penn State Special Collections of his stuff, I don't know if there is music there.

ME: OK. That's great info. I really would like to make contact and propose that idea ASAP.

GC: There is also this: https://www.kbjournal.org/carroll. When you want me to contact them to introduce you let me know.

ME: OK maybe this week while I'm in Toronto. I like new targets so sooner is better.

GC: I'll check with you early in the week and you can tell me when to go ahead.

ME: Ok, great! Suffer me (if you will) and read this journal review of my opus from 2005. The piece is aging like a fine Scotch. This would be my calling card to the Burkes. You may share it if you deem that proper.

GC: Thanks. Glad to have it to read. I just sent an initial and preliminary query to the Burkes to see if they are interested.

ME: Thank you. Btw: That opus was commissioned based on the merit of a previous Mingus program I did for Jazz at Lincoln Center. Stanley Crouch had this to say:

Dear Westray—

Congratulations on a major achievement in your Mingus arrangements. I hope you are commissioned later to do versions of "The Shoes of the Fisherman's Wife," "Open Letter to Duke," "Tensions," "Alice in Wonderland," and "What Love?" Anyway, I want to talk with you about the recording because I have been assigned to do the liner notes. I have been a Mingus fan since about 1960, and found this work some of the finest that I have heard done with his music. What brilliance, what feeling, what dedication! You are part of the true vanguard: the serious ones, not the fakers or poseurs.

Someone who was less serious or less talented than you would not have even attempted what you achieved, which took music back to where it always stars—in hearing. Mingus would have been stunned by how well you heard the breadth and power of his material. Anyway, what you have produced is one of the best jazz recordings I have heard in a long time. I think, with BIG TRAIN and A LOVE SUPREME it is one of the LCJO's masterpieces (if not, all three are mighty close). Take care of yourself and work on that exceptional talent that you have.

It's the same thing that happened to Joe Westray:
Perhaps something about us Westrays makes others believe that we don't need any assistance (or perhaps don't deserve any). So I'm just trying to stay alive and do it myself ... lol.

I think I am ahead of the process; but it has, at times, been hell.
What is the "it" I speak of?
True acknowledgment.

GC: Wow. I know SC well enough to be certain such an acknowledgement is both rare from him & absolutely honest. Thanks for sharing that. I visited him a few months ago in a care center. He's a diminished version but still thoroughly SC.

ME: Indeed. Oh man I was not aware of that. That saddens me; but, as you have just reported, I know he is still SC.

* * *

Will I? Never!

ME: Let's say that I'm special. You would expect that I would have some idiosyncrasies; and you would expect that my mate would understand those things. So, essentially, she doesn't respect my speciality. The problem is that she patronizes me at other times. But that's not an idea that I should have to sell. Who needs a mate like that?

T: How does she benefit being with you?

ME: She has benefited far, far more than I have.

T: I'm not sure you are ready for the truth.

ME: I love the truth.

T: You cannot handle the truth.

ME: You don't even believe that. Tell me. What's this truth?

T: You exist at the center of the World you have created.

ME: I've been with enough women that fully appreciate me to know how I should be being treated.

T: Here comes the Motherf★★★ing Truth!

ME: Bring it!

T: I do not want to be the one.

ME: It's OK. I would love to know.

T: Even if it doesn't feed your ego? Be honest with yourself, Ron.

ME: I'm living it every day. I have no problem with honesty. This is my truth. I've been good to her. I'm just looking for some basic respect from this woman. My consolation is that I don't need anything from her. I give credit where credit is due. I would love to say I can't live without her because of this or that, but there's nothing there. I've read enough history to know that my ego is a liar. I'm a scholar, baby. I understand things outside myself.

T: What difference will it make?

ME: Bring it!

T: OK, you are f*cking with women with low esteem, and you give nothing of yourself but your dick. And you ain't sh*t on the human level of companionship!

ME: You just called me out (and cooled me out). Thank you.

T: Stop expecting more than what you give, Ron!

ME: Ah … so … Well, it's not conscious.

T: Well, it's obvious. Pay for sex and keep it moving. Otherwise, you are ruining the lives of women who care for you, and that is sheer evil.

ME: I don't do the "public" sex thing. I appreciate the objectivity.

T: You surround yourself with people not as smart as you because it's easy.

ME: Life is hard enough.

T: You are smarter than that.

ME: I'm also around a lot of people who are smarter than me. I inhabit both of those worlds

T: Ah, the twins!

ME: Yes and Yes.

T: What difference will this epiphany make?

ME: It's already making a huge difference; and I thank you. No one ever told me that. I'm going to digest it and be aware.

T: Who are you?

ME: Hey, you got to keep something for yourself. People taking all the time. Some people keep *this* much some people keep *that* much. I keep *this* much.

T: You're a pimp.

ME: Thank you … 

T: You use women for their very essence.

ME: I also bring a lot to the table as a man. I'm not the pimp on the corner. I'm a very focused person. Most of my energy has gone into my art. I have a little bit left over for relationships, and that's it.

T: You keep telling yourself that horror story. Women do not benefit from being with you. You will continue with great creativity, but I want you to be better.

ME: You've known me since I was a boy. Why *am* I this way?

T: Just stop being an ass (smile).

ME: Ah so …!

T: Your mom gave you so much love. But due to your dad's death, you didn't witness a giving relationship between two people. Therefore you have no template for what a relationship actually takes. You are what is referred to as a creative, and you also have no clue what it is that *you* need.

ME: Perhaps.

T: F★ck you!

ME: No, really, no one has articulated that to me. I have never been to an analyst. Though, I think I'm good now, lol.

T: Everyone is in your world. But how much greater you could be if you … (fill in the blank)

ME: Cared?

T: You scare me.

ME: I don't mean to scare you. (I'm sounding like Brad Pitt in *Meet Joe Black*.) It's all I know. The human thing, you know? All I can do is let art speak for what I can't express. To me, that is enough.

T: How will I benefit from blessing you with this insight?

ME: Just know that you were the only person to ever articulate that to me.

T: Obviously!

★ ★ ★

L.: Lol! Today is Sonny Schitt's *[inside joke]* birthday! You know you wanna laugh!

ME: Hi. Just got your messages. Call me when you have a moment. BTW: If you don't want to talk, let me know when you are available; I will text you briefly.

L.: Hey! I will call tonight around 9. Is that ok? I have a late eve.

ME: Ok phone died. I didn't want to end up on a negative tone. My apology

L.: That didn't go well. Maybe another time. A little raw right now.

ME: Pick up.

L.: Raw for quite a while now

ME: Phone hung up pick up

L.: I couldn't hear you. Just say goodnight

ME: you couldn't hear me? whats the last thing you heard?

L.: Nope. You were saying that you love me!!!

ME: Precisely

L.: Oh wrong conversation

ME: Always been crazy about you. Just wish you were too oh well

L.: I do like your piece, though. Never misconstrue that!

ME: So what you sayin?

L.: Can you put it in a box? Like now?

ME: Let me call fedex.

L.: I'll stay up. Ain't got no toys, contrary to belief

ME: Face timing you

L.: No! Imma mess! Can't let you see me

ME: I know how you look, pick up
L.: Gimme 2 min.
ME: K
L.: I see what you do in your spare time, though! You funny 😂
ME: Hmm what do I do? Messy is good
L.: You like to look at faces! All kinds a faces!
ME: I plead the fifth amendment.

★ ★ ★

ME: Good morning darling. My mornings feel so much better knowing that you are mine.
L.: Yours alone! I really miss you
ME: Nothing more important to me and I miss you way more.
You got me about to send our eldest some money. Stop it, woman 🍸😂
L.: Send her hugs and kisses!
ME: Will do baby. I'm going to say from mom and dad LOL
L.: Yes! She will have a good laugh

★ ★ ★

ME: Ok. File closed. They have agreed to give me my retainer back. My dumb ass. LOL I love you baby. I just can't exist without you.
L.: Wow! You never cease to amaze me! I feel the same about you
ME: We are so much alike. That's the funny part. You're a narcissist! (*smile*)
L.: Yeah! Thinking about when I can sit and spin! I knew I missed it, just didn't know how much until you put it in my face! Good lawd!! Why come my 7 pm rehearsal not starting til 8:30 on count of black folk?!
ME: Brown people unite, tomorrow!
L.: I love you Ron Westray!
ME: You and the girls are my everything.

★ ★ ★

L.: Hey baby! You're up! Been up since 5:24 thinking about you!!
ME: Yes baby just up.
L.: My body misses you
ME: And how, baby. I got plenty for you.

L.: I know
ME: All this love.
L.: You got "the meats!"
ME: lol. I know
L.: Not just for sandwiches
ME: You're funny.
L.: I'm hungry
ME: So, I see. Soon come, baby. With yo' fine-assed self
L.: Almost forgot. Gotta get the girls up!!
ME: Ha ha, ok baby, thinking of you every minute of every day, somehow someway. Kiss the babies for me.
L.: I think I will bust when I get to you!
ME: Well I'm gonna bust for sure LOL
L.: Crazy!!
ME: Yazz
L.: I miss your hands, your mouth
ME: All this love is waiting for you baby.
L.: I miss your total package—my beautiful wife.
ME: Yeah baby! Just wanna lay next to you, under you, in front of you
L.: It's raining here I need you
ME: Soon baby soon.
L.: I'm excited to hear you play! Love your music!!
L.: Thank you sweetheart. Means much ❣
ME: You ARE the love of my life L; and we are inevitable
L.: I love you ♥! Nothing left to say
ME: Never Goodbye, baby—Always Hello.

★ ★ ★

Rest, Jimmy

As a young musician, Jimmy Heath showed me so much love and respect (and the tritone substitution). I am forever grateful to this jazz master. Rest in heaven, "Little Bird." Jimmy used to post his home number on his website. Having met him, I called the number on a whim. He talked to me for two hours about life, love, playing and composing.

It was not our last conversation. With years having passed, I would randomly call him. He was always the same: "Ace-Duce-Tray!" he would proclaim. Thank you, Jimmy.

Another time, another place, I had the honor of being invited to sit and eat with the Heath brothers. I'd only known Jimmy, not Percy and Tootie, so I was thrilled to be in the company of all three giants. Each brother had a distinct personality. Amid various tales and lore concerning our shared Carolina roots, the subject of fishing came up. I believe it was Percy who asked me, "So, do you know how to fish?"

I arrogantly replied (sounding like an intellectual Bubba Gump), "Yep, I fish *all* rivers, lakes and streams."

PERCY: "Oh, that's nice."

JIMMY: "Okay, Tray."

TOOTIE: "Aw, man, that sounds like some of that old Teddy Pendergrass bullshit!"

I was so embarrassed—then we all just laughed and laughed. Now *that* was a Carolina moment.

Chapter 49

It's cold and rainy this November day, 2019. Through the glass of my front screen door, I am looking outside. To the right of my front stoop, the nandina bush and the American holly tree are both bearing fruit. The berries have turned from green to orange and will be blood orange by Thanksgiving, Chinese red by Christmas. Inside, where I am standing, near the front door, rests a picture of Mom sitting on my front stoop. Two dimensionally, she stares at the very spot where she used to sit; and I need all of this to mean something.

Oh, how wonderfully it all begins. All through my formative years (including my introduction to the professional world of jazz), my talent and dedication seemed to expedite the upward-mobility process for me. Not until my thirties did this process reverse, demanding that I earn my position in the profession. Though there are indications that I did that, I'm still not sure how well I have done it. Perhaps that is a virtue—not really knowing. False patronage gets all up in there and distorts the whole thing.

I was born a man of this world on June 13—that's one day before President 45, on the 14. Since he is such the *winning* narcissist, theoretically and numerically I am the *losing* narcissist. I'm good with that; because I never wanted to be that kind of winner. That being said, I offer you this partial account of my times before, during and after life "on the road".

★ ★ ★

These days, every direction I turn, there is something (or someone) waiting to draw a reaction from me. It is as if people already know that I will intellectualize offense. I will most times defer to rationale and/or empathy. Due to a series of unfortunate events (some of which you shall learn of in the chapters that follow), I have been following a low-income lifestyle. Accesses and pleasures past, now denied. Ironically, I am making the most money I have ever made. It's really hard to grapple with that fact. I'm not getting any returns on my investments; but I am excessive. I have two of everything—*every thing*. Go ahead, name something.

I regard myself as having an exceptional sense of humor, and I can dance. In my youth, my friends used to like to see me make up moves at the house parties. In undergrad, I was part of the choreography committee for the frat *and* the marching band—this in addition to being the first neophyte president of the Zeta Eta Chapter of Kappa Kappa Psi, National Honorary Band fraternity, and the president of the SCSU Marching 101. That probably makes me sound loyal, but I really haven't kept up with the frat or the marching band. Having made the jazz draft, my career rearranged my associations—seemingly overnight.

This reminds me of L.'s thing with that picture of hers. Occasionally, she will show me a younger picture of myself and say, "I miss *this* Ron." I find it preposterous that someone would expect another to be as a statue inside of their perception from a previous era—which allows them the convenience of not having to acknowledge another's personal evolution.

Perhaps others assume that your success is based on your ego. Perhaps there are those that have achieved success using ego alone. Seemingly, people will love you, people will hate you and people won't give a damn. For me, right now, preparation trumps acknowledgment.

In many of my interactions, other people's opinions, assumptions and pandering have ignited in me a myriad of literal, figurative, subliminal, negative, positive, patronizing, verbal, social actions and responses. Ironically, my reactions (as opposed to responses) reinforce assumptions.

I'm not trying to be famous; I'm trying to be great!
If you can't stand my idiosyncrasies, I'm not special.

My mom bestowed upon my sister and me an artistic and philosophical bearing on people, places and things. I set a few goals and gained entrance to a professional world of experience and notoriety.

★ ★ ★

There is no point at which you can exit the bus called victory. Tradition is a killer; and retrospect is some bullsh★t. I sin for the convenience of my emotions; and because people seem to glorify whatever virtue is convenient for the stance at hand, I don't mind being perceived as the "bad guy." People want to be eligible for all positive descriptions. Then, there are those who are, admittedly, "Not a role model" but still running the little league team—for what, exposure? It seems that everything is established on contradiction. If you understand anything about life, you understand that you are always in class, that there is always a principal, that your ex-wife and your mother, sometimes, represent the same (type of) person. Oh, and that there is no facial expression that will justify a mug shot—try it in the mirror sometime. Doing that reminds me of the feeling of the end of a relationship with a scorned woman. I have never been in an exclusive relationship. I guess I grew up too fast to view monogamy as a *special* thing. With dad gone, there was no model per se. I'm not making excuses—that would indicate guilt. There is nothing to defend here. Aside from my mother's hand, I am a self-made man.

I lost my virginity around age 10 with a girl my age—she was not even a virgin. Then there was reefer at 12, alcohol at 13, (consistent) orgasms at 14, crabs at 15, all-night parties (on a weekday) at 16—oh, and I started at McDonald's at that age—juvenile arrests at 17—this along with working at Burger King, bussing at Red Lobster and being a "stock boy" at Winn Dixie—and suspended license at 18. At age 19 or so, between my freshman and sophomore years of university, I worked for a job service that placed me on many arduous jobs, ranging from office-furniture moving to light construction. My schizophrenic college bud, J.D. was working with me on the summer job. Things were going well until he forgot to take his medicine and showed up to work in his birthday suit. Another time, back during school days, J.D. came to theory class with no shirt on. I gave him a sweatshirt I had handy. Does all this sound like a horror story?

I was always duplicitous. I generally pulled this stuff off while maintaining a fair grade-point average and manners to boot. I suppose my type could be called "not today's bad boy." Video cameras were barely invented, much less mounted everywhere. I would still be in prison if that were the case (pun intended). I was also the one left behind when the dust and clouds of disrespect and defiance would settle in the classroom, filling the slot of the sacrificial lamb. It may sound like a cop-out, but I guess my shy and passive side would at times clash with the wild dog within me, always leaving me to choose a path.

Sometimes the crossroads were good, like the times I would sneak through LG's bedroom at 3 a.m. on a Wednesday night during the school year, only to see her in the morning in the hallowed hallways of the "get high" school we attended. She showed me the way. She was hot in the seat, and I had the curiosity, the nerve, the testicular fortitude and the ejaculatory viscosity necessary to complete our, now, history. Sometimes the crossroads were bad, like the time I was arrested in a stolen hotel room with my girlfriend. Luckily, we had completed our "mission" before we got the big bang on the door. That would have been really embarrassing. After I graduated from high school, and during my first year in college at SCSU, the hotel warrant led to an attempted arrest. Yeah, things were still chasing me from the past, and this pattern didn't end until I became aware of the part of me that was responsible for this duality. Or did I? Hmm, I can't remember.

I can imagine that I'm beginning to sound misguided, right? Well, I'll have you know that I was brought up by the finest parents, and reared, after my father's untimely death, by a mother whose motto was "I can't afford to make any mistakes with you kids." And by golly she didn't, in terms of pure unadulterated parenting, with summer vacations, new clothes at the beginning of every school year—well, kinda the end of every school year and a size too big to accommodate the growth spurts during the summer. It was up to you to decide whether or not you would wear those new sneakers during the summer or those new Levis to the back-to-school party the day before school resumed.

My sister was not as strong in her resolve to save her new clothes till the first day of school but instead found exciting combinations of every year's collection of new gifts in a way that transcended newness-versus-oldness. Well, in this way, Mom saved money by shopping ahead, V. and I didn't have to worry 'bout no swapping and I learned my first lessons in how to force retentive behavior on my own self.

Ever noticed how the word "won" is in own? It's like with my name—"Ron" and "nor,"
meaning neither, implying both. Like "dog" and "God," something lowly, something high,
both wrapped up in a word.

★ ★ ★

Mom said that I'm lazy when it comes to picking girlfriends and that this is the reason I've never been totally satisfied. Never really taken the time to find what I want and pursue it. Now, I don't like pursuit.

It naturally puts me at the disadvantage, and I hate placing myself in that position. "Well," you ask, "how have you ever met anyone?" I guess things happen for me like they're supposed to. The guys think I'm a mack, but I mack for convenience and that can be a little noninspiring every now and then. I have become less tender as I got older. Time keeps going by. Mom told me from a very early age that I was here to lead and be an example. This placed me under a great deal of pressure during my youth, when I wasn't prepared to "stand out" just yet.

★ ★ ★

Because the strength of the constitution with which I was being raised gave me a vision beyond the immediate juvenile follies in which I was participating I ended up standing out anyway. Every now and then I would have a run-in with people who suspected that I was a double agent, for good and bad things.

I have many bumps and bruises from those literally trying to take me out, or at least take something from me. I'm talking age 8? My nephew doesn't seem like he is in the same type of struggle. But that could be a misperception.

Still, by definition, I'm sure I was (and am) a loner. Some would say this is not true. The fact is, I'm both. It was soon clear that I did my own thing when the other boys grouped. I garnered respect anyway for the sheer guts with which I discovered my own folly and extended beyond the familiar with the best of them. In our young way of thinking, we were taking it to the next level. But the next level, for *bad* boys, always equaled breaking something—if not some tangible material thing, then, at least, the law. I remember the feeling of falling in love with a girl named Diane around age 8. We kissed during a field trip while sitting in the space-observatory theatre. Carly Simon's "No One Does It Better" was playing overhead as we snuck a kiss (for about 1.5 seconds). Now that I'm an adult, I realize the teacher probably saw that … oops.

Fast-forward 11 years, and lots more focus, and I entered the professional world of jazz via the Marcus Roberts Ensemble. I managed travel and study well and graduated on time, in time. Then I went off to graduate school. After that, I toured with the Jazz at Lincoln Center Orchestra for 12 years. And I, somewhat unwittingly, entered academia as an assistant professor at the ripe old age of 35.

* * *

BILO

These days, I can't even mop the floor without backtracking. There was a time when I knew how to mop. I was a young man, working at the Winn Dixie on North Main Street. I believe it's a BILO now. Anyway, an ex-con showed me how to mop smoothly, when I was a stock boy at that old Winn-Dixie. "Set yo' bucket way back behind you, son. Ring your mop well, no dripping. Now, go back up there, start your line going left to right, smoothly. Swivel that handle and flip it over to the other side, without lifting it once it streak' the flo'. After two or three flips, you need to go rinse the mop, son. Now start at yo' new line, and bring that line back to the bucket like that. And don't you even think about going back making *co-rrec-tions*, Hollywood. Know what I mean?" That's what they called me, "Hollywood." This is not to be confused with "Hollywood Cold"—that's different! With me, it was because I always wore shades, day and night. I corroborated the nickname by being cool and efficient.

That wasn't my first job. My first job was caring for flowers at Robert and Ruby's plant shop on Two Notch Road. They were Canadians who had settled in Columbia. Mom spent a lot of money with them for her "garden room" (aka "Florida" room). Consequently, they liked Mom. They hired me at age 14–15, during the summers. I dug that job.

Back during my road years with Wynton, I was on the phone with an old girlfriend from the South. Midway through our conversation, she asked me if I would be playing at the BILO Center anytime soon. "Babe, maybe some trombonists would, but Ronald Westray don't play at grocery stores." Turns out that her town of Greenville had constructed a cutting-edge convention center/ sports arena called the BILO Center—I understand that you have to follow the money, but what a dumb name. Years later, I was able to apologize about that, and we laughed and laughed.

You know we go way back. I haven't forgotten. I remember that rainy morning at your boarding house when first we hooked up … I think we were in love?

I don't claim to know a thing about, well, *staying* in love—and most certainly not back then.

⋆ ⋆ ⋆

The Living Years

Every generation
Blames the one before
And all of their frustrations
Come beating on your door …
Say it loud, say it clear
You can listen as well as you hear
It's too late when we die
To admit we don't see eye to eye

—Mike and the Mechanics

11/4/19:

Oh my … I'm sorry, man …

Keep your head up (as he would want).

Wounds heal—Ron

Hi Ron,

This is only to let you know that my father passed away last night. I don't have words but I know you understand.—C.

10/31/19:

Hello Ron,

This is great news: you married L. again! I am so happy to hear this, congratulations to both of you! We wish you the very best, love and joy and happiness, zen and good luck and whatever you may need to feel good and stay together. Believe me, Ron, very often I feel exactly the same about my marriage as you do about yours. Very often it doesn't feel right. But then again, that's mostly me and my doubts and my troubles and obsessions, and maybe it's just the way things are. You and L., you certainly deserve each other, you deserve your love and a little bit of acceptance, and well-being. I don't believe too much in taxi drivers (ha ha), I believe that what is, is good …

P is at the door urging me to finish so that we can go (see, that's what I mean). We will spend the long weekend in the village of her parents, so I will continue later … Just wanted to tell you that the news of you being married again is news of happiness, you and L., you are very lucky, and very very courageous, my respects for you. Please be happy, both of you. Somebody told me not too long ago, the secret of a good and long relationship is the ability and the determination to forgive and forget, again and again, that's all. We are all so fragile, everybody, and so much in need of love. I will write again very soon, kind regards to L., and a big hug for you.—C.

7/30/19:

Hello C,

I am doing well. Yes, long time! The girls are doing very well. A. is a junior in University and then there is Amalya, the 12-year-old, and Ariele at 10. Yes, kids, kids, kids. Thank you. I too am glad you had the chance to meet mom. I'm still very sad as well. Brief encounters with sadness is how

I deal with it, if you understand. I'm still watering her plants over at the house. It's now a museum, ha ha. I'm glad to hear that you all are thriving Wow, building a house, amazing! Having lost most of my close relatives, I remarried the mother of my children, L.

The reunion has not been 100 percent blissful but it feels like something bigger than us is keeping it together; and the kids of course.

At times, I feel silly for remarrying her (a cab driver told me not to do it because "nothing would change and in fact it would be worse." Well, he was right). But perhaps I owe her another chance, too. At other times I feel like I did the right thing. "C'est la vie …"

So glad you latched on to Trane: Welcome. You and I are on the same frequency; I have been living and supping with Trane for about three weeks now. Inside of a very meticulous and complex transcription process that is my own. I would love to talk further about exposing my transcriptions (Ted Talk or Conference). I'm only attracted to the most complex solos. The sheets of sound. This process changes my brain every time I immerse and resurface. I am literally smarter … lol.

I thought about Mom a lot during these transcriptions. She loved to look at the notes and would expect me to still be transcribing. I'm going to attach to this email my rough draft of probably the most complex Trane solos I've done lately. Enjoy the view. The point is that music is math, and that improvisation is real, not imagined: Coltrane is not making it up. He is playing what's there. And he is the Supreme Manifestation of jazz improvisation. Have to debunk this at a conference. Let's do it and reveal my never-before-seen collection of solos!

I just finished in the morning. Yes, please, let's talk soon. So much to talk about. If you want to follow along with these transcriptions the title is "I Want To Talk About You," one version is from Stockholm 1963 and the other version is the more popular compilation version from "Live At Birdland." I will also include a blues called "Sweet Sapphire Blues" from "Black Pearls," 1958. YouTube them and follow along, haha … The ballads are sans solo cadenzas. May do the cadenzas … All to say yes I am a Coltrane *geek* and one of his scribes left on earth. I am able to do this stuff cause I am on sabbatical again (*smile*), and it folds back into research requirements. But it is *still* a personal passion; that makes it very rewarding. I am sharing these because I need an audience; esp. someone who knows work. Thanks! Give me a ring sometime. But text me B4 so I recognize the number. Right back at you!—Ron

5/30/20:

Hello Ron, my friend,

How are you? It has been a long time since we talked or mailed, is everything fine with you? The music, the girls, little and big ...? In these past years I've become sort of a playground man, there's almost no time for anything else but kids kids kids ... But I still think a lot about you, and I also have very fond and warm memories of the brief encounters with your mum, still feel very sad about her passing, and I often wonder how you deal with your loss.

D, M and A, are all doing well, the three of them are attending the same pre-school now. D is learning to skate, M and A are discovering the bike. Yesterday we had a Star Wars party on a playground nearby, I had the Obi Wan Kenobi part (could have been worse).

P is ok, too, she's still looking for a job, but [prospects] are low, so we are planning to build a house in the little town where her family lives, two hours south of Madrid but close to my job.

When I find some time, mostly on the train on the way to university and back, I listen to a lot of jazz, I try to listen to all sorts of stuff, but it's mostly Coltrane. I am so deep into Coltrane that I don't find other things that interesting. Remember when you told me about Coltrane? I've been reading some books but I still feel so ignorant about it all, it's funny. Tomorrow night P and me we have a rare night off, some baby-sitters, we have a couple of tickets for Herbie Hancock at the Auditorio Nacional ... I just hope he will play some romantic stuff, it would certainly help to clean up the terrain. A big hug for you—C.

Meanwhile, after Mom's death, a former friend of the family that had produced a film short on my mother's art sent a blurb to me for review. She wanted to publish this nonsense.

Rancor: Spring 2019

I do NOT approve of this blurb or ANY OTHER BLURB that trivializes my relationship with Mom. It was not complicated. It was true love between mother and son. All due respect, but you don't know enough about that relationship to casually state things like that for the public.

As well, I do not approve of this sentiment: *Ron and his mother had a complicated relationship. He was divorced with two children and an ex-wife who lived in DC, but he owned a house next to his mother's where he spent summers and school vacations. Ron exemplified the saying, "Every boy is a mama's boy." Ron and Ginger were always edgy with each other, always fighting.*

What would make you think that I would approve of such nonsense? And this is not accurate or true: *Ginger asked him to move some paving stones and Ron got upset. The stones did look heavy. They were snapping at each other, while Lynn was balancing a heavy camera on her shoulder. V., Ginger's daughter, was exclaiming, "Artists! They're always being difficult." The weather was hot, the traffic was noisy. I was wondering how the shoot would end.*

I did stuff like this with mom well before your low-budget camera person showed up, and I was not upset. If anything, I was frustrated by your shallow, "Now, pick up a rock, Ron" scenario—which in and of itself showed a lack of true understanding (as did L. asking Mom to pose with a fake copper penny in her hand at shoot's end). Mom never forgave her for that underestimation; as you shall not, ever, be forgiven, by me, for yours. You would have been far better served leaving me and Mom to our own devices out back.

Do you think that that microcosm of an experience really informed you about me and MOM'S YARD WORK to the degree that YOU COULD MAKE A SWEEPING STATEMENT? You need SO MUCH more data, and you should know that. SO, due to your lack of real understanding, DO NOT refer to me and mom's relationship in your document, AT ALL. Btw, actually, I have three daughters, not two; and my divorce did not make my relationship with my mom complicated.

This is a HUGE overstep. I am both shocked and surprised that you would think that I would approve of this nonsense being spun out into the public! Think of it like this: You do not know anything about me and mom's relationship. Your observations are topical and trivial. Presenting a half-cocked description of me and my mother's relationship to the public is not something I will allow. Ask me some questions for your next book. Ginger Westray would NOT approve of this fickle description of our relationship. I believe you know that.

In the words of my dear mother: DO NOT CALL MY NAME.

The most startling part of the naivety of your authorial attempt, amid the misperceptions and the mis-observed, is the fact that you would underestimate my ability to have an opinion or even be aware of the type of damage (and impressions) that could be created if I did *not* have an opinion regarding such a sensitive matter and implication. That's the part you need to think about. Stick to describing relationships you understand (eg., you and your son). Don't worry about Ginger and Ron-Ron. You are, officially, banned from Mom's premises and my presence. Now, be off! Go on, shoo!

★ ★ ★

Meanwhile: Spring Semester 2019

To the Employer,

It is a distinguished honor to represent York University as the Oscar Peterson Chair In Jazz Performance. It is both exciting and inspiring to witness the progressive effect of "new information" upon the development of students' abilities, and the impact of teaching upon my own development as an educator and as a person. Teaching at the university level inspires my research, bolstering the development of an effective didactic process. The fostering of healthy relationships with students, colleagues and other professionals is my *main imperative*, and I am aware of the limits and degrees of interaction needed for success.

With regard to the described context and nature of the accusations: That is not who I am. My artistry, creativity, research, my decisions and my experiences all have a bearing upon my interactions with colleagues and students; the art of balancing a dynamic life with professorial responsibilities defines the metric by which I evaluate my moral standards. For instance, there is not a day that I report to the campus of York University that I assume I can just be myself.

I am acutely aware of who I am, how I am perceived, and of the power of my position (and even my presence). I am mostly aware of the vulnerability of my position with regard to offending students, and it's the factor I think about far more than lesson planning.

That is why, after teaching approximately 4,000 students, over 10 years, at York, there is no record of my berating of students or colleagues. I am, also, the father of three daughters of various ages. I appreciate being liked by my children, and my students. I have a productive relationship with my students; and *all* of my classroom environments are consistent, controlled, engaging and fun. I accomplish this by not throwing my weight around, and by creating a collective environment in which the student wants to take ownership.

I cannot, however, control timeliness. The down side of not always "wearing" authority (eg., "fun" prof) is that there comes a time when you have to claim the authority. This was such a time. However, prior to this verbal reprimand, there had been clear mediation about my expectations with regard to punctuality in our performance ensemble. The issue had been escalating (almost like a direct challenge), and the two students that showed up late that day pushed back in a way that I felt was not in line with them being students and leaders (4th and 5th year), or in line with them respecting my credibility as a professor and as their course director. The loss of my temper was an anomaly, and I am, personally, embarrassed by what occurred. I expressed my embarrassment, and apologized to the class following the "outburst."

Finally, the thing that makes feelings, feelings, is that you cannot control them. But this accusation has been discussed out of context, with total subjectivity on both sides of the issue.

I would appreciate being measured by my successes.

Ron Westray

Chapter 48

Hi Ron, my friend,

I am so sorry to receive the sad news of the passing of your grandmother. I remember her very well, from our visit to her house. It was difficult for me to understand everything she said, but somehow it worked, and I remember that she gave me a very warm feeling, I felt immediately at home with her. And I had the impression that you loved her very much. To lose two so beloved persons, your mom and your grandmother, in such a short time, is a very hard blow, you must be devastated. I hope there are people near you with whom you can share your sadness, your feelings, and who can give you a hug when you need it. I have told P., she sends you her warmest regards. Our condolences, and be sure that you and your family, including your mother and your grannie, are in our thoughts.

We are all fine here in Spain, kids are at school and in the kindergarten, I am at the office, semester began couple of weeks ago, business as usual. I am still doing some research (same thing), less than before since D., M. and A. need a lot of support and company. Last Monday we all went to the Prado Museum, which is just a little walk away from our home in Madrid, that was great, lots of fun (A. shouting out loud all the time, she seemed enthusiastic about Velázquez and Goya). My arms are still aching … Summer holidays in the South were also really nice, although P. and me we need another break now, batteries are low by now. P. is looking for a job, but there are few offers, circumstances are not favorable: age, kids, two years' break. We'll see. It would be nice to see you again, will you come to Europe someday? If not, I will have to fly to Canada, or to South Carolina.

All the best, C.

* * *

One More Once!

ME: Feel better; We may not like each other sometimes, but the love is there. I love you, L. I go off. Then I think I am going to lose you; then I go crazy … At times. I am such a fool. Once and again, forgive me. I cannot live without you.

I think I was in DC about one day too long; I don't think it was so much about us. Just too long. Too long as in that visitor status feeling; hotel/ house, back forth, etc., also trying to be too helpful; should have let the guys do what they do, stay out of the furniture business. Like you say, I have my way and it works for me. I get you, L. I get *it*. Its just that I'm used to operating solo. I will be less criticizing … How are you? I need to hear you. What's going on w/ your health? Are you pregnant … (*smile*)

One last thing: I have a way of rationalizing conflict that I have developed that involves going ice cold; in the process, I forget, for a very short period of time (short temper), how much you mean to me; then I remember, like David Banner, post HULK.

Then, I feel bad. If we get through this one, we can make it, promise. You know my heart, L.; you have told me so. You said we could talk. What's up? What changed? Why are you communicating with silence? Does that mean it's over? I know that the silence is my punishment, but it's not going to help anything; I can only guess that it means "figure it out." Unless you tell me otherwise, I must come to my own conclusions …

I can imagine you are opting out of any of this convo in lieu of family time. I get that … But it's not helping this. I would like to know if you are IN or OUT. I don't want to leave you again, but if you are DONE, then there's no point. To me, one week of silence, 'cause of a verbal altercation is a little extreme.

For the record, this is my recollection of our disagreements since marriage. They certainly did not revolve around any one issue:

1. Holiday Inn: Ultimately I got pissed cause of the references to other-guys stories in relationship to something I was trying to express.
2. Did not realize we were on an open timeline regarding when you all would arrive in Toronto (found that out after marriage).
3. You texted me to say that I sound unhappy w/ you "and you know I am going to do what I want to do (like I always do) and I know where to get it."
4. My recent EXPLOSION because you tried to "position" my "preferences" as our core issue. You dig?

5. Leaving my door unlocked as I slept—in an apartment, knowing how I feel about that. What was that?

Those are the issues leading up to last week.

★ ★ ★

ME: Hi. How are you? Happy Thanksgiving. You could not possibly think that I don't love you. My mother cursed me out before. I've cursed my mother out before. But we never doubted our love. Love is trust.

Can you get over last week? Or can you not get over last week? Should I take your silence to mean that you cant't get over this? Or you just don't want to deal with any of this on Thanksgiving? Not really trying to deal with anything. Just trying to say hello. Hello? I thought maybe you were just tired of texting. So I called you. I see you're not answering your phone either. I can only assume the worst. Be well.

I wish I knew what to say to reassure you. I too need reassurance from you. I need to know where you stand. Leaving me to my own thoughts is not a good idea right now. I have apologized. What do you feel I am not acknowledging?

My manifesto was my natural defense as a person and as a man as a human. But I also understand why you think about the relationship in the ways that you have described. I am trying to intellectualize this dilemma, as I do all things. Your silence ultimately will only lead me to one conclusion. Perhaps that's the conclusion you are trying to indicate. According to your only correspondence with me you said you are OK with any decision I make. That's unusual for you to say. So I know it's serious. I'll take the blame. It's all my fault.

I don't want to lose you again. But your silence can only mean that you are very unhappy. That makes me unhappy. So there's no need for us to be unhappy. I was already unhappy by myself. Love is not based on whether I curse at you. That's just a reflection of the passion I have for you. Love is based on 100 percent trust. Respect is a different issue. And that was not respectful. And I regret that. As I have communicated.

If you accept me as the creative dynamic passionate artist, as you say, why can't I be allowed any idiosyncrasies? To me that means it's all pandering. You don't actually see me any differently than any one. Not to mention the stress and stresses I have endured this year.
Where is the (or any) empathy?

★ ★ ★

ME: MONDAY:	I drove all day; you opted for David's party; I slept alone. I was fine with that.
TUESDAY, DEC. 25TH:	You never greeted me that morning, till after the girls opened their gifts; had to ask you to open your gifts, some hours later; not even a card from you. I was fine with that.
WEDNESDAY:	Only day we spent alone together.
THURSDAY:	Cooked breakfast with girls (you did not warn me not catch on fire this time).
FRIDAY:	Came to house before noon; house all day; Mom downtown ride; night time at hotel (we just slept).
SATURDAY:	Went to house early. Cooked breakfast; that's when I got offended at the fire comment. Why this time? The sweater was not that loose, and it is made of acrylic; it doesn't combust. Then the drawer-closing thing—what gives? I was not curt. I simply said I was 48 and did not need that advice; I was done with that. Took W. to Sears. Sat night @ hotel. (You and I just slept.)
SUNDAY:	At the house early; had a fine day with you and the girls and Granny B. (and a little bickering about the sofa at your mom's).

I was fine. Sunday night you came to the hotel and accused me of treating you some kind of way and being curt—and texting someone from the house. Btw, I was telling V. all about Granny on the porch, and she was "blowing up my phone" (as you call it). I was offended, and I tried to defuse the situation. I said let's talk tomorrow; and you said, "or not!" I stormed away. What can we do to make this situation better?

The reason I got out of the car like that was because you had been cross with me earlier; we couldn't even agree on Cecil Taylor sucking! I wanted to kiss you but I didn't want one of those cold kisses from you (the one where I kiss you but your lips are sealed). I just got out the car. It feels like I am chasing a dream (you) that I cannot have. It's been twenty years and this is where we are (and to think this is all my fault—nothing to do with you—wow!) By "micro-managing," I meant basically bossing everybody around all week (just like you drive). So I said I'd "defer" to you (by which I mean, absorb the constant bossing and lack of flexibility, and avoid arguing), and you said don't do that either. What do you want? I can only hope that you are not teaching my girls to be strong by presenting ME as your example of the type of man you do not tolerate.

I would like to meet the type of man they should meet, if so. I know you always talk positive, but I think you are inadvertently giving them the message that I'm not the kind. Are you sure you mean to do that? Do YOU own ANY of our issues? Or are you just that perfect? It's all ME?

When you said, "So, this is the part where you go and get with some other women?" I wish I could have been cool enough to reassure you that was not the case. Instead, I fought fire with fire. I should not have said what I said. I apologize.

The silence needs to end. It's deafening. It took me a couple weeks to calm down—but I am always willing to try again. We aren't even together, and we still can't appreciate each other when in person. What to do? I want to get this right this time.

* * *

Now, Granny Neal

V: Hi. Granny's system is getting weaker. She will be moving to in-patient hospice. She called a meeting yesterday while I was visiting. She went over her will and I have a copy for you.

We are named on behalf of mom with things split 50 percent to Bubba and mom's portion divided, 25 percent each to me and you. Just wanted to tell you what her last will and testament includes. I pray you will be able to see her before she transitions.

Just think about it … you can visit early or late. There are no set visitation hours. I hope to see you later. Got some food for hip chick too. Have a blessed Sunday! 🙏

ME: Thank you. I've been scarce because I have a friend visiting all week. But thank you for keeping me up. Not good news. Wish things were different.

V: Oh ok. Thanks. Hi. Took a break from hospital. You still have company, or they coming in tomorrow? Let me know if you want to visit Granny. I'm going back down there later on.

ME: No… Company is here. I will defer. I have chosen to remember her as she was the last time I saw her.

V: Ok. Respect your wishes. No funeral either?

ME: thx. No

V: Ok

ME: Not mad. I just meant what I said.

V: Got it. Ok.

* * *

V: Good morning! God is Love (not division and discord). All I want to say is that I love you Ron. I pray that the spirit of anger and temper be removed, because we can communicate on a higher level. There is no division—not necessary. Let us not have any force divide our family. No one is against you. This is a difficult time and yesterday was difficult enough but I had to press on as a mom. Just know I come in peace and Jesus is love 💕. There is no y'all *vs.* you. I'm your blood sister and there is no animosity or discord in my heart. I wanted you to know this no matter how you may feel. All is well on my end. I had to say that. This is a new day that the Lord has made. I will rejoice and be glad in it. Wishing the same for you, my brother! Have a blessed day, in Jesus' name, Amen. I'm headed to a real estate conference call; take care.

ME: Thank you. I'm just chilling; and I don't wish to interact right now. Your son has no respect for anyone. I get that; but I can't deal any further. He's walking around with my last name; but he not listening to me (like I'm some bum off the street) I'm out. I get the no respect thing; but don't pull that on me. You act like a man, you get treated like a man. It's not just anger. I keep my jobs a long time; and I function at high levels without problems. You need to account for the fact that you (and yours) seems like y'all are on another planet. Lacking understanding (and interest) of simple things. Like we not even from the same Mom. Mom dealt with it in her way. I'm not trying to be understood, anymore. Get with it. Seem like nobody understood what mom was talking 'bout—tuned her out—especially you and your children. I'm going to deal with it like this. This ain't confusion and discord. We were never a family like that. I'm through compensating for peoples personalities. I'm taking names.

You struck out and did your thing a long time ago. I will admit; I have a lot of resentment. It's best to leave me be. Before she died, Mom told me that she hadn't seen G. for a month or more. M. never liked being there. She said she hadn't seen you either. I'm not going there. I have my beliefs, though.

You spent more time with Ms. D. than you did Mom. Mom felt that way. You were doing shit for her you would not even do for Mom. I have a lot more that I won't say, because it is subjective. I have made certain decisions. You will see a change. But I'm not mad. Btw, G. was asking for that for 20 years. Same reason he keeps getting towed … His lack of respect for me comes from you. You have always been very competitive. I don't know why. We are total opposites in any ways that would count professionally. Come at me correct or stay away. You are a nice person in all the ways people say you should be nice, but you lack SOUL. Get some soul, sister. And thanks for all the NICE stuff you have done. I hate to come at you like this at a time like this, but the disparity has always been there. I'm done faking. I'll be doing what I do when I'm in South Carolina. Y'all do what you do when I'm not here. Your kids don't do shit for anybody, anyway. Okay, I'm done venting—later.

ME: That's been brewing a long time. Long ago, I told him that would be that—not because of what happened—because of all the other dumb shit that happened. You say I had my troubles at his age? Yeah, but not like that. Those episodes slowly killed Mom. There is no need to be around me. I'm not mad, I just don't feel connected to y'all, right now—other than by definition. I'm here. I'm glad y'all are. Be best. Gramma basically gave her life up for G., and this negro got the audacity to tell me, "I ain't even listening to nothing you sayin'." They are just like you. Not to mention that I'm not the average uncle off the street. But he doesn't feel that way cause you would have had to help with that. But you are so competitive; why would you do that? I have thousands of students listening to me every year. I can't cuss them out. That's why he got his ass cursed out.

He was standing in the way of me cleaning my own daddy's grave; I didn't like that playful shit. It's all symbolic to me. He has brought a lot of stress to the family. My mistakes were, at least, countered by achievement. Just like Mom, my friends and colleagues can articulate far more about who I am than my family. You still stuck on "GreenStreets" and "How's Wes?" Please. It's just like the mopeds when were kids. I'm already up by the 7-Eleven. You, still at the park.

As far as what the hell I really do, "My brother knows the chords, though," does not suffice. I wish you understood what I really know and do—not for me, for you. I held this while Mom was living. Cause I didn't want to ever disappoint her with division. Now, I don't give a damn. Her death must provide something. For me, it shall be liberation from holding my tongue with the family.

I know I'm rambling. That's just for the memoirs. Mom would be so upset with me venting on you like this: She'd say, "Nobody better not bother V." I get it. But I'm not killing myself holding shit in.

⋆ ⋆ ⋆

V: Good morning! Love you … unconditionally. We are all grieving. Just want you to know I'm not mad either, and I'm here. Just want to stay connected in the spirit of peace. I come in peace … Praying for peace as stated before. Jesus is Love 💞.

ME: Yes, he is. Love you too … and I've said my piece.

V: Amen, brother. I love you, thank you💞 💞 💞. You've expressed your opinions and I may not agree and that's an individual right. My whole point is only to say that I don't want you thinking I'm angry. We can agree to disagree on perceptions and feelings. All I know is that there is enough division in the world. I refuse to let the enemy take my brother from me and cause us to have strife. I'm an individual and we may do things totally different. I'm ok with us being different. God didn't make any two people alike. I'm sure you don't want anything to happen to me and likewise. I'm trying to get to Jesus so I can see Mom again, and I will do everything to do things pleasing in God's sight. He is who I aim to please. I went to bible study last night and I prayed for our family. I'm asking for a renewal of the heart and mind! I keep Mom in mind too … She's looking down. Let's keep doing things pleasing in The Lord's sight.

V: Love is stronger and covers a multitude of sin, saith the Lord. It did my heart good to get a text back saying you love me too! 😍 loving you always …💞

⋆ ⋆ ⋆

Emergency Run II

V: Is mom ok? She sounded like she had shortness of breath

V: If she needs to go to urgent care I can take her

V: She's had this lingering cold for a couple of days

ME: Heading to Dr.'s care on two notch

V: Oh ok. See you there

V: Don't have that. I have the pads and we can make it

ME: Ok

ME: Get icy hot patches?

ME: The Vicks is not strong enough

ME: We will make whatever work just follow instinct
V: Pharmacist says that icy-hot is not to be used
ME: K
V: Go with Vicks
V: I just confirmed
ME: We have that here
V: Oh ok. I'm bringing the pads that stick
ME: Get the liquid Vicks?
V: We will get it
ME: Maybe a newer one will be more effective this one is old Vicks capo
V: Liquid mucinex
V: Ok
ME: Vapo
ME: And liquid Vicks if available
V: Don't see liquid Vicks. Looking
ME: K. Get new one small one
V: Ok
V: The CVS you get more than Vicks. Same ingredients and strength
V: But I will get name brand for this
ME: K

* * *

ME: I think Mom wants to be by her grandparents. Because she buried daddy way out there under different circumstances and I don't think she ever intended to go out there
V: It's best to have them together I think. I don't want to drive to Springfield when I visit dad which I do often. Let's keep them together but let's talk tomorrow. I'm drained
ME: Is there a will
ME: Ok
V: She's a Columbian, as the art house says. I think it's fitting here
ME: Ok agreed. You're right it makes sense
V: Yeah. Let's just always think this through and try to agree. Emotions high and I'm still in shock.
ME: Will do
V: G. taking hard.
ME: Just remind him grandma always said she was just a living memory.
V: He sent me this
ME: This is what she meant
ME: No Facebook post of any kind. Make sure G. and M. know

ME: And make sure your pastor knows we don't want this to be public information yet

V: Done

ME: K

V: "I am definitely praying for you and your family.
Please let me know what I can do to help." 🙏
This is what he said in a text and told him she was private and we are wishing to keep that way until arrangements made

ME: I'm not condoning telling your pastor anything. That's your style. I don't believe in that kind of stuff but just as long as he knows it's not public

V: He does

ME: K

V: He deals with family wishes all the time. He even met her and she visited Bibleway and enjoyed Services. He is a state senator and professional

ME: I don't know him

ME: I can't see where he has done anything for me or Mom but that's your pastor

ME: Not to get into that that's your belief

ME: I'm just nitpicking. I get it. It's a common tradition

V: I know but she did and he visited G. many times in hospital ... we are members there. That's the relationship of having a church family. I know where to draw line

ME: That's your church family not mine

ME: Let's just go with Greeneview for the service

ME: No viewing just the service and the burial

V: Ron, greenview may not be best. Viewing at Palmer memorial with viewing to family only. They can do two services for Family to view and others closed casket

V: We need to discuss in person

ME: There's no need to view but we'll talk about all of us again I want to lose all of the posturing let's just keep it simple

V: Let's just rest in that. Too soon

ME: This again. OK

V: I do want to view and her grandkids should along with her mother know matter how we feel

ME: View at the funeral open casket

ME: Think about it Mom wouldn't be into being viewed. Let everyone get your view at the funeral. Old-school

V: Viewing can be controlled for immediate family as well. The chapel people can tell us and go over payment processes as well. We need to go simple and all in one for then to visit at a chapel

V: I'm sorry. Drained Let's chat tomorrow. So many options

ME: Ok

V: Let the funeral director folk talk with us. They have many options

ME: No because they just gonna blow it up into a bunch of bullshit I want to keep it simple

ME: I'm not interested in options V. I'm interested in keeping it simple

V: No they really don't

ME: This is not a vacation plan

ME: Yes they really do. I'm not interested in their freaking plans let's keep it simple

V: I know about this not talking about it like a plan. They can keep it simple as we want

ME: Great

V: We can talk with them. I like Palmers and Bostic Thompkins

ME: Ok shall discuss

V: Good night … tired of texting

ME: K night sis

ME: Moms up there partying with daddy at some nightclub 😊

V: With a can of orange paint

ME: Yes

⋆ ⋆ ⋆

ME: Morning. I just tried to start moms car the battery is dead. I will charge it today. I was going to pull it down into my yard. It was hard being at the house. I always told Mom that we would leave everything as she left it in the house not withstanding a little pick up here in there

ME: Mom's battery never dies. Go figure

ME: But by the same token being in the house was cathartic. Everyone's going to have to

V: Hi

V: It was hard sleeping man …

ME: Mom is everywhere!! Praise God. She is already speaking to me quietly listen

V: I know !

V: Things will never be the same. I pray that we can hold on and not let ANYTHING keep us apart. We are all each other have.

ME: I really want to push to have mom's property labelled as a historic house based on her teaching and her art in its uniqueness—and being a native South Carolinian

ME: There's nothing to fall apart we just keep everything moving as it is house payments etc.

ME: Locate the insurance policy if you can because we need to find out what's there and what part we might have to chip in for services

ME: No rush but start thinking about harvesting this information

ME: Mom's stone is garnered by I would like her to have a Garnet casket what do you think. I would also like her to wear her Garnet headscarf similar to the one she had on when she came to your car. It has garnet stones woven into it

ME: I'm glad they decided to do the autopsy. We really need to know in detail

ME: Again you were right

V: Yeah garnet is nice … let's start talking and listening to each other's ideas because we both have great one … these funeral directors handle a lot. Let's not get bogged down right now. It will be nice to allow them to tell us what they handle and let them assist us because we need to keep this costs at a minimum but have her style woven in with class simply.

ME: Mom is alive in all of us and the grandchildren. her DNA goes forth

V: Amen!

V: I'm just shaking all over. M. and G. really came to my side last night. I needed that

ME: Yes agreed, sister.

ME: That's the beauty of motherhood. Mom was very proud of both of us and got to see our assent to the top of our careers and she believed in us

ME: That's the first thing everybody wants to know … what happened

ME: I'm having trouble getting over the guilt of mom dying slowly right in front of us and us not realizing it. Should've put her in the car and took her to doctors care but there's no need to dwell on that. Things happen as they should. I guess. I feel guilty but I know she would not want us to feel that way

ME: I think mom was an anaphylactic shock the whole time, should've noticed it. Having trouble resolving it

ME: I will never understand why she didn't go to Dr.'s care with me but decided to go later on

ME: It was too late. I should've put her in the car. I feel so guilty. I hope I can get over it

ME: And Mom was trying to walk it off. As she did everything in life

V: Listen I know you said I need to not turn this into a spectacle which I agree … we cannot control who sees and hears things. I know it appears no one visited but mom was loved and respected by people she opened up to! We can set times for viewing and hand pick those persons for the wait and the chapel can arrange however we want it. There are a few have picked selection that a chapel can handle and we keep it more contained and private. Greenview church has too much bias and stuff attached. I think the chapel would be more neutral and self contained. We are the children but let's embrace input from Granny if any is rendered but we will make final decision

ME: I agree with everything you just said. Except embracing input from Granny. She didn't even know how old Mom was. No

V: We cannot exclude a mothers love however that may that be. As a mother I have to understand that love from a mother

ME: V. that's philosophical. The proof is in the pudding

V: Respectfully I know what you are saying but maybe Granny can finally get it right now with god and herself

V: And we need to give her a chance

ME: A chance? She had 74 years V.

ME: We can tell her what has happened and that's it

V: I can't judge it and she won't make any decisions. The autopsy will be a week or so. Granny needs to know today as we planned but let her know we will be planning everything

ME: If they didn't show Mom love in life I'm not for all the posturing

V: You are angry I understand that. But I'm speaking about a mother and what ever she wants to communicate. Let's listen

ME: Especially C.N., who was jealous of Mom her entire life!

V: I know how they did stuff but we must forgive and do things respectfully

ME: For me that's the part that may fall apart. Not sure I want anything to do with that side now Mom is gone. Nothing but fakeness and deceit and envy

ME: Mom wasn't for taking off from the world. She was protecting us from people and unfortunately a great majority of them are in the family

V: We are better because of how we were raised. I will not show any contempt even if I feel they did her wrong. Let's just get through this bruh and we can control this in our own way. We have the power. They won't be able to tell us how anything goes but we will listen and act with how we move

ME: I respect you and I promise to be democratic. This is just my perspective

V: I understand

ME: Thanks

V: I am the eldest and would like that lead diplomatic role with all due respect to you as the man in the immediate Westray trio … I respect you as well

ME: K

ME: Want to try to contact MJ and BB, see if they want to be pallbearers

ME: And CC, me and G. Or some combination.

ME: In my opinion I don't want a lot of speeches built into the program. If things happen spontaneously that's fine

ME: Specific speech is me you, G and perhaps one good friend

ME: Just my opinions

V: Yeah those are the logistics I want to help with. I'm good at that. That is the hand picking part I can help with but we need to create order and uncle as half brother needs a part in it as pallbearer as well. All men in family.

V: We will let that flow

ME: Yeah he's not healthy

ME: But we can extend the invitation

V: J. is my choice. Has known mom since 1st grade

V: I know the way they move. Mom visits her and likewise. She talks to her regularly

ME: I'm fine with that. Even though J. mistakenly left a voicemail … and Mom overheard her referring to her as crazy as hell and not the compliment

ME: And I quote

ME: That's what friends are for

ME: I respect your desire to create a program I just happen to know the truth

ME: I think Miss J. is also a candidate, even better

ME: I will follow your lead on this. I'm just putting that out there

V: I don't … but again let's not dissect that just let's go with who we know mom had laughs with and we will extend. I know K and VT up here by me would like to be there.

ME: Yes

V: Not a program. That is something that funeral home can help with. That's not hard. It really can be short as we need it. A chapel can give us that small feel … I want mom to wear her hair that she talked to me about if she left us. I want to have input on that and pick her best pair of shoes or buy the outfit … she loved a good pair of shoes

ME:

V: Mom visited Bibleway in the past when we were young and last few years went to services on New Year's Eve with us and listened to pastor J. on radio. She enjoyed his sermons. I could just check on his availability or associate pastor since she didn't have pastor per se … would have to check on process but our fees would be minimal since I am member … we need a pastor for eulogy … just thoughts. So much to consider.

ME: I've never had my heart broken before until now

ME: Mom was a very forgiving person

ME: That's the first thing Mr. Eulogy needs to know

V: I would like to go in together in house if you could just wait on me … I will be there in about an hour or so. G works at 12. Granny needs to know autopsy may take too long. I don't know if we need to call B. first to brace because granny's health is fragile

ME: We can call him from around there

V: I just don't know

ME: It is what it is she's gonna find out either way

ME: Let's just control the information as long as we can. We are in control, V. I'm not concerned with courtesy as I said. Not much courtesy was extended to Mom in her life

ME: I know I'm still on the ship but I'm not concerned with how comfortable people are about protocol is. we are in control

ME: I thought you said the medical examiner will call you today

ME: Let's see who all sent mom a Christmas card this year. I think that's an important list in a random factor that may be a good guide

V: Yes they called me last night and doing examination this morning. And will contact me

ME: K. Mom gave everything she had to us, that's all she knew.

ME: And at least she didn't have to live to see one of us perish or the grandchildren … and she's outlived many of her colleagues

ME: Just talking to myself trying to resolve the matter

V: Yes. Mrs S. passed last year

ME: And many of the neighbours have passed

V: Her pelonians loved her

ME: Thought I had more time to prepare for this possibility

V: They Facebook me and say she was their favorite teacher

V: I know

ME: Yes and still a minuscule fact in the total spectrum for Mom

V: Facebook can't know. My classmates make all these announcements but I dont want that at all

ME: No, no social media. Mom would be pissed LOL

V: Exactly

ME: Not now or for the funeral or anytime we must agree on that especially the kids got to chill. L. and the girls the same thing

V: I have guilt too but that coroner put it beautifully … she may have known.

ME: Yes she got in her home and we were both present and I'm rarely here on her birthday since moving to Canada

ME: She was so happy I was here this year. God worked it out

V: 🙏😢 Crying

ME: God tried to tell me in a dream. Or maybe he was preparing me

V: My heart has a void … just praying for peace

ME: Mother has cut us loose from the spiritual umbilical cord Val. She is with the ancestors now.

V: That's hard to swallow bruh. I just knew we had more time with her

ME: Isn't that what we've heard so many others say? Here we are and we are the closest thing you're going to get to her so let's do this

ME: You know Mom wouldn't want us to miss a step you know that

V: I know. I owe my strength as a woman to her and God. Period.
ME: She was all I ever cared about
ME: I have to pray to continue caring about anything right now
ME: Please pray for me.
V: I am definitely doing that. We gotta be strong for each other right now. I'm praying and praying, warriors you don't even know are praying for our family
ME: And you are next in order so don't you go breaking my heart. Take care of your health, V.
V: Crying Ok
V: she built a good mini soldier
V: Her strength carries me more than ever
ME: Mom thought you were strong as hell
ME: We would laugh about stuff you've been through and how you bounce back and how good you are on your feet
ME: Who, lady V? I don't talk about lady V. LOL
ME: Nobody better not say shit about V. LOL
ME: Mom will fight to the death for either one of us and the grandkids
ME: In fact that's exactly what she did … peace
ME: Great picture. Do you think we could use that for the obituary
ME: Or maybe we could use that picture from 1965 that she loves, that gorgeous picture of mom.
V: She said in her famous words, I don't drive used cars. You need reliability as a single mom.
ME: Yes
V: My spirit is broken but she lives in me. I will hear from her every day of my life. She wanted to get a passport and travel when kids graduated … we would talk about it. Come to Canada
ME: Yes. luckily Mom came to Canada in 2001 when my appendix came out. they flew her there and we spent the weekend in a hotel downtown before I knew I would live there, but God is good
V: Just like y'all heard that wooden flute. I'm waiting to hear from her
V: Think Thanks!
V: Another famous quote
ME: You will hear her voice tell you exactly what to do just listen and ask yourself what would she say
V: She loved God and he is hers
ME: She really did, since she was a child
ME: And the celibacy: incredible!
ME: Unreal. Mom never let any man touch her body except our father
V: That's why she will be by him
ME: In the general sense and in the not so general

ME: Like I said mom is in the same ilk as Harriet Tubman, Sojourner Truth, I know she really is

V: She loved that man and all marriages have problems as we know

ME: The fact that she never remarried says it all

V: Love is …

ME: When should I contact L. and them

V: A series of ups and downs …

V: When we get arrangements

ME: Ah yes

V: Or a little more arranged

ME: Mom is looking down on us I assure you

V: We don't need a lot of voices

ME: Dad already put a hedge of protection around us now we have double protection from the heavens

ME: Save this text because you let your man will need to know some of the sentiment whatever you choose

ME: This is real talk what we're talking about see

ME: Speaking of the eulogy

ME: And nobody really knew mom including us let's face it

ME: she will remain a mystery on many levels like all great artists

V: Do you know anyone better to speak from clergy … Granny will probably want Greenview and that would probably save huge costs who knows. I don't know

ME: Come on Val you know I don't know anyone. It's not up to granny to decide

V: I kind of go there. but Greenview is not real

V: I say Greenview is out

ME: If it's going to be bibleway then go thru them

ME: Agreed

ME: Like you said mom always liked bibleway

V: Granny spoke to those people about mom in a different light

ME: Yeah I know and not just them

V: They don't need to be orchestrating them

ME: That's not even a thought to me

V: G. found this in his phone

ME: Ok no more media right now please do a little bit at a time

V: Did a video on taking her to ihop one morning

V: Ok. Sorry

ME: OK see you around noon time

V: We trying to come sooner

ME: Well it's important that we expose ourselves to that stuff to heal but I've got my pace

V: G. has to be at work at noon

V: M. went to get hair braided. Has appt

ME: OK all good no one's on a strict schedule let the chips fall

V: Hey ron. You ok?

ME: I'm fine. I was only trying to talk in a language that granny could understand when I said that but in addition to telling the first person to call to say that is not tolerable

V: Yeah well Granny felt a little intimidated and I know emotions are running high. I told her you're ok. She really said she didn't mean to upset you like that. Let's stay on our course … all is well

ME: Intimidated? What's that supposed to mean I can raise my voice is the free world

ME: And you are passing that on to me as if

ME: did you and G. think I was going to attack when he knew why were you all evened up that was ridiculous

V: Nothing intended at all. Just sharing

V: No! We both told her that!

ME: like we were in the street, I was simply raising my voice. you all the ones that exaggerated the moment

ME: Thanks

V: I'm just sharing. She's fragile.

ME: We all fragile

V: I will see you soon

V: Yes we are. She keeps saying she is 97 and one word is just what she says and meant no harm

V: It's cool. All is well

ME: That's not how you describe somebody's death, your daughter, to a non-family member

V: I understand

V: It's too late to correct Granny now at her age

ME: No it's not

ME: She can at least hear it

ME: Who's next?

V: I hope no one but we agreed to be diplomatic and respectful last night

ME: Oh yeah that whole thing

V: Let's move forward. So much to do

V: I'm good and so is everyone over here

ME: Oh she's intimidated like I'm some gangster off the street wow

ME: Talking about Mom with no dignity. Just like anybody she would be talking about.

ME: I'm not trying to hold grudges here I'm just saying

ME: You can tell granny I've never laid my hands on any woman. And she wasn't about to be the first, tell her that

ME: Who beats up a 98-year-old grandma, and again I didn't appreciate the way you hyped that like I don't have any self-control wow

V: I didn't hype. I'm sharing granny's hype through text, which is not good. I will stop texting now and see you soon 🙏💕🙏

⋆ ⋆ ⋆

V: Good morning Ron! I hope all is well. I am running around researching and handling errands to include getting information about selecting a funeral home to take mom today. It looks like Leevy's will be a good choice and do everything there within the chapel. This will be the simplest and most efficient manner to expedite everything in my opinion. As moms personal representative, I'm reviewing documents and will give you a full report later today. I am in business mode all day in addition to securing things with my job for this week . I will be in touch! Love you 💕 Ron!

V: I just tried to call but running errands and researching costs … will give you full report this afternoon

ME: 👌

V: Once I get confirmation of best funeral home to go with today, we can set a time to meet with them and go over the whole process. They pretty much go over their process with us in full detail.

ME: Ok. Car payment and house payment due date?

ME: Well electricity and house, car is paid for

V: We will discuss in person later today. There are several options on how to handle. I would like to discuss in person … driving.

ME: Ok

V: Have you told the girls yet and L.? Are we still waiting to notify once arrangement made?

V: They may need to start planning for travel but I should have more definite info when we meet later today

V: I'm in transit, so I will be in touch as mentioned

ME: I haven't told the girls yet. But probably will call today

V: Ok let's call after I get you the most information I have available with day this week once i get to talk with Leevy's Funeral Home

ME: 👌

⋆ ⋆ ⋆

V: Hi. How you.
ME: Hey I'm ok
V: Ok 😭😢
ME: I went down earlier. Now I'm up
ME: I know it's very sad. It's going to take a long time to accept it
V: Same here
V: People close to me are really hurt for us.
ME: If ever. Mom seemed invincible
V: They knew how much I talked about her to my friends
ME: Talked to the girls, they are devastated. they are coming down
V: G.'s alpha brothers are calling me and they want to be there. They said they talked about the warmth of her house and uniqueness overtook them.
V: They been talking about her house since they met her
ME: I know
ME: You OK up there
V: Not really
V: But I gotta be strong for my kids
V: As always.
ME: Yes
V: Mom did the same for us when dad passed
V: She gave me those genes … survivor
ME: This is the feeling Mom has been living with … trying to explain to us about losing dad and now we are feeling it
V: 💔
V: My rock
ME: Queen Warrior
V: She got to see all of us before she left us
V: That makes me smile. She knew we loved her
ME: I know she was fighting to the end. She was fighting so hard that we didn't know how sick she was
V: I even prayed for her while putting warm wash clothes she instructed me to do
V: We followed her instructions to end as well
ME: Yes
V: Everything she asked for we gave it to her
V: In those two hours … Filled humidifier up with water. Thinking the wheezing would end
ME: Yep she figured out how to let us love on her one last time
ME: Rub the salve on her chest
V: I just knew she would live another 20 at least!
ME: Wasn't ready for this
V: Me either

ME: I can't get this right in my mind. I probably will need counseling

V: Yeah me too

ME: This is the first time I've ever felt like I needed counseling

V: I am really lost but trying to just keep it all together. This is like no other issue we have faced

ME: It just hurts me that mom had to feel the sting of death at age 74 in front of us

V: This is the first time I prob need. Hard liquor

ME: I feel like I would have rather taken it for her

V: 

V: 

ME: But then that would devastate her so can't win

ME: And she never had to live to see one of us perish including G.

V: So many emotions … love anger hurt guilt all wrapped. The guilt is normal and we just always let mom tell us she would be ok and we believed it. Why not??!!

V: She was my super hero

ME: Yes

V: I just hate I couldn't have just been stronger and more forceful to just put in car!!!!!

V: Period!!!!!

ME: I think she was avoiding doctors care because she knew that she was dying

ME: Same here I wish I had just put her in the car because she told me to call doctors care and want to call and got the address he said no that's OK I don't feel like

V: But then I say … mom wanted to be nowhere else than in her house daddy put her in at a new bride of 21

ME: Yup God let her make 50 years. she was so excited about the 50 year anniversary

V: You wanna see a pic

ME: No

V: I came across

V: Ok

ME: OK hit me up if you need me sis, got to get off the subject for a second

* * *

V: Good morning. Praying for you and me! I'm at funeral home right now. I got Friday date for us. They moved some things around

V: 🙏❤️🙏

V: My phone is losing charge. I will talk with you this afternoon

ME: 🙏

V: Have you eaten? I can bring you something. I haven't eaten yet

V: My appetite is gone …

ME: Same here. But I'm OK use this as a time to clean out and turn around. no more fast food on the go

ME: Mom's favorite hymn, know a verse in it that goes, he walks with me and he talks with me he tells me that I am his own. that's the hymn that we should use

ME: You can bring me a dozen eggs or more. that would be great. that's all I can eat

ME: "In the garden." That's Mom's favourite hymn!

V: Got you!

V: What else can I bring you. I'm in grocery store

ME: Gallon of milk. Loaf of bread

V: Ok …

ME: Grab a box of cereal too. maybe Froot Loops. the girls are on the way down

V: Bottled water

ME: No. Sprite or Coke

V: I will pick up snacks for them too … tv dinners for girls.

ME: I have plenty of bottled water

ME: K

* * *

V: My heart aches 💔

ME: I'm just starting to realize that it was Mom's time, believe it or not. we had our time but it was her time

ME: We just can't accept that it was her time but it was. everybody has a date

V: I'm not there yet

V: But sure I will be

ME: I just realized it

ME: Nobody dies before their time

V: Little too fresh

ME: I got to get to it

ME: Otherwise I won't be good

V: Yes

ME: So I am going to believe that date was already assigned just as her birthday was

V: Faith heals.

V: Let not your heart be troubled. Mom just spoke

ME: Yes yes
ME: Did you get the email?
V: Not yet
ME: AOL
V: Ok
ME: The picture is the one that says Ma 8283 I think that's the one
V: Ok you want to go with that one, not the cropped picture by the car. They can crop it but I still want the others you had
V: We can go with this pic
V: I'm using other one for easel
ME: Ok
V: Send me others for my files though
V: That we were gonna consider
V: Not tonight if not up to it
V: Got time for that
V: Oh I see them
ME: Sent three pics altogether. Ok

★ ★ ★

V: Hey Ron! Just checking in … did visitors come by your place? I'm just getting up but so drained and heart chest hurting right now. I checked on Granny and she asked about you.
Will you call her just to let her know you're ok? I'm going to lay back down brother. I love you and wanted to make sure you're good. Peace and love.
ME: Hi what's with the heart chest do you need to be seen?
ME: I'm good. I love you too
V: Not that type pain, just heavy
V: just wanted to touch base. In bed. When I'm up I will get down there. Tell girls hello. Just decompressing since it's the day a week ago that I saw momma and losing her. I wish I could be down there to be with you as well but glad girls are there with you right now. We will talk in our own private space at appointed time. It's best that we get our private time to just talk but I did not want you to think I'm closing up today just time to come down and breathe a moment. I'm in lots of pain on all fronts.
ME: 👉❤
V: 🙏❤🙏💕
ME: You are a soldier just like Mom. Keep pounding

V: I appreciate hearing that 💕 I got her house built back and had to handle all of those type things in all aspects of operations and knew a lot about Ins and outs . This is a lot different but the estate must be protected the right way and that's my expertise and lane which I plan to execute with her desires communicated to me.

Please know that when this soldier starts getting the second phase going I will need your full cooperation and let me run with torch. I'm proven on that end and would never do anything outside of respecting her wishes that we had to discuss for many years with my legal obligation to her and the process. We will talk, Ron, but we know the woman and how private she was and so that is why we will and must talk on certain levels that's just between us and tighten this up like she had it tight for us!!! I love you so much and we gotta be patient and there for each other. I will wait for our time together but can't do with others. Just you and I on deep and real matters that only we need to discuss. I respect the code mom engrained in us and me with the assignment of Lady V. We will protect her legacy and all of her assets like the Queen of England! She's our Queen and will always be honored!! 🙏

ME: Yes I concur. You'll have my full cooperation

V: Thank you!

V: 🙏♥🙏♥♥

ME: But we are together on paying off the house correct?

ME: That's a yes or no question

V: Yes. We are together on that

ME: Cool

V: I am weak. Typing slow.

ME: It's OK

V: And also we agree that we will never sell the home … it will remain in the Westray Estate along with all other heirloom assets belonging to Mom. Again these are two confidential topics to discuss more in detail privately but glad to confirm with each other this way right now. Correct? Are we good with this agreement as well?

V: It appears this needs more conversation. For now let's leave ALL of her assets in place until we talk not text. This takes time because of grieving. Just promise me no movement of anything until we talk as mentioned in earlier text. No problem. Again, I want to handle all property matters like the Queen of England and how aristocrats do because she thought of her belongings that way. As we both know. She's our Queen. God bless

V: Can this be agreed to?

ME: yes most certainly

V: Wonderful comments left on Leevy's site! I emailed you the link

ME: Thanks

V: Have girls call me before bed. I'm going to church in morning so I will see them in morning

ME: K

★ ★ ★

V: Hi! Checking in. My computer acting weird. Running a few errands. I will bring you macaroni down later as promised

ME: OK great. Mom's white boys who laid the tar for her came by with some more tar. they were all devastated and crying

V: Oh wow

ME: Yup. Cowboys out there crying like babies

ME: Everybody is devastated it's just a tragedy

V: I know. 😢💔💔

V: I'm literally a zombie these days. Trying to make it. I gotta press through and do what I do, like when house burned down. her legacy is what matters

ME: Right now it feels like I will never resolve this in my heart

ME: The more we can celebrate her legacy and let others know about who she was the more the pain will go away perhaps

ME: Like any great artist and teacher

V: I'm headed to gravesite … heavy heart

ME: What's going on out there

V: I just want to go. See how it looks. that was painful to see the breakdown with how it was supposed to be as well

V: I have flowers came to house. My therapy will take many forms

V: Wanted to take out there. It was a disaster to watch lowering malfunction. That hurts me too

ME: There's no need to fret on the lowering malfunction. if you want to talk about how things were supposed to be Mom is not supposed to be dead. everything happens as it should and Mom was used to having to do it yourself fixes she would want it corrected in the way that we try to correct it just like stuff we did in the yard there's enough to get over rather than making that the issue I don't get that

ME: To make that the centerpiece of the ceremony doesn't do it justice it was a classy ceremony

ME: Like I said I would love to worry about that but mom's death is enough for me

ME: Don't get me wrong it hurts me. But I know it was just a physical malfunction. I'm not going to make it the whole story. we do what we have to do. that's what mom would have wanted us to do

ME: Choices were to leave it as it was or to do what we did in closing the lid

V: Oh I agree Ron. I'm not making choices here. I'm grieving differently. Some things I guess you don't see my point on

ME: That comes with the package of not having a vault we had a plastic box

ME: So we should just start again, have a vault if that's gonna make you feel better or us feel better

V: No that's not true. I've talked through this with other funeral cemetery people. Leevy's tried to blame

ME: Greatest tragedy is that Mom died. All this other stuff is after-the-fact so I have to choose my battles do what you think is best

V: Some protocol was not followed but I can talk about it later. Yes it is not equivalent to mom's death. You know I'm not saying that

ME: I don't like what happened either but I know that everything happens as it should for whatever reason and that's what happened

ME: But I do follow it up in terms of protocols and adjustments

ME: They should have simply requested a new lowering mechanism before proceeding

V: They've been doing this over 100 years. Time and place though. Driving. Talk later

ME: But let me tell you it would've been much worse and we left earlier

ME: Ok didn't know you were driving. No texting!

V: Yeah at gas station. I had just got in car … was parked. I know

ME: 😬

V: I'm headed that way with macaroni and stuff for you

ME: Ok.

* * *

V: Morning. Starting back today … 2nd week of classes. It will be in a skeleton schedule with flexibility. Just introduction to classes, etc. first class at 9:30. Will be checking in.

ME: OK sis praying for your strength

ME: We shall continue to snatch victory from the jaws of defeat

ME: The only man to fear is the man in the mirror

V: Thank you. I have no fear of who I see in the mirror … thy rod and thy staff. They comfort me … will fear no evil. Psalm 23 🙏❤️🙏

ME: ❤️

* * *

V: Hello. Hope all is well. What are you up to. Still on campus at moment

ME: I am just at the house. I had a stomach virus all day feeling terrible. Just having a really bad day missing Mom as well

ME: Cold sweats on and off all day

V: I hate to hear that! Do you need juice or anything? I'm at Allen about to leave campus. My mind is not clear. Just gloom and tears as well. Trying to hold myself together. Ran so much all last week with no decompression. Still all inside on auto-pilot

V: I can't get in sync with rhythm for organizing classes because I missed a week and hate being behind but colleagues jumped in. Most students didn't come to campus until after MLK day on 16th when I showed up

V: All is well. Just trying to stay encouraged …

ME: Yes. It's just hard to accept I'm really having trouble today. start to feel a little better I think I can make it

V: 🙏💔🙏

V: You will. We all have to. With God, all things are possible!

ME: Yes

V: Hardest thing that's happened to me to date

ME: I just feel empty

ME: There's no higher level for me

V: We need the counseling like you said before. Grief is real … I know. We were taught to forge and press forward

ME: Yes I'm sure I do. I'm just empty. I have no interest in anything

V: I have some information that MetLife sent when you're ready. Let me know. It's a free service

ME: Ok

V: I will definitely be looking into it as well

V: I can't get anything done. I went into autopilot with funeral and it hasn't stopped. No time to really release and when I do my heart feels like a deep hole is in it

V: Funeral arrangements and dealing with all that

ME: I know we haven't even processed yet and I feel it and it's not good

ME: Having diarrhea all day has not helped at all

V: Well if you need juice or anything let me know. I can just stop it by. Let me get you something for that. Imodium

ME: I'm actually doing water so that's ok you've done enough Val. Get some rest.

ME: I've gotten through the worst part. I was in bed all day. I'm still in my pajamas

V: Ok. I'm a phone call away

ME: Thank you Sis. Love you

ME: My apologies for the recent tantrums. I'm just a little messed up right now

V: I know that 🙂💜😊

V: You're welcome. Love you more. 🙏💜🙏

<div align="center">★ ★ ★</div>

V: Hi. I prayed all last night that God would get you to feeling better! How are you? 🙏

ME: Thank you. Feeling a lot better 🙏

ME: I think Mom had a taste of what I have. Same symptoms and her body would not have been able to handle this at her age

ME: In fact I came down with this after I used fruits she left in her hanging baskets in the kitchen to make a smoothie. Next day I was down

V: I'm glad you feeling better. yeah this bug has been going around. It's all over news. it's really bad! So glad to hear you better!!!

ME: I really think mom died from influenza induced heart failure. Just like the coroner said when we first met with her

V: Mom never wanted flu shot. yeah that doctor said flu could take seniors out and it is known to be harsh on seniors

ME: Mom didn't even know she had the flu. Therefore we didn't know she had the flu. we didn't know how sick she actually was and she didn't show any signs. Her warrior quality worked against her on this one

ME: By the time she show the signs it was too late

ME: Mom's heart would not be able to tolerate influenza

V: 😢😔😞

ME: I know

ME: So that's what I want to hear on the toxicology if they should say that they saw influenza I know that that's what did it.

V: Granny Neal just called. She asked for your number and has been asking me about you. Just FYI that she may call. I'm letting my thoughts strictly be from love and what God requires no matter what I may personally feel towards others.

 God is Love and he will have to work on others in his own timing. We can only do what we do and do our part in forgiving … let go and let God. That's what I plan to do anyway. I just hung up with granny because she went on to barnwell for a few days to get away and deal with her grief. What would Jesus do? I'm not preaching or lecturing. Please know this. Just trying to heal and share loving thoughts and kind words during this difficult time. I 💜 you. My love doesn't change or waiver … ever. Jesus' Love is greater! I look at this painting I bought over holidays that says "Be the change you wish to see in the world" by Ghandi. I love it … powerful message

V: Going to lay down… getting dizzy and lightheaded. Need to take my blood pressure also 🙏
💕 🙏 Talk later … love you Ron

ME: Hey how are you?. I'm feeling much better. Yes thank you for your words of encouragement. Unfortunately I'm not him. But I love the guy 🙏

ME: The only thing I can talk to granny about is the reason I have decided not to ever speak to her again. Which really has little to do with two weeks ago. It has to do with the fact that granny hated Mom since the day she was born. And she badmouthed her her whole life and even in death the first words out of her mouth were derogatory. I will not be forgetting or forgiving that. So don't think we could talk unless it's for me to articulate in detail the things Mom reported to me. If you like to hear some of the stories give me a call

ME: The only person I respect is aunt Q. She loved Mom. I want to invest more time with her. Also next year we should conduct the Christmas Eve dinner at Mom's house. After all Mom started that tradition and it was only after she was hospitalized that granny took it over one year, So let's go back to Christmas Eve dinner with the Westray's to let the Neils do their thing. I would like to have a media fest during that location for the family, when we show all of the videos either during dinner or after dinner and various other forms of media that Mom is represented in.

ME: You're not mean enough to exact it (which, is, really, no punishment). Because they don't give a f*ck anyway when it really gets down to it they always done there own thing; and, granny has no respect for anybody. So you go on being the diplomat you are. And I'll go on being the renegade I think I am. I was having this conversation with mom a few days before she died and I was telling her I was ready to be more real with the so called family. Just been too much time

★ ★ ★

ME: Morning. Stewart, Dad's old EMS buddy, contacted me on Facebook. He said that dad was "talking" to him the same day Mom died. Via an article and pic he stumbled on. 😮 Don't you know dad wanted to drive the ambulance all the way from heaven LOL

V: Hi we just getting out of church Garrett said he texted and called you. Trying to catch up with you. Check your Phone. Call him back. He wants to get together about hip chick and feeding her … he had a conference 10a–2p and free now

ME: K just texted him

V: Hey! Forgot vacuum and bringing plate I fixed I forgot to give you. Be there in a few

ME: K

V: Tell me how you like those meatballs. Special sauce. I made the cabbage. Ran out of rice

ME: Will do

V: Last but not least I have been praying that you will reach out to Granny. Let it all go … mom would not want the strife. After all, she dealt with whatever with grace and never wanted us in the middle of that. Just consider. This isn't diplomacy … let's just do it to honor mom and how she would want us to handle it. Just consider this from big sis. Life is too short and we've all said or done something Granny has been asking about you and it would do my ♥ good to see you get on that plane with peace towards her … let Jesus in you allow this to happen. If you disagree, we can but I just wanted to share my thoughts. Mom would not want this discord or at least for us not to fight for her. In my heart, I know she forgave … even from others who may have offended her. She was that type of woman! Let us forgive and move on … so we can be blessed for it.

V: Just saying … sisterly love 💕

ME: Meatballs are amazing.

ME: Wow the yams OK Val

ME: Everything is really tasty. Me and Angela approve.

V: 😊

* * *

V: Hey! Just want to say that I love you and pray you have safe travels back to Canada!!!You didn't respond to my suggestion as it relates to Granny Neal but hope you at least consider it. 💕

Another consideration is allowing me to exercise guardianship of mom's jewelry while you are away. This is simply a request as we discussed a few weeks back so we both have joint access to her belongings as our MUTUAL desire is to protect her treasured belongings. I have a hole in my heart and the memories I hold with how She felt when the fire happened and I reminded her the next morning after she spent the night here that she didn't have her jewelry and she was forever grateful to me for taking her back to get them out the ashes. I just want to guard them (like I did in 2008) while you are away and it would help me feel connected to her in a mighty way if you don't mind. 🙏

That's it. my SENTIMENTAL self and wanting to connect through our woman bond with jewelry as women do.

I will gladly return for your safekeeping when you return but I would like the torch respectfully given to me and entrusted to watch over like you've had over the last month. If you can, just let me know the place you will leave in mom's house that ONLY you and I will know. With you gone, I would feel much better that I safeguard … We should have a mutual place we can agree to on this. Your house will be locked and like we said, I'm not comfortable going in your gun case or your home while you're away … unless an emergency arises. Not sure if you leaving keys in coat like you used to. I will also keep you posted when life insurance checks come to handle as agreed! THANKS a lot for letting me handle logistics and business aspects of making sure we protect the legacy. I remain committed to this … with you! Oh, the login to cameras as well … best for me to have eyes on this also since you are far away. I can respond quicker here if I see something. I would have preferred to discuss this in person but it wasn't the right time with kids around or while you had company. Just know we will get through this together and you are forever in my prayers and thoughts … all is well! Love 💕 you brother!

ME: I don't like that idea of leaving the jewelry in the house when no one's there. I also don't understand this need other than the fact that the jewelry is safe, so no I disagree

ME: It's not about who has the jewelry. It's about the jewelry being safe. the jewlery is safe locked in my safe in my house, not at mom's house with no one living there

ME: Although I understand your sentiment I disagree with the idea of just handling the jewelry. That's not what I've been doing I've just had them put up. There are eight pieces including Mom's dental bridge. Whatever rings you have, one or two

ME: That's when things happen, when you start passing items like that back-and-forth. right now there are no issues all the jewelry is intact

V: Ok. Thanks for understanding my sentiment. That really means a lot. I suppose you didn't take a picture on your phone of them you could send though? You're probably on way to airport so I feel good that you listened to my side without any explosion. Thanks for sharing your view.

Love 💕 Sis. Safe travels! Peace and love 🖤 Mom always called me a sentimentalist!! I guess you never really knew that side. Let me know when you get there safely … talk soon

V: Thank you. I was with her for at least 5 if those designs created by Andrew's on two notch. Does my heart ♥ good to see this memory. 🙏 thank you

ME: My pleasure Sis. Just trying to keep things simple. Love you

ME: 😘

V: 😘

★ ★ ★

V: Hanging in there?

ME: Yes. I'm just counting the days till I can get back down there

V: Yeah. I understand

V: Emma just called. They had to take Granny to ER for chest pain. Running test right now at providence downtown. They said they would keep me posted and call back once doctors talk to them

★ ★ ★

V: Hi. Just up as usual. Wanted to check in

ME: Morning. Yeah I went down early. Hope you're doing OK. One thing about it is that it would've felt the same way whether it was 10 years or 20 years later it would be the same feeling there would be no time when it would've been OK

ME: So painful. But the pain we feel is a measure of the love she left behind

ME: And we didn't have to watch mom slowly decline like so many people with their parents. God took her while she was still up right and functioning

V: Yeah. I hear you and true about never being ready! I just knew she would be here a lot longer but we don't know. I could never be ready. God's time is not ours … we have to just go with the days granted and making sure we're good in our hearts, mind and soul so we can return with Him to the most high! I know she's in Heaven. There is no doubt in my mind … "love covers a multitude of sin" saith the Lord. She was such a special soul

ME: Yes indeed

V: By the way, Granny had a aneurysm in her stomach area and they won't do surgery at her age. They are just monitoring and safeguarding what they can … please at some point try to forgive and call Granny … she's still asking about you and saying to tell you hello. It's best to just let go and let God! Forgive … like we all have been forgiven did things said or done. It's just something I want to encourage you about if nothing more than to be the best of how Mom raised us. She never showed strife or acted with disrespect towards Granny in front of us no matter her feelings. Let's just work towards peace … that's all.

ME: Yes. I am not mad at Granny. I just have nothing to talk about. Tell her I said hello

V: 🌎 Ok I will

ME: Mom didn't hold grudges She just didn't deal with that person anymore. I'm not trying to be her and I'm not acting in her behalf. It's just a real space

V: Time will heal and hopefully you can get to a real space and still get to a speaking point. It's just unfortunate that mom's death created a void … just a year ago you were helping Granny so much and going around there. Time will heal … gotta run have a good day! 💜 peace and love 💜

V: "Big sis" outlook … 😎

ME: I was helping her before that.

ME: Just like with mama, help can't be quantified. I've been helping granny thru years.

ME: I was helping her with the same knowledge that I have at present. But with mom's death it just created a resentment and it didn't help that going to disrespect her on the phone in front of me.

V: Yeah help definitely can't be measured. I will pray that the resentment is lifted is what I want for you. Not healthy. I do get the human element though

ME: That took me over the edge and it brought home all of the things Mom had already shared with me

V: All good. I'm out … have a good one 💀💀

ME: 👍

★ ★ ★

V: Hi. How you doing?

V: Not to worry you but … Doctor said I had abnormal EKG. Sending me to cardiologist

V: God got me. I'm trusting and believing in HIM. Keep me in your prayers. I went due to chest pain

V: She wants to pull me off job but I gotta make it work

ME: Hi. Ok praying 💜🙏

★ ★ ★

V: Thought you get a laugh. Mom got her escrow returned of whopping $3.50 since mortgage paid in full 😂

ME: 😂😂

ME: And she would've been so serious about spending that

ME: Hope you are feeling better. I had abnormal EKG in my 30s, probably still abnormal. This usually not that serious. The chest pain not sure could be digestive

ME: About to crash. Talk to you over weekend ♥

★ ★ ★

ME: Morning. Hey maybe just save that check. It's a hilarious memento

ME: And its signed Valentine's Day lol

ME: Any word on the toxicology? It's been seven weeks. You know what I just thought about? Mom was never a person to linger. She left as she always did. Unexpected. Think about it

ME: And even if Mom had survived the heart attack the possible brain damage or disability would've been more painful for me than instant death

V: Hey! My heart ♥ is just still so heavy. I'm not in total acceptance … seems you're a little ahead of me. We go to same physician so I told her and she was saddened to hear. She says they always put cardiac arrest on death certificate when they arrive and patient was non responsive because heart did stop. What messed me up was she said any cold medicines could have triggered reaction. but she said it's hard to say.

Mom was just talking to me in normal voice at 11p that Friday night and again around 9a Saturday morning. It was too sudden. Something did a 360 and it's all after fact now. Just should have called ambulance but mom was saying she was feeling better while I was there. I'm getting sad and got a lot of grading and stuff. I definitely don't want to text … I'm following up on toxicology too. The autopsy report was requested in writing before they would send. It's sad that I saw mom and did CPR and all this. It was very traumatic and I've had no time to grieve. This is unlike no other experience in my life. I know I'm supposed to be strong and I will but I'm human too. It's tough.

ME: Yes I understand. I just happen to think about it in different ways to try to resolve it.

V: Everybody does a second guess of what they could have done. I get that … just gotta get through one day at time.

ME: I'm over the could've would've should've stage. Just trying to accept

ME: I think Mom had a stomach virus or flu which stressed her system to vomiting first, heart could not handle it

ME: That same stomach virus I came down with

ME: Will stay strong. You know mom would want us to keep it moving. I got to go in now for auditions for next year ttyl

V: Well try going there and being here waiting to get a call or when you pull up … you waiting for momma to come outside … my heart is so heavy bruh … went to April tax like I always do for her and took her stuff into be filed. She broke even like usual … they were very saddened too. Yeah, that's what I keep telling myself.

V: Ok. Ttyl. Chick digging bad by that tree in his pen. Gonna get G. to put cinder block in that hole she keeps digging … just FYI. I found one on back lot that will work … know she misses her friend too!

ME: I totally understand. OK also use any pine straw that you can get it for her holes

⋆ ⋆ ⋆

V: Hi. I see I had missed call. I was away from phone. How are you

ME: Doing okay just checking in You hanging in there?

V: Yep. Hanging best I can. G. headed to Germany next weekend over spring break for a week

ME: Hey. OK great I was wondering when the trip was.

V: Been out with him most of day getting appropriate warm gear for that weather over there and business casual attire. He looked at some Stacy Adams today that he really wanted. I only chuckled after thinking of mom back in the day during her Stacy Adams years with you …

ME: Lol ah yes

V: He's in Germany March 10–18

ME: Cool. That's huge. Happy for him.

V: Yeah great opportunity!!!

ME: Well stay strong. I'll be rolling in four weeks.

V: Ok. We been trying to hold it down. I filled in holes in chick pen with straw and stuff … she's had a lot of good home food leftovers past few days

ME: Oh great

V: Need you to connect with that SCAD contact when you go to Savannah for M.

V: She got award for self portrait she did and in honors art class

ME: Ok will do that next week

ME: That's super!

V: Just trying to see if they have a summer art program that she could participate in. I think she is leaning towards graphic design or mass communications

ME: K

V: By the way. Check out 8a or 11A service with pastor Jackson at Bibleway BWCAR.org tomorrow. Think you will enjoy the live webcast. Click watch live link!!

⋆ ⋆ ⋆

V: Just finished helping G. pack for his big trip. He's excited
V: Mom was looking forward to seeing him leave for first trip out of country 😢
V: She gave him a great map that they put over his bed ... she loved geography and maps!
ME: Yes I'm sure she will be with him.
V: No doubt! I feel her presence driving home now
ME: Yes she's everywhere.
V: Living memory
ME: Yes
V: Watered plants today. Those on front porch really needed it and one on her bathroom ... they should bounce back
V: Totally wasn't going to front porch. Hard enough going in period
ME: OK. And the violets in the garden room window by the back door
V: Yep. Got em. They were cool
ME: Cool
V: Got to do nuclear stress test with dye next week and echocardiogram ... Cardiologist 2nd opinion. Doesn't like abnormal Ekg either
V: On mom and dad's anniversary 3/13
ME: I did that in 99. You'll be fine
ME: A's birthday 3/12
V: Yeah I know
V: Got it in calendar
V: They growing up!!!!
ME: I thought mom and dad were March 23
ME: Sweeties
V: Nope. March 11 marriage license and 13th was when it was officiated by reverend brown at granny's house
ME: 👌
V: I always called her and said happy anniversary
V: And she would say ... wow you always remember 😁
V: Granny had aneurysm in stomach but at home doing ok now. Looking for sitter full time
V: Ok nite ... been a long week. On spring break next week

V: The weeks get longer and longer
ME: K, Night 💕

★ ★ ★

ME: Wow great pic
V: Yeah
V: Glad he gets to see more out here than SC or United States for that matter
V: He needed this
ME: Yes he really did need this experience. nothing like getting out of the 🇺🇸 sometimes
V: Yeah. He even beat me to it! I'm overdue with getting this passport. Mom and I were just talking about getting ours
V: 😂
V: Yeah that's true
ME: Yes
V: He talking bout he is at a Irish pub drinking a beer. Some things I guess I don't need to know! 😡
V: It's 11:40p over there
ME: Yeah the drinking age is 18
V: What??!!!! 🙅! ⍰
ME: Europe yeah … and you can marry a 16-year-old
V: OMG!!!
ME: Same here in Canada 16 hee hee
V: You really made my day! 😡😒
V: 😬😩
V: 😂
ME: He would be at Irish pub in Germany. Germany is the beer capital of the world lol
V: Yeah I know. Was trying to forget
ME: 😂
ME: He should really try some German beer. lol
V: Oh I don't doubt he will
ME: Yes
V: Let me tell him to get on back to hotel!! 🙅! ⍰🙅! ⍰. This is why he said this is best of life
V: This knucklehead will be 21 soon. I might as well recognize
ME: Won't be long before he'll be dragging some woman home lol
V: 🙅! ⍰

ME:

V: Azalea called to check on me. She's growing up!

V: Sounding all mature …

ME: Oh nice. yeah I guess she is growing up.

V: I pulled him up on my location. At O'Shea's Irish pub in Nuremberg.

ME: Wow

V: Unbelievable!!!

ME: All Westrays are leaders and teachers and our children will be the same

V: Absolutely!

ME:

ME: Billy Graham only wanted one word on his headstone. Preacher. I think mom's headstone should say teacher

ME: Along with her name of course

V: Not feeling that one …

ME: K

V:

ME: I trust your discretion on the design. Something simple.

ME: Similar to dad's headstone in shape

V: Yeah. Yep

ME: And his headstone needs straightening

V: Wish I could bridge theirs together

V: Yeah I told guy that

ME: Maybe buy a new one combine them both. Because mom's name is on dad's headstone as a living person so it's obsolete

ME: And we could include the grands and our names

ME: Or don't include anybody's name as survivors. Because same situation with mom's name on dad's

V: Yeah that's a thought. It really isn't obsolete due to time and place and mom got that for dad on that time. It's still relevant … time and place

ME: Just throwing out ideas. Put it all together. I trust your discretion.

V: Yeah it will work out … these people do this all time and give good ideas and samples to view.

ME: Has the deed shown up yet?

V: No it has to go through proper channels according to Wells Fargo

V: It will be in mom's tin box with all these other docs I used to get all this stuff done … glad I was strong enough to pull through. Wasn't easy going through all the planning for the service but it worked out … my pastor said it was a wonderful service and he has seen a many

ME: You have done an incredible job under the circumstances. But you've always been a strong person. We had a great teacher.

V: Yes yes … She was my best friend … as far as a female friend in my life. She taught me well

ME: keep the vitamin D going
V: Yeah and my potassium was low
V: I'm under 50,000 units prescription … take once a week
ME: Oh wow ok
V: I'm on cholesterol medicine and a low-dose sleeping pill because I wasn't sleeping at all at one point
ME:
V: I was trying to avoid this cholesterol medicine but I won't be on long term. Messes with kidneys
V: I hate all this medicine. Trying to avoid blood pressure issues for sure
ME: Precisely. Try niacin. And red yeast rice after you wean off of the Lipitor
V: Yeah I'm not on Lipitor thank goodness. Milder one
ME: Niacin is the natural remedy.
V: Oh ok
ME: And niacin is the base medicine for a lot of the pharmaceuticals
ME: Small tablet tasteless
V: Well last but not least I have a huge dental issue in morning! I gotta get 7500 worth of work and coverage will only cover 2100 with insurance. Dental is always lousy
ME: Oh my
V: It will take most of my tax return
V: Yeah thank god I got a good return
V: It's inevitable
ME: And that's what money is for.
V: This is what being without insurance looks like for preventative things
ME: Yes
V: So two root canals here I come and on spring break to get done. All I can say is forever indebted for you picking tooth up out of Liston but the torch is even further now.
V: Like mom always said I ain't gonna be bald … well I ain't gonna be snaggled-toothed
ME: Lol you've done well. It was the least I could do LOL. OK good to catch up good luck in the morning. Love you talk later.
V: I'm in front of folk for a living talking. Too much.
ME:
V: Alright bro. Same here … those are the two … hee hee
ME: That Millie Lewis smile LOL
V: Ha ha … gotta protect
ME: You and Denzel Washington LOL
V:
V: Well beauty secrets are well earned. Later
ME: That's a great quote. Later

V: Thx … learned from that teacher of ours.
ME: And part of being a woman is knowing when not to be too much of a lady. Ha
ME: Always love that.
V: LOL … I had that in my head last week. Crazy!!!
ME: Mom. And you were as welcome as you feel.
V: There willl never be another
V: We had a treasure in so many ways. Her spirit lives always
ME: Yes. She is now mystical.
V: Creative and original all wrapped up in one
ME: Not even trying. Wow
V: Indeed. End on this note. Talk soon 😍
ME: OK bye
ME: 👍❤️
ME: Wow beautifully blessed
V: Yeah I just told him. he's a little put out with the way the whites are acting cliqueish since it's only him and a black girl out if 20 in the group. We both know how white folks can make you feel less than worthy to be somewhere where only they think they belong! I know what he's feeling and you at UT Austin and me when I was a student and worked at USC. Story of our people. Mom in Pelion as only black teacher for years. He needed to see all of this to get his mind right for workforce.
V: Sad but true. My heart goes out to him but i know how they have that unspoken bigotry especially at USC but he's worthy to be there and in the school of business just like Them! Told him to keep
ME: It's a very important lesson. So he has to recognize it and maneuver around it
V: Exactly
ME: And Eastern Illinois and York University. And J@LC and savannah jazz white people
V: I told him the same thing
V: Ha ha. Yep!!!
ME: It's called America
V: I know right …
ME: Mom was a white person expert. And she passed skills to us. God bless her soul.
V: But they think because they cut up and go out in five-points that all is well. They are ok until you end up somewhere they think is only entitled to them
V: She definitely was
V: and I told him he was from that stock and to recognize and move within it. He understood

ME: Tell him to Google the Orkney Islands. We have plenty of Scottish blood too
V: I will

★ ★ ★

V: Had been looking for this. Mom put in a card and I came across recently. My 50th birthday card
ME: Oh yes. I have this on my hard drive
ME: Oh wow. She was right on time. She made exactly 50 years at the house
V: Yeah. Still thought she had so many more years
V:
ME: I know
V: She has that never ending spirit. Would be around forever
V: And literally she still is
ME: She is alive in us.
V: Just never will be the same
ME: Still can't wrap my head around it. And as hard as I try
V: Yeah. I'm gonna get with a grief counselor. My doctor strongly recommended to me
ME: If I have accepted it I have not resolved it. I don't think I ever will
V: Since I was so up close in bathroom and witnessed it head on. Very traumatic
ME: I can imagine. No less for me from my perspective
V: Did CPR on phone with 911 operator
V: Yeah I know
ME: I can't get the image of you holding her on your lap. I knew she was dead the minute I saw
V: You don't want that image. I think I knew but was in shock and holding on to hope so desperately
ME: I still can't believe it
ME: I do but I don't
ME: I do think Mom knew more than she was communicating that week
ME: Saturday morning she called me and said she had a panic attack. But I think mom had early stages of the heart attacks started Friday night
ME: I think mom had blockage complicated by either the flu or some type of virus
ME: Most people with mom's condition already had the stents put in place and going to the dr. every other week. Mom did not that
ME: We all have hereditary high cholesterol. We may have to get stents in about 10 years

V: Could have had pneumonia. She sounded like herself when she called me that morning … then that cough syrup could react with her blood pressure medicine. They tried that

V: Something did a 360 very quickly

ME: I really don't think it was the cough syrup. I think it was pneumonia and or blockage

ME: Cardiac arrest is defined by the unpredictability. And the sudden onset

V: But she jumped up from her bed like old times and walked normally to the back like ol times. saw it with my own eyes and was thinking she was ok and we would go on to Medcare like she agreed to

ME: Mom had all the markers for cardiac arrest. Did not like going to doctors. And would not communicate about her health. I know

ME: Is devastating.

V: But she complained about not being able to urinate. That's kidneys which tie into heart. Renal

ME: Precisely

V: Backed up fluid. Went to lungs

ME: I think Mom had small heart attacks leading up to the big one and she didn't know what was going on

ME: She told A. in a casual conversation earlier that week that she almost left here one night

V: I'm glad we were there and did everything she asked of us in her moments before leaving. I even prayed for her in her bed and didn't know why. I felt compelled to

ME: Mom knew something Val

V: I touched her whole body and prayed with the pink washcloth she told me to get out of her bathroom

ME: I put the vapour rub patch before I left. that was my last contact

V: Yep. I know

ME: She was lying in the fetal position on her left side when I left the house she looked like she had given up. I can't get that out of my neither

V: God wanted her with him more

V: I Remember she helped me get her humidifier hooked up. I added more water. she said that felt good and she could breathe better

ME: But overall Mom lasted much longer than most with her life story. she coulda left here after dad died. she coulda left after the bad accident with the car. she coulda left that day at Granny's house. she coulda left those times she had to have blood pressure and had to be taken straight from her appointments to the emergency room. and other moments that we probably don't even know about on the road. the wheels off for that thing. For us. She stayed around for us. Mom had plenty opportunities to leave over the years

V: Then she had me get her washcloth. She specifically said to go get one out if her bathroom and put Vicks on it

ME: She rode the wheels off of that thing they call life

V: God kept her through all that and we don't know why. but God knows and he makes no errors as hard as that is for me

ME: That was her only prayer, that she stay around to raise us. she said it all the time

V: My faith is all I can hold on to … she always gave the best

ME: She took us well beyond

V: Always giving always doing

ME: She couldn't do anymore

ME: All she had to do was stay alive. But Mom was finished

ME: Mom died with no pain. She did not fear death. But she loved life even more.

ME: I will never get over her I feel so alone.

V: Yes she loved God and knew him. I know where my momma is

ME: Yes and we will see her again one day. one day we will all be together again

V: I am empty too. So broken

ME: Sometimes I feel like a motherless child

V: I have the picture from Leevy's when I went by there, but can show you when you come home. May not be a good time

ME: But we have so much time with her, it would never have been enough

ME: You can send it

V: When they dressed her. I look at it often.

ME: Yeah I need it for the archives. And I'm curious. I know it will hurt but I have to see it

V: I haven't shared these with anyone. Just for us.

V: She looked so peaceful. Leevy's did a good job. You ok?

ME: Oh OK. Thanks for sending. I'll hit you back in little bit. I'm ok

* * *

V: You alright?

ME: Yes

V: Ok. I was not sure you would want to see via text

V: But thank goodness for technology in this century

V: I'm still not into social media and posting my whole life story like some people I see put there

V: Meant to tell you … Toby sent us a very nice card from penitentiary

ME: Oh wow! 😬

ME: My man

V: Yeah it was touching

V: He said he wept for the loss

V: She was like a second mom to him

V: I remember her helping him or sending things by B. way back when, or sending scriptures

V: When he first got locked up

ME: Yes

V: He said she was like a second mom. His mom passed when he got locked up

V: What do you think about pictures of mom

ME: Is just as I remember it.

ME: I'm glad I saw them because I had forgotten the details of how she looked it was foggy on my mind

ME: But it hurt. Real bad

V: Yeah me too bro

V: You have no idea. I listen to art house every other day just to hear her voice

ME: But mom told me before she died that I was one of the hardest men she knew. And I plan to always be that.

V: Just short piece not entire video

V: What did she mean. Not showing emotion or what?

ME: It's a manner of speaking. You definitely haven't had much experience with hard men

ME: Like men she trusted along the way

V: I just never heard that expression

ME: It means tough Val

V: Ha ha. Got it 😊

ME: 💪

ME: But that really has sustained me. Because Mom viewed me like she viewed men she hung with. And that was based on actions. Things she has seen me do

V: Yeah

ME: She wanted me to know that she thought that I was tough

V: Got it

ME: As a man that means probably everything

V: I'm sure.

ME: And as a mommas boy well

V: Mom was good at always building us up. Always let us know

ME: There's a difference in building up, that's a stage. But acknowledgement comes after testing

V: No one did it better … and genuine

ME: Yes

V: Yeah I have some writing in cards of what she thought about my strength. Cried the other day reading one of her letters to me

V: She wrote her feelings out

ME: Precisely
V: She equated the magnolia in yard being same age when I turned 50
V: Funny
ME: Yes. That's what your plaque is on that tree
V: Have makeshift birthday photo with the limb making an "A" in the happy birthday card she made
V: Unbelievable
ME: A truly full life without a doubt. Just wanted more time with her
V: Very precise and abstract at same damn time. Who does that
ME: That's what the greats do
V: Well she's one of the greatest!!! No doubt
ME: It comes from knowing the subject, thoroughly.
ME: Accuracy meets freedom
V: Indeed. I told my class once in talking about success. Talked about you. Success = preparedness meeting opportunity. Must be prepared
ME: Yes she is one of the greats
ME: Like actually
V: I know. Glad we got to witness her greatness through childhood to adulthood. We're blessed
ME: Yeah we had plenty time
V: But like you said never enough to be satisfied. I saw her being here another 20 for sure.
ME: And this is the natural course. She is supposed to leave before us. We're both in or near 50
ME: And we were there. We are blessed
V: But god called her on home to be with him. Well I'm not convinced that it was her time. Only time and God can get me there. Her mom outlived her so. It's God's timing
ME: Yeah but that's not the natural course
ME: It's not possible to die before your time even if you jump out a window that was your time
ME: Basically that's what it is. But that's natural
ME: We are both used to Mom being a part of our future. Now she is indelibly a part of our past
V: I don't know if the kids that are innocents in a classroom who get shot and killed by a maniac. Is their time
ME: Yes that was their time that's the point
ME: It was already written
ME: Martin Luther King. John F. Kennedy. tragic but that was the time
ME: Michael Jackson. Tupac. Elvis. Sad but true
V: I will keep her spirit alive in me forever. Memories are what will sustain me …

V: I will get there, just will take time
ME: Well of course. But I do believe it was her time as hard as it is to believe
ME: We are so used to mom's uniqueness. And death makes her equal to others. I don't like that either
ME: But I have to swallow it
V: I can't put her in my past but I know she is gone
ME: Well that's all a psychologist is going to tell you
ME: Mom is a part of the past. 12 week has passed
ME: But our memories we have always had. her art is everywhere and her quotes are embedded in our brains and videos and pictures
ME: Like all greats she will live forever but I have to acknowledge time
ME: And circumstance
V: And it's ok. I just can't label it that way as I work through it. That's all
ME: It's too painful to try to pretend that she is not a part of the past
ME: For me. everybody grieves in their own way.
V: Yeah, we're different in that way. Sentimentalists like me. We're doomed
V: In a good way
V: I will get there slowly but surely … mom wrote once to me. You remember with the heart
ME: Sure it's cool
ME: And she called me tin man. You know what his problem was
ME: But I love Mom more than anything in the world. And I've never experienced grief at this level
V: He needed a heart
ME: I've never had my heart broken in my life till mom
V: ?
ME: Yes
ME: I'm not sure I knew I had one until Mom died
V: Wow. That's heavy
ME: I knew I loved mom. But that was about it
ME: She was only connection I had to what it could be
ME: Sibling love, that's different
V: Of course. Nobody love like a mothers love
ME: The only woman I've ever loved
ME: And now she's gone. I am empty
V: Yeah, I know. I hear you. And no matter what we think about Granny she brought mom forth and I'm grateful for that and she is grieving in her way losing a daughter. I believe that … she continues to hope to hear from you. She said that's her prayer every time I talk to her: How is Ron?
ME: I get that. And I appreciate you reminding me of these things. Still healing

V: I know. Only time. I get it

V: Yeah, nice person, she really appreciated mom for who she was

ME: She did. And she was mom's wheels at a time mom needed her. And provided good company for mom and I appreciate that

ME: And that has nothing to do with all the stuff you did for mom. That's a whole nother level

V: Oh I know.

V: I ain't tripping … I'm always the daughter and the September Song she loved to sing. She wrote that to me too

V: That's apples to oranges

ME: So that's my story and I'm sticking to it sis. Just trying to heal. I'll be home in 21 days

ME: mom loved us more than anything

V: I hear ya. You will. yes she did

V: And I love ♥ her for that … loyalty to her family.

V: Through it all

ME: It's just an overwhelming amount of love she left behind

ME: Just think mom already knew what it felt like from her grandparents, from Dad, from uncle W. The only people who truly loved her

ME: That's why Mom was the way she was. she already understood this level of pain

ME: She was trying to tell us that but I couldn't understand until now

V: Like she always says, you will understand it more by and by

ME: Yes. And here we are

V: Loved to say that

ME: But she prepared us for a death from the time we were young. She would always tell us so I'm just a living memory and she meant basically enjoy me now because I'm just a living memory I will be gone and she was trying to let us know for a long time

ME: And that actually consoled me that she told us that the consistently through the years I'm just a little early and now I know what she meant and it actually kind of helps she prepared us

ME: It makes so much sense now

V: Man I knew mom would not be here another 70 … just not January 6th after just talking to her and stuff … not ready for that!!!! No!!!

ME: She meant I'm alive but I'm already a memory.

ME: As odd as it is. That's a complete cycle, to die one day after the day you were born

V: Yeah … only time and God can mend this hole! ♥

ME: He let her see her whole birthday week, fried fish and drank beer that night

ME: But we will never be OK as Mom might say lol

ME: This is what it feels like to have a mom that great. It hurts

V: I talk to her all the time and play a song called "Safe in his arms" that consoles me! She is safe now by her shepherd who watches over her now by the meadow in the field

V: Psalm 23. Her favorite

ME: 🙏

V: Talk later, Enjoyed the chat. Garrett leaving Germany in morning. Gets home Sunday

ME: Great. Me too

★ ★ ★

ME: Well so be it

V: When I call she can't really talk about this because her church folk are there and she has to not let them hear her looking at bringing someone else in. She fell the other day and Deacon W. and S. were there. They had to get her a commode top.

ME: Okay

V: It was loose which caused her to fall when she reached for it. I check on her when I can.

ME: yeah mom's death has afforded her all the attention she ever wanted and i'm sure she is milking it … don't like that. not that she doesn't deserve the attention, but it's never enough for her and she will accept it at the expense of anyone.

V: Yeah she's fallen a lot and she said she may move in her little house next door. I got a property management company to rent her house so she didn't have to worry about it and she complains about all the cars (and the drug dealers) all the time.

ME: she has plenty of people supporting her. and mom was not on her list as far as she was concerned. she actually told mom she was having her removed from her contact list cause she too sick to do anything and don't answer the phone. that's recent like over the holidays, weeks before moms death. she has a lot to think about. hadn't been to the house in 10 years. that envy. she hobbles everywhere else she wants to go

V: I got that company over a year ago but their lease is up in May and she can choose not to renew it … all I hear are the stories of how she provided for mom and it was rough after L. died but she never lacked for anything. She provided and made sure she got to college

ME: that's not sufficient. there is even more to life and love. she despised mom from the time she came back to the city from Barnwell. mom didn't even know C. was coming into the world. one day much later they told her to go in and look at your brother

V: Why do you think? She wanted to focus on new husband and life with their child?

ME: Granny was doing her thang in Columbia and was into Mr. N. Land his child were dead to her. Yes, Mom was a part of her past not her future in a sense … and there you have it. So as for my part I plan to complete it. They have never done anything for us. What do I need them for? Mom recycled all this bullshit. That's who she was. My mother; the recycler of bullshit

V: This is why mom didn't want to put bias on us. She's still our grandmother and all families have something. Forgiveness is just our duty through it all. It protects our soul so we can go on and be with mom again. Just like forgiveness is hard. I can forgive; and mom just wanted peace and was always hoping change would happen. Keep hope alive

ME: So did Martin Luther King, Jr.

V: You're crazy man. Lol

ME: let me just clarify one thing: That spiel that granny gives bout what she did for mom as a child *is* your responsibility as an adult. Furthermore, it's no different that what you would do for a boarding student. Where is the love, baby?

V: I'm just seeing this. Sorry I didn't respond until now. Yeah I hear you. We can't correct it. I just want my heart to be right and love covers a multitude of sin. Mom reminded me of that verse a lot

ME: Yes; but like that story about Dad slapping her down to the floor … like, really? God knows who she told that. That Mom left us and ran off to California. Like we didn't know where the hell Mom was. Lastly, I'm not talking about Mom's upbringing I'm talking bout her down-low-ding; Tainting her name at Greenview Church over the years. I'm talking bout now. But Mom's now is no more. But I will control mine … I'm not mad at nobody.

V:  I know. It's so long ago but not right. We gotta not hold onto past with ignorance and wrongdoings. We gotta break the cycle. They waiting for us to go in and be cold now that mom isn't here. I won't give them that and more to keep mess going. I see your point though. I can be ok and still speak and love from afar … and be in touch or whatever

ME: I knew all this stuff the whole time I was dealing with Granny. When you speak of forgiveness, I've been doing it the whole time. That was my purpose. But to spit in my face like she did that morning on the phone will not be forgotten—Consequences. They can't do shit but talk about it either way. Bunch of cowards.

V: We have two different styles. You know I thought about that. When you said that's how mom passed away on toilet. She repeated what you said. But you specifically told her we weren't announcing it and that's what she ran with. She told the first person that called

ME: by which i meant seated. that wasn't the point we were asking her not to announce. it hit facebook right after that

V: ! ⍰ She later said that was her daughter and she was telling her closest friend ms Cunningham. And it was already known because we told her late

ME: Right; like fuck what you saying imma just tell the first person that calls. no tears no nothing. she was just flipping thru the rolodex to see who she could call. just like it was any old body

V: I can see how that could anger you. I've just grown immune to granny with no emotions or care and so did mom

ME: Well it's not acceptable because she wants to be perceived otherwise and thats fake as hell (pun intended).

V: Mom just did her part to remain respectful and remember that she was her Mother. At least that was what she always told me … I got it. Peace and love

ME: Hi. My heart is so heavy. Mom had been asking me to find this since the 1990s. I finally found it, and she is gone. This is the only song she played on piano; and there is a middle section to the song that she couldn't remember. I'm so sad that I will never be able to show her this—and play the B Section for her.

Look to This Day

For it is life—the very life of life.
In its brief course lie all
the realities and truths of existence
the joy of growth, the glory of action, the splendor of beauty.
For, yesterday is already a memory;
and tomorrow is only a vision
but today, well lived, makes every
yesterday a memory of happiness,
and every tomorrow a vision of hope.
Look well, therefore, to this day.

—Ancient Sanskrit

Virginia Ann Bush Westray (1944–2018)

So sue me if I go too fast
but life is just a party
and parties weren't meant to last

—Prince

Her friends called her Ginger. She often told me, "Anyone that calls me 'Virginia' better know what they are talking about." Mom was a black Ginger. She had the personality of the "white" Ginger; and Mom's style is imbued upon her home by the force of her personality.

Names have personalities; and Mom was one tough cookie—a *Ginger Snap*, if you will.

Speaking of names, Mom claims to have brought the Westrays to town. The town is Columbia, South Carolina. Dad was from Pittsburgh.

He was stationed at Fort Jackson SC when he met Mom at the intersection of Taylor Street and Harden Street—that's "downtown." It was more than a claim. Mom did bring the name to town. As a child, Mom grew up downtown (off of Taylor Street). But that's *not* why she was on Taylor Street at the right place, and at the right time. Mom was a student at Allen University. The school rests at this intersection.

Near this very location is a landmark-funeral-home owned by the Leevys (a well-respected black family in the South). Lawyer, funeral home director and House of Representatives member I. S. Leevy Johnson (deceased), of the 74th district, was the most well known of the Leevys.

December 23, 2017, was Mom's 50th anniversary in the Farrow Hills (subdivision) three-bedroom brick home that Dad had purchased for them. She reported that his instructions to her were, jokingly, "do whatever the hell you want to do with it, baby."

Dad probably never knew how much Mom appreciated him saying that to her; or maybe he did. She followed his instructions to the T: http://www.imdb.com/video/user/vi769438489/.

On January 6, 2018, Mom died, unexpectedly, in the home she loved. She had just turned 74 the previous day. Never remarrying, Mom survived Dad by 42 years. On January 13, we buried Ginger next to Ronny ("with the Y," as she called him) at the Gates of Heaven cemetery. Leevys conducted the service. Mom respected the Leevys a lot; the service was classy.

Because we learn by experience, not by definition, only now (and, seemingly, too late) do I understand the meaning of love and of loss.

Mom's favorite expression was "Why?" This is now my mantra, albeit for a different reason. Whatever the source, this was truly Mom's persona quantified. She would often tell me that when she was really feeling good, she would go to the bathroom mirror, look and ask "Why?" before she stepped out in any direction.

Perhaps she developed this open hypothesis while staring at herself in the mirror at her grandparents' home in Barnwell, SC, as a cared-for child. Or perhaps it was the mirror in that one room she had to stay in, all day, when she finally joined her mother, on Pine Street, in the city of her birth. Jennie Ree Wright-Bush-Neal, her mother, was working *and* expecting her second child. Mom once told me that the day her brother was born, she was still in the "room" and knew, not even, the reason for the baby bump, prior to. She heard a baby cry later that day. Sometime later it was tersely explained, "Virginia, that's your brother."

I always tried to be there for Mom. I never realized that this time I would not be. I wasn't expecting it. Mom's death has not stripped me of my confidence, per se. The incontrovertible has left me void of feelings and empty; if I can accept it, I cannot resolve it. For now, I can only hope I would, ultimately, become the kind of Dad that Mom was to me and my sister. By that standard, presently, I am not, even, close. The pain I feel at Mom's passing is a measure of the amount of love she left behind; and like her love, her death is, at times, unbearable. Mom could love you until it hurt.

Mom's favorite room in her home was her main bathroom. She once described it to me as "one big bathrobe." This is the room where Mom was found. I first remember seeing a glint of light from my kitchen. It was the rear lights of a truck of some sort. I leaned in to get a better view. There was a fire truck in front of Mom's house.

Just behind it, there was another truck—an ambulance. I ran out my back door and met them as they entered Mom's yard. I beckoned, "What's going on?" The EMT responded, "Patient unresponsive."

They attempted to enter Mom's side door but couldn't. I simply walked up and opened the door. It wasn't locked. They chuckled at themselves as they rapidly entered the home.

I arrived at the bathroom at the same time as they did. There sat my sister, V., holding our lifeless mother on her lap from behind. I knew she was dead the minute I saw her. I will never forget the tragic, yet wry, smile on her face. In my mind, Mom saw Dad as soon as she crossed over. It was the type of smile you flash when you haven't seen someone you loved, romantically, in a long time.

Stuart Platt, an associate of Dad's, contacted me upon hearing of Mom's death. He said my father had been speaking to him that same day, that he believes my father was "there" that day. This confirmed that expression on Mom's face. Dad was in the house that day.

Val reports that when she found Mom, she had fallen to the left, in between the tub and the base of the toilet. She then administered CPR to no avail. I can't get over the sight of Mom sitting, limp, dead, there, on V.'s lap. The EMTs quickly stretched Mom out on the floor. The space was limited. They moved her to the front room (her main gallery). Mom lay dead. They shocked her twice—nothing. Mom's stomach had filled with air; she spouted water, like a drowned victim, as they returned to traditional CPR.

Mom was dead. The scene was a mess. V. was screaming and, in his frustration, one EMT finally shouted, "All that screaming ain't gonna make her any more dead than she already is!" I chastised him without making a scene. He apologized and assured me that they would do all they could to revive her in the ambulance. Without asking her name, or ours, the EMTs hastily loaded her up. We were instructed not to follow the ambulance.

Though we had initially been referred to a different hospital by the EMT driver, we finally found a "Jane Doe" at a hospital nearer to the house. I guess those factors can change on an emergency run. The first person we encountered was the pastor of the ER. He calmly took us through various protocols to prove Jane Doe's identity and to corroborate our relationship to her.

Once assured of our identity, he announced to us that our mother had expired, DOA. We were asked if we wanted to view her. She was still in ER. They pulled back the curtain, and there she lay. She had the same tube in her throat that they had "installed" at the house. Her lips were pressed in against her gold teeth due to the force of the tube. Mucus and blood were seeping from her nose. I wiped the fluids away with my handkerchief. Mom's left eye was still partly opened, as it was when I saw her at the house. Before kissing her forehead, I closed that eye (her "lil eye" as she used to call it). Holding my mother's head in my right hand, I felt the weight of her precious knowledge and existence. This was the second time I saw Mom after she ascended.

As I think about it, Mom was never a person to linger. She left as she always did. Unexpectedly.

A few of Mom's mantras:

- I'm just a living memory.
- I don't care what you and V. do—y'all grown.
- Don't feel sorry for me. I'm doing just fine up in here.
- When you think you know, look out!

Through knowledge, sovereignty and wisdom, Mom thrust V. and me 20 years ahead of ourselves. Unfortunately she, too, traveled, using (or losing) 20 years of her own time in the process. This is why I disagree that 74 was young for Mom's demise.

It's all about lifestyle, baby.
Mom rode this thing called life and love till the wheels came off; dig?
My Mom did not have a "favorite chair."

My pain is not intensified by the yearning for unrequited experiences; it is multiplied by fond memories, abounding. Mom prepared us for her transformation from the time we were very young. This is what she would reiterate in casual conversation a few times per year: "I'm just a living memory." Mom did not fear death. But she loved life even more.

Three compliments Mom paid me prior to her untimely death have sustained me:
"I admire the way you care for yourself."

- "If I were asked would you be among the survivors lost in the woods, I would respond, yes; definitely."
- "You are one of the hardest men I know."

Further:

- Mom's and my philosophical departures were based on similarity not difference.
- All children fuss at their parents.
- Mom did not argue.
- She most befriended those who underestimated her.

Mom was always a part of my future; now, she is part of my past. This fact is painful. Mom was unique and irreproachable. She was not trying to be different, she *was* different. And like the cicada, death rendered her observable—now, mystical. Unless you have gone through this, it's a degree of suffering you cannot understand.

★ ★ ★

Winter Is Her Favorite Time of Year

She finds solitude and serenity in becoming one with nature, escaping from civilization, it's a beautiful sensation. Winter is finally here! Fireplace lit, just took a sip, as Jack Frost tiptoes through the night, twinkling candle lights reflect joy to the world.

On the outside her yard twirls with grandeur, garden mingling with Hydrangea, Ajuga, and Periwinkle, yet one could never detect how spectacular the inside would be.

On this winter morning it's the 5th of the month, January, having church, it's her birthday, sanctuary, spreading love like it's the 14th of February.

Heart is pure, so much in this world to endure, seeking God she always finds the cure.

Her teachings taught me to keep my cool; make sure to never argue with a fool, she said, as she tosses then turns the logs on the fire. Takes a moment to ponder whose woods are these? Yes, that poet, Robert Frost; one can no longer carry this cross. She seemed amazed when she noticed some sparse wiry roots laced with black moss, then gathered broken branches from her trees to create a birch harbor, don't be somber, there's always a silver lining, inside it there's a bright sun shining. Words she spoke strike your like heart keys on the piano, perfect timing, a glissando of truths resonate transcending as we converse.

Trees stiffen into place, a majestic scene as an artist she paints with ease, each brush stroke effortless yet swift. Always remember, life is a gift.

Oh Zion! From above, she shares her canvas for the world to see, colors brighter than a copper penny, sceneries sketched in memory, once transformed it encompasses an eternity, the same it will never be, paintings don't need a name, not looking for fame.

Forever evolving, that's the plan, her legacy with forever stand, such an abundance, one wonders where did she began. Her love goes beyond a life span!

Winter is her favorite time of year! Especially when those she loves came near.

—A.S.

Company

E: Hi

ME: Good to meet you today. I see you know my good friend, B.

E: Well she and I may have been together when we saw you with S. way back then.

ME: Oh, wow … B … yes! Great to meet. Hope to connect soon.

E: I will call you tomorrow to see what venues you are going to.

⋆ ⋆ ⋆

ME: Did you just go home

E: Dude, what's up with this image on your Facebook?

ME: 😎 I made the New Yorker in 2005

E: Ah, the image is from the New Yorker in 2005? Cool! I worked at The Royal Conservatory so I practically lived inside Koerner Hall, a lot of concerts, both classical and jazz. Humber since May 2015

ME: Ah, okay, I've seen you there then

E: Really how's that

ME: In passing

E: When?

ME: Not sure … lol

E: What occasion? Did I look familiar to you today

ME: Now that you say that about Koerner, you do … lol

E: Are you jiving man

ME: No, that's how my memory works.

E: Do you go there often

ME: Not too often, but several times, over time.

E: I see a lot of the jazz concerts. but this year's lineup not so great. I'm seeing Gerald Clayton in the spring and Lisa Fisher and Dianne Reeves in December

ME: Nice, I like Gerald. Dianne I know from my Wynton days.

E: You didn't attend the Tribute to Oscar. not this December but the one before? Gerald played, Kenny Barron, Benny Green, etc. Were you there, I was

ME: I remember that. Nope

E: Why not?

ME: Probably schedule conflict

E: Really, you're teaching that much.

ME: Yes, but it's not just that. I can be a bit of a homebody. I'm always with music …

E: I don't want to take much of your time

ME: Not at all, you are fun to talk to

E: Thanks! It was a pleasant surprise to me. I knew you from way back in Wynton's band.
I thought maybe somebody took your heart up to TO; and then you had to get a job up here and of course teaching made sense

ME: Wow. No. The gig is why I came to TO. How about you? Are you in a relationship?

E: Nope, widow

ME: Oh, I see.

E: Yeah, my late husband died 10 years ago and my daughter was turning 5 the next month. So she's almost 15 now. I tell people she's been to the Vanguard since she was 7 and fallen asleep and fallen asleep the last time we saw the Lincoln Jazz Orchestra maybe in 2008 or 09. Lol

ME: Oh, my, 15. Amazing. I'm not surprised, they've been pretty boring since I left … LOL

E: My daughter didn't fall asleep last summer at the Vanguard when we checked out
Terell Stafford and Tim Warfield quintet.

ME: I bet she didn't. Those my cats!

E: Hey how old are your children

ME: 17, 10, 8. Oldest went off to University

E: Eight? That's when you came here. You guys broke up right after her birth

ME: Yep. The transition messed us up plus the post-partum stuff. And i was completely absorbed in the new gig to boot. They still visit once or twice a year. But the problems started well before the move for us, btw

E: LOL. Well you look amazing

ME: Thank you! Actually, I think you are really pretty. I want to say cute. But I know that word is scoffed upon … lol

E: Were you at the Senator in the mid 90s? I saw Freddie Hubbard there and Tony Williams too

ME: Yes I was there w Marcus Roberts a couple times in the mid 90s. I was his road manager … lol. I had just finished Grad school. Me and Sybil got into a big fuss over the money. I hard-balled it … I was a kid … lol

E: So you and Sybil have beef

ME: Yes lol. She prob doesn't even remember. But then, she prob does. lol

E: She loves me! Remembers when I practically lived at the Senator

ME: So you can reintroduce us … lol

E: She means well

ME: Hell I grew up around Lorraine Gordon. No problem. If I survived her … lol

E: Haha, Lorraine Gordon she's legendary tough. You're an amazing player and if those cats are York U faculty, as a listener, is it OK to say you need better players??? They are old guys. They are burned out. And they all went to like elementary school together. You need Larnell Lewis.
Sorry!

ME: Yes it's okay to say … lol. I like Larnell. We've played together several times in the past. Good rapport.

E: He's my damned favorite. Lovely dude great attitude

ME: I see what you are saying … You have amazing hearing.

E: I don't go up to musicians in general but I go up and tell him when he's killing it lol. So you have to hang with me because they are playing at the Rex at the end of the month, Mike Downes' band. Larnell plays drums. Last time they played I was floored.

ME: Okay. Def wanna hang w/you

E: Gee thanks finally someone who actually understands my passion for jazz. Well of course for you, you live it! For me it's what I hear

ME: Yes m'am. You can hear!

E: Whatever age you are. It's working. Sir Mr Westray sir!

ME: You're a Foxy Lady.

E: No need to say those things. I'll hang tomorrow. Happy to.

ME: Okay, cool. Let me know what time?

E: So, Ervin comes from my first husband who was from Chicago. I was married to him when I was 20 for 7 years

ME: Oh, that explains … lol. Wow. You married a black man at 20 … wow … lol

E: How do you know he was black

ME: I'm psychic? No, that's a black name in the South where I'm from

E: Oh. Of course! My father in law is originally from Mississippi, not to say it's not also white, but my instincts said black. My mother in law or ex mom was from Alabama

ME: Yes. The South! But you went black. I was curious from the first time I saw your name.

So. there is some soul there … lol

E: A handful

ME: Had a great relationship with a woman from the Philippines when I was in NYC.

E: Really?

ME: Yes

E: Nice, what happen to the lady in NYC

ME: When I moved in 2005, distance killed it

E: Moved where

ME: I started at UT Austin as an Asst. Prof. till 2009 when I came here

E: Austin has amazing music scene from what I hear. And you've been hibernating since being in TO? I was trying to figure out why you would come here. Why York U

ME: I came for the Chair and I got it. that's all. Pulled tenure and Pulled residency. never heard of York before the gig posted. LOL

E: Amazing, Ok Mr. Westray, better shut down this conversation before one of us gets in trouble

ME: If you insist, but I'm enjoying every bit … Okay shall we resume tomorrow. I will await your communication

E: I have to go back to my cleaning and laundry so you would see me sometime tomorrow. There's a big band I'm curious to see.

ME: Okay, tomorrow

E: Would you like to do something else

ME: I will follow your lead …

E: I have comps to the Art Gallery of Ontario and there's some photos of relatives of slaves from the Underground Railroad you may find interesting … how about that?

ME: Sounds good

E: Where do you live and how will you get to the city

ME: I have to catch the Subway down there … I'm coming from York

E: Cool, that works. Should we set a time? I'll run in the morning and maybe church at 10:30 till 11:30 then I have to see what my daughter is up to then go from there …

ME: Okay that sounds good. Cause I need time to get up and running. So I will await your cue.

E: You don't gig. So you're not a night owl anymore. or are you still?

ME: It just depends on what's happening. I can be a serious night owl

E: Ok I'll say bye for now? We've been talking a long time.

ME: I know … nite nite.

E: Yes, nite nite see ya

E: Good Morning, Ron. Went to bed at 3 am after all the laundry and cleaning. I can see you after 12 like 1:00 or 1:30. Did you want to meet at the Market, grab food, and see Chelsea McBride Orchestra or scrap altogether and see the photographs at AGO. Listened to your album about three times and I think that you should make a submission to the Jazz Festival for 2018

ME: Hello, there … No I value your opinion. That's the Jimi record, right? Hey I went down far later than I expected too. In fact, I'm feeling quite lazy today. Would you mind if we rain checked? I have things going on downtown on Wednesday, the Wynton Concert. It was all I could do to get to the market on time yesterday. Today, I gotta rest … Want to catch up w/you later, though by phone. Hope you understand

E: Yes, it's the Jimi Jazz record. It's a great album of music but needs different players with you!

ME: Yeah you are right. But you are hearing what the budget could afford … lol. Larnell would have wanted fifty-thousand dollars and such, etc … I did that record for 5K. The other thing is availability. Those cats are so busy, they couldn't have done it anyway in the way that I executed those recordings. Then they want Top Dollars in the studio. So, I did my own thing. But you are right. Maybe I'll call Herbie Hancock and Wayne Shorter for my next CD, and maybe Christian McBride. yeah right. Can't afford those guys … they don't just play for music's sake … you feel me? same for all those people you named. too high post for my do it yourself attitude …

it's not like when a record company gave you a budget in the 90s and you hire the best players …

I really do know how to hire a band. What you see, including the band yesterday, are resource issues and decisions.

E: Got it! I understand. Of course you know how to hire a band. The material is amazing and you killed it of course but I guess you and I both know the level that it could be.

ME: Yes, you have great taste. I can't afford those cats.

E: Would love to come to see you but will not stay for LCJO. Maybe we can hang a little

ME: YES. Me and you! I will send you the details about my show with Share the Music Foundation. I've done this about 5 times.

E: My daughter saw me texting you and is rolling her eyes. She feels very jealous of any man I'm talking to. We'll give her the attention she wants. I'll let you go. Text me as soon as you have time later. We'll meet in the middle didn't mean to send that emoji … LOL. well maybe i did … LOL

ME: Sweet, you're good. Have I met my match?

E: Who do you think you are, Ronald Westray? Maybe you need to keep up with me!

ME: LOL, Okay, maybe I believe you 😐

E: Just kidding! I like to talk shit to keep people from knowing some things about me. LOL oh okay you had me going there. there are many facets to be uncovered, darling. Many facets, many sides, complex person. I want to be that guy you open up to, again, for the first time …

ME: We met for a reason.

E: Oh yeah?

ME: You see we nearly talked into the night.

E: You have quite the personality and I would have thought even at York women would be vibing you

ME: That's a more complex issue of expectations lol. but you could be the Yoko to my Lennon baby

E: Ha, take it easy Mr. Westray. Sounds good but are you always this serious or upfront with someone you met yesterday afternoon

ME: No

E: I look forward to people watching and laughing w/ you many times over …

ME: I'm flattered. So our first official date is Wed. after my thing @ Massey, right?

E: I have to be sure I wear the right thing on Wednesday

ME: For the record, I have women that I have known for decades in the U.S. Just girlfriends. True friends. Well I am a good-looking, heterosexual, artistic, hunk.

E: These are the surprises in life that bite you in the ass.

ME: I have no girlfriends in TO. Women here are scared of me lol. I'm too wild.

E: Well, you are a little crazy on stage which I thought was very cute 😊 That's too bad! They're scared of you … I don't even understand that. It's a front really. I feel you are a true Southerner, a gentleman

ME: I learned from the best. Frank Lacy comes to mind lol. Thank you for saying that. Means a lot

E: I'm pretty honest with you but you don't get to know me in two days

ME: Yes I understand. And likewise. I can't stop talking you. what is going on

E: You mean you don't normally talk this much???

ME: No

E: You love talking, was my impression when you were on stage

ME: Yes I do.

E: Don't you get bored?

ME: If so I don't realize it … lol

E: I have an active social life with my friends and colleagues.

ME: I am the King of Gemini.

E: Still in your jammies lazy bones??? On the ball in your jammies lol

ME: Yes. I mean NO.

E: Time to stop Mr. Westray. I have to clean my front garden, get to the salon to get my nails done, cook some more. And the work that's not getting done because you have taken so much of my time

ME: Lol, Okay, bye! You have to see my rap videos to understand me: http://traydeuce1.bandcamp.com/album/out-the-box

E: Ok will listen later for sure. Gotta get my work done first. See ya

ME: Enjoy. Talk later …

E: I think you're a little loco

ME: Yes, I am. But I have art to show for it.

E: Yes you do! Enjoyed your Jimi Jazz really want it presented with the right personnel

ME: Yes, thank you. Help Me!

E: The beginning of many great things

ME: Yes. TTYL

Chapter 47

This morning I feel as though I am struggling with a self-worth issue. Sparing myself definitions such as low or high esteem (which might produce similar results), I will simply say a fear of rejection. I had forgotten that the very artistic talent that I now wore as an emblem was designed to protect me and propel me beyond the possibilities of any such quandaries. That was a huge part of my motivation to be respected.

I was aware of this in my formative years. I never wanted the prom queens. I did not want to play the game. I didn't want my desire to be observed (which seemed to be the minimum requirement for the diva). Instead I would pursue the unpopular girl. In my own defense, I will say she did have to have a shape (or at least the potential to gain one).

Even through college and grad school, this was my pattern. I overwhelm. This, in contrast to actually learning the ballroom dance. I only interact, romantically, for convenience. A psychic once told me that I'm manipulative. Could (or would) a woman who would *not* tolerate my style make me happier? Make a man of me?

"Take your medicine?" "Get you a real women who's going to"—what? Make me into more of a man than I already feel like? The river of esteem flows in both directions. Do I deserve an heiress? I haven't been willing to work for it. I have made lazy choices with romance; but L. made me work hard for it. I misjudged her coyness for vulnerability. Maybe she misjudged my niceness for weakness. What I have worked hard for is the title of "American jazz musician." Those emblems have not erased the issue but have fortified my personality to such a degree that an esteem issue is out of the question to *most* who know me: To posture is to be.

Anti Depressant

No pain, no world
No world, no money
No money, no problem (mo money, mo problem)
No problem, no life
No life, no risk

No risk, no belief,
No belief, no faith
No faith, no hope
No hope, Xanax

⋆ ⋆ ⋆

ME: I DO talk like this when we are together. Think about it. This is just how it looks on paper. The one thing you fail to recognize is that I'm not always trying to share everything. I'm secretive at many levels—especially my true opinions. They are not always constructive. I know the candor you year for. I'm not capable of that right now.

ME: Well, there you have it! That's upfront, eh? The part you see is me wanting to give *that*.

AM: I haven't failed to recognize the level of secrecy you have in your life. We all have a level, if the one you think shares everything … What realities are you forced to deal with?

ME: my preference for secrecy and lack of willingness to be completely open … that's who i am … not something i'm seeking answers to, per se.

AM: I didn't attempt to provide you with an answer.

ME: it all has a purpose in forming how others view us … ike you said you know i prefer secrecy. but you accept that about me … so i view it as a constant not a coefficient.

ME: no, i didn't think you did … just saying i know you are like what is up w/ him … just one of those weeks where i want clarity in the few relationships I have … So, this is real talk to me or we can just talk based on familial templates … yay

AM: If this will provide you with that … ok. I can do either … Anything particular you need me to clarify, expound upon, share?

ME: in your case, earlier it was 1) Does she think I am insecure or unhappy? and now 2) She probably needs this type of nurturing relationship, and I am not capable.

ME: just little points that i could fluff through in conversation or open up and examine as i have today. Contrary to that analysis, i would ask that you think about the energy i do give in lieu of what i am describing, and perhaps there is some credit to be given there. I try to love those who love me. I have hard limits that are not personal but personality. personal then, our interaction is minimal comparably. so we are usually to focused on enjoying each other for a little time for any of this to matter. i like that. but this idea, is what i mean when i say we could never live together …

it's this mess i'm trying to describe … i like being not fully understood. and you want to understand; and I get that.

AM: Sometimes I do … it's who I am. But I don't always need to understand. I've learned its not necessary. As for a nurturing relationship … i might enjoy one, but don't know that i have the time or energy to offer to one myself. I like not living with anyone … don't want anyone in space, love my alone time … i get more than you know. As long as I'm not fully understood … you cant hold me to everything!

ME: lol oh, okay well that's where pisces gemini hook up right in there …

AM: Hey … I didn't mean that to be funny …

ME: oh really? Well, you should know the answer to that … Do I seem insecure?

AM: No … of course not.

ME: that's what the interviewer ask me over the summer. that's why i said funny. i had forgotten that he asked

AM: Yes … just a reminder of how great others see you … baby

ME: thanks baby

AM: When i read the article thats what came to my mind … last summer interview. I should say, how great you are at what you do … you deserve any and all praise.

ME: always good to hear. cause people usually don't give it up … thank you. look forward to our first pow wow when i get home …

AM: No they dont, but the truth can never be completely hidden …

ME: ah ha

AM: What you got for me?

ME: All this love is waiting for you—same menu.

AM: Lol … Isn't that a DeBarge song, all this love is waiting for you

ME: yes!

AM: That's my jam

ME: Mine too, lol.

AM: Love that dude … el D …

ME: Yes, he's one of them real ones.

AM: Baby, i'm going to need a different menu, this go round. somewhere between decompressing from work, answering a trail of emails from work and perusing facebook and, well, this … typing a description of that to you.

ME: Hmmmm, oh yeah, what? you go first

AM: Im gonna need you to take it easy … less beating, more slow stroking.

ME: oh, okay …

AM: More kissing … grinding … more body contact. I need to hold you … Yo turn …

RW: sure, that's just what i was thinking …

AM: Funny, Funny … 🙂 Come on now … what you want? You know dang on well that's not what you were thinking

ME: i try to avoid comparisons with you. i let you find your own comfort zones … i'm just a meat and potatoes kind of guy. a few things i like. and thats what i like … you do one naturally, one you don't and the other you will … oh and the fourth … well you do it for me but not for you. so that's different…

AM: Only asking you what you want … new on the menu conversation … Nothing that deep … thought we were going to have cyber sex … geeesh!

RW: lol … there's nothing new, darling—just things you like to do, too. i got you this weekend tho … lol worn out from the day … anyway, enough of this cyber stuff … the real thing is coming your way …

AM: I cant wait, get some rest baby, I love you! Had my two shots of shine … be easy! love you nite nite

* * *

AM: Good morning … happy Wednesday, make it great, and dont forget WHO YOU ARE!

ME: Thanks, I never do … The problem has been being myself—not not being myself.

I keep defending that; cause I have never had an issue with that. As a matter fact, it could be said that my confidence has created an effect of "let him get his own." So, I'm out here doing that. My problem is not me knowing; it's whether or not others realize. I can't go around asking, "Don't you know who I think I am?" Well, don't you know who you are? YES! Do you? It seems that people can only withstand so much confidence. So I be on the down-low with the blah, blah, blah. Maybe people are compelled to ask?

ME: Once an interviewer ask me if I know who I am? He asked me that because I'm treating him with respect and not being the dick I could (or should) be. People get it twisted. Man, don't you realize you could be acting like *this*!

ME: Meanwhile back at the ranch, I'm perfecting the same skills I always have, amid immersing myself in an amount of work that keeps me pretty damned humble. Don't get it twisted. I'm twisted. Conversely, I am arrogant. It's part defense; and it's part pride in my achievement. I treat people with respect. This fails, miserably, too. I've burned many bridges with this ego. At times, it's all I had to protect me—knowledge of self. See?

ME: Getting back to the topic, when the interviewer asked me that, I was flattered. Again, I was also mildly offended that he thought that I did not know. I'm so full of myself, people can't even see it. I can back it up; and that's the difference. Like a black belt I keep it concealed. You don't know until it's too late. Man or machine? If you have to ask, I have to explain. Once, okay; two times? Oh no, she must think I'm down on my luck.

ME: Okay, pardon my ejaculations. I just needed to get on the other side of that topic with you. That's that part I mentioned—What am I really thinking? There, you have it.

AM: Wow … Just so you know, Yes, I know you are arrogant (but not as much as you described). You keep saying if you respect others and don't act an ass, that somehow people are unaware of your level of confidence. You don't have to be an ass for that to be seen. If people are asking you the question, then they are just unaware of your awareness—not because you aren't acting out. Not all arrogant folks are asses. I get what you're saying, but everything doesn't relate to *everybody*.

AM: If you want to be an asshole, then be an asshole. You know what that would entail. If you want to walk around with your chest stuck out. Or, be on the DL about how you view yourself and your work. Whichever you do, just do it.

AM: True, people can only stand so much confidence; some can't stand but so much of the DL blah blah blah. So, what cha gonna do? Be true to you. Nothing matters.

AM: I just wish when we are around each other you would share with me in the same passion as you have on here. I don't think you are down on your luck. I didn't say what i said this morning because I think you have self esteem issues. But to what level does it exist? Good or bad … On the real, it's all of your personality traits and characteristics. You decide which ones people see—true awareness! I guess I coddled another "perspective essay" out of you. Thanks for the insight Ron … Love and much respect.

* * *

"Anybody that's ever loved me, still love me"

KB: Surprise, Surprise and Happy Valentines Day … 

ME: Thank you sexy … Happy Valentine's day to you 2!

KB: Sending you some wet warm kisses all over you. Holla when you come this way again would love to connect. Xo

ME: Oooh, loving those kisses …! I will def. reach out when heading your way! ditto would love to reconnect. Oh, what I would give to be there "catching up" with you tonight! …

KB: Me too!!!

ME: Soon cum, soon cum … lol

KB: Lol xo

ME: oh the memories … wow

KB: Yessssssss!

ME: your FINE ass …! had to get that out … lol

KB: Lol xo

ME: Well enjoy your special day and evening and we should def. be in better touch … set some dates … and you can always hang out in the 416 for a LONG weekend (pun intended) …

KB: Lol really loud. Lot of business happening now but we should set something up somewhere.
I think of you more often then I should xo

ME: lol well it's nice to be thought of. I will def make that happen knowing you are into it. i think of you quite often as well … hey we had a great time … unforgettable … Encore, encore!

KB: I concur!!! Say no more … so making that happen!

ME: It feels like yesterday I can't believe the time! Do you know how long it's been? I do.

KB: I know! Long time …

ME: Thirteen years—who's counting?

KB: Wow didnt know that! Well we will make up for lost time. On my way to dinner right now. Lets make it happen soon! Hugggggggggg

ME: Okay, yes … sooner than later! bon appetit! xoxo

★ ★ ★

L.: I am writing because I am frustrated, at this point. It is best that I not speak over the phone. I need your help to get Z finished with this school year and into York for the fall. Honestly, I don't care if she does music. She can do basket weaving for all I care.

I do not have money to pay for her college, and she needs to benefit from the wonderful tenure status you have. Having said that, I filled out admission stuff awhile back. I have not received further word on her status. At present, her teachers are not pleased because she has failed her senior hearings twice!

That means that if she does not pass the next one, she will not be having a senior recital, which is required to receive an Artist Diploma from the school. She is not prepared to do any auditions. Additionally, her grades are not up to par. I am tired of telling her to practice, turn in work, blah, blah, blah!

Although you already know she will not be honest, I need you to speak to her. I need you to tell her what her GPA needs to be to get into York. I need York to be where she is going to be. She will not be able to sit at home with me in the fall. I need you to give her a wake up call that Toronto will be her next destination, unless you have connections in SC universities with free tuition. I don't know if she is scared or what. I need you to do some probing as to why she is not trying to finish up this year. I don't know what your communication with her is like. It would greatly help if you could give her a better perspective or sense of excitement about being there in the fall. Again, I am burnt out from trying to pull her through this year. I need your help. She needs your help.

ME: Also I can't TELL her where her next destination is. There has been no push towards York. Only now, in the emergency sense (PLAN C). Meanwhile, I have had to entertain conversations about a dozen other schools and majors. Now it's YOU ARE GOING TO YORK! Okay? I will do my best, but don't expect miracles overnight. Everything has a process. Free tuition connections in SC? You're kidding, right? Simmer down.

L.: York has always been MY plan for all of them! I agree that she has mentioned other schools, but I have told her from the start, that if they are not full rides, I am not paying for college. She has not spoken to me of her conversations with you, and that is OK with me.

I respect her privacy in her conversations with you. Clearly, I am feeling some kind of way, because I don't see the effort on her part. She might be tuning everyone out. Maybe you have a better perspective on what she has said she is doing. Yes, everything has a process. Anyway, you continue to speak with her, because she might be communicating more with you. She seems to get offended when I tell her I haven't heard her practice in "X" amount of days, knowing that she failed her hearings. Keep talking with her. Yes, I was kidding about the SC thing.—L.

L.: Ok, I get it! Tone was all wrong!! Just got in a rant with Z and picked up the laptop to vent. Baby, please know I appreciate every effort! Your first child is driving me nuts with this lax, fantasy view of life. Maybe she doesn't get it. I do know that I am a little pissed with her. Again, I didn't know you all spoke. She is very quiet about her dealings. I am only dealing with it as I see it. I love you. I didn't mean to upset you. You work miracles in other ways! She just got the best of me today.

Thanks, Big Daddy, L.

ME: I'm okay … I love you too.

You're welcome, Lil Mama, Ron

Chapter 46

AS: Being in your company and hearing your voice yesterday hit me hard n my heart … this is so difficult bc the test of time has shown me that I really do love u, as much as I know letting go is best. I still think of u and how happy I am when I'm with u. I want u to know that I'm all f*cked up too, I have never been n love with someone who could not belong to me. It's all or nothing at all. I am all I have to give. When all those around know this is not your style. When all u know is nothing, because everything is uncertain. When all comes to you, can you give *all* in return? Does giving all make you feel like you are missing the pussy train? That said, if you have not found anyone that you can give all to, you are half-stepping through life, missing it all, a continuum of nothingness. I thought about u all day yesterday after we spoke. I'm n tears as I write, u may think this comes easy to me but really and truly I'm lost without u.

ME: Please come back to me … You mean a lot to me baby … You have treated me so well, and I realize that—Ron

AS: I'm loss for words Ron, I'm also afraid, u really make my heart melt, please I dnt want to hurt or to b hurt. I want to b happy and for u to b happy as well. I will give to u and continue to give u my heart.

ME: Baby, I will take care of your heart. I promise. I love you.

AS: Thank u Ron I believe u and I believe n u. I love u too … I hope I'm not being a fool for u, love scares me, where do we pick up from here?

ME: baby, we just pick up where we left off before the madness … i need to hold you and kiss you and talk to you. you mean so much to me baby. i will never let you go … just rock w/ me …

AS: Im fragile, please handle with care. Good night Mr. Westray, I feel myself coming bak to life. Only if u knew, how much ur words mean to me, and I hope u will never let me go I need u i know baby … thanks for removing the lump from my throat too …

ME: lol Baby I mean what I say. I never want to lose you again …

AS: lol … I'm really speechless, imagine that, me with nothing to say smh

ME: I'm so happy you came back to me … I missed you something awful … Caught me off guard … Now that we both know how miserable we are w/ out each other, let's not go there again, please …

AS: That's part of why I'm speechless bc I'm trying to figure out how I can please u n that regard without making myself unhappy. I really and truly don't want to go there again, so how do we prevent it, bc I dnt expect change from u

ME: just know that you mean the world to me no matter the circumstance. but i am more aware of what affects you and why. I love you and respect you and value your love and friendship.
I regard you as a very important aspect of my life, baby … you gotta always know that, no matter … i'm crazy about you … just know that … don't be insecure about my independence. just sit back and know that he loves him some me just know that … you are my angel

AS: Well enough, my dear Ron

ME: k, baby … can't wait to hold you.

AS: Yes, I didn't expect this … I will b honest I have been seeing someone else and recently I allowed him to hold mę in that way. I just want to b honest with u, we used protection, I dont like going bak and forth between partners and would b unable to b with you without you knowing. Going to bed—good night.

ME: it's okay baby … nite nite …

AS: ok thanks; my heart is clear, now.

ME: Is the relationship still going on baby?

AS: Yes, I began seeing him mid August and arnd thxgiving we proceeded forward. I will end it. I love you unconditionally.
(8:08 am)

ME: Morning, love … I'm feel blessed to have you back in my life … just wanted you to know that; I'm never letting go again …

AS: It's ok don't, everything has a breaking point so just bc I reached out to u doesn't have to mean anything to u. I guess I'm just another crazy bitch to u, but my heart is clear now I'm free.

AS: A word to my brother, lets b clear up front I know it's none of my business who you f*ck, but when u r going up inside me, and my gut instincts tell me that after getting the gig, that you are, now, fraternizing with the help. Ron, not trying to come off as anything but concerned for my own health and standards; so don't take my word to the wise wrong. I'm a true friend; and I have had this sick gut feeling all week I don't want to be in the midst of any sex-capades. I want to be free; and I want you to be free, too. Give your body to anybody you please. I realize I have fallen for someone that will never be *mine*. I know we talked about it and had an understanding; but when I entertain the mere thought of you and her fucking! I realized

I can't deal with your lifestyle. You are correct. I talk a good talk; but at the end of the day I can't handle it. I don't want to be *here* anymore. Even though I have tried, I can't fool myself. I'm human, too—Just like you.

ME: Haven't read your message; I probably won't. I'm not f*cking S—Thanks.

* * *

L.: It's late. Was listening to OP playing "Put on a Happy Face"! I thought about you. I remember when you used to call me "darling!" I used to think it was so country. My father's father used to call me that. Funny to think I didn't know what love was then … I do miss that country boy!

L.: Hey Professor! I know you are preoccupied with your move and all. Thinkin' about you! I hope all is going smoothly for you. If you get an opportunity, drop a line and let me hear your voice. Luv the sound!

L.: Hey, just giving you a heads up. It's been extremely busy and I haven't had a chance to connect. The girls will only be with you on Saturday and Sunday. I will be in Atlanta for those days and will travel back to pick them up, unless you can meet me halfway to Atlanta on that Monday. Arthur wanted to see the girls as well. We will be with him on the 4th. We will get back to DC on Tuesday so A. doesn't miss another work day. I know it isn't a lot of time. I will try to get back to SC before they go back to school. See you in the morn.

L.: Hey, I'm up and was thinking about you before everyone got up. How was your first day? I know it was awesome! The crisp air has me fiending! Miss ya Talk to you soon.

L.: So, it came yesterday! Flow was not as heavy as normal but consistent. Maybe i'm peri-menopause and finally slowing down! Love ya.

ME: hey, baby … missed you … I'm at Sterl's … Bout to crash out … Love you.

* * *

9/20/16:

Hi Ron, how are you?

Thanks a lot for your message and the information about the Diefenbaker Award, I checked it out, thought it sounded interesting, but then I read it is only for people who live in Germany and work at a German University at this moment … nothing for German expats … What a pity! For a moment I thought about living with P., D. and the twins in Canada for a while, I wouldn't hesitate. Maybe on another occasion.

P. is fine (huge), and so is D … The twins will be boy and girl!

The first of the papers is finished and revised, the people from the journal in Serbia tell me it will be published in December. I'll send you a copy, eight pages are about your Opus.

By the way, after a lot of problems, the people from the Archives finally sent me a digital copy of the recording, that's great, makes things a lot easier. But it took them three months, then they got things wrong, sent bad copies … Anyway, now everything is ok.

Now I am preparing for the conferences in Alcalá (near Madrid) and Berlin, with a lot of things about the piece as well. And this weekend I will see a friend of mine in Barcelona, this will be about your Opus as well, she is deep into the music scene in Barcelona and has promised to check things … So things are moving, very slowly, but steadily. Since August and until the end of November I am very busy, mornings at the university: articles, conference papers … but I hope I can push things a little more next year.

How are you doing? Lot of work? Any new recordings? I listen a lot to your CDs, the ones you gave me great stuff! And how's your family doing, girls, Mom?

Best, C

6/16/16:

Hi Ron,

Sorry for making you wait such a long time, busy times here … I had two jobs during the last months since September, in two universities, too much really. P. is ok, we are waiting for the twins, expected around December 27. They are going to be tall, so P. is really huge by now and feeling heavy. D. is fine, sporting around and singing and playing all the time, great fun with him.

No news so far but I am still talking to people here. Also working on the papers I presented on the conferences, people were really interested but they had little time to listen, I could only present small fragments. Anyway,

I'm working on it and will tell you how things develop. By the way, I had Charles Fambrough (Milton Nascimento composition), so far I have found more than sixty jazz compositions inspired by Don Quixote, some of them quite interesting. Did I tell you about the other jazz suites? There are some strange works, one by Japanese pianist Mitsuaki Kanno (1981), this guy had an excellent album in the seventies which is almost forgotten now (called *Busho*, or *Shisendo No Aki*), but his Quixote suite is not that good. Nobody has come near what you did though.

What about you, how are things going? Everything is fine with your girls? Love luck's ok? Your mum and grandma are well? My regards to them.

Remember when we talked politics when I was at your house? You told me a little about how you felt about the things going on in the States, and I could see some of it with my own eyes,

but still I was shocked when the results of the elections came out. This summer I read the Michael Moore article where he predicted this, I thought he was probably right but still couldn't imagine things had really gone that far. Crazy times …

Ok, we're going to the hospital right now, they're going to check the twins. P.'s preparing to leave and she is calling me to hurry up. Hope you have a good time these last weeks of the year, Christmas celebrations and so on …

All the best, C.

Hi, C.

I'm doing well, brother; thanks. Ah, Wow … that's a bummer, thought we might have a caper there. Well, another time, another place. Glad to hear that mommy and babies and big brother D. are all well. Ah, yes, I look forward to the publication in December! Wow, I could have given you a recording, I guess … Were you able to assist the institute in correcting their records?

Okay, slow and steady always works, man … Thank you for all your work. Yes, I am pretty busy. Or, at least, it feels that way coming off of summer break. But I am acclimating and regaining my appreciation for simply having a job. I try to remind myself each day. Did a lot of recording w/ the RAP guys during the summer. Got HITS coming soon!

Mom and everyone are fine. I sort of fell out of sorts w/ Mom at the end of the summer. I guess it was just separation anxiety.

This is normal. I will see them around Christmas. My girls are doing great. Sprouting up like string beans. I have a high school senior this year! Decisions … decisions … My ex, L., is doing great and looking better to me than ever. We are doing well right now, and from a distance … as always …

Great to hear from you, C … Be well and give my regards to your family.

RW/DQ2

6/16/16:

Hi Ron, how are you?

I hope you have recovered from our intense working weekend almost two weeks ago … For me, it was a wonderful, deeply impressive and memorable experience, so it took me about 10 days just to find myself again, I felt very tired and a bit dazzled when I arrived at New York after staying with you in Columbia. And today was already my last day in New York, tomorrow.

I will fly back home. I have been quite nervous about coming home in these two past weeks, I missed D. very much, I didn't expect it would hit me that hard, but that's how it was.

By the way, last week I suddenly became aware of a little misunderstanding that occurred while we were talking, I think it was Sunday when you told me about that psychic, remember? Well the thing is, I didn't understand you because I didn't know the word, I thought you meant a psychologist, psychiatrist or psychoanalyst or something like that. Then I looked it up in the dictionary and now I understand, and I agree that this is a bit crazy, not rational anyway, and I know that it feels bad being treated that way by someone you have worked for, and for such a long time. It is always awful to have the suspicion that things are being decided behind your back, but even much more so when the people who take decisions concerning your job and your life use that kind of supernatural bullsh*t, it's weak and it's mean.

I also wanted to tell you that just three days ago I suddenly found out that the Rodgers & Hammerstein Archives of Recorded Sound at the New York Public Library for the Performing Arts sometimes authorize copies (they call it phono-duplications) for scholarly research. I didn't know that, that information is not on the website but only in a small brochure they have at the front desk. I thought it wasn't possible but I asked, and after some urgent paperwork and a little insisting they have now authorized to produce a complete copy for me! I had to write a short email to the Music Administration Manager of JALC, but there was no problem, it all went very quick and easy, they also authorized me to present some sound fragments at the conferences in Berlin and Madrid. I have not received the copy yet, they will send me an email with a link so I can download it as an mp3 file, but I think there will be no problem.

So this makes things a lot easier because it is not necessary that you send me the sound fragments I asked you for (I only hope you haven't begun working on the files yet …!!!). Working on the compositions for me will also be much easier because I will not have to work by memory. Of course, I had to sign different forms assuring them that I will not publish your work nor make any commercial use of it, all the typical things. Anyway, I am happy about it, I thought they would not allow it. And well, I hope all this is ok for you.

What I really would need from you are the lyrics of the songs. And also I would like to ask you: could you scan the front page of the program, the disclaimer or legal notice page, and the contents page, if there is such a thing, and send it to me by email, please? You already gave me a lot of photocopies of that program: (musicians, abridgment of the story), but in my papers, I would like to use (and cite) this program as a publication of The Wooden Flute, that makes it more objective (it is sort of independent), and it is better than citing the texts on your website.

So if I had these other pages it would be easy for me to make references and citing in the correct form.

Ok, Ron, that's all for now, I hope you are well, and your family too. Please give my regards to your mother, it was such a pleasure to spend some time with her. And to your grandmother, too. Both were so friendly to me, I really like them.

Un abrazo, C

6/1/16:

Hi Ron,

less than 2 days left until our grand quixotic meeting … prepared for a 3-day interview? After having listened to your Opus every day for two weeks now in the Public Library, I am really excited about this. I don't know much about jazz, musical harmony and theory, and I don't know if I will find the right words, but what I can tell you is that this is a wonderful work, I am deeply impressed. More than once here these days, walking down some Harlem Avenue, or in the subway, or in the library, I have found myself humming, whistling or tapping my foot with this music in my mind, or in my ears. I enjoy it, and sometimes it moves me to the heart. So you see, I am really glad that I came here to work on this, I feel very fortunate for having the chance to listen to your music, and now, to meet you and to listen to you. So, we'll meet at the airport? Just look out for the helmet of Mambrino!—C.

Hello. Okay, sounds great. Columbia, SC (CAE) is just a hop away from NYC by plane. Call anytime.—RW

3/16/16:

Hi.

My pleasure. It's a long story … haha … I would be delighted to tell it to you. and, like many great works, It ends w/ me feeling blacklisted after it's premiere … yeah, insecurities, jealousies and such … oh and few outbursts during the rehearsals … LOL

You would do better to deal w/ me directly. I have the scores and the entire recording on DVD as well as CD. No one knows anything about it but me. Think about flying into Columbia, SC, instead.—Ron

3/16/16:

Dear Mr. Westray,

My name is C, I am a Professor. I live in Barcelona.

I will be in New York for a research stay at the New York Public Library (Music División), where I want work on a recording of one of your compositions, Opus 1. This is a part of a larger research project on jazz compositions inspired by literary works. As far as I know, the NYPL is the only library and archive that holds a copy of the CD of this recording; and I am really looking forward to listening to it, since it is one of the very few larger jazz suites inspired by a major novel, and as far as I know it has not been published, am I right?

After the first week of my stay at NYC, when I become familiar with your work, and if you are in town at the time (or some place not too far away), would you be so kind to receive me for an interview (30–60 minutes), to ask you some questions about this composition? I would appreciate this very much, especially because I am not a musician nor a jazz expert, so some first-hand informations and thoughts by the compositor would be of great help. This interview would have an academic character, and it would not be published. I would just use these informations (and mention the interview) in some papers I am preparing this year, for a conference to be held in Munich, and for a Austrian review for comparative literature. The papers of the Munich conference will probably be published in book format.

I would also like to ask you if you would allow me to copy a fragment (1 minute) of one of the most representative songs of your Opus, in order to reproduce this fragment at the Munich conference, as an example of your work and your reception of the novel. Thank you very much for your attention.—Regards, C

★ ★ ★

We Are the Martians

Enough of this relentless (and senseless) search for Martians on Earth.

First off let's get this straight; like other planets, Earth is *in* space (protected by a thin atmosphere called the Ozone layer) in a galaxy named the Milky Way. Your car harnesses the massive (and continuous) explosion of a volatile space element (petroleum) to propel you forward, in an airtight capsule within the Earth's atmosphere (in space). A tiny rocket, if you will. This ceaseless search for life from other planets only reinforces the fact that if people don't feel like they are in control of something, they will generally believe the computations and facts of those who seemingly do have control (harnessing the *same* potential as those in control). And why keep up with political stats and global understanding when you can simply keep up with *sports* in your region? Ironically, both require about the same intelligence. That's another subject, though.

That is, people who are independent minded
and cannot be trusted to be obedient don't make it, by and large.
They're often filtered out along the way.

—Noam Chomsky

For instance, this *type* of trend-belief brings us to a very comfortable conclusion about higher intelligence in our galaxy: It's *there*! Humans seem to be really good at Martian stuff: For instance, the 1940s brought about the Atomic Age, when humans showcased their ability to split the atom, therein harnessing the power of the sun inside of a nuclear warhead. Well, it looks like we beat the Martians to that ... Hitler anyone? Chemical warfare, germ warfare, mass genocides ... all the things we hear Martians are capable of. And even some Martians would be hard pressed to present something more awesome than the Bruce/Catlyn Jenner transmutation, as an expression of Future Possibles ...?

What are some other things we generally accuse Martians of?

Hmmm ... well, there's eating people: Along with many cannibals and cannibalistic cultures through time, Jeffrey Dahmer settled that matter for all time. Okay. Probing of the human body?

Again humans are great at probing each other's bodies just fine ... from sex to laser eye correction, to open-heart surgery, to open-brain surgery, to tiny robots that can go inside your veins and correct pathologies. Come on, people. Let's just face it. It's *us*. Then there's, well, cloning ... Michael Jackson, Little Richard, Ted Bundy and Charles Manson ... and Donald Trump ... That's your Martian, Jack! Oh, and how about the *gun*? Chinese-Humans created that (out here in Space), along with firecrackers, thousands of years ago, and it remains the most effective space weapon thus far. Yeah, gunpowder—from space. With the advent of real laser technology, conventional weapons are near obsolete. The only thing holding the United States up is a reliable battery for that amount of imagined disintegration power. Maybe the hoverboard battery is the solution? LOOK OUT Luke Skywalker ...! Then there's satellite technology, the iPhone. Jet propulsion and hovering drones. Okay, let's talk about space travel, like, umm ... NASA? Recent Mars exploration. Private space travel. Man even had a space capsule catch up with a comet and piggy back a ride recently.

Where are the Martians in all this advancement? *WE are ALL space travelers of epic proportion, traveling on our own spaceship, Earth*: Human advents, inventions, catastrophes, experimentation, exploitation and sacrifice!

If (other) Martians do exist, it would imply that their cumulative intelligence proceeds ours by, perhaps, eons. So, why would they want to f*ck with *humans*, anyway? I mean, would *you*?

Chapter 45

Dear Dean,

I am Ron Westray, Oscar Peterson Chair In Jazz Performance. My tenured appointment commenced on July 1, 2013. I would like to request a sabbatical for the full academic year beginning in the fall semester of 2014 and continuing through the spring semester of 2015. I will fulfill any outstanding obligations in the time before my departure, as well help transition my workload to any temporary replacements in a smooth and efficient manner.

I am eager to take this proposed sabbatical in order to refocus my goals in education. This proposed sabbatical will allow me the time to regain and enhance my philosophical clarity and professional goals, producing a significant and positive effect while away and especially upon my return. I look forward to resuming on July 1st of 2015 with a renewed and invigorated attitude for all that higher education demands.

My activities during the proposed sabbatical will involve (but are not limited to) the following areas:

PERFORMANCES
International Jazz Performances/Limited Touring
Commercial/Archival Recording Projects

WRITING
Completion of Brass Technique/Jazz Theory Manual (editing and inclusion of new transcriptions)
Editing of the first edition of my Contemporary Black Music Anthology

COMPOSITION
Completion of Leviathan—Contemporary Score (non-jazz)
Editing of Chivalrous Misdemeanors—Jazz Opera—for (tentative) FASI

OUTREACH
Coordinating of the 2015 Oscar Peterson Scholarship Gala
Coordinating of the Oscar Peterson Jazz Educators Ensemble
Continuation and Coordination of the Oscar Peterson JazzMobile

Thank you for your time and for your consideration of this proposal.

Ron Westray

* * *

The trees unwrap. *Gunpowder lifts every leaf into the air. His eyes glare with fire no desire to go this way. But this Thursday was the day, for he felt the tide turn just days before. I said, Thursday was the day. That night in Montgomery, Dr. King led the chant, "There comes a time when people just get tired." I said, the trees unwrap. Gunpowder lifts every leaf into air, barely escaped a cabbage-colored cicadas lickety-split, he'd just finished smoking a spliff, shaved three times, with three different size scythes, over three minding weeks, that explains the cut across his forehead, boy go head. Several months of mostly nights of pulling the gate closed for privacy, the needle perfectly placed. Coltrane's black and outstretched arm. Jumpy, the beat jerks him to his feet, without warning, A love supreme hemorrhages, midair. He had a great time that night she's wrapped pussy tight. Arrives from the slippery bleeding horn, he remains torn could it be the liquor—spinning in a glass or the trombone tired from a week's worth of work and no one to offer the door. Let's explore, so high, up in the attic, one blow to his head. He walks to the closet undrunk but woozy, the black gun, the one-eyed stopwatch, batting hand over his heart, Nina's ready, capable, locked and loaded suddenly exploded one after the next felt like sex. Every love-light in the world lit, daring ahead, not behind, everything at risk, to the left, to the right, really hate being polite, mentally he takes flight. It's almost a quarter til 3, mama's on her bending knee, praying "Oh Lord don't let this be." Just pull out your wallet, the blue lights map out your thumb, blazing the like a dark auditorium. The indelible blue ink still on his thumb, he dials 911 to his love. She goes to the courthouse in the morning the dew still sweating the grass, she dials 911 Jesus on the main line. Words of comfort he expels, don't worry my child I'm only chastising him.*

—A.S.

* * *

Yo, gentlemen. What you drinkin … Take a swig Ron-Ron. Okay. That's NC Shine.
God Damn. How'd you know? I know the taste of them radiators up there … HAHA …

* * *

Retrospect is some bullshit.
Tomorrow never comes.

* * *

Americans argue. Canadians complain.
It's been about a year ago since I stubbed my toe.
I just kicked it again.

* * *

I went to jail for the first time at the ripe old age of 45 (and deservedly so). I had been doing high-risk things as long as I can remember. But that's not how it happened, though: I was in my own fenced-in yard, shooting into a sand pile. One bullet defeated the sand and went through my wooden fence before striking a neighbor's front fender. Prior to this, I had successfully pulled tenure at York U and Canadian residency (processes that tested all of my morals and tolerances to the max). For instance, it actually took more time to achieve Canadian residency than it did to attain my bachelor's degree. And I rarely get to play with my "toys" at my home in the South.

Ultimately, that style of decompressing (in the suburbs) was out of (municipal) style; and being *well-versed* doesn't always show in your decisions and/or actions.

* * *

February 26 (L.'s Birthday), 2015, 8:22 a.m.

Columbia police officers uncovered a marijuana grow operation inside the home of a man who was allegedly firing several shots in a residential area Wednesday. Officers were dispatched to a residence on the 500 block of Floyd Drive near Greenview Park after receiving reports of a man brandishing a gun and firing several shots in the neighborhood. The bullets damaged a wooden fence and car fenders, but no one was injured as a result of the shooting. Officers identified Ronald Kenneth Westray as the shooter, and while searching his home they discovered a marijuana grow operation in his closet. Westray was charged with manufacturing marijuana, discharging a firearm within the city limits and malicious injury to property. He was transported to the Alvin S. Glenn Detention Center.

★ ★ ★

ME: CD release is tomorrow. Here's the iTunes preview: https://itunes.apple.com/us/album/magisteria/id962263038
love you—R

L.: Wow! I think I heard some of these in the initial phases. The little girls love It's Crazy and What a Guy! I have many likes as well, particularly the slower grooves. Congrats to you! As with many things, I know you've been waiting for this "release"! Luv ya back and wanna see ya soon.

ME: Okay, momma. Can't wait! :-P Reminder: Granny B. is 92 today. If you can't get out there, put the girls on the phone w/her after school. Great News—Conditional Release—60 days. Charges Dropped. No pee test … YAY! Thank you for your prayers. I Love You.

L.: Yes! To everything!! And we will call her, too.

★ ★ ★

AS: I see your point. I'm always progressing in some fashion. The lesson here is to gain satisfaction in changing my attitude and to allow time for contemplation rather than responding immediately.

You can see how i got caught up with this snafu because it was triggered by a compounding effect of no response. About riding back with you to eventually seeing her waiting outside glaring at me and not responding to my good night to seeing you walking across my car at the light after stating that you were "hanging out" with the cats. I'm not some crazy b★tch that doesn't get it) It appeared one way which sparked an emotional response that I otherwise would not have given because I'm fully aware that we are not exclusive.

Now that I understand that u r not n fact in love with me I can become cognizant of my emotions which will enable me to react with less concern towards you and anything that you do.

Because really and truly our friendship is what matters to me; and I admire you for being a guy who was upfront with me I like a straight shooter so don't sugar coat on my behalf; Say not seeing you on Friday or there will be some of my other b*tches there that night. You don't have to tell me your business; but it's good to keep me informed. Because you really don't know how these other bitches will act out; and that is real! I liked they way we were before. I need my independence; and your coming and going is perfect for me; because I don't like to feel constrained by a man; it's suffocating; and now I think it will be even better if we finally take this love shit out of the picture. That was my plight months ago; but you ignored it; and so did I. Thank you for the clarification.

ME:

you don't have to get over ME
you need to get over IT.
and roll w/ ME.

Is that right? I have been expressing my love to u n every way imaginable even n poems but most of all through my actions and u hav reciprocated it … didn't stop me to say I'm not n love with u A. I see where u r going but this is not that … I love u as a human loves a friend U know just keep it plain. I didn't just need to hear u say u loved me for the sake of it hell I've been n love several times I'm not n search of it I hate being n love and I mean that! bc there is no more true love n this world that is no where to b found … Men and women hav become lovers of themselves …

AS: Yes of course ppl hav human love i love him; but he has never heard me say that to him more than once all these yrs. there r other ppl u express human love to but I don't wake up n the morning tell them u love and miss them on a regular basis … Or give them cards expressing love to them.

Ronald the truth is that you do love me and I know u do u can down play this too but I know u do and i will never tell u how i know. So if u never say it again it won't matter bc I know it n my heart … and for me to cope love can't b part of this bc when I'm n love it's real to me n every fashion even now although I hav to let go i dont know how long it w b b4 u r out of my system bc I can't cut off love that's another reason why I hate it bc I hav no control over it.

ME:

it is possible to love many people.
when i say that, i'm not talking about romantic love.
i'm talking about human love.
thought you understood that.

AS: Thank u for taking time to explain but my view point was a little diff bc it started with u not responding when V. and mom asked if I was riding bak with u bc I had to work the table. I told ur mom that u never answered; so I better drive. She ended riding with me to save time for V. we as women we worked together. U could hav been candid with me and I would hav went on about my business only a gentleman would walk both ladies to their cars but if u r telling them both u love them I can see how the best option would b to opt out. I Just don't want to go through anymore changes I'm too old almost 50. I need time to recapture my heart so that I never fail myself n this manner ever again or put u through my anguish which under these circumstances not warranted. I hav to b careful bc the entire sum and meaning of my existence can b smashed and broken to pieces under the weight of giving my all to a man who is incapable I can't b denial about the complexity of what this really is bc in all actuality very simplistic … And I have to let THAT sink n and as u continue to stay the same I have to let go of loving u by allowing myself to date other ppl again at sm point. But for rt now i just need to b. I can't pick up where we left off bc it will lead bak to this point we hav got to kill this pattern I can't b consumed by emails.

I don't do this type shit … I really don't know how to pick up from here i would like to b able to continue if I could get u to stop saying u love me that might help me keep things n perspective.

As we both know the music has a tendency to speak so the song playing now after I've gotten off the phone with you is "Upside Down" by Diana Ross. I've heard this song hundreds of times but this time it fit you.—A.S.

Chapter 44

L.: hey baby!! Let bygones be be bygones! When do you want me, your babies and the dog to come back to Canada and see you? Act like you know who loves ya! Yo' Boo

ME: Hi, Les. Thanks for reaching out. As for the travel, it's a matter of communication, as usual. I'm only in TO for about another 3 weeks; then to US. On another topic: I could really appreciate you withdrawing the back-child-support order and let me do what I do. In addition to having embarrassed me at my workplace with several subpoenas and sheriffs in my absence, it has caused a logistical (and financial) nightmare in preparation to defend myself against such a general accusation. I'm not the kind of man that needs or deserves that in this particular case. The order, essentially, describes me as a deadbeat. That is offensive. I will not be present as a dad, but dealt with by the courts, simultaneously. If I am going to be labeled as a deadbeat, then I will let the courts tell me who I should be. If I am going to be present (as the past has corroborated), then, again, I could appreciate the withdrawal of the order.

L.: We are on spring break now, but of course I could have done better planning. I am glad that you are well, considering I have not spoken with you sense October. I will be honest in saying that I am not aware of the particulars of this support order. I applied for medical assistance for the little girls. In requesting that, I had to also be OK with seeking child support. I accepted all conditions that they asked me about. I do not have a "case worker" with whom I am in contact. Actually, I don't even know my so-called case number. It has been a long time since I have requested medical assistance. As far as I know, this is a course that has been rolling since I applied awhile back. I don't have a contact person. I am not familiar with what is going on, even as we speak.

★ ★ ★

Around this time, I reconnected with M., whom I had met in 1995 in Toronto while traveling w/ Marcus Roberts (just months before I met L. in Boston). We reconnected when the semester started, and it was just the interaction I needed to remain sane while being sued for child support by the ex (under false accusations) and precipitating an annulment (divorce) with R. M. She had been separated from her husband for several years now, though they lived in the same household. I didn't much care for the double-drama-karma, so the relationship didn't last.

* * *

AM: Can you please stop posting on fb, its making me want to see you … really bad! Thanks, lol:-)

ME: HAHA—Soon cum … ooops come. Let's get together for the Xmas HLDZ … for a taste

AM: What dates will you be home …

ME: From about mid december, til Jan 4. I will see what I can do … you know my child issues. will look into it for sure …

AM: definitely … we'll connect then. Ok … have a good one …

ME: You too, good to hear from you … XOXO

AM: Was listen to your cd … came to the Garden. beautiful flashback of when you packed a picnic and we lounged here one afternoon!

ME: Aaah … simple times … xoxo

AM: Yes … if only we knew … xoxo

AM: I sent a text to your mobile # did you get it? It contain pics. Let me know …

ME: hey babe … can't get text on that # … send to [mobile #].

AM: Ok …will do :-)

ME: Daaaym … okay … lol who is that? Bahahaha!

AM: Okay, I'm in that pose right now … minus hair, + oh say 60 pounds LMAO. did all three come through?

ME: Just go then … wow! That's when you came out to Illnois in '94 or '93 and my 1st european tour in '92 … you're goooood

AM: You sent me those pics … I didnt take them.

ME: we were so tight … Thanks for that, babe … what a blast from the past …

AM: Yes we were … hey I got a letter you mailed me … made me cry when I read it!

ME: Well, I am a man of words … You could have been my future ex wife … lmao

AM: Seems like a lifetime ago … yet like yesterday for some things …

ME: right, right … we are the same people in lots of ways

ME: So, when you coming to hang out w/ me again? be in the Metro by mid may btw: was there any fall out or acting out form "old boy" when you returned from our ron-de-vous

AM: just got other pics … raw steak on the plane to europe … yuck. we were too hot to trot

ME: Sooo young and full of life!

AM: I remember we had bake fish or chicken on that picnic!!

ME: Oh, okay … what a sweet letter. I was such a gentleman … Lot of good that did me, ultimately (not w/ you, but you know who). Met the ex right after this phase. still mister gentleman. she thought she had her one. so i had to spend 20 years proving that this ain't that, you dig. i'm still the gentleman at heart, as you know. but, i'm hard now. wow … my hand writing has deteriorated (damn laptop)

AM: The choices we make … a lot of moments that make up our lives.

ME: we would have been exes, too. so i'm glad we are still friends …

AM: I feel ya.

ME: I'm as hard as I've always been, just in different ways … different tolerance for different things … you know niggas have tested me. who saved my ass. not my words. I will hurt something. See, it starts in the heart. I have a warrior's heart. two extremes: on/off. the middle involves me, mostly, not fucking with lots of people, so i don't have to … See, a warrior doesn't show off, or boast, right? I just want you to understand that at this late date …

AM: Yes …

ME: Thanks for listening, babe …

AM: That was a conversation I would have liked in person… such as it is, thanks for sharing! and thanks for all the memories this morning!

ME: I'm glad you did … oh you are welcome! Thank you for the memories of the past … A friendship like this helps me to at least approach some semblance of understanding of what love is, or could be. I do not attest to really know.

AM: Wow … I get that!! I would like to think the bond we share (shared) is in some part an attest to what it is to love and be loved!

ME: i'm just glad we are still tight and didn't f*ck it up by getting married. know a woman may not see it that way, but … from MansVille, in other words, in retrospect:
I would have ended up in the same situation w/ anyone i chose. and I had my choices

AM: You didn't mess anything up with your marriage. We went in different directions. I've always known there would remain a connection between us. You don't meet, connect on those levels for it to never resurface. I own what did or didn't happen for us, but I love the relationship I had with you. I look forward to being friends no matter where we are … you have been an inspiration.

ME: well, thanks for that.

AM: You're right we probably would have ended up divorced, and possibly not friends, and that would be worse!

ME: You're correct xoxo—hope to see you over the summer

AM: Ok … I feel like I need a hug!! Lol. On that note I must jump in shower and go to work.

That would be great … love ya! Xoxoxo

ME: okay, no texting in while driving … you know you my girl.

AM: Stop in-boxing me then! Ok

ME: HA

AM: BYE

ME: BYE

Chapter 43

Gigs

David Lidov, Faculty Recital, York University.

Ron Westray w/ The York University Jazz Ensemble, The Rex Jazz Bar, Toronto.

Ron Westray, Savannah Music Festival, Savannah, GA.

Marcus Roberts Dectet, Florida State University.

Ron Westray w/ The Jazz FM 91.5 Youth Big Band, York University.

Ron Westray w/ York University Wind Symphony.

Ron Westray w/ York University Jazz Orchestra.

* * *

I tuned up V.'s 450 and my 650 over the holidays. The 650 almost killed me, it was so fresh. Popped out of first and it bucked up like bronco, right in front of the park. If I were not strong as hell and determined not to eject, that 650 would have come down right on top of me, upside down, in about the blink of an eye. I would have died or been paralyzed right there in front of the park, while visiting for the holidays. Instead, I dug my finger into the jagged, broken-off front brake clutch, bonding flesh with metal and held on while the bike leapt like a horse. I put my weight down on the tank. I felt the tires when they made contact. Stunned onlookers watched. I headed on up the hill to Aunt Queen's picnic birthday party.

She and J. were doing okay these days, and he was throwing her a picnic. J. had served a lot of time, but was doing well and had purchased a home in Greenview, not far from his mom's. J. was the first to jokingly point out some flaw in my deportment, as was his nature. In this case, it was the fact that I was bleeding—something I knew not. My heart was still racing 100 mph from the near accident and the adrenaline was surging through my veins as I successfully contextualized the mundane activities of children, family, and associates, and a bleeding pointer finger. I simply announced that the bike had tried to kill me cause I had added a little chainsaw oil to the old oil.

"Man, that thing grabbed so hard out of first!" I exclaimed, in the wildest, most country twang you could ever imagine. The older women were looking at me like they had seen this frequency before in really crazy men. I guess you could say I was proud of that. True to form, I went around talking loud, giving out cheek kisses and handshakes, in between sucking my own blood from a deep gash in the wrinkle of the under side of my finger.

J. offered me a towel on the inside. "You alright, Cuz?"

Yeah, bruh, I'm alright. This was by no means my first near-death experience.

★ ★ ★

L.: Kindly do me a favor. Please tell your wife to refrain from contacting me or my family or my affiliates. I totally understand what she is trying to convey here. She obviously knew that you did not tell me who she was. It is clear that she put it out on facebook, sent directly to my colleagues in an effort to "put it in my face."

Please assure her that me and my family are not interested in her invitations or her affiliation. You are two of a kind and should do very well together. Tell her to concentrate on her union, as me and my family are content as we are. Again, I urge YOU to tell her to refrain from imposing her psychological issues on me and my family. We are not interested!

★ ★ ★

OMG

Hi L.,

I hope you are well and the kids are well too. Seen photos, they look pretty. You look well and happy … I sent you an email to school and it returned …

I am sure Ron must have already shared his new news with you. I was hoping to tell you by phone and did not have a number for you. I was in South C with the Westrays and was hoping to see you, but we did not come to DC. I asked to see you but never happened, so sorry to miss you. I will be back in the US and hope to see you and the kids … the holiday to Melbourne is still open is you want to take a break …

Hope you are still teaching here in the school, if so send me an short email so I know you got this. The last time we spoke was in Canada.

I read and see all your fabulous performances at the Synchronicity ... keep it up and you look well. love to connect and hope to see you soon in the USA. Love to send the kids some Ausi stuff from Downunder and will post it to you to DC.

Take care and hope to hear back.

kind regards,

R., Melbourne

★ ★ ★

ME: I do find it interesting that you can take time to respond to this while simultaneously placing it in a context in which I have imposed "my business" onto you, but you can't take time to simply respond with a confirmation email regarding thousands of dollars being forwarded to you.

You can take time to imply that I am crazy, but I'm pretty sure you would not allow me any mental incapacity if I were not supporting you and our daughters in the ways in which I do, including health benefits and putting teeth in people's head. So a little respect would be cool; and remember, "I'm not crazy, I'm just horny and arrogant." (Where have I heard this?)

Rather than blaming ME for her actions (as if I would have you in my business if it were up to me), you could just address her when and if she contacts you, and let her know you don't wish to be in communication w/ her (like an adult/woman).

For instance, what you wrote me, you could have just as well written back to her. I have forwarded your response. That's all I can do. As I have stated, we are not in communication. Don't delude yourself into believing that HER actions are MY fault or design ... You should know better than that. I don't have time for those types of games ... you know that ...

You see what it is, so you might want to rephrase this: keep me out of your business. Be for real. Trust, when its up to me, I do! Again, please don't create some bull ..., like I'm egging her on or something ... I DON'T HAVE TIME for games, trust!

★ ★ ★

R: Ron, After careful consideration to your ongoing request to end/annul the marriage, Ron I agree with your proposal to annul the marriage. Please proceed and take the necessary legal action.

ME: We should annul, ASAP.

R: Ron, I need you to tell me this ... Which way do you want to go with the USA marriage? If the marriage is legal, what do you propose we do? Will help the process please advise asap.

ME: My bank account is for RW, not silly assed affairs. Hey, works for me, I wasn't raised to need a woman for anything financially. You must be thinking about some movie you saw ... Didn't need you before I met you in 2001, and I don't need your worn out ass and your fat purse to match. Prestige, baby ... check the books.

ME: You filled out the same box I did in Buffalo: not married. So, that will be proven when my D Cert. is shown with a date of 2001. I was never playing games. You will find that out in due course.

R: F*CK OFF RON!! AND STAY OUT OF MY LIFE TILL I FINISH THIS!!! SEE YOU SOON!

ME: We both have the same emails. I don't see anything to be concerned about in the emails except your numerous threats over 2 months, now. I have nothing to hide, and look forward to defending my innocence against whatever party so desires and regarding whatever issue you have.

R: No you fucking fool I have nothing to hide from the law in any country, it is you who lied and a dishonest man to the court house! You have given me enough emails and reasons ... I do need to give out more now! Wait!!! Tell your attorney to stand by please xxxx

ME: Yes—IN YOUR OLD, FOOLISH MIND, HUZZY. I AM ALIVE—AND WELL—and innocent.—W

R: Money you have nothing Ron!!!! No human qualities, and no soul!!! You are—barely alive! Now get fucked I am DONE with you! I don't need you! You are a loser ... All the Government dept, child support, YORK, USA COURTS, DC COURTS ... let's get it out there! You will be paying back more money than you are now, after I am done with you dirty dog! You are already in trouble with the law right??? In the USA??? Wait Ron!!!! Stay tuned! I am making plans for the trip and I am not coming alone! So I will meet you at York first!

ME: It's not hard to find me, and I have nothing to hide, so do your fucking thing. I look forward to making a complete fool of your ass when it is time. Music has nothing to do with this. That's what I do. I always have money. I do more things with my money, honey. I've never had a wife.

R: Negro go play more music ... make some real money so you can have a woman maybe one day!!! Sorry, I'm not interested in a prostitute. Wife basher!! Stinking ... you are a sick negro who has lost his soul. Only jazz will help you … you are nothing Westray, you have nothing!!!!!!!! Let's see who will be suing who ha h ah ah a!!!!! You have no money to scratch your ass!!

ME: Huzzy, You must be thinking about some movie you saw. My sister and I have more education than your entire family. There is not one thing that I have done illegally. So you serve me justice with no fucking case, you tired assed bitch. You WILL BE sued for slandering my name w/ my employer. Meanwhile, York payroll won't do anything without the legal process being equal, silly rabbit.

R: You are a dumb ass too not just sick in your head from smoking pot since 10 year age … and now 43 yrs old!! And three abandoned neglected children and bashed up wife … shame on you!!

Just tried to rip off the new wife too! Wife basher you are Ron … I am now heading out. Let start the process and I will make sure we have enough media coverage in USA and CND!!!

[X, Y, Z] and more who asked me not to marry you, and was so angry with me that I did it with a untrustworthy man like you, are forming a Facebook page to make sure this never happens to any women … All my phones and stories will be posted … emails … Thanks God for friends!!

Stay tuned Ron!!! I have all the time nowwww!!!

ME: The Westrays never needed your approval. How dare you betray me like this after spending time with my family. Pay out from who? F*ck off, as you say. You have no more grounds for a pay out than I do. No judge is going to honor a payout after 16 days of being together in 14 years. I will let my attorney do the talking on that. That's silly.

R: Fucked up Westrays from the South with no money, no hope!!! Listen Negro I will deal with you and serve you justice!!!! Let's see what happens to your f*cked up game! Low life you are.

ME: As for my family, they only care about my well being. You, they will forget; no real impression was made there.

Anything you have paid for involved both of us. YOU DID NOT PAY FOR EVERYTHING ON THE HONEYMOON; you're exaggerating. I have over 3K to 3.5K worth of receipts of MY OWN from the supposed honeymoon. I don't know of any cash exchanges. I certainly am no wealthier. Where is all this money that I have "grabbed" from you?

R: You are a fucking money grabber Ron … you made it tooooo obvious Ron!!I was paying for the whole wedding you low scum!! "My ceremony" … African American style is it Ron??? … paid for you all the way, you got me to fund the honeymoon … you are f*cking LOW!! No respects for you!!! You know how much money I have f*cking wasted on your ass!!! Forget it loser! You not worth my sh*t!!!

ME: You haven't paid for sh*t for me. Your purse? I didn't need it and don't need it. As for opinions of your family, I don't give a damn. I don't need a woman to support me, and I never have. You haven't funded anything for my family, so save it. I haven't needed you purse for anything. What have you paid for? My family is not affected by your opinions. You do what ever you need to do. The truth will be there to confront you.

R: What are you talking about Ron, class??? You are a non-trustworthy, deceitful, cunning man … I am sick in my tummy! When I see you in CAD soon I will have a chance to look in your eyes … None of your family could not even come for your own wedding … Only interested in name titles … sad babe!!! I am sad for YOU!! I know enough now. 3 months was enough Ron!! You are as good as your family, we all know the Westrays from the South now LOL. I think I will make this my next career move and use this for a screen play! SAY NO MORE … Your activities, actions, behaviours have spoken for a life time, Prof Ronald Westray …

Let's take this all the way Ron … I, my family, my friends, my guests, the involved body corporations, all are very supportive, corporative and giving me the strength I need to go through this nightmare!

This just the start Ron! Heyyyyyyy you may like to talk to V. for a little advice right?? I have sent V. the guest email, so V. is fully aware of the Ron dramas … The belly flop wedding … Ha ha.

Did you tell them even the truth Ron?

You still have time to tell me the truth over the phone, all your reasons, and we come to an mutual agreement … If not I will take it through the right way as I have NO CHOICE!

ME: >My attorney will handle your church.
Church and State don't mix in North America, by the way. I have broken no laws. In fact, we have a marriage certificate.
As for your friends and family, I will be waiting for any slander and libel issues. You are insane.

R: hey no time for this game anymore … I am taking this forward and let's see how it unfolds. sorry you have not been a man and be a dishonest man. I am very sad I landed myself with this shit … you are NO husband to me, you have been the biggest ass and this is not the first time … You HAVE NO CLASS NO STYLE and let me down … the wedding got cancelled b'cas of you. you f*cked it all up … NEVER WANTED IT RIGHT????

I had to write a statement, the church has got involved, I tried to tell you big head man WITH A FAT EGO … you will find out all about it … You cancelled the wedding as you are not able to face anyone Ron I have had enough of this WESTRAY style … HOW CAN ANYONE PUT UP WITH YOUR MAD ASSED AND LOW WAYS?

R: you have made a great impression on everyone here … people are in disbelief I married you … I am paying the price now as I am getting hell from family and friends as no one wanted me to do this, most of my friends were upset, they know what you are like … now I am facing all of them … and it is hell Ron … you have shamed me, my family and treated me like one of your low life women … you were mistaken … I am not your type Ron … you have tried again to fuck me up … you are sick man. all the answers I have asked you and you have not been able to show me, tell me, will be told and seen, since you have messed around with me, family have taken over, friends have taken over and this will be very bad now … you asked for this the way you have carried yourself … very poor!!!! no class …!!!

I will never never forgive you ron for this and the hell it has been for the past 2 months dealing with you!!! I am coming to deal with you face to face and this will happen soon.

Don't think you can do this kind of shit to women and run away … NO WAY!! YOU DEAL WITH THIS IN A DECENT MANNER WITH ME AS I WILL NOT LET THIS PASS MY DEAD BODY! IF YOU WANT TO HIDE AND NOT CALL ME … GO FOR IT!

See what happens … you have had enough time!

I am extremely pissed off to see what happen to the f*cking wedding, your true self, and the wedding you never wanted … Played me out again!

ME: In addition to waiting on my own approval (whether right or wrong). I HAVEN'T ADDED YOU because we are separated and in a negative relationship. Why did I come back into your life? Well, it wasn't for any of this. I did my part. I married you. No secrets—W

R: No, I need to talk to you nothing to hide Ron … Let's do this nicely or you may need representation. Send me your number I will call you.

ME: I don't have anything to say. I will have representation when it is time. I will present my divorce order if it is called upon.

R: RON CALL ME ASAP … IT IS VERY URGENT AND YOU ARE CRAZY TO GO COLD … PLEASE CALL AS THINGS ARE ALSO OUT OF MY HANDS I NEED TO TALK VERY SOON. THANKS

R: Ron, I hope you are finally happy my wedding got cancelled … this is what we had to tell the guests, as we were not able to tell them the church issue!

R: Please give me a call at home … so we can chat about this matter asap.

R: Hey the silence game will not work so please let's talk and I need you to respond back like a husband would do! Let me know the time you will call as I will not be home all day.

R: Dear Ron, It is with deep regret that I have to bring to your notice the reception to be held on the 28 December 2013, has be cancelled. Under the Australian laws the church has declined to have our marriage/blessing due to the deficiency and deficit of Ron not able to surrender a copy of the divorce papers thus far, which also happen in New York Buffalo USA on 19 August 2013. Until you are able to show proof of this critical document and full conformation of your legal divorce, the marriage in question will be referred back to Buffalo NY via Melbourne church. The matter is out of my hands now and I gave you enough information and reasons for asking … The divorced certificate can be obtained via online (USA Washington DC Courts or births, deaths and marriage office in that State) within a 7-day time frame! Let me know your thoughts and thanking you in advance for your full corporation.

ME: Back pedaling? We are already married. Everything I have told you is true. The fact is, YOU don't believe we are married. I don't want to be married AGAIN in AUS, which is the real reason you need the BC. The ceremony to celebrate our marriage was fine, but not another legal marriage in another country. If YOU need to fight to find out that I have been honest, then YOU fight. I have no interest in fighting, but I will present the facts when necessary. I have taken enough bashing. I am also tired of your orders. You should know I'm not into that role.

BTW: I'm not going to send emails back and forth this time. Tired of that pattern. You tossed your accusations and venom, once again, but I will not try to defend each and every accusation, this time around. Many of your accusations are old topics that we were supposed to be over, but you are still scarred by YOUR OWN BELIEFS (stemming from your insecurities). What you have, effectively, done is turn me completely off; when all I was trying to do was honor our decisions.

R: Dear Ron, I am no longer interested in your warped principles (you have zero principles), unsubstantial excuses on every important matter in relations to our marriage and the law.

Again you have failed to produce the straightforward information any wife will ask and MUST HAVE … the divorce certificate which any one would expect to have with them.

And if you don't, you get one online, period! I don't believe a word you say and never did or respect any of your dishonest stories anymore.

I have learnt, and observed that you are someone who has no respect for the law, no respect for other humans, not give a shit about anyone! It is a damned shame you are not able to get the divorce certificate online without any further fabrications, as it has opened to some lawful and valid question from the church and R? In September you failed again to produce the copy of the "removal of your common law spouse in your PR application," and we battled and fought throughout September, and then you tried to call off the wedding in many ways, as you were back peddling, lying and unable to show your wife any paperwork. Later sending me "cut and pastes" as proof, I have lost all my respect for you as this is pathetic, dishonest and NOT acceptable AT ALL ...

To date you have not included R. in your York profile, not notified the Canadian High Commission of your marriage to R. in USA, lied to the USA courts that you were never married by not showing your divorce papers, and asking me to lie that I was never married (even though I had no reason to lie, for you), and now NO divorce papers ... all lost. This is a serious matter and a felony. What are you covering up? Let's talk about this first ... NOW!!!

ME: Come on, R, I have a legal divorce certificate with me, so I have no such complications! What are your complications?

R: You do have a chance to be honest with me for the last time? Until all my questions have been legitimately answered by you, Ron Westray, with the paper work that I have asked to see, this matter will not be put to rest, Ron!

I know more than you think I know, about what you are up to??? If you want to fight we can ... Let me see your honest side and the highly educated and respectable professor Ron Westray, so you can shade the truth here before it gets tooooo complicated! I trust you will cooperate, Ron ... Thank you.

ME: It's not about secrets. It's about principles. This is a conversation we could have had in SC, before we went to NYC; not now that we are married. There are no secrets, here. I'm just not going out of my way to do that because it indicates a change in plans, two legal weddings. I don't feel that is necessary. Any time you want to rummage through my papers in SC and read the orders of my divorce, you may. We don't divorce papers need that to have the Priest's blessings. Why are we talking about divorce papers. We did this already, babe; We are married. It's real. You produced a birth certificate in 48 hrs because we WERE getting married. Now, we ARE married. It's not the same scenario, babe.

R: Hey Ron, I will not get in to your usual debits and side talks to try and by pass the real issues. I produced a birth certificate in 48 hours been in Sri Lanka, so let's get real Ron and please don't insult me. I don't see why you are not able to get this online. I want to see it like I said, and I have a right to ask you this Ron? So let's stop this secretive games and I want your divorce papers please. Let's keep this simple. Thanks babe, R.

ME: Babe, I have no plans on marrying twice. There is no purpose in me being married in AUS. We have wed in NYC, and it is legal and sufficient. I asked you to say not married, so we wouldn't have to enter into any inconveniences. Also, I couldn't find mind in time. Come on, R. Mainly, I don't see where divorce papers have anything to do with the process as we have a marriage license. Again, I will not be able to produce that. Use the marriage license. The same that will be used. Initially, you told me the Pastor needs our marriage license.

R: Hey there … I have just answered in yellow as I am a little rushed honey … Please reply as you ignore my emails most times, I have noticed this and

R: Hey babe this should not be an issue or too complicated as you can obtain a copy of a divorce certificate online from USA DC courts. It is a simple process and please don't question the church. Ron I brought my divorce papers to USA and they are in the yellow packet, and you have a copy. By the way babe why did you tell the NY courts that you had never married before, and you asked me to say the same??? Why did you do this babe??? Since we do not belong to this church and this is a formality here and is common. There should not have to be a debate or issue on this please. I am kindly asking you to get one online. We are married already, however this is requested by the church and I will not question the priest. I hope you don't make this an issue as it is a basic and simple request, and I obeyed it too.

Hope to hear back soon … Your wife, R. xxxx

ME: Hey, babe …

I don't have my divorce certificate. I can tell you, I won't be able to produce that; it's lost in paper work in SC … No way I can find that, now. If I had known, I would have worked on this earlier.

Why did you not approach it as not previously married for us, like in BUF? In BUF, this related to State laws, I though this was a church service, not AUS gov.

Again, I don't have that w/ me in TO, and even in SC, I don't know where it is. I looked when we went to BUF.

Technically, we are not getting married twice, okay? This is a church service, right. All we should need is our marriage license from BUF in order to have a service. NYC has already married us. Our marriage certificate should be our validation for a church "service" … not divorce certificates. We already passed that phase of the legal marriage—Ron

R: Morning babe, Hope you had a good night sleep … I had the church meeting with Pastor Lucky and went over the Order of Service and details etc. Babe please scan and send me a copy of your devoiced paper please, as part of the administration systems they need both our divorced certificates. Please send asap babe … and I will send the admin office.
Everything is fine with the service and it should be good!

R: Hey Ron, You may like to add your preferences for those categories you are referring to, add to the Order of Service. Put it in a different colour, I will pass it to the church. This is the church services put together by the Pastor Lucky. (I have my walking in song on CD and will give church.)

Just email it back to me once you are finished as it might be our only option with your busy schedule. If you have time to talk to me and go through this, it would be my ideal preference, however, I will leave it to you Ron. Many thanks and miss you,
Your wife,
R. XXX

ME: Hi, babe. Pardon the delay; incredibly busy week! Midterm examinations this week and recitals … I thought you would fill in most of the form, but we can discuss that together … I have few preferences for those categories … Miss you heaps, too, babe—Ron

R: Hey babe … How are you doing? I am sure you are doing fine and enjoying work. I am not sure what's going on, but we are hardly in communication and long periods of silence … Silence is a harmony killer, and I am reaching out to you if you and I can talk, email or network me??

I have been fortunate to get your calls this week and thank you Ron … Even though it has been rushed … And really with little or no time for us to chat … I hope you don't mind me asking for a little help here babe … thanks! Ron humanly and as a woman I need our communication line to stay open and flow, and be able to talk to you with out fear, share and express … I hope I am not asking for too much babe. I miss you and words don't really mean much too right … when you are so far away … Hope you will have a little time today (Friday morning for you).

ME: Hey, babe. Sorry about that. You know my home service is out 'til Tuesday. I can only contact you from the office or other places I can get wifi … Right now, I'm at a performance using the wi-fi. I have been running all day. Just got your emails on the break at the performance. Babe, I miss you too! I will go to the office tomorrow (sun) to try to catch you either at 11p/12a or 6:30 am Monday, MEL time. Just work w/ me 'till I get my new service at home, Tuesday.
Your husband,
Ron

R: Hi Ron, I am trying to call you babe, are you able to call me. I really need to talk to you and I have no way to reach you over the weekend. is it ok that I want to talk to you babe …?? I sent you emails with no replies … Love, your wife, R.

R: Darling Ron, I miss you lots and it was beautiful to hear your voice over the phone yesterday … You sounded sooo sexy babe and amazing voice

… just like when I used to call you to NY apt, and I used to hear your voice …

You sounded like a school boy when I spoke to you yesterday, excited and playful … I miss not able to hold you babe, and kiss you. Know this.

Been your twin and a Gemini "I," "We," mirror each other … So keep this in mind babe as I am learning through science and astrology.

What time were you born? Send me the time I can give you some useful knowledge on us both …

Love you genuinely, Your wife, R xxx

ME: Good Morning I will be there on December 28th. Yours, Ron

R: Ok thanks for explaining and I am sure we are the ONLY two people who can work this out … and I am more than happy to share with you what I can do and not able to do …
Further I will wait in Aus till my Visa is through and then we can more forwards if that is what you want?? If not good then you may suggest or make your decision based on what is good for "You."
Thanks,
R. xx

R: Thank you for acknowledging. I really do understand the importance of our wedding ceremony. Yes I agree and understand all your concerns and yes we must talk babe … I am on the same page … "I am no more sure how to handle our current state than you are"—you not wrong Ron!

ME: I'm not trying to pull out of anything. My pride is on the line here, too, R. I simply don't want to be unreal about the relationship potential.

ME: You know, I really do understand the importance of our wedding ceremony, but I feel like the relationship has been spoiled. Let's face it, no matter who is at fault, the bickering did not just start. We are too far ahead in life to be unhappy. So, before you dismantle anything in your life in MEL, we need to make a decision. I am not anymore sure how to handle our current state than you are.

The biggest issue seems to be the fact that I cannot control or determine the timing of the CAD issue: This has caused you change your plans (selling vs. renting). I get it; makes sense. The financial burden now rest solely on me, which was never plan A. That's fine, I can support my lifestyle as it is … I understand that this is because I could not give you closure soon enough as weighed against your financial risks in MEL. That's fine; I get it.

You have also stated that you are not going to remain in a marriage in MEL, beyond thus and so date in the New Year, even though I can't determine when the CAD issue will resolve; and, you are not flexible to being in MEL beyond thus and so, then who's fault is it? and nobody said any of that would actually be that prolonged; it's out of our control …

We were only talking Plan B's and C's, that's all … At present, we are still within plan A. I want to be together just as soon as you do, but some issues. I cannot control. I thought you understood that.

BTW: Your WP solution does not work within what I understand about my profile. Around this time, I'm supposed to graduate from the Work Permit to the Perm. Res., not add to the WP …
That's what I'm waiting on.—Ron

ME: Hi … I am doing fine, R. … None of our conversations have gone well for two weeks, now. So, I guess I'm a little turned off from trying to talk. My home internet service will end on the 17 through 22. (changing providers). If we talk it will be from the office.

R: Hi Ron, I have not heard from you at all and wondering what is going on? Why are you silent and aloof on me again, hey is this marriage babe …You need to communicate with me considering we are so far away and you cut all line of us speaking to me … I am very confused, alarmed and need you to talk to me asap and tell me what you plan is?Is your work phone working now or you are incontestable still? Hope all is going well and I look forward to hearing back.
Your wife,
R.

* * *

Actually, L. and the girls were visiting during his time, but R. and I were having too many issues for me to try and incorporate that into the conversation. The out-of-reach thing worked for one whole week. The girls' visit went well, and "sex with the ex" (with an estranged, second wife) is the best. The rest of the week went to hell, as usual. But I saw the little ones, and teeth were fixed, using the benefits; and that's what's important.

* * *

S. (R.'S COUSIN): Hi Ron. Yes, I agree it's a confusing time for both of you and this is the time that you should put your heads down and work together! The reason you both are arguing is cause this is a stressful time and you both need to stay calm. Have you ever asked R. what her concerns are? Why do you keep pulling out of the 28th December? R. had sent me your emails and I was able to see both sides of the issues …

Pulling out of a wedding date is not a very respectable and decent thing to do Ron, not in our culture. I was under the impression that you and R. had agreed to this wedding and that is why R. asked my family to come to Australia to be in the wedding party. We have booked our tickets, other people have done so, and this is not very nice … so I really ask that you do the right thing and email or talk to R. … I will NOT tell her all this as this is NOT my job. I am here to help and support both people.

Why will you think of cancelling a wedding rather talk and work things out together peacefully … this is a very new marriage, and R. has committed to a lot Ron, leaving everything behind. Stop and think Ron … ask your friends and mother if this is right???

I was quite upset to read that you are unsure if to go ahead with this or not!

Ron, I am quite surprised that you should make a statement like that as no matter what you both are married, you cant take that away. I would have thought that you would want to give it your 100% before you say such a drastic thing. This is only going to add to R.'s doubts and worries. Even if R. has decided at the moment that she should put the sale of the house on hold. Why should this change any of our plans?

Surely you can rent a bigger place and make R. happy until she gets on her feet or is that too much to ask for? Please don't misunderstand me but it almost feels that you were totally depending on R. to finance the move to a bigger apt. Can you see why she feels so anxious as you have not clearly explained or discussed what plans you have for her. […]—S.

ME: S., thank you for your words. It is a confusing time right now. We are in a cycle of arguments, and cannot communicate effectively. This will certainly continue on. I don't know whether to proceed or not. R. has changed her plans so many times. This is why the move to Canada is now a stressor. Originally she was selling, meaning saving in CAD. Now, she is renting (meaning, potentially one salary in Canada). This was never plan A. Plan B (R.'s insecurity which has damaged the marriage). She is renting because she began to think that I was hoodwinking her or that I had no plans to add her in CAD. She has stated this in different ways in several conversations; even our last conversation on Friday. I have only defended myself against these absurd allegations (many of which are in writing per emails). This was never supposed to be an issue in our marriage; but, because of it, I have seen a side or R. that concerns me; and again, in defending myself, I have been labeled insecure and an abuser? Furthermore, after all of the arguing, neither of us was certain that she should sell or do anything. Now she's pressing me about the CAD thing; which is out of my control (a fact she knew before coming to the USA). Now the issue is my salary? That was never the plan.

Now, I'm not even sure if we will make it.—R.

S: Hi Ron,

Thank you for all your emails and I am saddened to hear that both of you feel so stressed and unhappy at the moment. Being away from each other and the only method of communication being skype doesn't help the situation either.

I have spoken in length with R. after reading the contents of all your emails. Whilst R. must be coming across to you as being impatient or demanding she has explained to me the real reasons as to why the conversations get so heated and escalates to another spat!

Ron, you must understand that R. has suddenly had to make some life changing decisions in a very short period of time. You both got married in Aug; and since her return back to Melb she has had to deal with lots of emotions and major decisions; and moving from Oz to CAD after nearly 25 yrs would be a daunting task for anyone (if you know what I mean) R. also feels that both of you are not able to have a conversation without feeling like you both a head butting …

So I told R. back off and do what she is doing until Ron is ready for CAD. I guess some of her fears and anxieties are validated as anyone in her situation would be stressing out. I feel these are the issues that's causing her the greatest fears and worries and I have listed them for you so you can get a better understanding and appreciate the stress she is under. R. also feels like she is carrying all the financials and without a job how she will manage in CAD …

The fear of the unknown is her greatest worry and if you can give her some reassurances I feel that she may be able to make up her mind and move forward with her plans. I feel that both of you should be calm and understand where each other is coming from and work towards a common goal post. Remember now you both are married no matter what and you should always remember that you are two players on the same team. You both should not be fighting each other, instead work together with love being the common denominator and care for each other. Speak to each other with respect and at all times try not to say anything hurtful to each other which may cause you both so much pain, when both of you are so far apart. R. is very sad and not herself I noticed the other day …

Right now, being away from each other doesn't help at all and for that matter the time zones that you both live in is not helpful either. All I can say is you both have something beautiful to look forward to in December and a lifetime of happiness together to look forward to so all I can say is don't let these initial stresses keep you away from each other and your happiness. Everyone goes through issues in any marriage and we need to be able to communicate and resolve these issues before it blows out and gets to boiling point. Let me reassure you that R. is 100% committed to this marriage and the relationship that you both have entered in to and she has told me that she is looking forward to starting life with you as a married couple.

Ron, please let me know if there is anything else I can help you both with as I am here for both of you, remember that!! Please keep writing to me as I want to make sure that both of you keep the communication lines open … This is all confidential and between you and me ok. Take care & speak soon.

Regards,

S.

* * *

R: Hope your Thanksgiving weekend was good catching up with friends … You were going to email me with a time to chat over your long weekend … you must have got to busy … That's cool. It's my work week and the time difference is very challenging to keep up till 11 pm just to hope I can chat over Skype, which is about 8.00 am for you. That is if we chat at 8.00 am … so hope you understand my predicament? Enjoying the Melbourne weather and day light saving—extra day time now! I am just heading to BT, so chat when we connect!! Take care and I miss you Ron.

Send me a kiss xx

R: Hey darling … I am so relieved, happy and so overwhelmed after reading your rich and loving email … I really needed that for my own confidence with this … babe … thanks for the beautiful words … and the reassurance. I sooo needed to hear this from you my handsome husband …

I needed to know that WE are on the same page … So thank you honey.

I am over the moon you feel the same way Ron … You mean the world to me and I don't want to lose what I waited for so long … the thoughts and desires I had after meeting you for the first time in 1998. Your email was so meaningful and promising just when I have been feeling suppressed with many fears, worries and emotional confusion due to my own believes and vulnerabilities. Thanks for trying to gain a perspective through my "women world," as I know it is not easy … I am insecure and anxious about many things … I am afraid and unconfident about many things … Only time will help this for me, so this is my own issues as a person, 47 year old woman … Entering in to a new marriage and moving to live in a new country, giving up my home … etc. I also know that we can be in bliss like you say and have a wonderful and interesting life together. This is what I want … if we can understand and support each other when possible like you say; it will work and add so much value to the investment and partnership I think?

I will make a conscious effort to understand your "man ways & style," so I won't react to you and feel you are nasty to me or feel you are growling at me LOL. Your old soul, our romantic night, your soft side … the "real Ron Westray," the crazy jazz trombonist, the handsome man … This is the man I remember and recall from that night in Sydney, and keep going back to the first page of the love novel … This is the man I fell in love with and always had you in my heart …

This is what we did on 20 August 2013; We rekindled our love back and this is what is called, human empowerment (HE) back LOL Babe I love you a whole lot more … For many reasons …

Help me to underrated your heart and soul Ron! Until we chat again … Good Morning babe … YOUR WIFE R. MISSES YOU SO SO MUCH!!

ME: Hi, babe. This is all designed to keep us from our bliss. Let's just keep moving towards our goals, R.

I will also take this opportunity to say that I have been unable to view things through your lens until right now. Within that, I will admit that I have been insensitive; I apologize, R., my wife. Let's just be more supportive and less demanding of each other. Remember, when you awake, I'm dragging in from work; and when you're getting morning coffee, I'm getting sleepy. It's not the best time to discuss sensitive topics …

All dates are set, and I am monitoring the spouse addition issue in CAD. Right now, it's tough. When we are together, we will become one.—Your husband, Ron.

R: Darling Ron, Thanks for coming on the network and talking to me. I feel the past two weeks of communications and emails have caused a lot of stress, hurt, uncertainty and upset for both of us.

I understand your upset and concerns about my emails, as I have been very forceful and upfront in communicating my message. I was also responding to what I was receiving, the uninterested attitude and the content … I can only apologise for my actions.

I have never been in a long distance marriage and relationship like this and never expected to face my own challenges … To add to a new marriage I have had to deal with Visa issues, X spouses, learning to be the "Westray wife," you expect me to be …, learning over a network how to read my husband and deal with issues etc. …

I am sorry I have not been able to make you happy babe, and kept failing … If you feel you want to end things as you have lost interest, just tell me … It is OK!

Nothing I can say or do at this point can change the reality of our emails, reactions to each other and the confusion and pain it has left in our hearts … I am happy and pleased that you are still committed to our marriage and want to proceed with our plans and relocation. I feel the same and that is all we can do, however, if you feel otherwise make sure you feel you can talk to me … Let us not allow things to escalate to such levels … Babe … I feel the same energy you feel, I feel the same things about the emails and our current issues and worry … my doubts, concerns and fears could be all genuine or based on my own inner insecurities… and you will have the same concerns …??? How can this rule and influence our real love for each other? All we can do is be honest to each other and true.

I miss you even though you would rather I not hear this … I miss our face to face interactions, touch and eye contact. Since you have told me to not worry about Visas, I will now be trusting on you to lead the way. Until such time I will do my daily routines. I love you Ron,

Your wife,

R.

ME: Hello, R.—With all the confusion, I wasn't sure. I am still committed. Ron

R: Hey Ron my husband, I am not sure what you are talking about???? "You are just angry because YOUR ceremony got cancelled?" Hey who cancelled the ceremony?

I didn't, I am committed to what I signed on 20th August 2013 in the USA, the wedding on 28th December that you agreed to, and all the plans you and I committed to? If I remember you signed off on the band, cards, and the whole wedding as this was the "official wedding ceremony" and not the little room I was taken in to for 8 minutes to sign a wedding certificate? This was not the agreement babe …

If you have changed plans and not able to hold the legal commitments, then I suggest you talk to your wife soon, as this matter will end up escalating. My family also wishes to talk to you Ron, and appreciate some type of phone number, as any of the phone numbers given to me by you are not answered and never been answered. So as your wife I am not able to call you period! Please contact me asap and let me know, if you fell like a chat on the network we can do this too.

I will be heading out soon, it is 11:20 am on Sunday, so respond back please.

Thanks, your wife, R.

ME: You are just angry because YOUR ceremony got cancelled, not because I did anything to you. You know it wasn't working. You said, verbally on record, "it's not working … and maybe we should rethink what we are doing …"

You said that in our last conversation, R. So, how am I such the manipulator? You are just trying to punish me because you sent invitations out, and now you feel embarrassed. I am embarrassed, too! But that embarrassment will pass. A lifetime of unhappiness and discontent is far more serious than an invite or a hotel reservation. BTW, I don't know of many hotels that will not give refunds within 24–48 hours notice, much less 3 months!—Ron

ME: I will be happy to know of the options, but I am prepared for either route. I am guilty of nothing. We were not happy and I said there is no need to have a ceremony. That's all. This mess you are stirring up is all yours. This is not about any of that. It's about the fact that we should both be happy.

You are just digging a ditch for yourself by referring to me as malicious.

This has nothing to do with that. I simply refuse to be in another argumentative relationship.

And this is far worse, due to your aggressive personality, sharp tongue and recent stresses. So, if this is my punishment for deciding that this was not a good idea, you go right ahead. We will see where the maliciousness is really coming from when others judge the situation.

My office phone has been in disrepair since the school year began; I have no one to hide from, sweetie.—W

R: Hey, no, my parents have not called you. I called you and left a message on York answer phone. Interesting that no one can call you, ha ha ... great method to bypass ha.

Ok when you're feeling calm and cantered we may be able to discuss the options best for both ... but this will not go on Ron ... I'd rather be dead!!

I am off to bed. Thanks, R.

ME: I have nothing to hide from you or your family or any other agency. I proceeded with my knowledge of the laws, and will discuss any discrepancies. There is no malice from my side. The malice stems from your side, with the threats, which are documented per all your emails and now trying to frame me based on my good intentions. WOW.

Have your parents contact me on my home phone. Office phone is off for repairs ... Ron

R: Hello Ron,

A message has been left at York on your voice mail phone. Please contact me asap as I wish to discuss my intentions to move forward and give you some time to consider the options. Due to the serious nature of the matter which has taken place, the manner, the malicious nature it is not promising. I have spoken to my family and inform them of what is happening and they have not taken it lightly either. Not wanting to face my family will not help Ron ... This is a pretty serious matter even though it is nothing for Americans and a man like you! When free on the network, over the weekend, you can let me know.

Thanks, R.

ME: For the record, I would like to say that I was very proud to make you my wife, and I thought that we were, indeed, a lot alike. Somewhere along the way, we got tangled up in a web of common accusations and insults which caused us to lose the very thing we both wanted: Respect.—Ron

R: Ron we are married and you know what you were doing to me!—R.

ME: This is the most absurd statement I have read all year.—Ron

ME: L. has been removed, but I have not requested that you be added, because of the current conditions. Furthermore, I have not been confirmed as a resident yet, and I was not a resident of CA when we married. I told you, before you came to the USA that I would first have the X spouse removed THEN have you added. I told you that I did not request both together, initially, to avoid confusion. We never made it around to the second request to add you. That's what's happening. I would never be so silly as to try to hide such obvious facts from the CA gov.

I haven't done anything to you, R. I am just as disappointed and embarrassed as you. Stop the blame game. It will not be respected in a legal situation. We were equally invested in our decisions … Well, your commission needs to be ready for my side of the story. Have them contact me. Use my home address and email. It will arrive faster that way. I can't understand why you think they will only respect your side of the story. Furthermore, we have been married for 7 weeks, but we have been apart for 4 of those seven weeks, so no court is going to view this as an abusive marriage. That's absurd …

We barely know each other. That's my defense. It's not really 16 years, in analysis. It's 1 night in Sydney, 1 night in NYC, 8 days in Toronto and 3 weeks in USA. That's a total of 25 days together over 16 years … Unfortunately, I have to defend myself with this reduction, since you are labeling me an abuser … I have no prior allegations such as this, in a marriage of length and cohabitation. By the way, I was the plantiff in my last divorce. NO abuse then, no abuse now. You use curse words just as well as I do … It's called 50/50%, not 100/100%.

R: Ron, please send me a copy of your declaration to the Canadian High Commission with the notice to change your X Common Law Wife L. Westray and add your NEW wife R. Westray. Please send a copy of the completed notice and this end is asking me.

It is too late to Ron … "I would prefer to bow out in a peaceful way," Ron we are married and you know what you were doing to me!

Send me the papers as the Canadian High Comm in Australia is helping us and our application needs this documents asap. I am waiting or shall I email all your work details and they can email you. I have NO anger towards you Ron Westray, just spoke the truth and how you have treated the marriage and your new wife in 7 weeks, as this is not a test drive … you are 100% going to take responsibility and I am going to take 100% responsibility!

Ok wait to hear back—R.

ME: I was trying to hold on, but your threats, and assaults against my character and good intentions, can only be compared to the dismay you must feel with regards to your anger and disrespect towards me. There is no way I could ever be happy in this union again.

You probably feel the same. I would prefer to bow out in a peaceful way, but if you feel that I must learn some lesson about myself, then you go ahead and teach me. Meanwhile, and in the aftermath of whatever you can dish out, I will remain focused on who I think I am and what I must do to survive life and people. —Ron

ME: YOU KNOW THAT I AM NOT "ON THE RUN" FROM ANYTHING. WHEN IT'S TIME TO DEFEND MY POSITION, I WILL DO SO IN THE SAME LOGICAL MANNER I WOULD DEFEND ANY BELIEF. I HAVE NOTHING TO HIDE, FROM ANYONE. MY CONCERNS ARE LEGAL AND PERSONAL, NOT MEDIA HYPE OR LIVE TV, AS YOU CALL IT. I CAN'T EVEN BELIEVE THAT'S YOU SAYING THAT, R. SOUNDS LIKE A HOOCHY-MOMMA LINE: In my opinion, you have had a meltdown that has severely damaged our relationship. What do you need from me?

I feel your proposed agreement is lopsided; I can not agree to those terms at this time. To answer you previous question, at present, I have one loving wife, and the relationship is going smashing

R: No demands Ron, simply logical the way you are treating me … I desired a little better … don't you think …????? After my painful history with you for 16 yrs …

ME: You let me know. You are the one with the demands. All of your email threats are only assisting me; as, I have nothing to hide. If you must, L. is prepared for your venom. I have the same emails you have, R. I can't see where I've told you anything misleading in the emails, starting Aug 1 thru today.—Ron

R: Let me know fast … as all guest who have paid for the 28th flights/hotels will be reimbursed by Prf Ron Westray. I have all the emails you agreed and signed off the wedding party in MEL. This is not going to be ignored and think you will forget this … If you have any style, work with this to the end or face all the moralities and the damage caused!

Do not let this get dirty pleaseeeee as I know you DON'T CARE ABOUT ANY ONE … it is in YOUR BEST INTEREST AFTER WHAT YOU HAVE DONE! Really darling … Do you think you have treated me respectfully, caringly … No. Is the how the Westray men treat their women? You have nothing for me or anyone!

I WILL BRING YOU ON LIVE TV ON USA AND CAN … SO YOU NEVER DO THIS AGAIN TO ONE MORE LADY RON … YOU ARE SHOCKING!!! LET US SEE THIS RON … now!!! You are caught out!!! I will be sending all copies off all emails so this will protect her and the 3 kids. HOW MANY WIFES DO YOU HAVE????

NO I WILL NOT PAY FOR ANY HONEYMOON, RON! YOU PLANNED ALL THIS KNOWING WHAT YOU WERE GOING TO DO TO ME??? NO … NOTHING! ALL COST WILL GO TO YOU.

HOLD THIS … THERE IS MORE! R.

R: Ron, Please confirm the Canadian notice that you had advise to remove your X "Common Law Wife," Ron this is not a joke anymore. You not cooperating will ONLY make this large than ever!!! You married me in NY, how long were you going to hide the marriage?

Please send your email conformation asap as requested 3 times now, and still avoiding. All out of pocket cost and your process to this marriage will be examined. I am for the last time asking you confirm your paperwork. If you make this more difficult than you have for me … this is no threat, a honest word! I am going public, to both families, US and CA authorities, friends, all social media … You X, your friends, your work … so the true story will revel and this is deadly to do this to women after women. Do you think paying me pack a few hundred $$$ will I let you get away with such nasty, dirty plan. WHERE IS YOUR PROOF!

Let me see the Westray true character … RON NOT THS TIME

You have disgraced yourself, my family, the Westrays and all your jazz friends.

ALL THE LIES AND THIS FAKE MARRAGE WILL BE OUT! ONCE YOU GET BACK, I WILL TELL YOU WHAT I WILL DO!

R.

ME: Since things are getting petty, here are my meager expenses, to the tune of 3K, bet 8/5 and 8/22. I understand that you spent double, but we had already discussed that openly …

WOW … If you spent 6 and I spent 3 (approx), then there's 3 left to divide from the money-moon expenses. That's $1500 … I get it.

I do not owe you any information from the CA Gov; I have no need to alter facts. I haven't responded because I find your accusations preposterous. I don't not owe you any information from the CA Gov; I have no need to alter facts. Your recent words, threats and actions reinforce the fact that I/WE made a bad decision. Though I did look forward to meeting your family, there is no need for interaction with your family in Canada, at this point, R. I will have representation when it is time.

I certainly did intend to attend our ceremony. In addition to not needing to lie, I certainly would never have asked my Uncle if I weren't.

My intentions were the same positive intentions that inspired you to be a part of those plans; and everyone knows you are no fool; so save anymore sarcasm and insults. I don't have time to play games and hustle women or people for chump change. The fact that you have accused me of such will never be forgotten.

Finally, I haven't responded, to most because I'm done defending; not because of teenage angst. —Thanks, Ron

R: Hey, all the wedding photos are going up on Facebook, and I am connected with your X, so you better break the news to her. If not she will not be happy and it is a little respect …

>>I do have the confirmation from the Canadian Gov regarding the removal of my spouse. The removal is complete.

Good, send me a copy of this if so Ron? I have asked you twice now!

>>What you have described were, and are, not my intentions.

So then what are your intentions???

Please reply to this email below and do not avoid the content, so we can make the next decisions and you will know them too. Be a real man Ron … Respond back to the real substance in the email without running away like a teenager LOL

This is worse than CCH, the worst that could happen to a new bride … this pattern has been consistent since I met you in 1998 … sad.

ME: Stop comparing to CCH, and look deep within for once in your life! The next step would have been to add you to the CA profile. It seems we did not make it.—Ron

ME: Okay, R. Sounds like you have everything written up to suit your purposes (sounds like the CHC report) This time you are wrong, however. What you have described were, and are, not my intentions. I do have the confirmation from the Canadian Gov regarding the removal of my spouse. The removal is complete.—Disappointed, Ron

R: Dear Pro Ron Westray,

You came back in to my life, lied to me, and then proposed to me. You put a ring on my finger. Then you made me pay for both flights to New York, honeymoon accommodation, car hire, majority of food and I went along with you believing you had taken marriage seriously and I was not getting used up! I proof on my Visa statements so I am not lying.

I also thought at 43 years old with a rough, turbulent and distrustful relationship with your X wife, 3 kids, that you will have learnt how to treat a lady by now and value marriage as you got a second chance … this is not the case? It is disturbing, worrying and very sad the manner you have treated me in the past 4 weeks … like a piece of shit!!!

You suggested we marry in New York and we did this in NY as it suited your purposes … I trusted you 100%. You were well aware of what you were doing to me, the laws, your X, common law papers, child support, and the intention to marry me and bring me to CAN. You had your X wife on your Canada PR immigration papers as a "Common Law wife," even when marrying a new wife in New York. You lied to the authorities and the State of NY as you had a common law wife in Canada to suit your budget and child support needs … Hey you got something coming … if you feel I am going to go through this again with you …

WHY HAVE YOU KEPT THE MARRAGE A SECRET TO DATE RON WESTRAY??? Not informing L. and the three children TO DATE? I was asked NOT to post any wedding photos on Facebook as you did not want your X to see anything yet?? When were you going to tell L?? Not informing the Canadian Authorities for Visa purpose THAT YOU ARE MARRIED TO R? WHY have you not logged the Spouse Visa??? WHAT WAS YOUR GAME RON THIS TIME WITH A SECOND WIFE? No one from your family is willing to attend your wedding … I am speechless and so sad for you babe … I mean that! You have No interest in me, the marriage, my family, have no care or respect, for that fact ANYONE, BUT YOUR SELF… SEND ME A COPY OF PROOF THAT YOU HAVE INFORMED THE CAN HIGH COMMISSION AS YOU HAVE TOLD ME? I NEED PROOF THAT YOU HAVE REMOVED YOUR EX.

Ignoring and playing the silent game will not work Ron. I am in disbelief you can do this and think you will get away Ron. You had no intentions to attend a wedding.

You will be liable for half the costs for any financial loss, and I am not threatening you, just simply informing you.—Thank you, regards, R.

ME: Hi, babe … Just got really busy; early starts, late finishes. How was the first day @ work?

R: Ron when do you hope to contact your new wife????? as the silence will only create some unwanted and problems for you, so I would think it would be better you get in touch with me asap please.

R: Morning Darling, I was exhausted last night on SKP as I had done a 2 KM swim in the day, house work, church and later at dinner till late, it was 2.30 am in the morning in Melbourne … I had to get off the line … By the time I had a bath and went to bed, it was close to 3.30am … very tired today … I just wanted to clear what I was saying about gifts as it is a Sri Lanka culture to give gifts to loved one and family … and I thought you would take that as "one of the gestures," in our connection … however, thanks for explaining that, you don't view "receiving gifts as a connection in the mind or a good relationship," rather a "GIFT."

Thanks for sharing how you feel about gifts, as I am only new at this and still learning.

In reference to what I said, "I have not received a gift yet from you," what I am saying is; "I don't have a point of reference to this subject as exchanging gifts," and it is not right or wrong, simply factual. There is NO judgment or expectation, as I married you for a higher purpose babe … (not for a gift) OK darling xxx

I have no doubt when I am with you in CAN, you will pamper me the way I love, massages, flowers, pick nicks, facials, nice underwear and dinners … I need to be connected with you in the MIND with your music and understand Ron Westray …? I thought I got that "well," as I am cooperative to support and work for your Jazz life … Hey I am your biggest fan and if you remember I have offered to all of the below:

- Pay and help with the new website
- Marketing for new business gigs in Toronto
- Plan Sri Lanka tours and hotels for Jazz shows 2015
- Travel with you and look after all the admin
- Talk about you to all my family and friends and your talents

I am sorry you don't feel I am connected to your MIND as yet. Babe it will really help if may write what that looks like for you, so, I can meet your needs as a wife, and not keep failing. So, let me know, so it is all clear love. I hope you can help me as I am on your side and support your life and soul in Jazz. I do know and aware that your music and work comes first, and I am OK with this babe … I have my hearing at FWA very early tomorrow, and have to get up early … So I will have 8 hours of sleep today, as I have been running on 5–6 hours lately … and I am dead beat!

Have a great day and send me some luck for the hearing … Hope to hear back from you honey.—Miss you, your wifey, Mrs R. Westray xxx

R: "In my culture giving gifts is looked upon as an act of love and neutering …"

ME: This will be hard to accept … lol

NEUTERING: definition

castrate or spay (a domestic animal): (as adj. neutered): a *neutered tomcat.*

render ineffective; deprive of vigor or force: disarmament negotiations that will neuter their military power.

ME: Nurturing?—Why, yes!

Ron

ME: Hey, babe … Thank you, sweetie. I have an alternate bible with me here. Will check that out … Just awaking, will get on the network in a bit …—Ron

R: Darling my face and heart lit up seen you on the network last night … you are so beautiful to me, handsome and my life partner … Baby, I wanted to share my morning reading with you on this page. Please read the full page …

Ron did you bring your bible from your bedroom in South C?

I am reading Deuteronomy 8, if you have your bible, we can be reading the same holy book at the same time, it is VERY POWERFUL FOR OUR MARRIED LIFE AND THE BOND OF MARRAGE (babe you will see the grace & love, blessings, gods guidance against all odds, and a permanent happiness within) If you have your bible … if not I would love to get you the Joyce Meyer every day bible with life points after each chapter … let me know babe what you think???

Hope you had a nice meeting and dinner with your friends,

Your loving wife,

R. xxxx

R: Darling babe, Good morning … I was reading this prayer today and wanted to share it with you. I am your soul mate, your twin, and friend. I feel your sadness and inner pain, as I feel the same way inside Babe open your heart and mind to your wife … let me open my heart and mind to you … we will never stop bonding … We are only human darling, in each other's lives now to learn and evolve together … Please forgive my imperfections and help me when I am week and fail you babe …

Your wife loves and misses you … Let me know when you are up babe—R.

ME: Thanks for this, R. and thanks for your words. I, too, apologize for failing you at this point. Our LOOK is amazing—but the minds? At this point, we have to be happy.

Makeups are always sweet; but I will not survive this cycle of war, then peace.

I have to head in rel. early, so I won't Skype; can't get too wound up before work. The whole thing has already negatively affected my "vibration."

In relationship to the Perm Res. thing, my advice would be to not make any move (house, moving company, etc.) until I hear from Canada. This would/could involve not selling, etc. until the New Year (i.e. whenever you are a PR); and assuming WE make it, of course.

Love,

Ron

R: Hey babe … I am so lonely without you darling and miss you deeply … I feel such a failure and loser … with no words to describe the pain I feel babe … I am so sorry I have failed you.

When I repeated my wedding vows on 20 August 2013, I said "I will," and I hoped it was till the last day … of each other's life's …? I hope the bond and promise of our deep love for one another will sustain, conform and hold us close even in times of despair and sadness …

Your lonely wife …

God Bless, R. xx

R: Babe … hey I wrote to you with no remorse, an open dialog willing to talk and share and responding to your email. I was trying to explain to you as we are million miles away … not for you to take it as "another fight," or you reading it wrong. Baby give me a break please …

All the things I told you in the email, that I would only marry you, that I have always loved you is NO VALUE TO YOU … as you think otherwise …

I didn't compare you to anyone … I was simply sharing about the past story and what happen … I cannot write anything you misread it … OMG …

When I say I love you, you rip me to pieces … The email was not meant to be to get you more angry … I really thought you will respond back simply by sharing and chatting … but it seems to have got worse …

I really don't seem to be able to do anything right here Ron … I am sorry that we have not been able to even dialog on email … I am sorry you have added your own meaning and interpretations …

Then you say … I say you are not worthy of love, OMG why are you misunderstanding me … and hitting me back … everything is an opinion … yours or mine …

Babe PLEASE COOL DOWN … Don't blow it out of context … when I tell you how I feel, you take it as I am putting you down … I opened up to you now … I am on your side and you seem to be on another side … So feel betrayed … thanks babe … I thought you were close to me too … I get it we are on opposite sides …

Can we not even have a email chat if we cannot chat on SKP? Babe what's going on … I wrote my email with no attack, no anger, and you are again so mad with your replies …

After the card title mistake, I corrected my mistake, emailed V. and apologised, re sent the cards written correctly to both, sent Mrs Westray a little hand written note … with a little apology.

I am so numb I have no words to say … very sad! It's not a good day for me …

I am way too frightened to say any more … I hope you can take some deep breaths and keep things in perspective babe …

Yours,

R.

ME: There is no way I can recover from this dialogue.

Ron

Later, I realized that deception was involved. It's not just me.

★ ★ ★

R. is argumentative. I am defensive.

Open Letter to S. (R.'s cousin)

There was sexual tension left over from a spat in 2010, so I reached out to R. and a sort of spark reignited, but also contained a slight demand, in that, "I'm not coming all the way to the US [this time] just to see you and come back."

I knew what she meant. This time, the issue was marriage. Marriage was the last thing I was thinking about. However, in reuniting with R., I began to believe that this was, indeed, the time to break the cycle with my X wife and began anew with R.

The second marriage, for both of us. I had had two unsuccessful attempts with my ex wife (and mother of my three daughters) after the divorce, culminating about six months ahead of this next major decision (so, basically from one negative situation to the next).

In thinking about R.'s inference, I decided that this was the time for me to marry, again. The cultural integration with R. was very appealing and influenced my decision greatly. I thought that maybe I would or could do better with a woman outside of my culture, this time. In addition, I have a genuine attraction to R.

R. travelled to the USA on Sept 15th, 2013, and I followed through with my promise to R. and we wed on August 20, 2013 in Buffalo, NY.

Even within a compromising effort, the latter phases of this quickly-decided upon, long-distance marriage have taken their toll on each of our tolerance and endurance. At last remains independent mindsets of two one-time divorcees in their mid to late-forties.

Things went downhill when, after the honeymoon, R. returned to Melbourne to settle matters in preparation to move to Toronto, to be with me, within the same year. The main matter was to have her registered as a spouse on my residency app., within this time.

I gave R. full disclosure of how I would proceed; which is about the time healthy communication broke down. I had been informed that my (applicant, not actual) spouse had [finally] been removed, per my request, and that I was the sole applicant for residency in CAD.

I am presently on work permit awaiting residency approval. The next step was to add R. as my spouse, when the paper settled, and in prep for her migration to Canada from Australia.

We talked about these matters before R. even travelled to the USA for us to wed., which was what we had agreed upon.

Each time we would argue, R. would mention that we should decide what we are doing; because her relatives had booked hotels and flights to our post-matrimony-ceremony in Melbourne, and that she was selling her house, etc. and everything …

I pleaded with R., for us to not try to "figure things out on Skype" each time we talked. But, each conversation, R. persisted, trying to micro analyze and predict my every intention, when my only intention was to follow through, as I had by marrying her.

If I were not going to follow through on ceremony, it's very unlikely I would have followed through on the marriage. The ceremony was in retro-respect of the solemnized marriage. This is not a case of groom doesn't show up.

I was ALL FOR IT, and excited about traveling to Melbourne to celebrate our marriage, primarily with R.'s family and friends, and my Uncle as a best man.

Well, sparing all details, R. and I had our 5th or 6th, and final spat: In the final conversation, I simply said that there was no need for me to attend the ceremony (three months away) if we can't get along, and that we are already married anyway; and that we needed to figure out what we are doing from the marriage standpoint; and that the ceremony was just an aesthetic, but that our happiness as people was really important right now.

That's when she went all "Medusa" on me; because invitations were sent out and her reputation was at stake (age 47, second marriage)

The next things to surface (in her anger of my rejection of the ceremony) were all conspiracy theories about why I tricked her to marry me for some unexplained gain that I have yet to figure out.

This is just as big an embarrassment to me and my family, but that's not the issue. The issue is R. and Ron.

So, I am being punished through Slander and Libel, all to say it wasn't R.'s fault this time?

When in fact it's nobodies fault; we have to be happy, and I refused to attend a post-matrimony-ceremony if we can't even get along (on Skype) …

The fact is, we are still married, at present; and I do not have any other registered spouses or wives anywhere in the world.

★ ★ ★

R: Dearest family, cousins and friends,

I hope all is well with you. I am happy and blessed to announce that my long time soul mate, Ron Westray, Jr., and I have married! We are now Mr. and Mrs. Ronald Kenneth Westray, Jr. We were wed on Tuesday, August 20, 2013, at Four PM EST, in Buffalo, New York.

We are both very happy to finally be married after 16 years of being in love on separate continents! As you might imagine, our joy is indescribable at this time.

Please enjoy our pictures from the past few days, including the (Magistrate) ceremony in New York State, USA.

R: Honey I will have to have a wedding in Melbourne as my family will not hear of it otherwise.

So, December 2013 if you come we can have the wedding, I will do all the stuff, so you don't need to stress OK? Is this Ok babe? as my culture is such I have to tell my family and relatives …

Don't worry I will tell all the guests—no gifts, cash ONLY, so the some of the wedding cost will be paid by the guest … Ha ha (ROI) return on investment!

Love you,

R.

ME: Hey, babe … Remember to pack you birth certificate and bring your divorce declaration, in case it comes up. We are both going to register as NOT previously married, but in case the legalities are rigid, we will be covered. For the hotel, we just need a full sized tub, not a jacuzzi, right. There are a lot of nice, simple hotels at a nice price. Or do we want more of a "Suite" feel? with garden tub or jacuzzi; it's three nights there … Let me know.—Ron

R: we just need a full sized tub, nice clean room in a nice place … will be fine babe. I didn't like the hotel we stayed in 2010, it was not a nice hotel … This is our special time together, getting married … and space to finally celebrate … so do what your heart feels right Ron

Let's do what we can only afford at this point in time … honey. I loveY …

R: Hi darling,

I miss you toooo very much! And I am in love with you too sweetheart … I have had a long day … 6 hrs sleep again helping Shen pack, and dropped her off at airport. I am very tired from all the late sleeps pass 2.30 am all week …

I have booked the Clarion hotel for the 21 December 2013, 4.30pm for our wedding babe, and U. will email me details.

The rest, I have people to do it for me at a reduced off retail rates, like flowers, cake, photos etc I am so excited Ron and can't wait to be with you … it will be a great wedding on an international level LOL. With my dream come true man …

On another note: I think it is always good to have an open, non-judgemental, supportive, communication policy for couples.

So this way we can share, talk and express what is going on at any given time. I want you to feel that you can tell me anything any time, so we don't hide anything from each other.

So … I was not going to tell you anything about my work issues as I did not want our happy energy to be ruined. However, since I am leaving to see you soon and lots have happen today, I

thought I will tell you now. I will no longer be working for CCH and they have terminated me. I was offered $40K to resign and I asked for more due to the matters involved, and the offer was withdrawn … 3 weeks ago.

I miss you, Yours R.

ME: Hey, Sweeety. Wow … that's a lot of work drama … love. But I know you will come out on top. I'm up if you want to Skype. Babe I am so in love with you. It is truly a bliss and joy to have you in my life forever!!! You are a gift from God to me … I know this 100%.

I am blessed to have you. Send me your ring size when you can.

R: Hey darling can I give you the ring size on Monday. I have to do letters of consent so S. can act on my behalf in Sri Lanka. I will step out tomorrow and go to a shop, then email you.

Thanks babe,

Missing you xxxxx—R.

ME: Darling, send me your ring size when you can.— Ron

ME: Darling thanks for that, now go back to sleep, I will talk you once you are up baby xxx I know it's been a long time. Just thinking about you and wanted to say hello. Hope to hear from you and that you are happy and well.

Are you still angry with me? I apologize for what happened. It was a stressful time for me, and … I really enjoyed what we had, though.—Ron

R: You're a great musician, jazz artist and professor; and your acting skills need to be endorsed by Warner bros … LOL I am not sure how you can miss me???? Ha. BECAUSE I didn't get a chance to enjoy you and … I can miss you because I am a forgiving person. I think you are too—R.

ME: Give me another chance, R.—Ron

R: Ron how can we pick up and more on, we live miles apart and I am not having an email relationship with anyone … If you want to come to Melbourne, then we can talk. You have taken me by surprise, from left field … Why did you suddenly contact me now Ron?

ME: Sweetheart, I truly miss you, and I feel like we must continue what we started. Can you come to the States? I will fly you.

I go back to Toronto around the first week of Sept. (That would be plan B.) I know you already came to me once, but I have so much going on in North America, babe—just my same responsibilities (Daughters, Alpha Male stuff in South Carolina—Mom, Sis, Niece, Nephew, Grandma—and the gig in Canada); nothing new. But, I mean I can't come to Melbourne, right away, sweetheart.—Ron

R: Ok let talk about it tomorrow as I am not sure how I can help you … I don't think I will come back to Toronto as I have bad feelings about that place … Maybe US??

ME: Sweety, don't feel that way. We can undo those feelings by having a better experience in Toronto. But US is just as well if you can get here before I head back to Canada.

HELP ME … O:-)

Ron

R: Hi babe, I am back, just dropped off my cousin at a wedding party. It is raining like crazy here and cold side …

Ron honey I am so excited, happy and feel amazing about wanting to see you again … I feel so connected to you and with you, my twin, soul friend, sexy hot stuff man … Thanks for paying for me to come and see you babe, it is so gracious and gods gifts for me—ha ha (for being a good girl). I am totally over the moon to have a chance at our long loved love for each other, and exploring deeper … what is true … and all that magic …

I am home for the night, come on SKP, so I can see your beautiful face again!

Love,

R. xx

R: Hey Good Morning babe … hope you had a good sleep, I am operating on 5 hours sleep.

Hey after you return back to York, when is your next break from work? What month?

I have lots going on and just mapping my current stuff in Melbourne … that why I ask I don't wanna see you in Aug … and then not see you for half an year babe. I am trying to keep things real, in perspective and what we both want in this time in our lives! I really think we can make it happen as we are both very powerful individual with many different aspects to our physic.

You look so good Ron, can't wait to get all over ya and indulge in you babe. I'm always yours—R. xxxxxx

ME: Baby, I want you to know that you are my "dream come true." There may be times when I am not as poetic as other times, or distracted by responsibilities, but always know that you are my dream come true in every way.—Ron

⋆ ⋆ ⋆

Afterthoughts on the Westray Cycle

R.W.'s triad combinations (extensions welcome) sustain a rich, dense harmonic space where reflexive categories of "right" and "wrong" notes must yield to artistic feeling for better and worse notes.

My experiments with his system necessarily involved me in fairly exacting and perhaps exasperating notation of a piano part. Though it may work fine as written down, it is not intended as obedience training. I would simply caution that the holy law of embellishment and variation still applies: Understand what's there before you change it. Players on other instruments are more on their own. A possible start-up figure was shown for the drum kit. (Maybe smoke and hisses should absorb the beat in no. 2.) Others should spend a little time with the theory chart at the front. Some may want to master the calculus of intervals. Some may prefer to depend on their ears. The page is not blank, but there's room to write on it.

[…] So far as I, still an outsider, "get it," the core genius of jazz harmony is what I might call "semiotic" rather than "architectural." A basic, European classical building block of three "functions"—II, V, I—remains a vital core after a century of jazz, BUT the means of representing or evoking those functions has often been refreshed.

That's what I find Westray's harmonic cycles can do, Piece III being the demo for that viewpoint. Westray combines triads with roots a major third apart. One way he has extended the concept since I tried it out is realizing the third layer one more third up. The way is open.

—David Lidov, Professor Emeritus, York University

Chapter 42

Gigs

The Marcus Roberts Ensemble, Jazz at Lincoln Center, New York, NY.

Ron Westray Quartet, The Pilot Tavern, Toronto.

Ron Westray, Savannah Music Festival, Savannah, GA.

Ron Westray w/ The Jazz FM 91.5 Youth Big Band, York University.

Irving Mayfield and the New Orleans Jazz Orchestra, US Touring.

Ron Westray w/ The York University Wind Symphony, York University.

Ron Westray Quartet, The Pilot Tavern, Toronto.

* * *

Afterthoughts of Unrequited Love

ME: Hello there. what up?

S: Nothing much what's good with you?

ME: Everything is swell … Living in Canada for two years now; they treat me nice here … lol

S: Nice, I'd like to visit there one day. How did you end up in Canada?

ME: Big professorship; Oscar Peterson Chair in Jazz @York U …

S: Congrats … you are doing the thing huh?! I'll be back stateside by October.

ME: Oh, yes … cool; after how long?

S: I've visited the states off and on for the last 6 years. But I'm just ready to be home for a while.

ME: Dig … all is well w/ the marriage thingy, though?

S: Nope, we're getting divorced.

ME: I see; good, if it's not happening.

S: Yeah, he says he does not want to be married anymore. So I'm going to make that happen for him.

ME: Excellent.

S: I'll be returning back stateside better than when I left in 05.
ME: Can I take "that" for a lil test drive, to celebrate your freedom, when you are back in North America?
S: Yes you can—as a matter of fact.
ME: Excellent. Can I get that in writing?
S: I've been sexually deprived for 6 years with lousy sex; you are so silly.
ME: Oh, no; please save that patient for me, K?
S: I've been getting it in at the gym, down 16 pounds and back in a size 18 Yeah he sucks at sex, oral and intercourse.
ME: Excellent; keep pushing it.
S: I got my 2 mile run in today actually. I'm still thick though. Some things are just here to stay.
ME: Well, I'm a handle up on that asap; wow, you are doing it …
S: Ass or breasts or both both, we grow them big down south. The waist is getting smaller though no doubt; I'm getting much attention over here
ME: We have some catching up to do; we had a strong sexual vibe, remember?
S: Yes, yes I do.; and I'm in my sexual prime, something is just different when you hit your 40's. got to be a beast.
ME: Yes. so, i'm waiting, ok?
S: Didn't you get married?
ME: No, my family moved back in w/ me for a while in '09, but we didn't remarry
S: Gotcha, well I'll be returning stateside, single, no kids, plants or pets and debt free with a nice bank account. So it's all good!!
ME: I'm so there. reserve that "space" for me, a'ight? You can come check me out in Toronto, too. Will you be in Cola, SC?
S: Of course, have passport will travel. Yes I will be in SC. My mom is too excited. Randall is home too.
ME: That's excellent; glad to hear that.
S: You'll have to give me your email so I can send you some pictures.
ME: lol please do, babe:
S: Too many people are telling me I need to start modeling;
ME: Send me some pics to my email, so i get hype on that shit in addition to pics of you … lol
S: Here you go. you'll have me flying back and forth to Canada. How long is the flight?
ME: no time, 2 hrs. come on …
S: Oh no worries; anything beats the 24 hours it takes to get stateside from Bahrain.
ME: OMFG; i know about those types of flights; but once it's done, it's done.
S: yes it is; but it's draining though; and the jet lag is a beast; but when I get back that's it for me,

ME: Just pop the melatonin when you touch down
S: It depends on what time the flight gets in true … It takes a while to get back on stateside time
ME: You will be aight in about a week, Hehe.
S: Yeah I'll just be up at 2 in the morning and out by 7
ME: When was the last time we've seen each other? 1986–87?
S: yeah …
ME: Wow! We had the hots, though. that's a long time. I still remember how wet you used to get; and how big your ass was, and how we had good conversations. does it still get that wet?
S: It's been a LONG time i tell ya. I sent you a pic.
ME: oh yeah, long time, boo; that's good; and can hit that way better at this point. LOL
S: And have me all strung out …
ME: Yes, but i will take care of that … if it's working, i'm there; we can talk specifics later …
S: Gotcha, check your email
ME: Nice, pic! you don't have far to go; lookin' good.
S: Thank you.
ME: Nice.
S: I shave everywhere.
ME: Love that. Are y'all still in the same house?
S: He is at work and thus and so? We are cohabitants. I live on one side and he is on the other. he has his room and I have mine
ME: eek …
S: It's been this way since January; better than having to pay a bunch of separate rent. I just ignore him.
ME: Been there, done that, bought the t-shirt, took it back for a refund, bought it again, faded that one, bought another one, then returned that one, and the store is closed.
S: Yeah it's something else I tell ya. I've quit cooking and everything too.
ME: I hear you; just ride it out and get in shape like you are doing
S: Oh you're making me blush.
ME: That's gone be nice, babe.
S: What's that?
ME: That's a lot of ass, girl; that's what's up.
S: The thing that I have not gotten used to is having other women tell me how pretty/beautiful I am. This is coming from women on the military base of course;
ME: Well, you are exotic—over there, and in general. They want some of that soul, girl.
S: I'm always getting compliments on how good I smell.

ME: You're the total package—a true diva; and I always get what I want
S: You do?
ME: it's a gift … lol.
S: promise?
ME: Scouts honor (all three fingers) hehe; bye, Ron

Chapter 41

Gigs

Ron Westray w/ Mitch Butler, The Speakeasy, Columbia, SC.

Ron Westray and Thomas Heflin, Smalls, New York, NY.

Ron Westray, Jazz Faculty Recital, York University.

Ron Westray, Savannah Music Festival, Savannah, GA.

The Marcus Roberts Ensemble, Jazz at Lincoln Center, New York, NY.

The Mike Murley Septet, The Rex Hotel, Toronto.

Ron Westray and Thomas Heflin, The Rex Hotel, Toronto.

Mom's H.E.A.D.R.A.G.

Mom adopted an acronym that matched her personal style spelled H.E.A.D.R.A.G.—her last automobile had the personalized tag to match. It actually stands for "He Adores Righteousness And Glory." Certainly this is what Mom was trying to convey in her living. Furthermore, that "understanding *is* the mellow prize that *will* last" was one of my mother's most profound quotes and beliefs. It is how she proceeded through life—and in love. Mom was rarely, if ever, ruffled by the assaults of enemies, or so-called allies. This mellowness is captured in all of her writing, countered by a *rough and ready* perspective.

The things Mom wrote about were highly personal; and it has been said that you can't be a writer if you cannot be fully honest. As a panacea, Mom engineered a style that encrypted truth and meaning inside of an accessible yet convoluted style. In this way I believe she was able to strike a median between evasiveness and candor. The fact is that no one will ever know her deepest truths; she took them to the grave. However, her free verses, limited in their publication, grants us, at most, an opaque view of her soulfulness—and at least, a partial account of a seemingly unlimited understanding of self.

★ ★ ★

"This 'changin' gears' is all you got."
"You got to be a leader sometimes"
"To be angry is to be powerless"
"If i didn't see it, it doesn't exist"

I was lookin' at you when you heard that i knew:

Cash Registers

see, i told about mr. joe—but i saw him through the eyes of the other kids—what they may have been thinking. Cause he'd stop what he was doing to service you. Those cracked-open oil-black cuticles. oh, thank you mr. joe: 2 mary janes, 2 squirrel nut, and one cookie.
see i told you i saw mr. Joe. Cause see mr. joe knew that i always requested cough drops … wright bros. Cough drops, the black ones … that's for my money now … about twice a week, the reds on occasion.

★ ★ ★

what is all tis world to me? Just to be prepared in body and soul.
It ain't nothin' sensual about it.
We tight like a braid, and that takes three strands. Don't cross over yet, get it slick.
I want it slick. (Property: fall lift and cat cleaning, trim and repair.)

I thought the cat would get you man … But I saw you take a leap. Man, you looked like a frog in a contest. A leap, deep into the periwinkle of which there is no shortage. The light of the car blinded the cat—I pondered a moment, turning in the driveway. Next morning, I saw who you were, there on dad's border grass.

Don't be glad to see me … Be glad that I came, because it's worse than whatever you think.

How about you? Need someone to help preparing the props. Selection will be based on the depth of the lies you tell during the interview process, which is on going, even.

"I'll open anything you package."
"A shop for papagallos": Black silk-dress with huge cabbage roses.

A proud woman feels like a "hat rack" … Her people wait their turn on the wide wheel …

You send it out—I'll pick it up … I've got a receiver in my mind. I've got a cup, I'll pick it up.

I hear your cough, I hear you rappin. I hear your wheels turning on the road.
I know your name, and soon … ah! Soon, I call your game.
You can't hold me. I aint tame. I know you like I know my roaches mr. man.

I love Liberty, because it affixes itself to any preposition without changing its relevance to the user. For you can be either in, on, of, from, to, with, and at Liberty. Only the self is the executor. So that's what prepositions are for, to only precede the word liberty?

If you don't want to, you don't have to get in trouble.

Haay man! That's a stud?
Way I recall it, you can get it down … but the studs, they gotta straight up and tight.
He ain' the stud. That's a prop. A prop for aspiring producers. Taxes for musicians, ass always.

Pat a cake
Pat a cake
I'll pop a punk
Pop a cake
Pat a cake, Ugh … Slam Dunk
Give me the money I didn't bet.

I would love to have seen you come back across the street old man Brown
Tore my ivy down
Pat a cake … Pat a cake.

Think Thanks—in advance. Thank him whom you have not seen.

This is the first Autumn of my life.
I'm trying, for the first time, to sneak into winter …
Eagerly planning for spring.

So, that's what all the Spring Lit. is about?
Well I wish I'd known before know.

Actually, it's worth living too ... New Life.

Hey you there inside your imagine nation ...
It's just my imagination i'm sure ...
You ___ that thing you imagine for me.

That place in my head where you want me to be ...
You must imagine yourself thinking.
Now tell me what you think I just said ...
You out here on my mountain, but don't you think about it.

This, my man, is image nation

⋆ ⋆ ⋆

On Day Care

Coming here, you say, involves the same process as a day-care pickup from wherever he is.
Well as long as you think that, prepare yourself, mentally, for a child who doesn't want to go home. Try to hear this and feel good, "I don't want to go home." Like I said ... There's listening and there's interpretation for what you need.

I can give you either one you want:
yo mamma
yo daddy
yo slick in the alley
I'm yo Soul Woman
Thank you God

⋆ ⋆ ⋆

Unsobering: 4:33 in the Morn. Jan. 3, '04

I'm so glad to be hear until I've chosen an un-sobering of many things.
For example, I should destroy last year's lyrics ... Unsobering.
I've done it before only to hear again that much takes a long time.
Time makes much. Time on it's own is much.
Much and Time is as sober is un-sobering when one overlooks the other.

You go too deeply: want to live, to love to forgive, to forget and to accept soberness as the much that time works well with. I Love You.

Now, to you I say… Create something greater than your change and your need.
Visit Soulville … find out the way there … your own.
The place is true … but as it is written you can't be known there.

But, you wait and I'll wait …
What does waiting mean? You'll know.

Soulville has a flag. No insignia. A flag.

Time of Day—Oh I can pretty much tell.
Without a watch towering over me—
My appointments are few.
Time to know and believe the things you woke up with this morning—
that is your art … if you will.
Don't be afraid of it now.

That is you isn't it?
Well, if it's not.
Be very afraid

(and thank you for letting me be myself again on the sly stone)
I'll take it from here, Sly.

Just remember, live it once and carry the flag.
Why? Cause to surrender the flag is not a victory.
You can go all around the town as a World.
Try to get home … That place not built by hands—
no Amen necessary.

Just thought I'd repeat for myself the rules of Astromeria Day,
I don't have my official book,
but rule #2 is:
Set the stage for your show.
What's #1? …
Glad you asked.
Simply,
No Carousing.

Why is #2 so crucial?

Well, you can't set no stage, you constantly getting hurt.
Take away the hurt—

and if you walk in from a stage obviously angled—too bad.

Rule 2 again, for you—where's my guest book.
You're still on the list—just know I'll do anything for you.

Everything I do is for me to you.
Bless my soul. It's true—for me to you.
Its' a matter of a preposition for—which one is you?
To you
from me
for me
to you
It's true.
word!

Questions?

You're still Chief Cook
I ain't adding no *thing*
to your pot for me. Nothing. Cook—
I may not eat—but since you Cookin', Cook.

Chapter 40

Gigs

Irving Mayfield and the New Orleans Jazz Orchestra, National Touring, US.

Ron Westray w/ Sunny Albeau at the Revival Bar, Toronto.

Ron Westray, Toronto Public Library (Black History Month Celebration).

Ron Westray, Dr. Norman Bethune C.I., Bethune Music Night, Toronto.

The Richard Underhill Quintet (JUNO), Mississauga Arts Center, ON.

Ron Westray Quartet, The Pilot Tavern, Toronto.

The Richard Underhill Quintet, Jazz FM studio, Toronto.

Ron Westray Trio, Cultura, Mel Lastman Square, Toronto.

Ron Westray Ensemble, Picton Performances In The Park, Picton, ON.

Ron Westray w/ York Jazz Faculty, York Foundation, Toronto.

Ron Westray Ensemble, Toronto Center for the Arts.

Ron Westray Quartet, The Rex Hotel, Toronto.

Ron Westray, Kincardine Music Festival, ON.

The Mike Cado Dectet, TD Toronto Jazz Festival, Toronto.

Ron Westray Quartet, The Pilot Tavern, Toronto.

New Orleans Jazz Orchestra, Jacksonville Jazz Festival, FL.

New Orleans Jazz Orchestra, Playboy Jazz Festival, Hollywood Bowl, CA.

New Orleans Jazz Orchestra, New Orleans Jazz and Heritage Festival.

Marcus Roberts Ensemble, Seven Days Festival, Florida State University.

Daniel Schnee, PhD Recital, York University.

The Barry Elmes Sextet, TD Toronto Jazz Festival, Toronto.

The Barry Elmes Sextet, Faculty Recital, York University.

ME: Hey You …! You don't have to have a New Year "like this," but you have to contextualize your demands, sweetheart—Happy New Year!
I have been traveling for near 48 hrs now, including bringing in the New Year w/ the girls in D.C. You know I drove from SC to Canada, right? I just made it to my home in Canada.
Have a heart, babe. There will be communication gaps sometimes. This one was largely due to transit. I don't want to feel like I have to explain these patterns. That's why I try to give you as much info before hand as possible. I pick the girls up at the airport tomorrow.
How's Bangkok? Relaxing.
You shouldn't be stressing over my emails, baby. Our love is more powerful than that. Thinking of you, heating the house up.—Love, Ron

R: Hey I had my new year 24 hours ago, I have not heard from you … no call or email to even wish me? Is this my reality for 2010? how does one manage this?

R: hey babe, I have been thinking of you all day… I miss you SO SO MUCH.
I'm leaving the hotel in about 40 minutes to hit the air port, my flight leaves BK tonight midnight and now it is 8pm here … just had a hot bath in candle light reflecting 2010 and my plans and goals!!! I am leaving soon. I love you and miss you.—R. xxxxxx

ME: R.,
Hi … I think you are overreacting. We never discussed the fact that I would call your cell in Thailand. We didn't even know you would have service. I do appreciate you finding a way to contact me while you were traveling, but I didn't realize you were taking such detailed notes on what you were doing tin comparison to what I was doing, or not doing. Besides, you have had more time than I have had to not only rationalize the situation, but also call me.
Coins? Pay phone? … Not on the same page, because I didn't go out of my way to call you, in
another time zone, and with many things going on, for New Years?
Come on, boo—Ron

R: Wanna see me naked lol. You are something babe …:)
Ok, give me some time. I need a shower now. I will wear some nice underwear for you. I want you inside Ron—All over me. I need u so bad now!!! Miss you my sweetheart … It's been a long time; I can't wait to kiss it.
R xxxxxxxx

Success is to be measured not so much by the position that one has reached in life as by the obstacles which he has overcome while trying to succeed.
—Booker T. Washington, *Up from Slavery*

ME: Hey Baby. Welcome back! So glad you made it home. I miss you too, so much, baby.
The girls are home, and are fine. Things are noisy now. Snap me a sexy photo and send it to me. Really sexy, like naked … lol

R: Hey my Ronski BOO … I am home now and so HAPPY:)
I thought about you all the way on my flight darling … your face, your luscious lips, your beautiful eyes and your manly sexy body all over me LOL I will write to you later. Hope all is good at home and the girls are back at home. love you babe!!!
Yours, KISS … KISS R. xxxxxxxx

R: Westray you are way too f★cking hot for my p★ssy right now … considering my p★ssy has been deprived for so long. Your are lucky to indulge me, taste my true essence, the sweet nectar I have cultivated …
Try me Westray …
Kiss xxxx

ME: sweety, we think just alike, and i want you so much right now. i want to suck on your p★ssy so bad. i plan to cum with you, for you, in you and on you … lol
you first—Ron

R: Hey my darling,
You write so beautifully. I just woke up to a sunny Tuesday morning in Melbourne to read your sweet words … you really make my day and help me to get through all I need to do. Just when I read your sweet poem … You and I are in this together … I will stay with you forever. Our love is so special and the bond we share is not to be forgotten. Yes, we are so far away from each other, yet so near. Not a moment goes by that I don't think of you. When I open my eyes, I look at your photos, your smile and I feel your soul. My room is covered with your photos, our photos … our amazing love. I feel your presence in my room so strongly and dearly I know you and I together can make this work, we can get through each day,
Honey you are not alone, I feel your pain and I feel what you feel & say … I am your twin in this life time … Babe you are mine … you were always meant to be with me. Time will bring us together I know for sure. Be strong, have hope, have faith that we will one day be one! Your sweet love carries me through each moment …

Just when I feel sad that you are not near, I read your words and get inspired, holding on to your love and the cosmic connection. Our love is all we have for now, I embrace you, I adore you and I love you my handsome man.
Yours R. xxxxxx

baby,
i wish i could be with you; and you alone.
i feel your presence in my life so strongly, though you are so very far away.
i feel the immense love you have for me, though i am not yours alone.
i see the dream you have for us.
i feel your soul.
i believe you.
i, too, wish i were yours; and yours alone.

⋆ ⋆ ⋆

Thinking thoughts of love, and how.
How did this happen?
Just when I had given up on those things which I never controlled,
You returned with your song.
The song of my life
In my mind, I plan for a future with you.
This, only knowing certain things about one another
The things I do know could carry me through two life times of happiness with you.
All I need do is hear your story. I know that you are my destiny.
I know that I am not alone.
Indeed, I have found a partner.
You have reinvigorated my life, my mind.
Like a Queen, you have adorned me with your emblem.
A emblem that has marked my heart and my soul, making the future seem bright
What makes ours everlasting, R.?
I feel that I will always need you.
I don't want another time when we are not each other's.
You are the Queen of my dreams
You are part of my life
We are; so, I am deprived, right now, without you—Ron

⋆ ⋆ ⋆

Hi R.

Wow, what a pleasure to hear from you. I thought of you recently and wondered how I would ever catch up w/ you again.

I'm not on that tour with Branford. I left NYC and Wynton's [Branford's brother] band in 2005. I moved to Texas to start a professorship @ The University of Texas, Austin. I was there from 2005–2009.

Now, I'm a professor in Toronto Ontario @York University.
In 1999, I had one kid, and was in the middle of divorcing. The divorce was final in 2001, but I have had two more daughters with my ex since then. Ages are 10, 3, and 9 months. I have not remarried, but my spouse and the girls are w/ me in Toronto. That's the short version. So, new house? Great!!

I would love to see you again someday. So let's remain in touch this time.

Talk Soon, RW

Dear Ron,

How are you doing and hope all is well with you. I was looking to get some tickets to see Branford Marsalis Quartet, who will be playing in Melbourne next year. This remained me of you and I did a Google search and found your lovely website. Are you coming on tour with him too?

It has been a long time since we spoke. I last saw you when I was in the US in 1999 when we met up for a drink down town NY. I moved to Melbourne in 2006 and bought a beautiful home etc.

Send me an email if you have time and tell me all your news. How are your kids doing? I think you had two kids when we last spoke and you were remarried I think?

Look forward to hearing from you.

Take Care,

R.

★ ★ ★

R: Good Morning baby,
WOW … I loved all your tracks and had it put on to a CD. Guess what? I played it in my car and it is amazing … I have a BOSE hi-fi in my car with a sub woofer, and the sound is breathtaking, magnificent and your voice is so sexy. I am so crazy about your music and had it on repeat … I will be taking it with me for SURE! Thank you so much for sending me the best songs … I loved the words and it is soooo romantic … I would love to be kissing you listening to this magic ha!
I can't stop thinking about you and "us" … a part of me scares me, as I am so into you. I am so looking forward to seen you in Feb 2010. I have spoken to three of my close girl friends and they have all told me to go and see you in Canada.
I will call the agent tomorrow and ask them to give me a quote for a ticket.
I have to attend the CCH sales conference in Sydney from the 29th January–4th Feb 2010. I will be getting an award called the "rookie of the year" for 2009. This is an award given to the best new staff member for performance and results. CCH is making a video of me for this conference—called a success story! So, if I get leave I will have to leave soon after the conference to see you. If Feb dates don't work out for me, when is the next best time for us?
I keep reading all your email a hundred times, I look at your photo all the time, and now I have your music on in the background on repeat … is this normal to carry on this way LOL I feel like a young girl who's head over heals in love with "the man" of my life … this is a real love story and not a made up one … No one has had this type of effect on me for the past 13 years since I have been divorced …
Most of my friends call me the mystery women, as I am always seen alone at parties, events, holidays etc. … people ask me "how come you don't have a man"? "you're a good catch" …
I was waiting for you babe!!!!
I was very emotional after you left Sydney as I felt a part of me was gone!!! I use to visualize us together as a loving couple happy and doing well in life … I hope my imagination will turn to reality and this is not an illusion or fantasy. I guess time will tell?
Darling you are very special to me and I hope you know this now!
I love you babe,
KISS xxxxxxx
R.

ME: Hey darling, you are not going crazy. We're just catching up with destiny. I know I have a lot on my plate, but I feel that you and I must complete what we began. I must have you again. I must feel that magic again.

When we are together, we are one. I now know that you have wanted me as I have wanted you.
I have never stopped thinking about you, and the thought of holding you floods my imagination.
There is so much I want to do with you, too. Don't feel guilty soul-mate. You will not cause any problems in my family life. Actually, knowing that we are reconnected enhances everything about daily life for me.
My responsibilities will always be a part of my reality, but I want you to be in my life R. I will always have to manage the reality of my family, but I want us to have our own thing "down under."
What if a child came from our love? Does the thought scare you?
Don't feel guilty. You are not causing any problems in my family life. Any problems that exist will and have always existed. You are a solution not a problem. Knowing that you are mine cures a thousand ills.
I love the pictures baby. Your home seems to be calling me. I know that I will be there in person sooner than later. At the very least, what we do will be a long distance reality, most times. Can you deal w/ that?
Darling, I desperately I want to come to Thailand w/ you, but these ticket prices are extreme, now. I have checked many airlines, and the prices are outrageous. Right now it looks like it would cost from $4500–7500 dollars. I will keep looking. If you know a cheap source for tickets, let me know.
If I don't make this trip, just know that reuniting with you is very important to me, and will happen. Again, just know that I really, really want to be with you.
You are so beautiful, baby.—Ron

R: I can't believe you say you feel this way for me as well … how can this be mate LOL I always had a big soft spot for you and just kept it to myself as you were involved. It feels good to hear you feel this way to about me, and I hope it is real and from your heart. I would love to see you again and just hug you and hold you. I will never forget the night we spent together in Sydney, that was magic.
Well I don't have any complications I guess, kids, boyfriend, partner etc, so meeting you is easy for me. On the other hand you have a lot on your plate and a lot to deal with … If there is anything I can do to make you come to Phuket let me know. This is so amazing … as I booked my holiday and offered two girlfriends to join me. I even said to both that they don't have to pay
for the room and all they needed was the ticket. Both my friends were not able to afford the air ticket … I told my self that this is for a good reason and I should go alone.
Honey please look into this ASAP as you don't have much time with the holiday season so near.

There's so much I want to tell you, so much I want to do with you if I ever had the chance. I feel terribly guilty after making my confession to you about my feelings, as this will cause trouble in your family life. However, I don't think I can hold back as I feel so strong about you; and this is not just a feeling.

Are we able to talk? If so, send me a number. Here are some photos of me and my home. Send me a photo of you so I have something to look and hope for!

ME: Venus in your love zone gets a kiss from Mars, the planet of All Things Hot Stuff, today, and if you think that sounds promising in the Ooo Er Missus department you're right (and if you don't know what I'm talking about, let me put it like this—Venus and Mars are the lovers of the zodiac, and when they connect, as they're doing now, it gets very exciting for all and sundry. Aries, Libran, Scorpios and Taureans tend to feel it most but in this case, because Venus is in your House of Love, you're in line for some good things re love and money as well.)

Astro theme for the day …

Moon into Capricorn. Moon Meditation: "Romance alert! …" The planet of love, Venus, and the planet of sex, Mars, meet tonight in a rather tender moment, promising we mere mortals down on Earth a chance to connect with our soul mates rather in the same way as these two soul-fully aligned planets are connected with each other. Everybody say "Ahhhh …!"

It was a fellow called Hermes Trismegistus who is credited with being the father of astrology and with the line "as above so below" which says so much about astrology.

If that last sentence means nothing to you, worry ye not. It's still a romantic night. And if does mean something to you, this is the night to raise your vibrations to make the most of the celestial offerings. And remember, we're all vibrations.

* * *

Baby

I knew it then, and our imaginations turned into reality the day you contacted me 'gain, for the first time. The happiness we feel now IS what we have, which can't be found elsewhere, and remained elusive 'til was ripe. Indeed, you were a mystery.

A mystery to my heart in the form of a question.
Where doth my love reside?
I know now.
Like a schoolboy, I brood on our love.

I dream dreams that I have dreamed, but I know the mystery now.
I stare at your pictures, your features.
I know that you were meant for me.

* * *

I look so forward to seeing you ASAP in 2010. I will not change on YOU.

February is the time I want to see you, simply because it is the soonest.

At a glance, though, if you came in March, I would be teaching, but it could work; as, working gives me an, almost, daily excuse to "be away, all day." You would have some stretches alone, but I could be, virtually, "travelling" during a given Fri, Sat. Sun. Then, back to "work" on Mon. Thurs., with may "another gig" on Fri. and Sat … dig? This is definitely plan B, though. I miss you so much, my Queen. We will talk later on sweetheart

—Ronald

* * *

I love you and I miss you sweetheart.
Thinking thoughts of love, and how.
How did this happen?
Just when I had given up on those things which I never controlled,
You returned with your love song.
The love song of my life
In my mind, I plan for a future with you.
This, only knowing certain things about one another
The things I do know could carry me through two life times of happiness with you.
All I need do is hear the story of your love for me, I know that you are my destiny. I know that I am not alone.
Indeed, I have found a partner.
You have reinvigorated my life, my mind.
Like a Queen, you have adorned me with the emblem of your love for me.
A love which has accosted my heart and my soul,
making the future seem bright.
What makes ours everlasting, R.?
I feel that I will always need you.
I don't want another time when we are not each others.
You are the Queen of my dreams

You are the love of my life, R.
Again, we are.
I am deprived without you—Ronald

★ ★ ★

Hello Love: That horoscope was amazingly accurate …

Darling, I have to decline your offer and follow my intuition, which is further justified by the internal flight dilemma. I can't come to Thailand. Don't confuse my decision with how I feel

about you, R. I too have visions of staring into your eyes, holding you, making love to you, sharing experiences, and just looking at you.

We ARE ONE in heart and mind. You say, "well why aren't you making this happen?" The answer is that I can't, logistically.

My choice was to "go against the grain" (including trying to run to the int'l terminal in 10 minutes) in order to prove to you that I am in love with you, that I want you, and that I want to be with you; or "grit and bear" a wiser decision for myself.

I have searched long and hard for a flight that would place me in JFK in enough time to check in for the intn'l flight.

I believe I mentioned that I would use that as my "omen" of sorts.

One other thing that I totally forgot about is the fact that I have work to produce for classes next semester in this two weeks. The travel would not allow me to execute any of that work, either (i.e. curriculums, compositional editing for jazz ensemble concerts next term, etc.)

Also, my 89 year old grandmother has just been released from the hospital, and it would weigh on my heart not to see her this Christmas, as she is expecting me. Also, my travel would forfeit any gift giving to my daughters and other family, as well as the aspect of not being contactable by them; this would be abrupt and strange.

I want us to have a smooth start to being together; and though Thailand certainly provides a great "backdrop," my circumstances, my time-line, and the internal travel dilemma says "not this time Ron." My heart wants to drop everything and fly to you, but my brain knows that it's not a good time.

I don't want to raise any eyebrows (w/L.) so early in our (you and me) reuniting, so that we may have smooth sailing when we do "set out to … See."

The one thing I am most concerned about is you thinking that I don't want to be with you. So, if you are still thinking that, don't that. I know how easy it is to get fixated on something going a "certain way." I hope you can transcend this disappointment, just I will have to transcend my own melancholy at not being there. I know your heart recently set on the idea of being together next week, but just know that my feelings for you do not have an expiration. I know you will yearn for me while there, as I will yearn for you. I will think of you each day and night, all day and all night. Just know that my not coming to Thailand is not a reflection of how I feel for you. I feel like you. I know that there is a great destiny for you and I.

This is NOT God telling us that we are not meant to be. We ARE meant to be. I know that, and you know that. This is, simply, a test of our patience and steadfastness. I WANT TO BE WITH YOU MORE THAN ANYTHING RIGHT NOW. However, I cannot forsake my God given wisdom, least I falter.

It pains me not to be able to accept such a grand offer. (You have no idea. Maybe you do. Basically, I feel like you at hearing this news, though I be the harbinger)

I want see you ASAP (this trip just came up too soon). I would really like the Feb. dates to work out if possible. Will you look into whether or not you can use your Jan. leave in Feb? Otherwise we will target March/ April.

Soul mate, I Love You. Call me as soon as you get this.—RW

R: *The mutable air sign of Gemini is tuned to the level of the mind (represented by air). There is restlessness, a need for variety and a basic urge for diverse contacts and relationships with a natural ability to do two or more things at once.*

Hi my darling,

It was so nice to get the chance to talk with you today. Honey thanks for all your sweet emails. You did put a smile on my face and I feel nice to read all the lovely things you say you say to me … I know this is from your heart …

Like I said I was sad last evening that I was alone here … I was feeling really lonely … mostly at night. anyway I had to deal with that feeling and I ended up in my room listening to your music, looking at your photos … and thinking of our future together … I am so in love with you that I really can't express this in words. Thank you for been so sweet and sending me all your emails as it really makes a big difference. I know you can only tell me all this in words and emails … I believe you darling … I know in time I will not need to feel so concern and worried …

I want to make you happy … I want to be your dear friend, lover, wife, playmate, confidant. I want to be all this and more … I truly see a bright future for the two of us … I know this and I want to be a part of this with you …

I know you and I will make a great partnership … with minds like ours, any thing is possible … I dream about the 11th of February … you never leave my mind honey …

You know what?? I bought you a great Rolex watch … you will love it. Silver/sports. I will keep looking for a wallet as I didn't see any thing with a good leather … will keep looking.

Darling you are thought of every moment … I miss you my babe!!! I want you so much … LOL (you know what I mean). I will talk with you again soon and know that I am for real and this is all real … you and me!!!

KISS, I love you.

Yours, R.

R: Sexy man … you are mine …
you know what keeps me going??? your words, emails, your actions, your poems … your music … your love, your caring…
I want you, I yearn for you in side/out!!!
Missing you Ron … all the time!!
R. xxxxxxx

ME: Miss you madly, baby.
Believe that—RW

R: Hi Darling,
So today is 24th eve here and it is about 8.00pm … I got back very late from the tour as our boat had problems and we were stranded in the middle the deep sea LOL … I will tell you all about my day when I call you ok … I love you too a lot … a whole lot … I thought of you all day while I was on the boat … every one was with there partners etc. … as usual! I want you too so much … TONIGHT! this is so crazy … we can't even be together?
anyway … Yours—R. xxxxxx

ME: Hi Baby … I love you. I'm going to bed. Had a pretty busy day. Wanting to be with you so much.—Yours, Ron

R: Hey Ron,
How's it going and glad you enjoyed my long email … did you not have any sort of response to what I was saying?
I did a full day boat trip to James Bond Island today and did a lot of swimming. I am very tired as I had a late night last night with some Ausi's I met here … went out till late and had to get up early for the trip.

I got on the pill yesterday as I had my period and this is the time to do it … however, it has made me feel ill all day with a bad headache. Since it is about 7 years since I was last on the pill, my body is not used to it. I am not willing to risk any thing and take any chance so that is why I am doing this … I will take it for 7 days and If i still feel ill, then I will stop it. Hope all is well with you.
Miss you,
R.

ME: Hey You … Thank you for your wonderful message of love, baby. I keep reading it over and over. I love you.—Ron

R: Hey Ron,
I have tried to call you several times and your mobile has been turned off! I did leave you a message and the rest of the time I hang up. I guess your back to your reality now.
I won't trouble you, just wanted to wish you a very happy new year and drive safe please. If you have time to talk to me give me a call. I am in BK now.
I love you a lot,
R. xxxxxx

PS: glad you found the photos babe!

ME: R., Guess what? I found the pictures from '99, on a whim. There are three poses. We are so cute!
You look splendid, and haven't changed much. What we have is so strong, sweetheart. I love you and I miss you, baby.—RW

R: Hey Ron, I am not sure how you perceive me as "demanding"? This is the second time you have called me demanding. When I called you from Phuket, and you were doing something … you told me you had 5 minutes to talk to me, and then i was upset and said I will call you back if that is the case … I call you all the way from Phuket, walking miles to find a pay phone … not sure how this is seen as demanding? How many times have you called me or how much effort have you put in to calling me?
anyway … yes, I knew you were going to DC, that you were driving from SC etc. I knew you were going to be with the girls … all is cool. I never asked for any thing from you, to be called demanding. I didn't ask you to send me a dozen red roses, a phone call every day … nothing!
What really hurts is you seem to not be able to even make just 3 minutes to call me for new year and wish me … and you say you're in love with me? I find this strange. surely you have a car, two legs, what would it take to get to a pay phone, put a few coins and call my cell—"just 3 minutes." I don't think this is a lot to ask for Ron? You know I was not able to call you, as your phone was switched off, and I was not going to call you … anyway.

I have called you every day since the 10th of December, most times I have called you twice a day … I found a way to find a phone card, walk a lot to find a working pay phone, paid a lot of money to call you just to hear your voice … I don't think you and I are on the same wave length babe? I should not have to remind you of this and the simple things you can do. I have not asked for a lot rather, really put my self out for YOU. I offered to fly you to Thailand, no questions asked, then I offered to fly all the way to Canada and never asked you to take half the cost of this expense … I don't think you even appreciate me, appreciate me calling you … I guess it is just taken for granted.
You say in your email that I should have a heart … I am speechless that you see me in this light! If I didn't have a heart, I wouldn't have taken this on with you, and all the complications and a full family you have … You don't seem to even give any consideration that I have taken on a long distance relationship with a married man, with a wife, and three kids and a complex situation … why do I need to take all this Ron?? why?? think about this? you have not once stop to consider this right?
I love you and I love you more than you will ever know. I am so offended the way you perceive me Ron …
I am not sure if I am built for this type of complex situations … I try to live a simple life and one of the reasons I have never been involved with a married man is, for this very reason …!
Yours, R.

⋆ ⋆ ⋆

At the end of this Ron-dez-vous, R. called L., introduced herself and told her we'd been "cooped up" in a hotel for two weeks—all this because she opened my email account while I was away from the room and read a flirtatious email I'd written to someone during her visit; though she's the traveling mistress; though I stressed nonexclusivity, from the get.

Chapter 39

Gigs

Ron Westray Trio, The Trane Studio, Toronto.
Master-class w/ [saxophonist] Stephen Riley, Dept. of Music, York University.
The Mike Murley Sextet (JUNO), Faculty Recital, York University.
The Mike Murley Quartet (JUNO), The Pilot Tavern, Toronto.
Ron Westray Quartet, The Pilot Tavern, Toronto.
Time Warp Orchestra (JUNO), York University.
The Richard Underhill Quintet (JUNO), Concert/DVD Shoot, Lula Lounge.
The Marcus Roberts Ensemble, Chicago Symphony Series.
The Irving Mayfield Quintet w/ The Minneapolis Symphony.
New Orleans Jazz Orchestra, New Orleans Jazz and Heritage Festival.
Ron Westray, Next Generation Jazz Festival, Monterey, CA.

★ ★ ★

The job came through at York in Toronto, and I decide to take the girls along for the ride.
We are living in Maple; the suburbs thirty minutes north of downtown Toronto.
There is a very liberal feeling in this department.
The students have flexibility, and I have a light schedule—this semester.

★ ★ ★

Man or Machine? It's a Fair Question

—M.M., AJW

Ron Westray is one of those rare individuals who breezes into town for a while, assumes the throne of Jazz Royalty, and then leaves for greener pastures when the "Live Music Capital of the World" reveals itself to be ... well, something other than that.

Ron is an amazing trombonist, and we were fortunate to have him with the Austin Jazz Workshop on two seasons (Ellington/Strayhorn and Rahsaan Roland Kirk). I learned a lot playing alongside him and consider myself extremely fortunate for having had that opportunity. A University of Texas professor while here, he has since moved on to a tenured teaching position at York University in Toronto.

When Ron was in town, he would often drop in at the jazz jam session on Monday nights downtown at the Elephant Room. I was there one such night, sitting in on alto sax. Ron came in, walked past the bandstand to the "warmup area," and pulled out his horn.

The warmup area is really just a dead-end corridor at the end of the long basement that is the Elephant Room. It's a handy place for people to lay their cases and wind players to warm up their chops.

Ron strode directly there because, as a member of Jazz Royalty, he knew he would not have to sit and wait through several sets to get up and play. As soon as he was warm, he was good to go. And sure enough, he soon joined us on the bandstand.

There is a lot of psychology to the Tradition of the Jam Session, and tales of novice players being "schooled" are legion. In fact, one of the reasons jazz music has managed to maintain some degree of integrity over its history is the Jam Session Final Exam, which has played itself out nightly across our country for the past ninety years. It goes something like this:

1. Spend as many years as you deem necessary to master your instrument and the principles of jazz improvisation (a minimum of ten is a good start).
2. Step onto a bandstand.
3. Get blown away by players many times more skilled than you.
4. Rinse; repeat.

Of course, there are many for whom Step #4 is "trade in your instrument for a bus ticket out of town," thereby maintaining the Integrity of Jazz. See how simple? See how effective?

Anyway, on this particular night, Ron stepped onto the bandstand after his warmup and called the tune "Donna Lee"—not a blues to ease into it, not some medium-tempo standard, but "Donna Lee"—a fiendishly difficult head followed by a challenging set of changes, generally taken at a preposterously breakneck tempo by its composer, Charlie Parker, who played the alto saxophone.

I looked down into my hands. I was, indeed, holding an alto saxophone.

I looked across the bandstand. The five other horn players who had been crowding their way into "C Jam Blues" just moments before had scattered like dried leaves, no doubt rushing to the bus station before it closed. It was just me and Ron. Ron gave the patented Manhattan count-off ("Eh, eh, eheheh") and we were off. The audience, NASCAR-like, leaned in and licked its collective chops in anticipation of potential bloodshed.

Now, the mechanics of playing the trombone are quite far removed from those of the saxophone. While saxophones are built for speed, trombones are built for ... well, I don't know what exactly, but I doubt speed is what they had in mind. But Ron was not one to let the mechanics of his instrument stand in the way of his desire to nail "Donna Lee" to the wall at 240 bpm. Which he proceeded to do, with me holding onto his tail for dear life.

Here is where my years of jazz training really kicked in. Firmly believing in the adage "the best defense is a good offense," I knew exactly what I had to do. I had to take the first solo.

Because if I had to follow Ron Westray on "Donna Lee," I might as well catch a cab to Greyhound that very moment.

So I dove on in and took three hair-raising choruses, about as much as I dared. No sense in pushing my luck, right? I'm sure the rhythm section appreciated my brevity. At that tempo, three choruses flashed by in less than two minutes. Still, I was panting when it was over and appreciative of the audience's polite applause.

Then, Ron started to play, and play, and play ... After about the tenth chorus, he bent forward with the bell of his horn facing the ground. People began to clap. I thought, "Wow, that was incredi ..." But he had come up and was blowing again. He was just taking a short breather.

I lost count of how many choruses he ended up taking, so let's just call it "many." When it was over, the audience stood up and cheered like Ron had just single-handedly won the Super Bowl. Which I suppose, in a way, he had.

Later at home, I pulled out my tattered Charlie Parker Omnibook and my metronome. Rinse; repeat.

Chapter 38

Gigs

The New Orleans Jazz Orchestra:

Essence Festival, New Orleans.

Coronado Theatre, Rockford, IL.

Grand Theatre, Wassau, WI.

Orchestra Hall, Minneapolis, MN.

Holland Performing Arts Center, Omaha, NE.

Krannert Center, University of Illinois.

Faculty Jazz Ensemble (University of Texas at Austin), Trinity Jazz Festival, Houston, TX.

Knoxville Jazz Orchestra, Tennessee Theatre, Knoxville, TN.

The Marcus Roberts Octet, The Allen Room, Jazz at Lincoln Center, New York, NY.

Ron Westray, Next Generation Jazz Festival, Monterey, CA.

Jazz at Lincoln Center Orchestra, Cross-Canada Tour.

Ron Westray, The Fort Worth Jazz Orchestra, Fort Worth, TX.

Timothy Ishii's Jazz Faculty Recital, The University of Texas at Arlington.

★ ★ ★

L and the girls are living w/ me in Texas now.
What a grand experiment. L. and I are like fish.
We have no memory until the next painful hook.
A. has started fourth grade down the street from the new home.
In not even three weeks L. and I have argued several times.
After fourteen years I now realize that she and I see everything
oppositely.

This disparity completely describes this absurd attraction.
Deep down, we really want to hear the other side, but we don't like it.
L. and I do not like one another, but are attracted to one another.
Explain that.
It's so easy to say "I Love You," but saying "I Like You," and meaning it, is a real mother for you.
That's where kids come in they give you an aesthetic to hold on to, at the least.
I'm here for the children, including, the unborn child to come.
L. lies pregnant again with #3; Saaaweeet. Like just now …

I entered the house from the Garage, where I have been exiled because of my smoking habit.
I was smirking at a wry thought upon entering the house.
Seeing my profile, L. asked, in a spiteful way, "What are you smiling at?"
As in, "what could you possibly have to smile at now that the girls and I are here?"

What could I possibly be grinning about?
This is when that divorce really starts to pay off.
We are still divorced.
Maybe that was what I was smirking at …
Maybe she could see that in my face …
In retrospect, I realize that she saw exactly what I was thinking.
But, who would admit to a thought like that.
She thinks I might, but I did not. Tough shit.

⋆ ⋆ ⋆

To L. and Back

Running out of time, as in, get it on paper before the money hits.
What if it never happens, as in, give up on it happening and sign up; then it happens.
I rather wait 'til it happens. If you win the lottery do you have to include me? As in, I'm waiting to "hit" and not include you? How are the pros and cons of making money in DC alleviated by us being married on paper? Isn't that just a fact with in itself?
How does marrying me alleviate the need for your own?

Why marry if I can't provide a salary on par with what you could earn OYO?
You just want me on paper. You don't give a crap about me.

★ ★ ★

One by one, I watched my Latino neighbors conduct garage sales. Always on Saturday, when I want to get up early and mow the lawn. Instead, I defer to the eager vending preparations going on directly across the street—under, and out from, the two-car garage.

Why defer? Well, it would be typical to forge on with my plans as a homeowner, regardless of the parked cars and little babies yawning and learning. Sure, they'll hear plenty of lawnmowers, including their father's, in due time. They won't hear mine. Not dis here morn. I gon' postpone my plans 'til the sun go down. Come Sunday, that yard gone be tight.

These lonely Saturdays smoking, drinking, thinking, blinking, dreaming, scheming,
priming, trimming, grinding, rolling, lifting, sifting, yanking, thanking, cranking,
mowing, placing, sewing, patching, matching, scratching, cooking, smelling, reading,
spelling, hearing, watching, seeing, doing, running, pumping, calling, stalling,
talking, walking, planting, ranting, raving, craving, paving, braving, saving, caving,
chillin', killin', drillin', pay-billin'—
These lonely Saturdays have made me hard.

Chapter 37

Gigs

The New Orleans Jazz Orchestra:

Mondavi Center, The University of California, Davis.

Zellerbach Hall, UC Berkeley, CA.

Stephens Performing Arts Center, Pocatello, ID.

Ellen Eccles Theatre, Logan, UT.

Kingsbury Hall, University of UT.

The Austin Pops, Ruta Maya, Austin, TX.

Ron Westray, Next Generation Jazz Festival, Monterey, CA.

Ron Westray, Carolina Jazz Festival, The University of North Carolina, Chapel Hill.

The Creative Opportunity Orchestra, Vanguard Theatre, Austin, TX.

The Creative Opportunity Orchestra, G.W. Carver Theatre, Austin, TX.

* * *

Around this time, I was asked to address the graduating class at UTA.

Congratulations! By virtue of the fact that you are here and not at the main office, you have prepared for this day. Now, the opportunity to assist and inspire mankind is before you.

I am—the world is—proud of you. How do you feel? You are among America's—the world's—future. This search for meaning—part of which you are completing—what will you do with it?

The knowledge you have attained is one thing, but your ideals are another. This will shape your decisions; and your decisions will form your reality.

And, as the road called life broadens before you, remember this: Service accompanies knowledge, and knowledge fosters discretion; discretion, in turn, encourages tolerance, and, from tolerance, emerges humility … a virtue not foreign to the scholar.

As scholars, you have learned to be responsible. The virtues of responsibility and service will be a "guiding torch" in your service to mankind. Because, many times, the greatest gift you can give is to help others help themselves.

You might say that life after college is a lot like any exam you've ever had. The better informed or prepared you are, the better you do. It's that simple. When you cram, you get "crammy" results, and when you prepare … you are satisfied. Now, you need opportunity.

In my formative years as a student of music, the skills I needed for success were described and demonstrated to me by my teachers and mentors alike. Heeding most advice, I pursued knowledge and developed the musical, physical and neurological agility to be in demand as an American jazz musician.

Contrary to popular belief, the American jazz musician—those with street cred—is a highly skilled and studied human, who searches endlessly for new answers to questions posed by people like this: Louis Armstrong, Duke Ellington, Thelonious Monk, John Coltrane, Charlie Parker, Bill Evans, Max Roach, Art Blakey Elvin Jones … to Bach to Bartok.

This dialogue with history is inevitable and of utmost importance, no matter the career. Call and response, I thinks it's called (metaphorically speaking). Those of you who took Jazz Appreciation (Jazz History?) will recognize some of these names. Any Jazz Appreciation graduates out there? Well, that's the legacy of my career. My quest, the study of American jazz, is a journey as challenging as most; and, at times, my career is as risky as a game show.

Well, it is music. So, it can't be but so "risky." But, risk is fundamental for discovery. I speak of healthy and/or creative risk—not negligent and reactionary decisions. Along this path, then and now, I remember what was told me: "Luck is when preparation meets opportunity." This axiom has provided a good deal of the fuel I've needed. That's in addition to still having a passion for what I endeavored to become. By cogitating on that old saying, I became an in demand trombonist/composer in the tradition of American jazz music. One hundred years of tradition has embraced me because I embraced it. I don't have enough time to articulate the rigors of developing in music, in jazz, in general—not to mention acceptance into the work stream. Trust me, you have to know "what's happening."

In jazz, it's not as simple as showing up well dressed. "Can you play" is the proposition. Do you know the code? The American Standard Song Book, for instance, represents "hard data" for the musician. These are the questions I had to answer before being allowed any experience. See, that's that part after opportunity. But you can't get to that without preparation.

Here are a few things I suspect you have all heard before:

1. You must have accurate information.
2. You must be able to apply the information in the form of a skill.
3. You must gather fresh information.
4. You must refine your ability … always.

You see success in action all the time, perhaps on a social network.

It's easy to recognize it in others but difficult to produce from within one's self (which will require turning the network off … for a time). For me, part of the battle was won because I knew what I wanted to do. For many of you, this is the case. For others, maybe not so.

Those of you who already have a goal:

1. Remain diligent.
2. Consult history.
3. Innovate.

But, what's your real interest or interests? Not the things you did throughout school, the other things. Is your core interest one of self or of service? If you answered the latter, well, then, good times, good times. You're gonna need that "good times" attitude while in service to others. If you answered the former … at least you're honest about it. Fortunately though, we all need someone. (Wouldn't it be a pitiful world if we didn't?)

Growth requires sacrifice. Many of you will be educated, working people, with checking accounts. Some of you will go on to achieve greater knowledge in your chosen field, and in related and non-related areas of endeavor … not to mention accomplishing the great things you haven't even imagined or dreamed yet. I implore you, make your chosen endeavor or endeavors your life's work, and grow in that work.

The quality of your ability should inspire others … as we observe in the superior athletes of the world, for instance; Or as observed in the revolutionary ideas of our recognized, and unrecognized, scientists, musicians, tech innovators, literary geniuses, and so on.

But, if you googled a question like "Who am I?" or "What are my interests?" or "What do I believe?"—firstly, you'd be at fault for consulting Google for that information. Secondly, you would not get an appropriate answer. You knew that right? Success can be compared to a search engine, like Google. You must have part of it figured out already.

Some of you may believe that, perhaps, by traveling across several continents with nothing more than a cell phone, as opposed to "going off" to med school or graduate school, that you will return with an answer about who you are. One thing you will attain is a huge cell phone bill … nothing against world travel. Meanwhile, this utopia of enlightenment you are searching for, might still exist at your room at your parents, or, perhaps, in the same apartment you inhabit right now. My advice is: Conserve your energy and prepare at home. Stay poised to meet the opportunity that will take you around the world, first class, for your first-class ability. An ability which only you can foster through Staying Started.

Graduates: In all your "after-partying," pause. In all your just plain living, Never lose touch with who you are (assuming you know where you are, and what, and whom, you represent). I and the world hope that what you represent will be good—and of service to others.

Remember this:

1. Sustaining a career is very much different from "working a job."
2. Sustaining a career requires passion.
3. Working simply indicates a "need."

Sometimes life doesn't give you a choice and you simply have to "work." That's nothing to be ashamed of. Even mundane work has dignity and passion behind it. When it's you generating your passion for what you do, that's a different ball game. It speaks for itself; and sometimes real passion meets real work: Da Vinci, Einstein, Picasso, for example.

1. Be a shining star inside of what you are, and what you do.
2. Earn your stripes the old fashioned way!
3. Bring it back!
4. Go old school on 'em!

In all your googling, gain understanding. Continue on in learning and in service: In service to our planet, in service to all humankind. Be the generation that will carry out new solutions regarding conservation, recycling, and the protection of this, our planet Earth's finite and vulnerable ecosystems.

It's bigger than you and me. And may The Force be with you!

* * *

Each day I could achieve only mild splendor. I found myself envying the youth and their carefree realities. Like I used to be—sad, right? The transition had kicked my butt on the inside. I was still observing life through the same lens. It's all I know. W. had effectively disassembled my NYC lifestyle and career. He could see the web I was stringing. W. also understood that JALC was funding that life and that style. In letting me go, he realized I would have to leave NY.

"Bruh, I'm doing this to spare you your dignity, okay?"

What? You are sparing my dignity by asking me to leave the band? Is that not the same as firing me outright? Thank the good lord I had the professorship waiting on me. My plan was to swing both careers. W. could see that far. At the top of my career in NYC via JALC, W. fired me. Fired me because of my hyper-competence, which happen to accompany a few opinions and outbursts.

I'm no punk. "Don't start none, won't be none." a.k.a., "You gone walk over, but you gone limp back." Despite my best efforts, the cats would always set me up for an outburst. And always over music—never bullshit.

Pluck at my pride—now you want me to show you my man. Well, you got it!

⋆ ⋆ ⋆

Now I was in Austin, TX— the South—the opposite of NYC. Not that I was so NY struck. Besides, I'm from the South. It was like being back home in a sense. This was not a desire of mine in '05. Having operated below radar, I had to adjust to life at street level again. Driving, grocery shopping, cutting grass and so on. "Controlled embitterment" would describe this phase: straight out of the stars to the common dives and the common experience.

Those who had only dreamed of the level of success I had, at a young age, attained, now studied my every word and deed to see what its made of. They ravaged me with spiritual, and physical, observation. Once my new peers had me all figured out, the attempt to exchange karma began. For some it worked. Some leveraged our association towards some new opportunity—that is, a nobody suddenly becomes somebody (in this minute community, mind you). You've just been jacked by the cat who used the information gained. Sound paranoid? Well, that's an easy way out, but let's keep it real. I ain't even talking about campus—that's a whole 'nother story to tell.

Everybody was gettin' a piece of me (as Mom likes to say):
The car dealers ravaged me; but I needed a new car.
The real estate broker ravaged me; but I bought a new house.
I had to get in. I sucked it up. I am conscious now.
It's okay. It's all just chump change compared to real money.

⋆ ⋆ ⋆

I yearned for my family, especially having purchased a brand new home. The house started closing in on me, and I found myself what they call depressed.

I reminded myself to be as thankful and happy as the first night I moved into my new home in the suburbs of Austin. That was how it really felt, but the splendor was veiled in the mess I had made between L. and me. I couldn't decide whether I wanted her back or not. I couldn't stop hearing the awful things she said to me about who she thinks I am. I could not forgive her. It didn't seem to matter to her, for she never called now. *Thinking back when we were just friends, before the love games began, talking, laughing, singing and dancing under the stars above, I begin to grin; then I remember to forget that I love you.*

I would speak to Z only, who would always be sure to remind me that maybe I could come down there this summer. She said that all year, up to the point I was able to say, "Well Z, it is summer now." She said, "Oh!" I began to accept that it was really over between L. and me, just as she said.

Well, it was indeed over if she was expecting me to sail through full of pity and apologies begging her to join me in my new home. She would have to want it this time. I was all for putting things back together, at my tempo. In my mind, L. owed me an apology and needed to make it clear that she needs me in the children's life, all bullsh*t aside. That's what I wanted to hear. Maybe she wanted to hear me admit that I had made mistakes. I admitted it all the time, by remaining open to the idea of having someone around me who despises me.

I'm so tired of thinking thoughts. It's all for me, I suppose. I need to write more. Instead, I spend the bulk of my time doing familiar things and surviving.

★ ★ ★

On the Road Again

Last week, on mentioning to Mom that I was going to return to the road for a 10-day stint w/ the New Orleans Jazz Orchestra, she commented that it would probably bring back memories of when I used to be on the road. Not feeling quite that old, I was offended and acted in my usual way. As it turns out, she was right.

Once reaching Sacramento airport, the first person I met was Nasa, the sound engineer for the NOJO.

R: "Hey."
N: "Hello."
R: "Ron."
N: "Nasa."
R: "Alright."
N: "Oh yeah."

The road had taught me long ago that fewer words were always the better option.

We sat neutrally as the Airport Shuttle shot downtown.

N: "I'm the sound guy."

R: "Ah, cool."

N: "Where you comin' in from?"

R: "Austin."

N: "Austin? I live in Austin."

R: "What?"

N: "They sent me to Denver at 8 a.m., where I had a two-hour layover."

R: "Really. I had a straight shot at 10 a.m. Wow ... what's up with that?"

N: "Who knows?"

R: "The Jazz Life."

N: "Yeah, guess so."

★ ★ ★

Having already hit the top of the mark as a touring musician with W., I reflected on older bands, like the Duke's, and how you would hear that his former all-stars were out and about with lesser-known organizations following their departures. Well, it's all really about gigging and paying rent. Let's not get it twisted.

Mervin, my junior by nearly 10 years, was now my boss for ten days. It hurt a little. I had come face to face with the fact that I had refused to sell my art with the tenacity required for success. Mervin had done it and was excelling as a band leader.

I felt as if he was more conscious of this position than I was, though I had not seen him in a decade. Maybe I'm the one who was more conscious (conscious, not jealous)—I'm well aware of where my efforts lay. The real kicker was that Mervin's former attitude preceded his status by about 10 years. That fact scarred my perception of him. Turns out that his ability finally caught up with his ego, which had earned him several bands, a touring schedule and the resources to hire me.

My ego is the thing that got me scorned in Ellison's band. Mervin knew I was restraining myself, because, every now and again, I would "go off." Viewing this little excursion as a re-baptism of sorts, I wanted to take my attention off me this time, in my mind. I seem to generate a form of energy that gives this fact away, though no real offense has been committed.

Maybe it's my facial expressions. I always felt I was pretty good at controlling that, though. That probably makes me pretty bad. I was conscious not to think it was about me anymore.

I'm just a C student. Who in the hell do I think I am? I procrastinate; and I still think that I'm *all* that?

Well, yeah.

★ ★ ★

As we entered the hotel lobby, Nasa greeted a gentleman of the band whom I recognized somewhat. He was sure not to send any greetings my way. That means, "I know who you are, or think you are, so take this: I don't know who you are." I felt it, and he eyed me as I headed to the elevator, not going out of my way to greet him as well. Near the elevator sat a gentleman that Nasa greeted as Victor. He did the same thing. I knew this face from former visits to New Orleans. He knew even more about who I thought I was, and his vibe was even more overt. Again, I headed to the elevator, not going out of my way to speak.

Oh, you don't know me? Then we'll meet when we meet.

★ ★ ★

I have earned several reputations (mostly positive, I like to imagine).
The negative rumors could be felt. I love it. Isn't that why we screw up anyway?
We want to say, "I don't give a damn." I love it. Vibe ON, mother★★★★★★s!

It's a matter o' the tortoise and the hare.
Let's say I'm the tortoise, and the story still ends the same way … b★★ches.
Yes, I harbor some resentment, and I don't mind admitting it.

★ ★ ★

Go West, Young Man!

There I sat in a new, now old, house in Texas. Mr. Professor is drinking a 40-ounce of Busch. This was the highest and lowest point of my life.

The neighbor's hound dog, now retired, sang with the passing ambulance; life ticked on. I don't want to talk money. There I was. I was asking myself, "Why do people lie about leaving messages? They know it's disputable, so they lie. Telling me you called would be enough. You don't have say you left a message …"

It was the end of the year. It was my first year of teaching. It was my first year of working a normal job, as a man. It was painful. Boss knew this when he let me go. He was sayin', "This Negro need to know about workin' a job—he got spoiled out here." I can dig it.

I don't want to talk about money. The year had not been comfortable. I was getting ready to go to SC to spend a few months off and with L. and Z.—L. and I had made up and were sexually involved again. This was our same pattern, even after a huge divorce. There was an assumed trust and an assumption of renewal.

Deep down, I think we both still had resentment for the past, but the growth of Z. and the general feeling of making up appeased us, and we were along the trodden path once more.

Just as in our first pattern, we were pregnant again. I treated the subject positively, while feeling insecure about what I should do. Ultimately L. gave me an ultimatum.

The first time around, I surrendered to the idea of matrimony, though I wasn't ready. It didn't work. I made mistakes, and so did she.

Chapter 36

ME: Marriage is not a responsibility; it's a choice. Not remarrying you is not simply a thing of being immature or cowardly, or preoccupied with fancies. A person has to feel like they would be happy with their partner. I have never been happy with you. Even when we were dating, it was never comfortable. We became pregnant, tried marriage, and it did not feel good … never has.

I am exactly who I am and have always been. My career change has little to do with "settling down into my paternal duties." I could have done that on the road if I thought I had someone on my side. I stated the importance of being in A.'s life as a general observation, and in terms of the sibling thing, you also hinted at the fact that your "time line" was not getting any longer. It hasn't been two years since we reconciled, it was only a year and a month or so before things went "out" as usual. I didn't consider myself to be proving that I wanted to be a family. I was just trying to reestablish a vibe with you. We became pregnant in the midst. I didn't say, "I'm not ready to raise a family." I said, "I'm fine with things just the way they are." Meaning, let's just keep on "vibing." Of course it was difficult to face the fact that I wasn't ready to marry, but I have never been a coward in relationship to anything you could propose.

I'm not saying you are fixated on the idea of being married to ME. Just being married in general. I personally don't think you care who it is. Again, this is not about "stepping up." This is about the right choice. Again, I have never been at peace with being in a marriage with you since the first go round. I haven't betrayed you any more than you have betrayed me, and my children are a part of my equation. Just not as man and wife.

You often refer to my child support as pennies, etc. I don't think you would feel that way if I had never paid anything, or stopped along the way. DC would be up my ass so fast, I wouldn't know what hit me. So while it sounds ballsy for you to discredit what I pay you, I don't think you take it that lightly when it hits your bank account. Besides, my salary at that time (Y2K) was higher than at present. I will be more than happy to adjust it to my current salary if you wish.

There are no facets in my surroundings or upbringing that allude to negativity, except the interactions we have had since day one. You never wanted me. I made you love me. I should have kept going when you gave me the chance back in '94.—RKW

L.: Hi Westray—For obvious reasons, I am compelled to respond to your letter. First, do me the favor of ceasing to continually portray me as some angry, bitter person that I am not and have never been, in light of my, once again, disappointment in your choices. As I stated before, I am doing well, and the fact that I have chosen not to engage in dialogue with you is simply because I realize that we are two different people with nothing in common except that we now have two children. If that makes you perceive me as bitter and angry, well, perceive as you need to.

I am not particularly concerned with hearing any more of your justifications on why you are not handling your responsibilities.

Secondly, I have no intention of recanting my words that I stated in June. You only validated what I wanted to believe was no longer applicable to you. You are still an immature young man, engaged in fancies of marijuana, pornography and various women. That is who you are and I can't change that, nor have I any desire to subject myself to being with a person of that nature. It isn't healthy for any sane person. As far as your dream is concerned, lose it. Trust me, I've lost any feelings or thoughts concerning us. As I stated in June, I am finished with whatever we pretended to have had.

Unfortunately, it took me 13 years to realize that you were never who you claimed to be. Additionally, I gave you the benefit of the doubt in believing that because you had finally stabilized yourself in a teaching position, you were ready to settle down and assume some paternal responsibilities. I do recall that you were the one who stated that it would be good for you to be more a part of A.'s life. You also were the one who constantly insinuated that A. needed a sibling. Well, here we are with that sibling. Believe me, there once was a time when I truly loved, adored, wanted, hoped in, and desired you. These past two years or so, you could not have convinced me more that you were ready to be a family. I never disrespected you. But the moment you opened your mouth, after A. and I had just spent time with you in Texas, and you stated that, you were not "ready" to raise a family, everything that I thought and felt for you left. You waited until I got all the way down to South Carolina to expose yourself. You confirmed to me the coward and immature person that you have always been. You couldn't even look me in my face earlier during that whole week and tell me what you had already made up in your mind, long before we arrived in South Carolina.

This was never about being married to you. Somewhere in your egotistic mind, you believe that I was fixated on being MARRIED to YOU! My dear, for the three years prior to our reunion, I had a wonderful person who adored your daughter and me, in ways you could never express. If my heart had been there, he would have married in a second! I held on to the hope that one day you would have matured and would have stepped up to the plate of being a partner in raising our daughter. When we got back together, I thought that we were building an honest love and partnership. You deceived me once again.

We could never have a friendship now. No friend of mine would ever betray me as you have. What could I actually talk to you about now, knowing that I have no respect or desire for even your mere presence? It probably won't be until you are late in your forties or even later before you realize and understand what I wanted to build with you. This was about family, A. having her father in her life, our having a relationship based on mutual love and respect! But, such is life. As I said, I'm not bitter or angry about the choices that you have made. I can't be. This is your life to live. Your little angels and me just don't seem to factor into your equation. I have accepted that. It is what it is. We really didn't have anything special. Westray, please don't misinterpret. The reality is that once again, I am stuck with the rearing of two of your little ones now. I'm not disappointed about another little one. If I thought you had your act together, I would have had three more with you. I've always loved children and family. That's what I came from. My father never thought of backing out of his responsibilities with his children, even after fifteen of us. I never disrespected you in any way to make you treat me like this. I never thought that I would be raising children by myself.

Trust me, the pennies that one sends in so-called child support could never take the place of being a real parent. Children need both parents and once again, you are "jipping" another one of your children. Be whomever you feel you need to be to appease your sensitivities. My responsibility is a full time commitment. I don't have a choice. I will love them the same and am happy for the opportunity to have had another child. A. will finally have the little sister that she has always wanted, and we all will be just fine.

I will never deny you access to your little ones. I never have. That, again, will never be me. You may visit, do and be whatever, whoever you feel you need to be to them. I will always be cordial in my conversations with you. One thing that is true, though: I no longer love or care for you as I used to. That died, completely, when you spoke what was truly in your heart. I know that this is what is best for you and me and our girls. You don't have to worry about negativity because I have never presented you with that as it relates to our children. Please don't try to make me out to be what you might have seen with others or have been accustomed to in your surroundings. I come in peace. I live in peace and I am raising my little ones in that same respect. I don't speak ill of you around A. and I never will with the next.

Wishing you peace and success on your path—L.

ME: Hi L.,

I keep having this recurring dream in which we kiss and make up. Each time this happens, I am happy and fulfilled in the dream. I think that in my heart of hearts this is how I feel. Though my indecision at remarrying caused a firestorm of emotions, I didn't think it would distort and destroy the friendship we had reestablished.

In your disappointment, you insulted me in many ways. It's taken me a while to forgive the insults, just as you are perhaps struggling with forgiving me for my indecision and what you might view as selfishness. After that day in the park, I wondered what would have happened if I had said, "Yes, I'm ready, darling." Would you have not thought of me in the ways you expressed immediately following my answer to your question that day? Looking back, it seems as if my choices were to remarry with you harboring this low opinion of who I am—or not remarry, and have you express it to me. I don't know which is the better option.

You also said that even if I had said I was ready, you wouldn't have believed me. This leads me to believe that you were just ready to marry me as a figurehead, a statue of a man that you don't even believe in, an insurance policy, something and nothing at once.

Am I to think that if we had remarried between then and now, that you would not feel about me as you expressed? Again, in retrospect, it's like, marry me and I'll pretend to love you, or run away, and I'll tell you how I really feel about you, mister. I'm glad it came out. I have decided to attribute your verbal assault of my character to your disappointment in yourself for being in the situation again, and in me for having a similar reaction as the first. The first time around I didn't want to see you hurt. This time, I had to really consider was it the right thing.

Though I wasn't ready to decide in June, I didn't realize the degree of negativity and estrangement that would follow.

I thought we could keep on working on rebuilding the trust and communicating effectively. I never insulted you during that time in June. I am willing to take responsibility for turning you into the bitter person I witnessed in June. However, it doesn't justify the defamation that followed and perhaps continues in other realms. In lieu of it all, I still dream of us being together, and I am happy in the dreams. It seems that this punitive approach of blocking me out of the experience of y(our) pregnancy, and its relationship to our oldest child is your solution. I have sucked it up and tried to pretend it's not happening in this way. I can do that. I would prefer

not to however. I am willing to forget the past and start working on our friendship again if you want.
I miss being a part of this pregnancy, but I guess that's my punishment. At some point we have to be able to create trust aside from the bonds of marriage. You once asked me, "When have I ever not been on your side?" Being on my side also means building me up, not tearing me down, not defaming my character. Perhaps to a woman, the greatest break of trust is infidelity, but to a man it may possibly be the type of betrayal I have felt, even during testy times. I know I have presented you with some disappointing and sometimes selfish decisions, I am willing to "come clean" on that, as you say. Men have done worst things; and their spouses have still turned the corner with them to better times. I have never been able to get you to turn the corner with me, L. You always turn against me …
"Who are you?" you asked me one time. My dreams reveal my heart of hearts. "How did you envision an ideal marriage?" you asked me once. I regretted not being able to give you a cogent answer then. I simply blew it off. Well, when I was young and naive, I thought you and I would just be in bliss forever. I think that you were saying, "You can have it that way." Can either of us really do what it takes to gain the other's total respect and trust, though, aside from marriage? We should consider some route towards reconciliation and raising these kids in peace. You feel like you gave me a chance, and since I didn't jump at this forgiving opportunity in lieu of our past attempt, to hell with me? Sometimes things aren't that simple. I'm glad that the ugliness reared its head again back in June. I would rather purge the relationship of that, even if for the second time. It took a lot for me to express these thoughts in writing. I had resolved, like you, not to say anything. I only write at the junction of a recurring dream.—Ronald

⋆ ⋆ ⋆

L. has taken on a self-righteous attitude regarding the downfall of the relationship, weighing everything on the idea of fidelity and vows and religious taboo, never realizing that the pain of infidelity was equivalent to the embarrassment of the verbal disrespect and slandering of my name. I have always resented L. for the way she responded *as* my wife. I always felt that she was trying to mold me into some statue of a man, being evangelized by an equally imperfect wife; infidelity is not the only sin. Then, as much as L. talks of her fidelity, I've never been convinced of this sterling chasteness in the midst of so much dissatisfaction with a husband, a man. Since the divorce, L. has often hinted to me that this wasn't the last dick left in town. I always heard the hints, though never reacting. L. had never learned to complete the turn with me, like two on a motorcycle. L. always resisted the turn, causing us both to crash and burn.

I don't mean to toss the blame. I have my demons, but when you know you have a good man, don't try to convince him otherwise.

Her solution was always loud and involving other people who were not involved. I could never trust her; there was simply too much bad blood. I felt that I was truly sleeping with the enemy. This time around, I toyed with the idea of reuniting at first, but my gut wouldn't let me submit to the idea. Well, at first sign of my hesitation, L. felt I owed her something from the first time, and I always felt like I gave as well as I got during the first time. I didn't view it like she did, of course.

L. went ballistic, reminded me of all my past indiscretions, insulted my talent, threatened violence, forecasted coveting the child and got loud with me in public. This is the kind of man L. actually wanted me to be, a man to be standing tall and proud in public disputing his business aloud with a quarreling woman. I guess this is the less violent equivalent of the women who instigate fights involving her man and other men. It's just a set up … to prove what? This is how you want me to show I care? Spewing hate allowed in public? Trying to unravel some bullshit in the park? I reacted calmly, but this didn't force L. to treat the subject matter more peacefully.

L.: So it seems as if my calls are being blocked? Is this my imagination or REALLY?! Anyway, my calls are not because I am trying to speak, but as always, I am the one to place the calls when YOUR little girls wish to speak to you. My only issue with YOU has been your unavailability to YOUR girls. I hope that you won't choose a route of non-communicating.

It won't benefit anyone. I don't have anything to argue with you about because I have no more vested in an intimate relationship with you. Therefore, all else should be cool!

I am also trying to see about possible dates in July or August when the girls can get back to Canada. I had promised them that we would go back. Look, I know I vented the last time you were here. I verbalized things I was feeling, that perhaps I thought I had suppressed. Honestly, I don't hate or dislike you. As I stated, just disappointed.

Perhaps the daddy-relationship thing just ain't your thing. I do know that three little people adore the ground you walk on and want more of it. If I could get you to open up and see only that aspect, then I, we could be cool. I know I bruised your ego once again; Sorry. Now, moving forward, please be OK to speak with me cordially, amicably, one parent to another. All hard feelings aside—L.

ME: I'm not blocking your calls, you can't bruise my ego, and I will call when I can, as usual. July/August, I will be in the States most likely. You really think that I don't know my girls adore me ... REALLY? That has nothing to do with what I do.

There I sat, another Sat. at home watching tv. I thought, "Ah, the Jazz Life."

My day started with a call from Mom talkin' shit. I thought, if only I would write this shit down, I could move on. Something always held me back from submitting to a writing task, sheer laziness. If only I would write this shit down.

Chapter 35

Gigs

Mingus Band: Malaysia, California and Alaska.

Faculty Jazz Ensemble, University of Texas at Austin.

Jazz at Lincoln Center, Dizzy's Club Coca-Cola, New York, NY.

The Wycliffe Gordon Ensemble, Body and Soul, Savannah Music Festival.

Faculty Jazz Ensemble, University of Texas at Austin.

Jazz at Lincoln Center Orchestra, Seasonal Events, New York, NY.

★ ★ ★

Just because I choose to go the hell off at a particular juncture in our conversation, my mother wants to be able to classify me on any scale at any time it's convenient to announce my flaws as a son—as if she's a saint. But I am to overlook all of her flaws because she birthed me in the world. Respect? What is that? "Do Know Wrong?" Just say what you want to, when you want to, reiterate as many times as you want, don't listen to the details, talk all over my topic, give solutions that I have not requested, coach me when I don't need coaching—I'm just reporting one day's reality.

"Tell it to your dog," say you, Mom? As if you don't call me with things you need to talk about. I will listen and not just start applying a bunch of old templates and solutions that are not organic to the matter at hand. It's just your way out of real interaction. I understand; you're burned out on really giving a damn. Just don't expect me to take kindly to the lack of sincerity when engaged in a seemingly reasonable conversation. I am in sincere conversations all the time; I know how they feel and sound. Be for real. These conversations ignite the same part of me as the most damaging conversations in my relationship with two ex-wives.

Conversely: Sometimes, I have to pull out my pimp hand and slap—MYSELF!

* * *

What I have imitated is the thing called Jazz.
My knowledge is Classical.
What I am is the thing called Hip-Hop.
Too old you say?
How old do you think Snoop is?
He can afford to think that way, you can't, you say?
That's like saying don't enjoy basketball.
It's just a way of perceiving life.

I don't like it when people correct verb tenses, slightly misused words (like "wheat and shaft" instead of wheat and chaff)—oh, and cursing, especially in the midst of a defensive outburst, and when they know you lead a stressful life.

My ex-wife used to do that in the middle of arguments, as does my mother. My mother and my ex-wives become more and more alike as time goes by. I believe that my mom now thinks that I am capable of doing anything at any time.

L. wants to win the lottery. I want to be great. I should reexamine my opening statement about preferring meaning and preparation to validation. That's not true. After all, who writes a book (much less counting off some jazz standard) without wanting some level of validation?

When I am in South Carolina, my life is essentially dedicated to household improvements and chores. Mom is in this mode all year round. For this reason, and like the changing landscape from season to season, her environment changes all year round. I have never observed this in any other environment, excepting ant mounds. Mom ends up make-shifting lots of things that work. This creates a serious conflict when it's time for me to help. I want things to last. Mom likes the "temporary permanent," as she calls it.

Mom and I just had another blowout. I told her that I only reach this tenor with her and my two ex-wives. She reminded me that, upon returning from the honeymoon, I referred to my second ex as "the other Mrs. Westray" when casually (and jokingly) reintroducing my new bride—so in that regard, she said, it was okay that I was once again comparing her to my exes. After this exchange, Mom said, jokingly, "I don't play, Ron." (Mom wants me to know that she don't play! Okay, boomer!)

A little while later, Mom dozed off watching the news. Observing her asleep, mouth open, gone to lullaby-land, often reminded me of the fact that someday, and given the proper sequence, she would, indeed, lie before me dead or dying.

I try to prepare my (future) mind for the inevitable, the incontrovertible, but my stomach still cringes at the thought. Mortality may very well have to do with this condition called depression. As the older folks in the South are apt to say, "When you're dead, you're done."

I have attained so many things. I have lost so many things.
Some things remain. One thing has not been lost.
And, "you can't give what you've never had" (Earth Wind and Fire).

I like to say I can't miss something I've never had. The gain balances the loss in the final equation, I guess. Mom asked me how I was feeling today. I explained that I felt fine, but that there was a feeling of waiting on something, or wanting something that I couldn't figure out; and that I had been waiting on this thing for quite sometime. I also expressed that I don't want to be siting around at age 70 still waiting on this thing. Is it fame? Or respect? I don't know. Got distracted. I can't really get down into this. I can't be honest enough right now. I figured it out this morning. I am waiting on happiness. I want to be happy. I can't seem to find it within myself. I'm certainly not going out looking for solutions. I have attached myself to people to find it, only to find myself even more unhappy.

And just above the surface of my reality lay an augmented reality—a deficit of desolation.
Alone again, I search for happiness.

⋆ ⋆ ⋆

Leaving The Band

By 2005 I had been in Wynton Marsalis's band for 12 years. During this time I had excelled as a trombone-section leader, arranger and composer. Along with such titles came the idiosyncrasies one might associate with a *creative*. Though I never had any "beef" with Boss, I had cursed out many band members and conductors in public settings.

Ahead of my Magnum Opus, *Chivalrous*, Wynton had asked that I not conduct the band due to my inability to separate my emotions from the process. He hired a mutual acquaintance, Bob, as the conductor of the piece. In order that he could be my surrogate for the process, Bob and I studied the score at my apartment in Harlem for weeks leading up to the rehearsals. I had a substitute trombonist play my part so that I could keep an *ear* on the process, without disturbing Bob. But when the rehearsals started, he conducted the piece as if he had never seen it before, and I found myself shouting suggestions from the back of the room where I had been sequestered with my score. At one point I finally approached the conductor's podium to offer assistance with a difficult section of music that was falling apart—mind you, they only gave me three days to rehearse two thousand measures of music, and this was the last day prior to the first performance. When I tried to help by pointing at different aspects of the score, Bob looked at me and said, "Westray, you're only holding up your own music." Well, I couldn't hold it. In a loud and thug-like voice I told him to f*ck himself and that it was my f*cking music. Further, how the f*ck can I hold up my own music? Wynton suspended the rehearsal and called me into his office as if he were a high-school principal.

W: Tray, you can't talk to people like that.
ME: But did you hear what he said to me?
W: But we had a deal.

In retrospect I realize that this was the "straw that broke the camel's back"—in addition to the fact that *Chivalrous* was a smashing success and donor eyes were on me now, too. About two weeks later, we were recording at a studio in Sleepy Hollow, New York. During one of the breaks, Boss said, "Hey, Tray, take a walk with me outside."

We walked and small-talked until we found a bench under a lighted street post. We sat down. Boss said, "Tray, I think it's time for you to do your own thing … You have your own music and your own concepts; you should do fine out here. Also, you can just say you left the band. I'm protecting *your* dignity this way, okay?"

ME: OK.

My interpretation was that he thought that he was putting me on the street in NYC (meaning no salary) to teach me a hard life lesson. He did not know that I had already signed a full-time contract with the University of Texas at Austin—as my recruiter was there, in the audience, during *Chivalrous*. The flaw was that UT Austin had insisted that I stay in the band to bolster the identity of my position at their institution; and I had been looking forward to having two salaries. But that was not to be. I had been fired from the band.

Anyhow, in the fall, I headed to Texas with all my accolades behind me—amid new expectations and responsibilities. The next time I saw the band, they were playing Bass Hall on the very campus where I was now working—a hall that I had played with the band many times in the past, never imagining I would be there in this capacity. I did not attend the concert because I had a gig at the local jazz club, The Elephant Room. After the concert the entire band flooded the club to see me. They had no idea I was there until that night, and I returned to the band for a brief time for a cross-country tour of Canada—at a time when, again, I couldn't imagine that I would be a Canadian resident in about another year or so. Somewhere along the way, some cat that I told the story told Wynton that I said he fired me—therein breaking our "pinky promise" from the Sleepy Hollow park bench, under the street light. Honestly, I meant for that to happen. I have never spoken to him since that time. In summary, I feel that I was not allowed to have an ego in his organization, though I always backed it up with innovation.

* * *

There is not a person in the world I trust less than L., yet we came together to create another child. L. wanted to wrap the whole thing into a package of, "you need to step up," while I wasn't about to be legally tied to a person who thought of me as L. had expressed in clear terms. I mention the disrespect because it does hurt. It's important for me to admit that, if even just to the page. I reckon L. knows that. She knows where to punch. Below the belt. To boot, as a grown man, with real responsibilities, I had to hear, "My brothers aren't going to like this"—are we in the third grade? Every scorned woman in the world refers to her old man as being a child, but realizing this does not help when your ex-old lady is calling you a little boy. I guess that makes her a child molester.

L. could always beat me at arguing, not that I couldn't go there, but because she had an extra ignorant gene or something. At some point, I start thinking about the intellect, meaning wanting to preserve mine through not sounding like I'm on Judge Mabel.

This doesn't work in "shootin' the dozens." You got to fight fire w/ fire. I never did, because that would mean that she won. If only I would compromise my style.

"What style, nigga?" That's what L. would say there. "You ain't nobody, I know you spent a lil bit of time w/ boss, but you ain't all that." She knew that would hurt the most now that I had left NYC and entered education w/ its hallowed, homogenous halls. Yeah the withdrawal from the "hoorah" of the road was a bitch. L. sensed that and targeted my psyche. She's good, but I'm gooder. My talent speaks for itself. She ain't the first scorned woman making light of the talent of her ex, but she was always so far behind compared to my career. Since having Z, she has tried to blame the failure of her ballerina stardom on me, as if at age 30-something, I was the reason she had to "slow down." @#$%^ please! That was her style, trying to flip the script.

I was burnt out from fighting from the divorce some seven years prior. L. still wanted to finish business from back then. I could hear it. Most of all, she wants me to lose my temper. She pulled out all the stops during this recent make-up/fall-out. All this led to a stand off.

I was glad I hadn't proposed again out of reaction to the same news but sad that I had gone backwards and picked L. up, like a cat, not even a kitten, on the door step. Or maybe I picked her up as the mother of Z. As the months wore on, I softened inside. The loneliness was trying to get the best of me. It, like L., just doesn't know who I think I am. So, on Yom Kippur, the Jewish holiday of atonement, I called L.'s personal phone that I hadn't called in months. She didn't answer, and I wasn't surprised, once I realized she was real, I submitted to the idea that this was going to be a fucked-up existence with this chick. What am I saying, it already was—all for that brief period of bliss that I, too, sorely regret. L admitted to me that she had prayed for my death. We laughed it off between drinking and creating another dilemma. Sick, right? Well, she was even more upset this time. I found myself imagining that she was praying for my death even more than ever, and that she might even have a mojo or some shit goin'—you know sistas and shit.

Damnation of Memory

Let us start with the fart off of a dead roach's ass (now detached)—
and the juices to simmer, therein.
Add a dash of rat's piss (add mold) before it gets cold, and that's just to begin.
Now, sweat of pig, rotten fig, and a lump of a decomposed bird.
That's not all, the jobs not done, now run and grab a possum turd.
Now what's needed is some pigeon shit, but it's still not time to munch.
Stir, sift, give it a lift, and add a little snot to moisten the bunch.
Lunch, anyone?

★ ★ ★

The leaves having turned; I looked out my front door in Austin. It seemed that this day held the potential to be the most depressing day of my life. I had seen so many.

Sometimes I wondered how I was able to survive. My life seemed so random and luck-driven sometimes. Yet at the core I knew my decisions were my own. I was spread so thin. There was the sublet in NYC, the mortgage in SC, the child support in DC, beer, smoke, the pay decrease and so on. I was still rolling along like I was making that touring money. My accountability at school seemed to wreak havoc on my psyche.

I guess it was just laziness. Not wanting to "give it up" just yet. I knew I would arrive though. There were periods in my life when things weren't so complicated. Things happen so fast. Ultimately, popularity is based on real or perceived victory, while defeat is viewed through a negative lens.

★ ★ ★

Then M. visited. It was cool. Sexually I needed the experience, but socially I could've done without the "little boy's eyes" bullshit from childhood. Old girlfriends always gotta remind you about some dumb shit from the past. Many women I meet can't really talk two feet into a real topic other than what they do at work or who their sister is dating or something. I pretend that I'm interested. Well, she did tell me I should write a book. And I figure if M. says to write a book, I should. When a person who is always imitating others tells you to do something, you should do it.

The house was owned by a church. Each Sunday I could hear a full Pentecostal service through the thinly paned windows. It was as loud as being physically in church, whether you wanted to or not. Some Sundays it was a welcome relief to hear the old familiar lopsided backbeat of the young drummer supporting all of three chords that the organist knew. The songs the congregation sang were mostly original and never fit the key of the organist, allowing the musical celebrations to sound both folk and atonal at once.

Other Sundays I was not as prepared mentally or spiritually for the abrupt end of silence to my Sunday mornings. Furthermore, I cannot explain to you the feeling of having sex with a girlfriend with the hellfire preacher's voice resounding in my den. At other times I wanted to watch porn (even though it was Sunday morning). It's not that I was trying to be sacrilegious. I just wanted to be in my home as I had been in all my other homes. I had never lived beside a church.

Though I had been raised in the church, I couldn't muster up the humility to go down and join the congregation in an original version of "If the bible is right, somebody's wrong," or "I want to be ready to see Jesus." After all, I was already a member of Abyssinian Baptist in Harlem, New York. Somehow, I had pulled away.

The preacher's evocations always touched my heart no matter what I was doing above the church, reminding me from whence I came. The church was waiting.

Wasn't this just like me, to end up living above the church? In my mind I thought that I was still being summoned by religion to clean up my ways and lead a fuller life.

I had never lived a life in concordance with all the virtues of religion intact. I guess that makes me pretty normal. The irony is that I was raised in those environments and had a firm belief in the principles. I could never fully submit though. As a child I had been saved and baptized between Baptist and African Methodist Episcopal traditions. At age 12, my brush with salvation lasted exactly two weeks before I found myself fondling the developing aspects of my hot young girlfriend behind some tree in the park. I knew that this would always be a struggle. I never could fully submit. My ex-wife could've forced me into a quasi-religious bag if I had let her. I remained semi-committed to my beliefs. I couldn't see where it had done her family any more good than any other family. They still had the same vices and issues as others. There was no way in hell I was going to live a fake religious life for appearances. I truly believe in a universal GOD, but I guess I always felt that my heart was good enough, even if my seat was hot. My dad struggled with trying to balance religion with the flesh. He lost. It wasn't going to be an issue for me to go crazy over; that was my approach.

I could still hear the two chords and the lopsided drumbeat from the church next door in TX, even though I was home in South Carolina. It reminded me of the fact that I was due back in Austin in two weeks.

"I'm gon' F you up!" I heard one of the young boys proclaim as they ran and played circling the church. The kids were out on break from the morning service. The playfulness worked itself up the hill to my front yard. The worst of the bunch started to throw rocks into the street out front. The house trembled and roared as I burst from the never-before-opened front door of the house next to the church. There I stood, in too little a T-shirt and some thin, high-water pajama bottoms. I also hadn't worn my doo-rag the previous night.

So it made for quite the spectacle as I stood, holding my screen door wide open, saying, "Hey! NO rock throwing! … Hanhg? … NO ROCK throwing! … how y'all doin? …"

In chorus: "FiiiiiiiiiiiNE …"

"Okay, no rock throwing!"

"He said, 'No rock throwin',"' one of the church kids translated for the rest as they headed back down the hill to rejoin service. I will not forget the children's horrified look at our encounter. It let me know, for sure, that I was pretty old now. I still felt young, but I had not been exempt from the effects of time.

As the children reentered the church, I heard the reverend proclaim, in a loud, sober and directed tone, "Rejoioioioice! … Rejoiooioice!"

He continued, "Let every thing that have breath, praise the lord!" Again, "Let everything that has breath, praise the lord!" Then, "Praise ye the lord! … Praise ye the lord!"

The women of the church, already simmering, were starting to boil with the spirit at the reverend's declamations. The organist, the two-chord maestro, kicked in. After a drum lead in (ooompa, ooompa, ooompa ooompa), the women of the church broke into song:

[call] I'm gonna praise the lord,
[response] I'm gonna praise the lord.
[call] I'm gonna praise the lord,
[response] I'm gonna praise the lord.
[call] I don't know what you gone do,
[response] I don't know what you gone do,
[call] you and you and you and you,
[response] you and you and you and you.
[call] I'm gonna praise the lord,
[response] I'm gonna praised the lord.
[call] I'm gonna praise the lord,
[response] I'm gonna praise the lord.

Having grown up in the church, I knew in my heart that the reverend was happy that his service had achieved "lift off" for the afternoon.

⋆ ⋆ ⋆

Getting back to that dualistic shit I was talking about some time ago, our second child arrived on January 9 of this year. L. and I were, as usual, at odds. I was not present for the birth. Z. called me later on that day. She asked me the same question her mother asked her mother upon calling D.C. from Harlem: "Guess what?"

Of course I knew, being the adult: "Whuuuuut, sweety?"

"My baby sister was born at 8:13 this morning!"

"That's terrific sweetheart! Is she beautiful?"

"Yezzzzz."

"How much does she weigh?"

"Um, I don't know … Nanna! … How many pounds does my baby sister weigh?" From a distance I could hear my ex-mother-in-law say, in a terse and pious style, "six pounds, three ounces!"

A. was here. I hadn't seen her yet. I still haven't.

Today I woke up thinking about a crucial difference between man and animal, as it relates to procreation. Animals have no rationalization process in terms of ejaculation. In other words, animals do not have sex for pleasure. Conversely, and whether with regard to suspension of mystique or just plain old pimping, I believe that men and women use the orgasm as a means of control. This gets us into a pile of trouble.

On one hand, in holding back, a man can exert the amount of power he needs to (in order to subdue the women toward orgasm, which, perhaps, will foster the emotional attachment he seeks from her). This is not possible to attain for the "minute man." On the other hand, the women can hold back her orgasm, therein creating insecurity in the man—notwithstanding such times as she chooses to expose her vulnerability or, at least, fake it.

⋆ ⋆ ⋆

I sat observing the students standing there: once peons, now standing with clinched jaws and poise—having observed tolerance and poise under pressure—now imitating an imagined advancement. Psychologists say that when you hold in your feelings, you project them onto others. Were these thoughts mere permutations of some insecurity I had developed?

I'm willing to investigate that. For now I'm going to say that if I had come in and really talked from experience, I could have shot 'em down and kept 'em down. That's convenient. I had it done to me and had transcended it.

I don't use it. I know it very well. Besides, I'm just not like that. Leaving room for discovery and truth, I tend to nurture. What does it earn me? Nothing. A smug look? False stoicism? I've seen you around. It's rampant in education. Some jive-ass undergrad workin at Jamba talkin' 'bout, "Hey, I know you. You play trombone. I'm in the drum dept." (which is on the same floor as my office that I have reported to for two years now, as an asst. professor). Workin' back there behind the counter at Jamba, he could not bring himself to simply say, "Hello professor, you play trombone, right?" Again, this is my reward for speaking or nodding politely in the hallways at school. This was my reward for dancing around all the bullshit—pretending not to hear or see so that others may be comfortable. This shit has not paid off.

I see so much negativity in simple relationships, in subtle ways. I try not to contribute. Having avoided the initial conflict (little things in conversation and basic interaction, little tiny things occurring all the time) you still have to pay the piper. When the person you are sparing from constant correction recognizes that you are willing to defer, they see it as an opportunity to go for more.

This juice-punk was, actually, trying to ask me for a ticket to get in the J@LC concert. You see? If I walked around all puffed up, pouty and over-opinionated, I could get my generic "respect package."

The dignity route will earn you a couple loyalists, but mainly a bunch of people suckling your tolerance while gaining strength in a more or less aesthetic fashion; but the thing that you want was earned. Be assured, peon, you will be tested, and it will not be comfortable.

If you be what you is, but you is what you ain't, you isn't.
—Bruh Rabbit

* * *

It was the beginning of summer. *Chivalrous Misdemeanors* had been a huge success at J@LC.

Press Release: *Chivalrous Misdemeanors*

Chivalrous Misdemeanors, a new musical by trombonist RON WESTRAY, is based on and inspired by the literary work *Don Quixote de la Mancha* by Miguel de Cervantes. Although musical masterpieces inspired by *Don Quixote* are mainstays in Classical culture, *Chivalrous Misdemeanors* may be the first composed and arranged for the complex jazz setting. The piece was premiered over three nights in May 2005 at Jazz @ Lincoln Center by the JALCO in Rose Hall.

The work is punctuated with narration and vocal performances in the roles of Don Quixote and Dulcinea del Toboso. The personification of the characters and the composer's personal impression of Don Quixote's state of reality are well represented. Westray is fascinated by the way Cervantes could "turn common conversation into literature, shedding light on human fallibility." For Westray, this is one of the key points of convergence between *Quixote* and jazz.

Unlike classical forms born in the parlors and palaces of Europe, jazz is based in the blues, and no more common a language has ever been spoken. Yet, from this fundamental vocabulary, art is born, Monk is born, Bird is born, and complex long-form, cohesively themed works on the human condition are born.

Chivalrous Misdemeanors consists of 23 selected tales derived from the famous novel. The tales put to the listener the question, which must certainly have arisen before undertaking this musical adventure: How can a jazz composer conquer a subject like Cervantes' *Don Quixote*? To the uninitiated it is perhaps a reasonable question; a work of this magnitude would seem more at home in a long-form classical context, as has been demonstrated by Strauss and Telemann, to name a few. But that, like one of the central themes running through Ron Westray's *Chivalrous Misdemeanors*, is a misperception.

Composer, arranger, and renowned trombonist Ron Westray insists that a Jazz Quixote is not only possible, but is long overdue. To be revised for its second performance run, the piece is still twenty-three movements, but with a newly edited abridgment, encircled by artful incidental music. As with the original score, the new version is performed in less than two hours, resulting in a condensed, complete experience.

One of the central themes in *Chivalrous Misdemeanors* is delusion—Don Quixote's singularly peculiar perceptions of the world around him and his penchant for action, based on those perceptions. "That is jazz," Westray would maintain. By virtue of an acute social awareness and a preference for the esoteric, the jazzman has historically represented this model. The jazz musician thrives on ideas and ideologies; this person is, by nature, a romantic. The task of the jazz musician is to approach a piece of music with his own Quixotic vision and take to arms in the form of improvisation, based on his/her own perceptions. In this sense, the jazz musician requires empathy from the listener, as does our hero. The avid listener follows the musical ideas of the performers as they transform sound into social and psychological metaphors.

Don Quixote reacted in opposition to 17th century Spain and its refusal to adhere to the ostensibly superior imperatives of an idealized time past: the Middle Ages as depicted in chivalric romances and in the lives of saints. Comparably, eras past seem to signal some providential unity between diligence and reward. Presently, the jazz musician prepares and presents his sonic emblem based on a premise that, arguably, only prevails in retrospect: Preparation Equals Opportunity. Like our hero, the jazz musician is at once heralded and unknown, but always inspired.

Together, the delusional and the romantic are the impetus behind *Chivalrous Misdemeanors'* two primary musical devices, consonance and dissonance. Dissonance (disharmony) represents our hero's knack for detachment from reality, as it does the jazz musician's proclivity toward chaos and complexity. Consonance (harmony) represents our hero's ability to be understood and the jazz musician's adeptness in logic and rationale. Westray brilliantly illustrates these neighboring conditions of Quixote, weaving seamlessly between the two over the course of the performance.

Like Cervantes' brilliant and playful critique of the vain books of knight-errantry, Westray sees his composition not only as a delightful musical tale in and of itself, but as an opportunity to incorporate and parody both classical approaches to DQ and jazz's approach to itself. The composer manages to expose the wit, irreverence and tumultuous reality of the central character without resorting to outright mockery. Cacophony and simultaneous harmonic complexity present a challenge to the listener, displaying invigorating compositional intricacies as an emblem, all the while inveigling the musicians to execute their convictions within the "Quaint Cloud-Koo-Koo-Land of La Mancha."

★ ★ ★

While preparing the abridgment for my Opus, Chilvarous, *I consulted my good friend Mike Romoth in Denver. Mike is a good writer and he offered some wise counsel.*

I'm kind of reading your position on the Don Quixote thing as you've bitten off a big bite and you're still trying to see if you can chew it all. I'm assuming you're still kind of in the development stage, so I'll throw out a couple of things you should consider at this point going with some of the stuff we talked about on the phone.

The most important thing is that you have to fall in love with what you are writing. That's why you pursue the Immersion. You must look for the noble, misguided Don in the world around you. Believe me, the story is there. That hopeless, heartbreaking love of a foolish old man for some barmaid he can never have. The crazy things he does to prove his love, his nobility. The Don is an old man trying to prove he is still a young knight on a horse, saving the world. He is a man so lost in his dreams that reality absolutely does not exist for him outside of these dreams. There is no fool like an old fool. I sure felt that to the bone with my last girlfriend. He doesn't see himself as a decrepit old man, but the rest of the world does, and that is essential. Go out to the bars and see how the way older crowd still dolls themselves up. You can learn a lot about what you want to write and say from the world around you. I'm actually fairly negative on the idea of just making things up. The best writers are keen observers of the world around them. That's where the emotions are. They take what they see and focus it down into what people call art. But all of it is derived from life.

Setting will be important. It brings up the issue of cliché right away. If you want to do a conservative take, you can go with a simple retelling of the story in its own time and place. Of course, an adaptation to another time and place and culture is what would make the project much more interesting. It can really be just about anywhere at any time. A modern setting (anything from roughly the 1900s onward, I'd say) would be nice for the art vibe. Could be a jazz or blues world setting, easily, from just about any time. Find something that excites you. Something that chips in to world culture as your own take on this story. Don't be afraid to try something challenging. Trust that your talent will rise to the challenge.

Clichés are the bane of the writer and must be avoided like the …! The idea for the artist is to create something new. And that means new. Don Quixote does not have to do battle with any windmills. He can get into a fight with some big guys who are windmilling their arms as they kick his ass. Your references to the action in the original text can be this subtle. Believe me, a literate audience will not only get it, they will love it. Or the windmills can be dancers.

So, too, with all the other aspects of the story. Simply by using the names for the characters, you will have summoned up enough reference to the text that everyone will feel the cultural reverberations from whatever story you create to tell the tale of an old fool who sets off to live the fantasies of his youth.

Let me know if you find these types of comments useful. If you like what I have to say, print this up and look at it again as you get deeper into the text. It's kind of like a long meditation to pull off one of these projects. Get into it as deeply as you can. Come up with ideas for places to observe. When you see it in the world, you will feel it. Then, the writing becomes easy.

—M.R.

★ ★ ★

The GURU Frank Lacy (we call him Roots) had lived with me, for a short time, during his time of need. We became great friends and it was great to hear from him intermittently.

The Big Band, World Tour.

Don Negro-tray,

HEY RON! I've been good, man. Got a LOT to convey to you … been a while. With me … JUST got to the point I wanted to be at concerning my exile in Europe after 5 years being here.

The WORLD is my NY NOW. I'm touring (mostly as member of quartet, quintet, and a few festivals) throughout the world (got connections in Italy, Spain, Iceland, Germany, UK, Holland, Belgium, Russia, Ukraine, Siberia, Bermuda, France), and trying to get in Australia, New Zealand, Cameroon, Mali, South Africa, and Senegal. And the States, of COURSE.

I'm like making 200–350 Euros a gig … anywhere to about 250–1000 dollars a gig internationally, as well as being in ALL the Mingus groups, and doing MY things around Paris (big band, small groups), and the BULLSHIT 50–100 dollar gigs in the States. Add that ALL, and I say AGAIN, I'm GOOD, man … for a BLACK MAN (NEVER can be ENOUGH).

Working on 2 studio projects in the R&B vein. One with this drummer producing it named Dennis Davis (played with Stevie Wonder, David Bowie). I'm gonna shop it in the UK (got some people waiting on it) and putting a project together with some Australians to tour there and New Zealand. Sue told me that the gig you used to have's going SOUR, man. She said that she had a meeting with Wynton and Todd Barkin. Sales have went way down for the concerts there, and the money's been cut in HALF. She's gonna do the Orchestra and Epitaph there in the future. Andre said the money for the band's been cut CONSIDERABLY also he's out the band to teach and he's doing that SF Jazz Collective gig. Heard them on TV at the crib … a concert in Poland. It was CUTE.

As soon as I get down there, I'll look you up. When will you be up north, or back to your home in South Carolina, or in Texas? I'll come and hang. Catch a bus to come see you, get a LESSON, hang, talk. Peace, ROOTS

★ ★ ★

Just now, while in the bathroom mirror, I actually had to confirm with myself that I was really standing there as a living man and that I just blinked, that I drive a blue jeep and that I am a composer, and that this is actually planet Earth. Sometimes it seems like it couldn't be this real.

I mean, aside from things we choose to engage in or goals and challenges we set—this nothingness. This used to be the way that I felt back in my mid-twenties, before I started smoking again. The smoke pulled me up from there and answered, "Yes, this is it. Now, make something of it." Now, I had come full circle, some 17 years later, still smoking, but, again, standing in the mirror thinking, *is this real?*

Before that, I was thinking about 1999 when L. and I had our first temporary hearing. I had to fly to NYC right after the hearing in SC for a concert at JALC that night. I sang a little number called "Swing That Music" with the boys, live on PBS, that night. I had the two little parts on the left side, etched in my faded hair cut. This look was a throwback to high school. I wore the two parts, pretty much the entire four years. Except, back then, I was singing Prince, not Louis Armstrong.

★ ★ ★

As I gazed from my hotel window towards the already searing outdoors, I observed a raven as it mercilessly tore the remaining flesh from recent road kill. It was as if this section of the road was part of a huge winding skillet spreading for miles through the bustling city. Though a lover of nature, I was somewhat taken at the ferocity of so natural an act.

My thoughts changed to symbols. The first idea that resonated in my mind was essentially the mortality theory. We are taught to respect death from a very early age. We are even taught to accept our own mortality as fact. Within this subtle silent acknowledgment, I withdrew to the thought of the seemingly mundane rhythm life can take on during less inspired moments … even for presidents, I'm sure. Confident that this was the very smallest price one might pay for being, I resigned to thoughts of love … mostly the unrequited kind.

Well, that brings me to present. Just moments before, I had escorted my ex-family downstairs of the hotel and outside to the car … my car … well my old car before the court order, the divorce. That was no issue. I have plenty of cars. L. and I were civil again after five years of divorce and fifty awkward exchanges over our 5 year old child, A., at the court-ordered location down south.

Anyway, we were cool now, and it felt good. I was in town on a surprise visit to my daughter's graduation from K to 1st. I thought it was a big step, so I was there. Everything went off like a hitch and we spent the night as a family and said goodbye again. I had created something—a family. As with many things in my life, the irony still rested in the fact that we were not a family any more … as family goes. Well, at least things were cool for now.

⋆ ⋆ ⋆

V: Hey Ron,

What's happening? Hadn't heard from you since we left … just wanted to say hi and make sure all is well with ya! G. and I thoroughly enjoyed being in NYC celebrating your occasion and showing our love and support for you.

I must admit that I felt some tension between you and Mom during the entire trip. I won't go into any details because this email isn't sent to lecture or anything else. I will say that Mom has been there for us when we weren't there for ourselves. Whether you care to admit it or not, she gave us our first concerts and shows on the Lane with first class audiences. It all began well before 2005. You know we don't really have any serious heart to heart discussions but if you ever wanna talk to me about anything, you can do that! Life has removed a lot of the sensitivities that were present early on in my adult life. I have had enough hard knocks and divorce court to toughen me up a whole lot. We won't have Mom around another 56 years and I know she is very opinionated and protective even now as we are adults, but she deserves respect and honor. We must honor her. (I didn't say reverence … save that only for God.)

I am hoping that now that your opus is behind you that time will allow you to spend more time listening to other things around you … oops, had to turn up daddy's song "Always and Forever" … it never ceases to amaze me that this song is playing when I am thinking of Dad. Speaking of which, Dad would be so proud of you. I am sure he was at Lincoln Center last week looking down upon you and just smiling away. "Take time to tell me … you really care and we'll share tomorrow together (my favorite verse).

But anyway, let's talk one of these days. We are both adults. I respect your opinions, don't have to agree but respect is due a dog … like Coconut. If we can chat without taking anything personally, let's do it. If it will involve you feeling the need to verbally attack me and my opinions, then let's not talk. I just want to understand what the deal is with you and Mom. She is probably affected a whole lot more then what she is letting on to. I can hear it in her voice. Enough on this, have a blessed day!

P.S. Results from physical were great … all is well!! Cholesterol is way down which I was striving for—Love, V.

★ ★ ★

Something had gone wrong through the years. Mom and I were not close anymore. I couldn't figure out any way to undo the misunderstandings, while Mom brooded and twisted negative facts into fatalistic judgments and sour resolutions. Things seemed as if they could never be the same. Sometimes I wondered, had that chick from '04 put some kind of spell on my relationship with my mother?

K. would always ask me how things were with my mom, as if she was waiting on some kind of confirmation that her spell was working. I would always reply, "swell," no matter how things were going with me and Mom. See, this chick had dolls and shit at the crib.

And it was an uncanny discovery the night I found that one of the dolls was wearing the same outfit I had on—namely, a red and beige plaid denim shirt, some jeans, a pair of leather bucks and a hat of sorts. She remarked at how unbelievable a discovery it was. We laughed it off and got horizontal on her already worn-out leather couch. There was also a doll in the figure of a mother on a facing shelf. Cliche, black-expo-type dolls, but well made though. And the mother figurine resembled my mom, with those Harriet Tubman like features of my mom's tribe. So looking back, I can see this chick being into some shit like that.

And now my relationship with Mom was deteriorating like a renegade meteor. We were opposed at all angles. Mom was still talking to me about religion and subduing the flesh. I had developed a shell as I had gotten older and was not always as receptive as she may have thought. I would always react in the way I had observed, which is to cosign in some subtle way that I "believe." Mom has a telepathic sense, as do all concerned mothers about what their children are doing. I think that Mom had maxed out the use of her spiritual binoculars, but, like a child, or an addict, she couldn't stop. Therefore, she exposed herself spiritually, through visions and dreams and voices to all of my exploits. It would always piss me off when in a casual conversation she would blatantly allude to an analogy that resembled the very course of action I had engaged in the night before almost to the letter, never having left her front porch. Like having a genie for a mom—it ain't cool.

I certainly resented Mom for being in my drawers all the time. She had done that I when I was in high school out of sheer responsibility, but she had maxed out in my young adulthood. I would actually accuse her of such, to which she would become incensed, claiming that I can't read her mind, meanwhile she's pimping my thoughts and actions as if I'm still a child. As I have matured, she has matured, and her ways, respectful as they may be, are still up in my shit. So, even this thanksgiving at the ripe old age of 35, it was suggested to me by Mom that I try to flee my fleshy ways. Boy, she's still right too. I just can't stop chasing that squirrel. Joe Westray and Ron Westray, Sr. both had a problem with it. They left early too. Her father was a sport too. She never knew him.

Well, I'm still here. I think that she thinks I'm a time bomb just like them. Joe made it to 60. Pops made it to 32. It's unfortunate, you know? Anyhow, life is hard by the yard, and you got to sketch every inch. Perhaps my sin had stressed the fibers of the relationship with Mom. I don't mind confronting that. I was raised with that post-baptismal guilt complex of the South. You never really shed it. I guess that's what religion is, something to remind you. In my mind, I had transcended that complex. My actions could attest to that.

This is not a confessional! Parents need to be for real sometimes. With exercise, supplements and an occasional prayer, I held up well through the divorce-post-divorce fog. That was a period between 1999 and 2005. I hate writing dates. They become old so fast.

It wasn't physical deterioration, that sagging embouchure, those worry lines, that dehydrated vibration. I guess it was just the number of relationships and the pace at which I managed them that sent my mom off into thinking I was a sex addict.

If I was, I was damned modest with it. But I bet my modesty is another's feast. I had noticed that disparity all of my life. I was raised to get what you want. The amount of business I had managed and the hours of earnest time obviously spent in preparation could never justify the fact that I had left one wife and was still living fancy-free. Being regarded as the foremost trombonist in the world paled in comparison to my reprobate lifestyle. Sometimes in the heat of an argument I would shout, "I'm just a musician!" To which she would cock her head to the side and ask, "Is that what you are, a musician?"—as if "that's all, not a son of God?"—as if because that's not the first thing that flowed out of my mouth, I'm on the wrong course? I guess had I only proclaimed that I was just a son of God at the height of my temper, we would be friends right now.

I guess I didn't want my parent to think anything was ever wrong. This drove me to work a little harder. Things were still very grueling to achieve. I had just taken on a professorship after freelancing for 12 years. My new boss in the Jazz Dept. would always say 11 years. I never corrected him. I suspect he wanted me to. I gotta watch my suspicions though. I'm a little paranoid. Enough to still be alive. Staying alive on planet Earth is not easy to do. We are just as vulnerable as the birds and the bees. I see it every night, well not every night, but that's because I don't watch the news every night. If I did, I would be more nervous than I find myself at present. People get taken out all the time, yo. Life is hard by the yard. You gotta sketch every inch (or die trying).

Anyway, this new pace was kicking my butt. It was just what I needed though. I was back in school. This time, I was on the other side of the desk. My career had changed and my salary had taken a dip. Well, it was starting to catch up with me around the Xmas holidays. All the creditors were chasing me for minimums and my discretionary income fell way below any recent levels. This drove me into a silent, nervous and depressed state. It was very difficult negotiating all my new responsibilities inside academia and juggling several waning bank accounts. Embarrassing comes to mind when I consider the flagrant ways in which I had spent the part of my income I needed now. I only learn the hard way though. Times were hard right then. The place I found in Austin was a rat hole as far as I was concerned, but it was the cheapest rent in Austin and the worst-looking house in Texas. I brought the inside up to specs. The outside of the place looked like a crack house. This two-bedroom was located atop the basement of the church which sat in the adjacent lot.

I've been wanting to work my way back where it all starts. Man, I could barely write this year. I'm so burned out it's a shame. I can't get my Jazz thing up. I'm toast. I need a new car. Then I listened to John Coltrane's *Giant Steps* again. My adrenaline rushed for the first time in months. Ironically, I had recently decided to slow things down in the harmony.

Hearing 'Trane just made me want to play sixteenth notes again. Well, I think I'll still slow it down. I need to hear myself again for the first time.

This is easier said than done, however.

I was also seeing Z.T. and got mixed up with R.O. during this time.

★ ★ ★

ME: Sweetie pie, I'm literally counting the days till I can see you. We are up to two visits. It's going to be fabulous to see you, touch, and love you. In the meantime I'm getting ready for this European tour and I see my reward for working hard will be a trip to be with you my phone and email should be working while in Europe. In an ideal world so I'll try to reach you. Until then be well and know that you are always on my mind. Enclosed is a copy of the benefit concert from last week. The performances were incredible, particularly Marcus Roberts, the Jordan family, Irvin and Paquito. Hope you can find a time to watch them. All my love.

ZT: honey, i wish i were there with you, too! so glad to hear you're getting your work out in … i take it your abs feel better? let me kiss them for you … thunderstorms here in new york but nothing like the thunderstorm we shall bring forth when we're together. right, my love?!
baby, this is a cute and fun animation at the top left of the page … it's of the dim sum brunch at which you were sorely missed. i'm eating, as usual. and my cousin surprised me and took this attached picture of some girl who misses you in every way. xoxo—ZT

ME: how are you? we made it safely and i just came off stage. we had to play the first day we got in. the brevity of this message cannot convey the full range of sentiment regarding my thoughts of us. the amount of words required to do just that exceeds my energy at present. so, i will simply say good night to you and tell you again that i miss you more. i thought to myself earlier, "wow!" if this loses you, think "edgecombe" mornings—wow!
i miss you Z. why? … because you're you, that's all
bon soir,
rkw

★ ★ ★

Hi darling:

How are you?? I'm so happy to be in contact with you!! Finally we could not meet us in NYC, isn't it? That's terrible!! I'm crying since Isobel told it to me … It's not fair!! Sniff.

well, first at all, I would like to congratulate you for your performance inspired in the Quijote, I've heard it was a huge success, and I've read some news interviewing you at the Spanish newspapers (i'll email you the link if you want to have this coverage), and it was strange to read this things about you, i dont know … special, ja, ja:))

regarding me, i'm nowadays at my home in Santander (in the north of Spain) with my family, and I'm coming back to Madrid in a few days (back to the reality) for working … And you? tell me things … i would appreciate to hear from you …

A BIG KISS!! RO

ME: maybe you can meet me somewhere. take a look at this schedule. let me know.—Ron

★ ★ ★

V.G. met me in NYC several times this year. We also travelled together in Mexico while I was on tour. I was seeing the actress K. around this time. She lived down in the 40's, Manhattan. As with all, this was primarily a sexual connection. I was never the type to just be friends.

Most all my interactions had to culminate in sex. That was always my goal.

Chapter 34

Gigs

Jazz at Lincoln Center Orchestra, seasonal events, New York, NY.

The Mingus Big Band, The Iridium Jazz Club, weekly, New York, NY.

* * *

When I first transcribed Mom's journal back in 2005, she was at odds about my interpretations—none of which were mine. My goal was to not disturb, yet codify her wonderful Zaner-Bloser handwriting, countered by an intoxicating scribble that was near impossible to read at times … Overall, very little deduction was required. Nonetheless, Mom maintained for at least ten years that the transcriptions were not accurate.

Mom was aware that I had included the transcriptions into my manuscripts along the way.

The night before she died, we were frying fish and drinking beer with a friend. Mom agreed to entertain the transcriptions one last time. What a thrill—as I read them with the ennui of a dialect-trained actor, careful to place the right twang and strain on the right words, and even imitate her voice, Mom would chuckle as a sign of approval. My dopamine could not have been higher. As I read on, she lent me her attention as if she knew she had to.

Long story short, when I finished, Mom said, "I really enjoyed those … You've got it, Ron. You've really got it." Mom never panders or patronizes; for me, that was a [sure] sign of approval; the approval I had yearned for in 2005, as I meticulously worked, in the "cracked" house, in my spare time, in Texas. I had never changed a word of the transcriptions until the day she heard them again—for the first time.

* * *

alamode

Ice cream or silk?

★ ★ ★

Let your freedom ring.
Don't know everything and I don't do Email.
and I quote …
Any city guy, I'm gonna fascinate you with my correct response.

You send it out, I'll pick it up. I've got a receiver in my mind.
I've got a cup, I'll pick it up. I hear you coughin', I hear you rappin'…
I've got a receiver in my mind.

I hear your wheels turnin' on the road and I know your name … and soon, I'll call your game. Cause, you can't hold me, I ain't tame. I know you like I know my roaches, Mr. Man.—Hamma
Z is in … you can retire your S's. Zurely you can join me for Zupper @ Zevin.
My Zmail address is Zixty … Zuper!—Hamma

Enough—on thos(z)e—You hear that Z?
The Z is end.
Azarri is horse of the year … Told you that … already the plant of the year.

I … Zmail!
you know I told Z is in.
To close out with this word
let me say this—
I'm this technical
and this only is it to me or for me.

This Pen.
That's high-tech where I'm from.
Out here—Z-mail is not for Private People

★ ★ ★

January 2, 2004

Again, Happy New Year to your soul and You … Auld Lang Syne … Horse of the year… Azzari.
Should old acquaintances of an ill nature, whether in thought or flesh, be forgotten and never brought to mind to weaken this bright and possible new year for you and your soul.

The soul is clothed with a body.
Auld Lang Syne. Oh my blessed soul.

As for this written word, it's the same as you've heard, or shall I say listened to:
I buried something in your yard. I burned it … then I buried it.
No, not that—you buried that … I, however, buried something you made to fit
me through your dirty, wrong thoughts.
You are a good person. I love you as I believe … and yet, I know that, even now,
as then, I cannot bear the wrong, dirty thoughts you build for your world.
Bless my soul in order that you elevate your thoughts. What can I do to impress
you as a builder? Select the thought for the day?
Why should I? You want to remember who told you, and you had it not for
yourself. I was sent to deliver, and you pretend to forget even sacred things.
Well, listen. No more free tickets to my show. Everybody knows what I know.
Then, there's no need to call me. Ask anyone.
Ask a wig? How soon you forget. Practice remembering.
Do you remember the lord? Or, do you consider that a given?

★ ★ ★

To Angel

Even After. (you know) There's no more.
We know.
We've spent our time—
but our real time,
I mean what you seek as the first plan is now … and tools…
Ha, no time… It's not like that either, ok?

Even after you know—When you think you know—Look Out.
-
If you like me, it'll show and I'll know …
Quiet … hear the wind blow?

Hold your head over
Rhyme … it's Time.

What about me? …
What about you?

Ask the bell.

Don't tone it out.

The bells got tone.
Rhyme time Hone.

The Bell.

Tisket, Tasket Basket … Ella knew that rhyme …
And the kids loved it first.
Mother Goose got put on a noose.
And the kids?
They're looking for the rhyme
Can you spell it?
I think it should end with an n
Rhyme …
Clear this with your knowledge.
The Hymn Rhymes.
Clear this with your understanding.

"Seen but not Heard"—(note from home)

⋆ ⋆ ⋆

Imperfect expressions of love 3, circa. 2004–2005

you know what?
I don't ever cry and sigh about not having a friend, and more so, not having "a man" here.
Wanna know what makes me cry? When … I'm getting my show ready, and all I need is an attentive but uninterested hand to assist with the props … briefly.
Don't worry about what you think.
Stay attentive but uninterested in my prop.
I'll be looking @ you when you get it.
I cry when I don't have "physical" help. I won't again.
I have discovered that this body is a working way to be around.
Somebody—And not.

A mother knows and must know.
That's why you'll find me here on this simple, wrought iron fence—

purchased way before its time—
with a worm in my beak to divide as needed.

Ain't much—cause much takes a long time.
I don't want much?
I just want a little bit?
Much don't come overnight.
So you're really saying you don't plan to be here?

★ ★ ★

Prop

clear straw from base of wrought iron fence.

No Trespassing:
It's rumored that I'll shoot you.
Since I shot Mr. Watson in the shoe,
decades ago now—
I can only say this—
I value human life
Never killed anyone—
have inspired some and
was injured in return—decades ago.
Of this you can be sure—
No Trespassing Means Just That.
There's just not space to put it all.
Who you want me to call?
I better get humble 'bout now—
if there's such a process as "getting humble"
Now listen here, I know things my dear and
man, if you don't know, you ain't gonna never know …
and Louis said it first.

You think you can trespass without my knowing it?
You see, I'm a woman of solitude.
I'm always working.

WHY NOT YOU?
I'm not an honest woman—not @ all

Oh, you think?
No Trespassing.
I don't pack on the Street
Just a lotta shoulders.
But I think you did.
Top of the page man …
Call it my "sound" in the air.

Something to me for me is why I do it.
In other words, kind is cool. Cool.
You say you've heard that all your life?
Must suggest that listen—interpretations change with your needs.
You ought to ask yourself, "how am I listening now?"
There are things to consider
Birth to 6—your "real" free time.

* * *

7/16/04

This isn't about my office teeth—
I'm not using that set …
It's about now, you, me, and things I can't forget.

Now and Me

This ain't dollar store
This is elsewhere
445 … no jive
It's the same time all over the world for soap girl.

Clean up. Drink Water.

* * *

I met A. around this time. We met in Lubjana, Slovenia. Later she came and stayed with me in Harlem for 13 days.

A.M. and I, from college, were also hanging during this time period.

G. and I hooked up several times during this year, too. I knew her from elementary school. She was recently divorced, too. The one thing I remember about her from back then is that one day she stood up and slapped the sh★t out of me for "playing too much" while sitting behind her.

There was nothing I could do. It was true. Now, some 25 years later, as I watched her achieve "multiples," I thought to myself, "I win … hehehe." We had a nice time a few times, but G. didn't hang around long. I'm not sure why not.

★ ★ ★

Zivjo (hello in Slovenian),

I was talking with a friend who told me that in New York, you can get an apartment almost for free from the Slovenian Cultural Department … so i will try to get it … if i don't get that, can i stay with you?

I was thinking about the end of September, October, or November …?

I asked about your flight … you can come first to London and then from London to Ljubljana, if not Vienna or maybe Italy, that is near enough for me to pick you up with a car.

So when are you coming, this week, maybe tomorrow, today? I have a lot of work to do so you cant come today … i hope you understand …

kisses, A.

★ ★ ★

"D" was an African American women (an MD) that I had been smitten with for a long time. She was smart, funny and gorgeous and now was our time. I was traveling across Europe, on tour, for most of our correspondence. We fell in love via these letters, and we met up when I returned to stateside. It was a very exciting and romantic time for both of us.

How ya doin' Ron? Wanted to follow up on my phone message Monday night … I wanted to forward a snippet of Misty's e-mail to you, but somehow in my reply to her, her original message got lost in cyberspace. The short of it is, she's going to the concert on Monday, Oct. 6th with a girlfriend or two, to return the "favour" of you coming to Thomas' gig. So, I suspect in true Westray fashion, she'll be sneaking in somewhere. But seriously, she did tell me to tell you to look out for her.

[What's up with women using me as a Pony Express delivery service?]

She plans on saying hello to you and meeting Silas. I should tell her to leave my man alone. Maybe she'll bring along some eye candy. I think she may have some knowledge of how to pimp a girlfriend. Catch you later. I have more to share later, but it is late, even for me!!!—D

I arrived in Rome, about an hour ago. It's raining and it's a very romantic feeling this Sunday in Rome. We play tonight, and travel to the UK in the morn. Didn't get many great meals. We've really been movin'!

I haven't gotten any work done. I haven't been feelin' the Don in a work sense, but I feel like I connected with something spiritually in Spain (no joke) I'm poised; and I've been able to shed in other areas like clearing the mind and contemplating the importance of patience and forbearance and forgiveness (daily) to myself and others. I feel good. I feel kinda transcendent for the first time (in twelve years) I could really absorb the reality of who I am and what it means to see the world, and how alike we all are. I guess I could always see the former, but something is more real than ever. I am humbled by the idea of humanity these moments, why? I don't know. I can actually communicate with all people without knowing the language. They talk to me as if I know their language; and I feel as if I do. It's weird. I can find the roots (latin, some french) and have a full length conversation. It's so funny! I am looking forward to getting back home.

Ron

Subj: Re: Is it real … (oh my God) Is it real …

Hey Slick, Are you and furthermore were you too musically evolved to have been doing the smurf to the Doug E. Fresh song (which I allude to in the subject title)?—D

>>>Naw, I was right in the mix.

I know the intro to the song has some musical significance (well, at the very least it is familiar and popular) and I have heard it many times but I cannot tell you it's famous origin. Nor can I write the musical notes to intimate the chords/bars to you. Nonetheless, the hushed chatter over that intro, before Doug E. starts his human beatbox is "Is it real, oh my God"—D

>> So I see!

You sound great. Got your message earlier. Just had you on the brain; Everything's cool. I find that i'm a little distracted over the pending legal matter. Didn't think it would be so un-nerving. But, I guess I'm use to being able to just pick up the phone and solve problems. This one is proving difficult to solve on my own. Got to pay an attorney. Nothing has changed since speaking with you. But, I can't catch up with an entity beyond a f------in' automated message in NYC human resources. Yeah!!! Anyway, that's enough.

D: How goes being with your fellow orphans?
>>> It's life on the plantation—as usual (and a lot of needless repetition)

D: hope you are making some music you can be excited about.
>>> Yeah, there are a few scores I always wanted to play. ie: Gil Evans, Sketches of Spain. We're playing two sides from that session.

D: I remember reading it had something to do with European influences.
>>Basically, it's Jazz music written by white composers; including Igor Stravinsky's attempt at ebony subject matter. ie: "Ebony Concerto"

D: I am a bit envious that you have the natural talent to create something new and exciting even if work doesn't allow you the opportunity. I am searching for my "talent" or natural affinity that will allow me to feel that liberation.
>> That's good to know.

D: I am good at developing or applying skill, but I feel I am still in search of uncovering that innate talent to which I can ascribe a name.
>>Hmm... I understand.

D: Can't believe the week is almost at an end. A. comes to you in a couple days, daddy! Soon your long hallway will be filled with the squeal of delight! Well, the youthful beautiful squeals and smiles of your daughter, that is! Do you like to be called Daddy? Or is baby or Big Daddy preferred?
>>> Daddy's cool.
Yeah, I gotta call to confirm.
Sooner, Slick

Hey you,

Thanks for the good vibes.

My work went well last night.

Amorous thoughts of you accompanied me on my journey, as always.

I wish you were here.

I'm on the Northwest coast of Spain at La Coruna.

I have a fabulous view of the Atlantic which I intend to dive into tomorrow before the gig. The ocean is literally outside the hotel's entrance.

The water is several shades of blue with little rock configurations similar to the configurations you would see sea lions gathering on (no sea lions though). The people gather just the same. The travel was pretty intense and I only got about two hours of sleep before heading to the airport. I'll catchup tonight though. well, I'm thinking of you and hope you're thinking of me too—Ron

D: O mas simplico, mi amor_

Como esta hoy? Bueno, yo espero. Que pasa en tu mundo? Yo quiero a habla tu usted, pero no puedo. Como esta la playa y mare (not sure if that is correct for sea)? Playa is beach.

>> >>uh huh.

D: All right I cannot think and write in Espanol with anymore facility than I just demonstrated. Do you read Spanish? I suppose you got the gist of what I was saying and asking. Mundo is world. Mi corazon de dolci is my attempt to say sweetheart … heart of sweet … the Spanish don't say papi like the Puerto Ricans and Dominicans.

>> that's okay, i get it sweetheart.

Nico IM'd me the other day and I was in the mood to respond. Dee is in Paris and I want her to meet Dee-Dee Bridgewater if she's around. Nicolas told me he'll be playing w/ W in Marciac and he's 10 feet over the moon. Will you be doing that leg off the tour or is W doing that on his own this year? Nico will also be visiting his sister in Barcelona next week. She's mad cool. I really like her and would love to help her come over to the States to work. She's pretty talented to be able to converse in at least 3 languages. I am so limited and have to try and see if she will help bring me along in French.

>> yeah, we are doing Marciac, so i probably will see him.

Back to us … my dad is back from Florida. There is no respite from the constant familial engagement that he and his wife expect. She said, "You haven't called me since we came back." Yikes, I'm losing brownie points!! Otherwise, I am doing well. Is your mom, sister or even A. on-line? Are you conversing with them or do you call when you have to be in touch? It's been a little while since you have been really out of the country … I don't really count Mexico. I am finally doing my paella tonight … I am leaving out the mussels and clams and lobster and rabbit. In V., they put rabbit and/or chicken in the paella. Mine is going to have chicken sausage, shrimp and chicken in it along with the real saffron rice. I am missing the white wine but alas, that should be all right.—D

>> no, unfortunately I can't contact them via email. I probably will not speak with them for these three weeks. It will be a first, but I'm kinda feelin that (no hard feelings). I talked to Z before I left town—Ron
Please write descriptively to me about all the good food you're eating. I love hearing about and imagining well-prepared food. I am a huge huge fan of tapas and some other Spanish dishes.
Baccala (baccalao, may be how they spell it there) is also known as salted codfish or saltfish to Jamaicans as it comprises part of the national breakfast dish of Jamaica. The Spanish and Italians for that matter use it a whole lot—D.
>> no great meals yet. i'm sure they're coming.
How are the performances going? Do I need to sign up to be a chaperone in the future to any young female vocalists? That's a gig I would entertain by taking a sabbatical. I might have to tell Frank I would be his apprentice for a short time. I feel my travel bug coming back! At any rate, I am sure you are enjoying your down time as well.—D.
>> What down time after the gig? I'm tryin to soak it all in.
So far, it's so good,; and everything's lovely. I'm off to sound check. I miss you.
Hasta hablamos, buenos dias
Have a productive day!
D.

Hi you,

So you leave NYC tomorrow? Or at the very least you'll be in South Carolina by Saturday. Will a pound cake or sweet potato pie be waiting for you after deal with your high grass? I am feeling a little overwhelmed by my schedule, unmotivated by my lack of good solid sleep and lack of appetite. I do however feel better when I have oatmeal. It weirdly seems to settle me. I have to summon up some energy to change things. I see the path so clearly for others, why must my vision become murky when I train it on my own destiny? I usually feel a little revitalized in the summer. No such feeling this year … where did the time go?—D

>> day by day we have to inspire ourselves to belief that today is a great day … sounds cheesy, but it works sometimes. don't fret over time past. each day we make a decision to do certain things and they accumulate into a series of days that we like to reflect on, but the decisions you make on a daily basis are relevant to who you are which directly correlates to where you are (spiritually and goal wise) make each day what you want it to be,

and cherish the day past. okay, enough dr. phil … no, no pies … just more tedious tasks as reward …

Have been watching loads of swimming. It is the breast stroke that I thought was the butterfly. Did you see the breast stroke? It looks rather frog-like in technique and is very tiring. I could only do it for 3/4 of a pool's length. I remember just hating the butterfly and somewhat refusing to do it. I hate the sensation of constantly plunging (okay, dunking) my head underwater to surge forward. I just like diving in once and using the dolphin kick to eventually surface towards the other end. Are you inspired to try some different strokes?—D

>>> hey, a little. my problem is consistent access to a pool. it's great in the hotels … how 'bout you? we should swim together sometime.

I hear men and spectators are tuning into women's beach volleyball in record numbers. I heard the Brazil v Italy game was like soft porn. Reports say, the bathing suits/uniforms were miniscule. Do you think Michael Jordan doesn't vote? Oprah tried to contact him to ask him if he ever had to get out of jury duty. She was actually really trying to get out of it. It was a good gamble to pick her. She's seen enough stuff to make her question things. I'm rambling …

>>> it's possible he doesn't vote … she's all the better having gone she says … i agree, she prob. needed a little reality …

You are 9 months away from giving birth to your magnum opus! I cannot wait!! I know all my talk of glad-handing and smoothing the way for great reviews can be a bit nauseating to think of. I know everyone will have to admit you worked your ass of and produced some great sh*t. But remember that the Academy Award Oscar went to Driving Miss Daisy, the same year "Do the Right Thing" came out. Most people stay with the staid and true as opposed to recognizing the truly challenging and magnificent.

I know even your smallest detractors will have to grudgingly give you props; but I want so much for those who like you and respect your work to be given the opportunity to tout your talents!—D

Thank you; you've been more than supportive … I'm starting to get those "will it be great? butterflies now … that's usually a good sign. like you, my summer was not as productive work-wise for me as i anticipated … but as i think of it, summer is never, ever that productive it's the fall and winter for me. i can see the production more clearly than ever, and oddly enough, it think i'm more finish than i realize. or at least that i have done enough work for a complete production. i have 9 months to just clean 'er up! i want to see it first … then display it. as oppose to rushing off the creative press so suddenly. anyway, I've still got a lot o' work ahead for my standard. I've basically been taking a little time to let people get a piece before I go "in."

Dee was no fool when she called me to tell me she got the E.R. gig. She knows I'll put out an informal press release and look for someone with a Nielsen box to ensure her episode is highly rated! I see the Wards throwing a dinner in your honor, replete with a bare-bellied harem girls!

>>> Now you're talkin'. I gotta bond with them more, man!

Physical was a breeze, like the office. checked out well from the office status. Doctor was impressed with my intonation—muscle intonation. He didn't like the six pack a day thingy; they never do. They always look so shocked.

>>>Yes, yes … I'm slipping … What tests did u have done? Did you say you smoked too?

No, but the fatty deposits you were referring to as it relates to alcohol occur on the liver which then turns sclerotic. He seemed almost encouraging when I told him it wasn't tobacco.

We had a nice interview before hand. He seemed to be nice and on the case. He said that I don't need a physical every year, but I think so. My levels will be in next week.

>>>Oh good. a consulting beforehand is a li'l rare these days. They seem to really want to grow the practice. If you are seeing other docs every 3 yrs is good up until the age of 35–40. Then that's when convention says every year; but it is good to stay with one doctor if you can. I would emphasize your travel schedule and they may try and work you in.—D

It's all the more reason *you* should be my doctor. Well, i guess you are in some ways.

D: They call me doctor love don't you know!
I will soon no longer be accepting any new patients
I feel special.

D: I guess I'd be relieved that you don't smoke tobacco after learning you drink a six pack a day!
I see your point.

D: Did he question you on the smoking? How old is the doc?

No; but he gave a facial expression that said as long as it's not tobacco. He actually waved his hand to the smoking—like he didn't wanna hear bout it?

D: Funny! I wonder what the laws are about learning of drug use during a physical in S.C. How old was he, would you guess?

He's an old dude. No, it was like "it's cool/okay." He actually mumbled, "that's okay"

D: Cool

Yeah. i really need that right?

D: Right, right

Subj: Re: m*ss you already!

Hey,

I got home and to work. Called my dad and finally called my mother. She gets real nasty and hostile very quickly. I hate that. But I took care of that and have to unfortunately see her today!! It's hot and humid and that will be an interesting combo. My trip was good.

I really enjoyed spending time with you! Simone, the hopeless romantic, also agrees with Keiko and says we look good together. She thought you were really personable. I couldn't tear myself away from you—whatever! Did I say that? I think I have a little problem developing inertia, whether it is to come see you or to leave you!

Thank you so much for feeding me, it really helped on Tuesday!—D

>> I'm glad your inertia is low on the back end.

I'm glad you want to talk to me and share things with me. It really does take two, regardless of how patient or interested or how nice I ask, it's great that you are willing to open up and talk.—D

>>You have a way with me. I trust you, so.

Am I a bit of a grouch in the morn? Yes, yes!!!! I now know how you felt trying to talk me through the logistics last night and this morning. I take it you don't like to see me stressed or concerned when it can possibly be avoided. Same with me in regard to you. It kinda allowed me to relax and de-stress (as did the morning air and sun) when you got concerned about me making the train. But then I wanted to make sure you became calmer! I think I stress a lot before I start moving and in the late planning stages. But once I am in motion, somehow I expect things to go my way. I needed you at the train station this morning! Thank you so much. You take pretty good care of me as I would have been at a deficit with no breakfast this morn.—D

>> I'm glad i tagged along too. You're lost without me it seems:)

I wish we had more time together. I suppose I have to get my act together and make more time for that.

>> Yes, let's map it out now—so we can have that to look forward too.

I, so, enjoy being "wrapped up" in your love.

You know if you had not stood in the doorway to look for me (us) we may not have connected Monday night as you didn't have your cell phone with you. If not for that, our great time would have started so much later and with frustration!—D

>>I'm always thinkin'—especially when it comes to you. I know how you can be ie: (had it not timed out like you expected) Imagine that vibe. (shiver me timbers) Okay, maybe not that bad.

That was really good and I didn't tell you it was really nice to see you at that very moment. I think because of that I relaxed and wasn't pushing to get anywhere (in the tent). I was happy to have connected with you and all was Kool and the Gang. Dare I say, you made me feel like a woman that was cared for.—D

>>I do care for you; and i'm glad you can feel it.

I didn't have to be the aggressor as I would with less of a man.—D

>> Thank you; you know I love being heralded above the rest.

Thank you and what a relief! It's been a little while since I've been in the role of being able to relax and not "having to" look out for myself in the littlest ways and instances. I think you get me and you're really trying to "get (at)" me.—D

>>Who, Me?

All right more later on the phone I suppose! I'm sorry I missed you last night my darling … I wanted to talk; but I fell asleep. I called over in the morning; but it was to late. I was sad; and I went back to sleep. Then I got these wonderful emails which provided instant re-invigoration.

Have a productive day—D

>>You too, love.

Hey,

Been thinking about our last conversation … wanted to give you my thoughts on it, but couldn't reach you later yesterday. That was bothersome. I was annoyed by you being concerned about my "overblown perception" of your sexual liaisons, proclivities or activities. I don't understand why you need to be concerned with that. Furthermore, I don't think my perception is overblown or all consuming, for that matter. You have made it clear that you are a highly sexual person and have "FSB's." What am I blowing out of proportion? Is it that you think I am keeping myself too aware of those facts? You said that you are not so active in that role now. All right, but I am not the type to concern myself on when you are or are not active in that role. Suffice it to say you have the capacity and that's that. I am not the type to take myself through "changes" based on our level of interaction. You alluded to addressing this sort of issue when the interaction level dips and possibly drops off with someone and things come to a head. I don't think that kind of thing should come to a head. It's a component and facet of this sort of relationship. I don't concern myself with what you are or are not doing on that front. Yeah, I've said it before … we don't have that type of relationship. Frankly, that's not how I interact in any relationship. If I were in an exclusive relationship, I would consider it a given that my man is faithful and that would be that. If I am in a get-together-when-you-want kinda thing, I would know it's a given that both parties are dating or sleeping with others, whether it's active or not. I don't like going on emotional roller coasters when it comes to any kind of relationship. Sure, the intensity level ebbs and flows, but there is that basic foundation of emotional connection ever present.

When we have a discussion like we did yesterday, that's when that stuff comes to the forefront of my mind. Knowing that you'll be seeing me in a week, I would think that's the last thing you'd want me to concern myself with. If you were telling me about your lack of activity to soothe the way, it didn't and doesn't work. That tactic is ineffective with me. And I do think you tell me some things for effect. You have made one such admission in the past and I know you are still capable of employing that tactic based on your comment on the Eva/Philly thing yesterday. Joking or not, you pulled it out and that was funny yet unsettling.

I guess you don't like the way I joke about those things (ex. when you were telling me about your sauna/fireplace hotel room). To be honest, the wish-you-were-here sentiment in that context.

I don't take it seriously; and that's my way of neutralizing it and saying that's an unnecessary comment. If it's sincere, you can just say so and let that go, as will I.

I do think there are a couple times you have reminded me of the boundaries inherit in this "relationship." Namely, you told me that I should be sure to call and talk to you in advance of seeing you in New York. It sprung from us joking, but you were clear to make a point that you were serious. Although, I understood, I wondered why you needed to make it clear. I thought I must have said or done something that crossed a line. I wasn't sure if you thought spending time with you in South Carolina gave me a different impression of things that you wanted and needed to clarify. I wasn't sure why you needed to make that distinction, but I certainly will (and have) adhere to that policy. I don't think you have a responsibility to be available to and for me whenever I call. And that doesn't stop me from calling. That's reserved for the exclusive relationship. I do think it's unrealistic for you to desire or expect of me, the things that come with an exclusive relationship inside of this relationship. If by happenstance you get it, well that's a fluke that may come inconsistently.

I know there were times you wanted to see me during the last 3 months. The fact that we didn't see each other would not vastly effect our relationship, I thought. Am I wrong? We did maintain some level of connection. I know you did make it painfully clear at times that you just wanted to physically be in the same place. I know my responses were inadequate at those times, but I couldn't give any more than that. I do care about you and you have no idea how much I wanted to see you in your glory during the Ornette Coleman performances. I really wanted to hear your arrangements and see you conduct. But I guess that desire is more friend-like than romantic. All the desires and behaviors you want me to express, I am not sure that I give all of that in this context. If you want more interactions like we had in Boston (as that was the most recent), then I can certainly give that. In fact, I think that will be the norm. The times in South Carolina and New York had similar elements as well. There was just more time behind Boston and involved in Boston.

My only concern with you and our times together is that I have to be uber-aware to clear the decks. I think you are very concerned with making sure I want to be with you and only you. I guess that's valid, but by the time I show up that question should be out of your mind. Neither one of us would do well feeling restricted or constricted, I think. I know I don't. At the same time, I want to be able to do other things when I am in your presence or spending time with you.

> You mentioned at one point in the last 2 days, that you were confused by me. That is not my intention. I don't know if my approach is too regimented. All I know is that it doesn't leave me open to confusion. The bottom line intent is clear and understood. Let me know if there's something you need cleared up.
>
> Now that I've let all of that out … does it read like venting? Right now, I am looking forward to seeing you and I am sure I will be anticipating your arrival to the Golden Gate City as the weekend approaches even more. I might even try for the Napa sneak peak. Looks like I will be doing Sonoma or Napa Saturday.
>
> See you soon, D.

★ ★ ★

ME: hi you! you good?

D: hey, yeah.

ME: you?

D: I was thinking fondly of you just moments ago. I'm just surfing (something I never do).
I talked w/my gyno. I have 4 tumors; the largest is 8 cm (about 3" in diameter). I go in Sept. for another ultrasound. I will just chill out about it and be watchful of any pain. So, for the sake of science I have to attempt having sex w/you again!

ME: Yay!! You know how athletic I can be. Now, I've gotta curb my whole dynamic and dig on the whole science vibe, right? Actually, I'm just the man for the job!

D: Oh, I forgot about your gymnastic like moves! Well, I don't know how fragile I am. (I get it, you mean fragile in that respect. I see) But yeah, I like it slow and gentle at first anyway.

ME: Bah, Bah, Bah. Ok, I'm going in!

D: Well, you'd be a good indicator. No need for me to dick around, so to speak (with smaller less painful candidates). I should go for it, right?

ME: Yes, you should. I wholeheartedly agree.

D: I should know my threshold …

ME: Sure you should.

D: YOU ARE, WHOLLY, SILLY, and you know that; I enjoy you.

ME: And I, you!

★ ★ ★

Hello from Slovenia,

I was really happy when you called me. I had a really nice time with you and was thinking about you a lot. That night I went back to that club just to say goodbay to my friends, but the music was so beautiful that I had to stay and dance even though I was so tired. We had that festival that i was telling you about and it was great, this year it was just one day, next we will do it longer.

I'm also helping at my fathers company and they all went on a holiday so I'm alone and have a lot of work to do. At the moment I'm writing a new comedy about love and I think it is going well. On Thursday I'm going to Serbia to one Balkan Brass festival—good music, great people, and I will probably do a fire show there.

About me coming to nyc … ticket is really expensive and i'm still a student; so, I don't have a regular job and that means no regular money, but I'm doing this big project that should bring me some good money that I first meant to spend for Cuba, but nyc became more important at one moment …

So I think I wrote more than enough for the first time, I'm looking forward to hear you, see you, read from you …—A

ME: I look forward to seeing you again. anytime you want to come to NYC, I will fly you in.

⋆ ⋆ ⋆

D: Ron,

How are you today? I know a sweet thoughtful missive from me is overdue, well this ain't it! Kidding! Now that I have relieved myself, of any pressure, I can relax and just get to it. I actually planned on sending you a little note to the Omni in LA. But as the weekend was fast approaching and I had not composed anything, I realized that my idea was going to remain a sweet thought and a missed opportunity, this time!

I wanted you to know that it was good seeing you last weekend. Somehow we managed to squeeze in a much interrupted 24+ hours. I actually didn't mind though. I got a chance to do just about everything I wanted to do and I unexpectedly enjoyed all the bonding I did with

Keiko. There wasn't a lot of me and only me time, however I did have a relaxing pace in which I didn't feel overwhelmed with someone else's presence and "stuff." Although, Keiko has made it clear that she wants to come here to visit. Geez, I feel the pressure to extend an offer and to entertain. I just don't think Connecticut is that great of a draw. I would be inclined to couple it—her visit, that is, with going to NYC or to some place in Boston/Cambridge or with going to Martha's Vineyard. We shall see.

I was really looking forward to seeing you and alas seeing you in San Francisco (and Napa) did not disappoint. You looked really good and I didn't feel any of that let-me-check-out-where-she-is-coming-from kind of tension. I didn't get enough time alone at the reception to stand back and check you out. It was good being around you. I felt like things were loose, comfortable and easy-going between us. I felt a tenderness from you and I hope you got the same or as much from my interaction with you. I was definitely wishing to have more time with you in San Francisco. Although would you have wanted to walk some of the city with me? See a little of Chinatown? Emphasis on the little as I am sure it would have been very crowded. I like being able to sense, see and feel the energy of such a place but I don't like being encapsulated by it.

Are you taking pictures with your digital camera? Are you uploading them onto disc or a free web-based photo album at such sites as yahoo.com or ofoto.com? I am bringing in that disposable camera of mine to get my pictures processed. I am excited to get the CD with the pictures. I'll be able to forward them without relying on snail mail. Yes, this camera has pictures from my South Carolina visit. Can you believe it?

So when is the next time—that I'll see you? I know you like that I am asking. After this tour you are back in South Carolina? You see A. and then off to Savannah? Hmmm … that puts us im mid-April?

All right, I am going to do my grocery shopping and other miscellaneous errands as Monday will be the last good day weather-wise. The sleet and snow starts on Tuesday. I see you have nothing but fog/smog and heat in Southern California.

Have you decided to keep mum about the glaring omission from the library of songs to be played in México? I suppose you would have to say something non-challenging that you want to be overheard that praises the song that was chosen instead of a longer possibly more difficult yet more apropos suite. I hate "office" politics!

You know the guy who had a son with fabulous eyes at the septet concert in Tanglewood? He's just now thanking me for the pictures of him, Nate (his son) and Skain. Sounds like he wants something.

At any rate, catch you later. I am going to forward this e-mail I got from Misty's Parisian jazz musician friends we saw at the Standard. Jean has a good manager. The interesting tidbit is that he mentions an upcoming performance with Marcus Roberts.

Be well—D.

D: Ron,

Como esta, papi? Bien? Pensado (now that I kinda made up to mean—I thought so). I realized when I talked to you the other day in México that I those calls or brief hellos are cheating me out of some wistful yet meaningful written musings. In fact, it has been a while!! Well, I am looking forward to the bounty of saved word attachments that will be sent forth once you're on-line.

Shoot, you think you're in Aqua-caliente (s) now! That's tepid in comparison. Seriously though, you have been slacking in that regard. You must think you got me or something. Should I consider myself woo-ed? At any rate, for whatever reason I feel the need to return to this medium, if even briefly. I do feel Spring coming on which makes me feel a bit free-spirited and energized yet i also feel the nesting instinct alive and well. Perhaps this is systematic of winter's unrelenting grasp on the Northeast. Either way I do find myself reaching out to folks through the written word and wanting that sentiment in return. Should start with my own family, huh?

Yeah, that's also a very serious and recurring thought!! Like I told you before, I am trying so hard to get a tight grip on my appetite/diet. It, my appetite, that is, just isn't really there and I find myself throwing away good healthy perishable foods that have gone bad.

I feel like there's a switch in me that somehow got turned off that I have previously disregarded as superfluous. Now I realize it should have served as an indicator that something needs to be addressed and it is quite more than a convenience. Sort of like a refrigerator light. Not a big deal when it goes off and doesn't come back on again. However, it is a convenience most people employ and take for granted. The fact that it doesn't work might be a source of mild irritation yet it may also be a signal that the refrigerator needs a little maintenance check-up.

At least I am operating from a source of a little knowledge of how to address my appetite problem, but the task still seems a bit daunting and sometimes counterintuitive to how I have been operating for many years.

Like your hotel card and Don Quixote suggests, sad times with food are less … By not eating well I am setting myself up to fall into a ditch when a bump in the road comes along. How poignant and relevant is that quote. What a reminder it is that there's always something in the little things—God.

Yes, my spiritual side is coming out. I think little things like that hotel card serves as a reminder that we are God-like and full of creation and creativity. A reminder that we must remember to create what we want and that we are fully capable of creating anew … for ourselves. Dream, create and move … I should save this note and send it to myself. I need to read this reminder everyday!

Wow!! I feel like I have digressed into something else, not intended but noteworthy all the same.

Anyhoo, as Deidre would say, I look forward to hearing from you. I suppose any medium will do.

I am excited to hear more about México and your impressions. I think this tour was really good in that you all played some music you haven't played in a while and got a good mix of that West Coast vibe.

Catch you later, D

★ ★ ★

The funniest thing happened today … I met this elderly white couple in the airport and their last name just happened to Westray. Here I go bragging about my friend that I met every bit of two minutes ago, "Oh, I have a really good friend with the same last name." The elderly man immediately said, "He plays the trombone right?" I was so shocked. I said "yeah, as a matter of fact he does and how do you know that?" He said his wife searched her family tree years ago and your name came up. They knew you were from South Carolina and everything. She said you once played in England (that's where they're from and live) and a friend phoned them and asked if they knew you. Isn't this a trip????

Anyhoo, they wanted me to give you their number and they said the next time you're in England give them a call. They're great people. I don't think they meant any harm whatsoever. It would be nice for you to call them. See, I didn't forget about you. Shout me out when you get a chance … Good day mate—Lady D

★ ★ ★

Comments

Hey there, ran across your site on the web. I'm Joe Westray's grandson.

You don't hear a lot about this great man; and as much as I know, I would love to know more.

I met Grover Mitchell months before he died. he was floored when he found out that I was Joe's Grandson. Ahmad, the same (due mostly to the long friendship he had w/Joe). Thanks for your contribution to his legacy. If there's anything that I can do or take part in, let's brainstorm.

My grandmother, Joe's ex, seems to think we are twins in all ways. (June Geminis). I guess we are.

I have a few of Joe's personal items down south (the organ for instance.) My grandfather was a real part of my life; At his funeral in 1980, I was 10 years old.

Joe and his son, Ronald Sr, my father, also a musician, never lived to see me become a well-known professional in my field, jazz. I noticed that you have Joe's interview listed as 1997.

How does that work (since he died in 1980)? Perhaps that's when it was filed? I would love to have a copy.

Ron Westray

Dear Mr. Westray,

Thanks very much for inquiring about the interview. It was fascinating to hear about your memories of your grandfather … The interview is, in fact, with Joe Westray's sister, Cathy. The date is 11/13/97 and the interviewer was Charles ("Chuck") Austin, who is President of the African American Jazz Preservation Society of Pittsburgh.

I am including Chuck as a "cc"on this note. I am sure he will be interested in talking to you at some point. Meanwhile, we will be happy to copy the transcript of the interview for you.

We would appreciate payment in advance. If you have any questions, please write to me directly at the above e-mail.

Best wishes, David Rosenberg

★ ★ ★

I never requested the transcript.
I thought they would be glad enough to hear from me to send me a complimentary copy.
This is around the time I started to wonder whether, or not (if at all), legacy suffices.
If so, why not now?—For me—When it mattered.

PHOTO SECTION

My sister and me with Dad (*ca.* 1972–73).

Leroy Leman Bush—Mom's father.

Mom's side of the family: Barnwell, South Carolina, 1960s. (Mom is the oldest of the cousins, more like an aunt.)

Musicians in Crawford Grill

Singer and Joe Westray Band.
Woman wearing light-colored gown with eyelet bodice singing behind microphone, with Joe Westray standing beside her and in front of his band, including George "Ghost" Howell on bass, Pittsburgh, Pennsylvania, 1943.
(Photo by Charles "Teenie" Harris/Carnegie Museum of Art/Getty Images.)

Dolores Ware performing at microphone between Joe Westray on guitar and Robin Webster on tenor saxophone in Crawford Grill No 2, Pittsburgh, Pennsylvania, 1954.
(Photo by Charles "Teenie" Harris/Carnegie Museum of Art/Getty Images.)

Joe Westray Band.
Group portrait of the Joe Westray Band, with Joe Westray on keyboard, William Biggs with tenor saxophone, Guy Hunter with saxophone on right, George "Ghost" Howell with bass, Rod Hawkins back left, drummer "Smokey" in back center, Stoney Gloster with trumpet and Reva George wearing a light-colored dress, Pittsburgh, Pennsylvania, 1945. (Photo by Charles "Teenie" Harris/Carnegie Museum of Art/Getty Images.)

My grandfather: Joseph Benjamin Westray, Punxutawney, Pennsylvania, 1948.

Me and my father, at Battleship NC, weeks before his death.

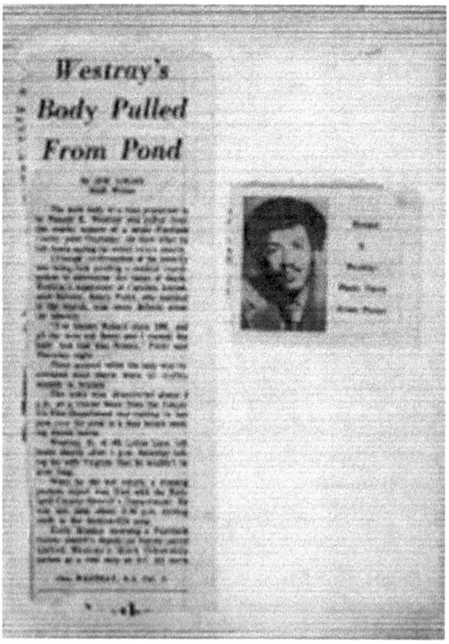

Westray's Body Pulled From Pond

Westray Found

The State, newspaper article, 1976.

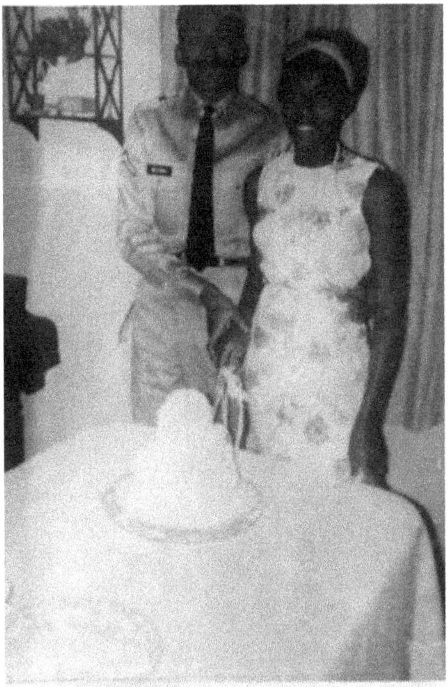

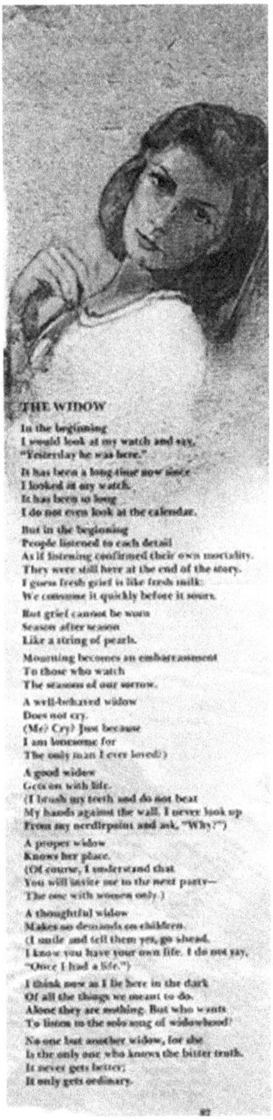

THE WIDOW

In the beginning
I would look at my watch and say,
"Yesterday he was here."

It has been a long time now since
I looked at my watch.
It has been so long
I do not even look at the calendar.

But in the beginning
People listened to each detail
As if listening confirmed their own mortality.
They were still here at the end of the story.
I guess fresh grief is like fresh milk:
We consume it quickly before it sours.

But grief cannot be worn
Season after season
Like a string of pearls.

Mourning becomes an embarrassment
To those who watch
The seasons of our sorrow.

A well-behaved widow
Does not cry.
(Me? Cry? Just because
I am lonesome for
The only man I ever loved?)

A good widow
Gets on with life.
(I brush my teeth and do not beat
My hands against the wall. I never look up
From my needlepoint and ask, "Why?")

A proper widow
Knows her place.
(Of course, I understand that
You will invite me to the next party—
The one with women only.)

A thoughtful widow
Makes no demands on children.
(I smile and tell them yes, go ahead.
I know you have your own life. I do not say,
"Once I had a life.")

I think now as I lie here in the dark
Of all the things we meant to do.
Alone they are nothing. But who wants
To listen to the solo song of widowhood?

No one but another widow, for she
Is the only one who knows the bitter truth.
It never gets better;
It only gets ordinary.

(Above) Mom and Dad's wedding reception at my Granny Neal's house (Mom's mom). (Below) Mom and Dad at Sesqui Centennial Park (Cola, South Carolina). (Right) The Widow: My Mom's Plight.

From left: Vernal Barnette, Ron Westray, Sr., Mom and Carol Barnette (Dad's step-sister) (*ca.* 1973–74).

Left to right: Ron Westray, Sr., Ron Westray, Jr., Virginia Westray, V. Monique Westray and Carolyn Barnette, Pensacola, Florida (*ca.* 1973) (Though trained as an EMT, dad had never learned how to swim.)

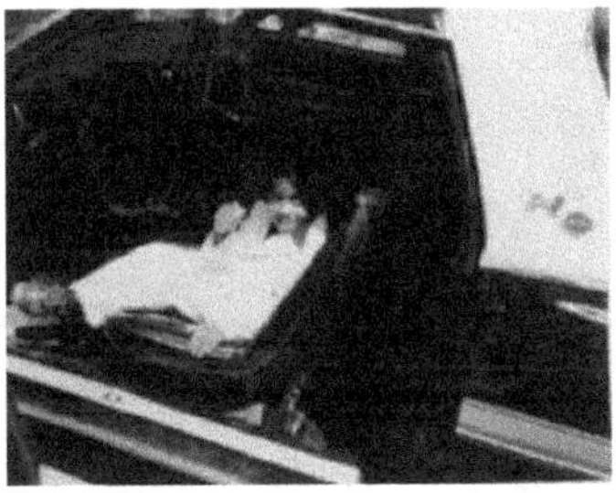

Sitting in Dad's 1975 Hurst-Olds.

Mom and Dad—the good times.

Left to right: Richard, Cousin Josie, Mom and Michael Bourne (*ca.* 1979). Richard is an engineer and Michael, his partner, teaches French at the same school Mom does (Pelion, South Carolina). My sister and I attended there until seventh and fourth grade, respectively. We were the minority, as was Mom (the only black teacher at the school). Cousin Josie (deceased) was a teacher too.

This is Mom and me, standing in the front yard of the home Dad purchased for her, 445 Liston Lane, in the Farrow Hills Subdivision of Columbia, South Carolina. I'm 13 years old in this photo and just home from public school.

Rob Middleton (a trusted friend of Mom's) showed me the meaning of strength.

This is Allan Horney (L), my graduate professor on trombone, and Robert Weidner (R), my music research and analysis professor. These men really helped me build a work ethic.

Mr. Sherrod (*ca.* 1980).

"Pete" in the 1980s.

Freddie Grace and Wille Lyles (my mentor), high-school band instructors.

Tim Hinton, my undergraduate trombone instructor.

"Resting" during a tour of Spain, 2005.

Me and Al McClain (1994).

Me and L. (2018).

Me and A.M. (1994).

Al Fulton, undergrad, Jazz Band.

Ronald Sarjeant, undergrad comp. instructor.

Me and my sister, V. w/ Dad in Hospital, c. 1972.

Granny Neal (with all her great-grandchildren), c. 2009. Mom is back-left in the photo.

Me and Sis,V. @ TWF c. 1995.

Me and my daughters, c. 2009.

Me,V., and Mom c. 2008.

Mom c. 1981.

My Daughters c. 2012.

My Sister, V., c. 1982.

Ron-Ron, age 3, c.1973.

Ron-Ron, First Grade Art, age 6, c.1976.

The Wooden Flute Jazz Club, c. 1995.

Some Things I Own (and Have Owned)

1984 CB650SC'84 Nighthawk 650 engine. Engine: 655cc; valves: 16-valve hydraulic valve adjuster system; power: 72 hp; colors: black, candy bourgogne red.

The Honda XL80S-82 was sold in 1982 and was available in one color: monza red. The seat was black with a white "XL" logo. The "80" logo on the side cover was white, while the "S" was red. The frame was red. The engine was an 80cc OHC single cylinder with a four-speed transmission and manual clutch.

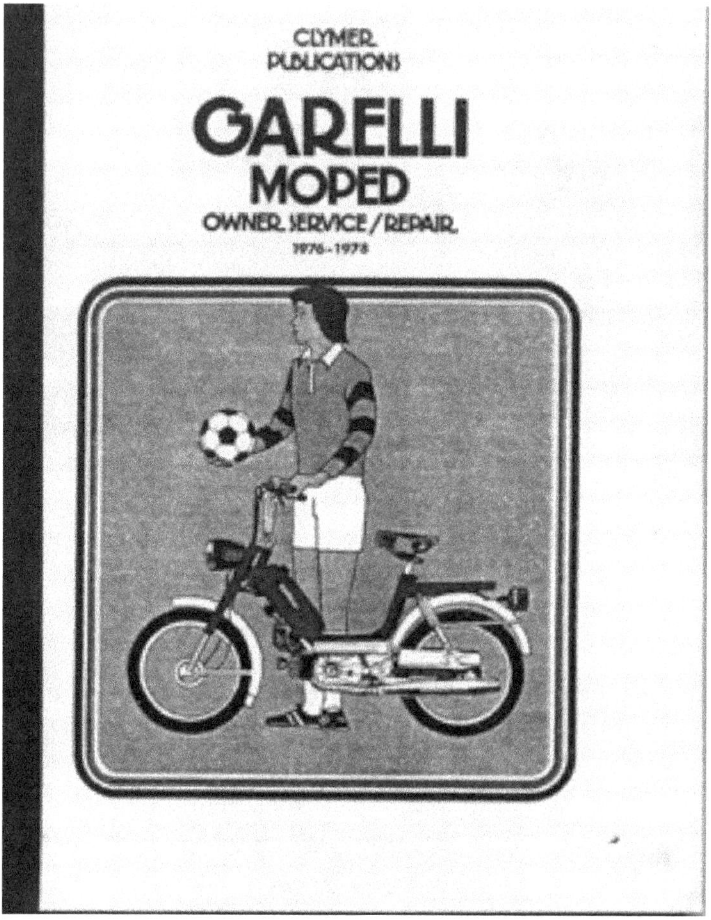

Garelli, an Italian manufacturer of mopeds and motorcycles, was founded in 1919 by the engineer Adalberto "Alberto" Garelli. The company produced small displacement two-stroke motorcycles and mopeds until it closed its doors in 1987.

Other Things

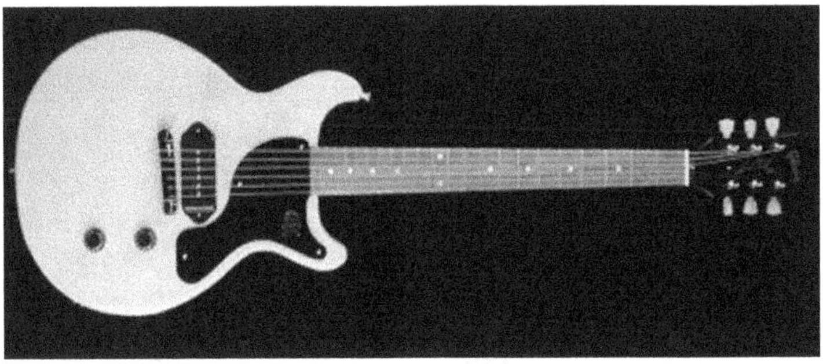

Gibson Billie Joe Armstrong Signature Les Paul Junior Double Cutaway Electric Guitar: The Gibson Les Paul Jr. was a solid body electric guitar introduced in 1954 as an affordable, entry-level Les Paul. It was first released with a single-cut body style; models with a double-cut body style were later introduced in 1958. This is just like Dad's guitar and is in pristine condition. Dad's is in good condition too.

Hammond C-3 organ, manufactured by the Hammond Organ Company (1935–85). Effects: vibrato, reverb, harmonic percussion; external control: amphenol connector to Hammond Tone Cabinet or Leslie Speaker. This is just like Joe's Hammond C3 and is in pristine condition. Joe's is in good condition too.

Four-octave clavichord. I own a similar one built in 1967 by Robert Oetring, London. It was given to me by the equipment man at UT Austin.

Marantz Model 2245 Receiver. Specifications: tuning range: FM, MW; power output: 45 watts per channel into 8Ω (stereo); weight: 34.5 lb; year: 1971.

Perpetuum Ebner 2040 full size turntable. VTG Turntable Perpetuum Ebner PE 2040 Germany. 33.3 RPM, 45 RPM, 78 RPM; Edge Driven Drive Type; Stereo L/R RCA.

Kimball 200 Spinet Series Model 200, 1962. 2-44-Key Manuals; 13 pedals; vibrato & reverb sustain percussion.

Chapter 33

Gigs

With the JALC Orchestra:

Kennedy Center for the Performing Arts, Washington, DC.

Theatre des Champs Elysee, Paris, France.

Les Grands Interpretes, Toulouse, France.

Concertgebouw, Amsterdam, Holland.

De Singel, Antwerp, Belgium.

Konzerthaus, Vienna, Austria.

Usher Hall, Ediburgh, Scotland.

Colston Hall, Bristol, England.

The Anvil, Basingstoke, England.

The Dome, Brighton, England.

Poole Arts Center, Cambridge, England.

Barbican Theatre, London, England.

De Montfort Hall, Leicester, England.

Alice Tully Hall, Lincoln Center, NY.

Supper Club, New York, NY.

Madison Civic Center, Madison, WI.

Chicago Symphony Hall, Chigago, IL.

Grand Theatre, Wausau, WI.

Fox Cities Center, Appleton, WI.

Civic Center, Peoria, IL.

Foelinger Great Hall, Urbana, IL.

Wharton Center, East Lansing, MI.

Peristyle Theatre, Toledo, OH.

Millet Hall, Oxford, OH.

Hulbert Circle Theatre, Indianapolis, IN.
Norton Center, Danville, KY.
Farthing Auditorium, Boone, NC.
Brooks Center for the Performing Arts.
Gaillard Auditorium, Charleston, SC.
Symphony Hall, Atlanta, GA.
Community Theatre, Morristown, NJ .
Miller Theatre, Columbia University, New York, NY.
Bone Structure w/ Wycliffe Gordon, Kaplan Penthouse, NYC.
Bone Structure w/ Wycliffe Gordon, Kansas City Jazz Festival.
Wynton Marsalis Septet, national and international touring.

⋆ ⋆ ⋆

So dear Ron,

I understood your comment about earlier this century … despite some popular belief, I am a glass half full kinda girl. Your "depends on the arrangement" comment was not made any clearer to me, however. Do you mean "depends on the arrangement" so you never had trouble kicking a babe out? I know what you mean. There should always be a known arrangement in place. Sometimes both parties do not have the same understanding of the terms … I guess I have had some disappointing stay overs, but generally, I try to plan smart. I have maybe suggested that a guest catch the next flight or what-have-you, as opposed to "original plans" (not very often though).

What's up with you being mine just musically? Catch you later. I have more to share later, but it is late, even for me!!—D.

ME: You know I wouldn't mine bein' your everythang. It's just that it would take too long to sign each letter with that description; so, "musically" means a lot, for me. This is actually Joe Westray's salutation. I saw it again (for the first time) and decided to employ it. What kinda salutation is that? You don't like that? Maybe you feel it's for professional use and not personal dialogue. Or maybe you are just joshing around. You know your satisfaction is very important to me. Don't be scared. Me, never … You da one.

⋆ ⋆ ⋆

ME: your message was perfect in timing, sentiment and length. Thank you.

D: For you, only the best. So, are you pre-performance or post, right now? Hopefully, you have gotten sufficient rest since this afternoon after that hellish bus ride. That sounded downright awful. Well, as you know, i'm just chillin at th' crib at present.

ME: Had no bunk, ya know?

⋆ ⋆ ⋆

D: Hi Ron, I am really happy to hear from you in any form and that includes e-mail. I am not feeling pressured by your e-mails this week … or by you for that matter. I suppose I would or do feel that way when I know there is some sort of an imbalance that I know will not or cannot be changed. I don't think there is an imbalance, at least not a significant one, between us at this time. Are you presently feeling like there is? I am totally not on that road either. Does my e-mail silence make you uneasy or make you wonder? What kind of response are you looking for from me? I am curious to know. You also alluded to you not not looking for that response right now or not being on that road just yet. Are you saying that my lack of response in a different time and week may raise an eyebrow or two for you? I assume so. That's fair. Context, right? All in all, I feel good, no pressure. I see a possibility or two.

D: Ron,

I don't know exactly what kind of surprise that I am thanking you for. But I am excited that it is a surprise. I left you a stealth cell phone message earlier. I did go out and now I am back in the house. I will have to go out again else I will do more shaking of the package.

Last night I was looking for a certain picture and couldn't find it … let me get back to you. Like that self-correcting mechanism, eh? I know you like it in yourself, do you give others the chance to self-correct themselves?

Are you patient? I'm sure you are saying, "Hell yeah, I have been patient with your behind!" I really mean in the regard of allowing people to self-correct … I am sure it depends on context.

As for the musically yours, yes I was joking quite a bit. I was taking the opportunity to boldly bait/tease you. Now that I know its origins, I totally love that salutation and welcome it. Please say that again! I look forward to talking to you later today.

Do you have a 2-year and 5-yr and 7 year plan? Do you look at life through age specific lens when setting goals or your level of attainment and achievement? Just wondering. we"ll talk later—D

⋆ ⋆ ⋆

D: hey sweetness … been back home watching baseball, oops you signed off … now you're back … you just keep signing in and out of my life

ME: ah ha. not by choice.

D: yeah, with the sniffles can you really say you have staying power? oh! stop it!

ME: yeah, play coy if you like

D: coy? i aughta …

ME: ooh, do you promise?! I'm feelin better. I had a good meal.

D: I am really happy to hear that … what'd you have

ME: sauteed spinach/garlic alongside salmon sauteed in scallion and ginger sauce.

D: That sounds so so good.

ME: I try. You seem in a bit better mood; how was dinner?

D: dinner was all right, I said I had an early morning but I just wanted to get home and watch the ball game and catch up with you

ME: awwh, i feel special

D: as u should

ME: i miss you

D: don't forget your hat; do you really? … even though we talk so much?

ME: what hat?

D: think—implication—timed expectation [no?]

ME: my hat??

D: you know: "get your hat before you head out the door" meaning: elude the subject sweetie, I think I …

ME: ahhhhh what? did you just slip out of an incomplete statement?

D: no … oh, the game, i forgot.

ME: hello out there in MLB land!!!!

D: I didn't slip out an incomplete statement … I was going to say that I look forward to the opportunity to spend face-to-face time with you.

ME: Subj: how art thou?

though speaking less, I must confess
my thoughts abound, in which you run around
sometimes questions appear, disguised as fear
not long thereafter, from you, I hear—Ron

D: Ron,

Haven't e-mailed you in a long long time! I've been spoiled, talking to you on the phone and seeing you face-to-face quite a bit in the last 2 weeks.

I can honestly say that I already miss the possibility of seeing you. When I said I was ready for you to go on the road, it wasn't for the reason that you revealed that you thought. Hmmm, sounds like you're rather confident in what you believe are my affections for you. Or is it confidence in your ability to affect me?

Truth is, I just wanted to get to the reality of the situation and to see how that felt or feels. After spending a bit of time with you, how would it feel to have you gone for a while and readjust to e-mailing and phone calls solely? It's still a tad too early to tell. I know you think I like to take the romance out of things.

That's true only to the extent that I like to the get to the stuff after the infatuation. After knowing that, I can settle in and get caught up in whatever romance there is. I do not think all romances for the sake of romance is worth the time and effort. It was great to hear from you last night and about your family day. Sounds like you three looked like the family on ABC's Schoolhouse Rock from back in the day … ya know the animated commercial song, "Three is the Magic Number"?

Ahh! I took a pretty long break from this note (an hour or so) and you rang … We got disconnected, but it was good to hear from you and it makes me hopeful that we will talk tonight.

Soon—D

ME: Hey, Sweetheart,

Thanks for the letter. Though my response be a little tardy, it's a really sweet letter and [it] made me smile today. I needed that; and since you were so fearless as to tell me that you missed me, you should know that I miss you too. (sounds cliché, but it's true).

Call you tonite, Ron

ME: I had time to think about (or as you would say cogitate on) something you said last night. You know, about how the the element of sex adds clarity or shines the light on the parameters or the is he/she is or is he/she ain't my/mine … If that is so, is it then unreasonable to think that things change afterwards? If he/she then expects different or certain things because of that element, is that not reasonable, albeit undesired or unnecessary? If it changes things in one sense for one person by giving greater focus or clarity and answering the is he/she is or ain't question then if it puts a twist or switches the focus of things for the other, what do you do? Just a thought …

D: Ron, even though I've said it before, I really do appreciate you extending yourself to my cousins. Seems like the clan, including me, are testing the depths of your grace. Thank you for going to Virgin records for me. I did go to the record store that Saturday I emailed you. They didn't have what I wanted. That's when I realize the artists were British and I didn't want you to think I just stayed in and decided to transfer errands to you.—D

Well, you'll be happy to know that not one but all your wishes have come true. The Garner was the last one left on a busy day. The others were stocked for the taking. I enjoyed being able to complete this mission for you.—R

I only have a small idea what you feel like when you say you are ready to come home. I know you're used to being on the road and unlike most travelers you often get a chance to retreat into the art, energy and integrity of your music. I can imagine having the clash of cultures and the incompetent hotel service as getting on your last note—and you just wanting to get to something warm and familiar.—R

ME: It's just a general feeling of being at home; yes, I like the warm and fuzzy feeling.

D: Do you speak any other languages? Do you have to marry in a talion wanted to learn the language? What kind of shit is that? I'm sure the fact that it is more difficult to communicate with my spouse would drive me crazy it's all gone. What's the point in that? I guess if the man is fine enough and I travel enough, when I see him we speak a universal enough language, right? Not! OK, let me leave you alone.

ME: Yes, I speak the universal language. I like it. It keeps things simple.

D: Do you speak any other language?

ME: No. I don't. I can, however, function extremely well he seems within cultures. I think it's the anthropological side of my interests.

Just got your call. Oh, you sound excited. Do you know what joy speaking with you has been and is? Well I can tell you it's significant. I guess it's just me and my imagination at work. You called for seven minutes?

D: It was more like 4 1/2 minutes, and I did say it was an unsatisfying tease. The kind that makes you pass up some good you know what because you know the denouement.

ME: Never you fear with a calling card, princess. I wish I could talk to you right now, in person.

D: Wish you were here run errands with me, seems like it would be fun. What do you think? Oh by the way we have been horrible at spelling conscious lately. What did we do before the time consuming spellcheck.

ME: This is my bad. How's that for eloquent use of Latin and English? I think I started the misspelling and you caught it. We are such nerds for even discussing this. I think we got cut off by the three-hour time limit.

D: Was that three hours? Yikes!

ME: That's three hours, discovery style. I love it. The glory phase: Oh how wonderful it all begins.

D: I am still trying to accept your theory about my mother's lack of consideration as a demonstration of control over her universe. But now it seems I still reject it out of hand. I did call her after I got off the phone with you. I just don't understand her behavior. I can only guess she didn't call because she thought I would disagree with what she has done with her day. She actually took care of some things that I thought she didn't. It seems to be she isn't too ready to throw away a new chance at the close relationship she says she wants. In the last three months, there hasn't been a day when we've been out of touch. This is a new way of life that I have committed to. I believe based on her words; she made the commitment as well. I feel like I'm trying to rewrite history create something that just isn't there.

Why should I suspend my belief; just because it involves a parent? I understand that a parent child relationship should be uniquely loving and what have you, but this one is not that.

ME: I feel you have demands that are, subconsciously, set up for failure by reinforcing your theories; therein, providing a justified "out" at whatever time you deem necessary. Am I completely off-base?

D: I do understand that this is a new concept for her and I have been trying to help her get, but left to her own devices, she doesn't want to try. It really is as difficult to her as simple as make up application.

ME: Don't try to change her. Work beside her. Be bigger. I know, I'm sounding like Dr. Phil; what the hell.

D: I cannot remember where I was going to take this email before we talked about my mother.

I know it wasn't here. Enjoy your last day in England. It was a good trip for me, too.

ME: oh yeah? Then it was double good for me, you.

D: Are you into aromatherapy?

ME: Yes and pretty well informed.

D: suppose you don't have trouble falling asleep.

ME: I go to sleep; there's no falling. I know where this is going, "Tina, I ain't on the narcotics!"

D: You're going to a part of France where lavender is bountiful. No need for you though as I can imagine you having your own brother herbs and plants to get you by.

ME: You know what you're talking about. How do you get so smart princess? That turns me on.

D: I am on the fence about going to Newport Rhode Island this weekend. Saturday is the day of the lineup that appeals to me. I also have a pool party on Long Island that same day. Can't decide. Just seems like a lot of traffic either way you cut it. I'd be pissed if I went to Newport and it was pouring. I suppose I'll decide soon enough.

ME: Take good care in making the right decision so that you can have optimally good time.

Talk to you later!

yes, you will—D

RON-RON: how adorable is that nickname? Hope you are feeling like you're falling into the, dreaded, friend category? All right then how are you RON? My last email was staggering?
How so in length or content? Too heavy? To reflective? I should've save a final copy for myself. I suppose you will use your famous and unmatched response style that I like. Does I'll get a chance to revisit those dolls. I was extremely tired when I finished it. And I wrote it it four times separated by at least two phone conversations with you. See what happens when you open up and give them a little more than usual?—D
>>Sends a brother reeling. I like calling card princess.
Do you invoke it because you recognize the deity that I am? Or is it just a term of endearment like baby? I prefer princess. Same amount of syllables. In fact, let me tell you how much I preferred not to hear baby. But I chose not to say anything when I did catch a point that you stated to me on the phone. I wanted to have a trip to London with as few layovers as possible. I just didn't want to disrupt our flow with commenting on that. However at this time, I tell you so we don't have a moment in which you used the term and I shoot you a look like you called me out my name. You know some ridiculous brushfire starting to look that we overly sensitive hormonal women are not to pull out a reserve at a blank. By the time you get this email you would have received my voicemail request. I imagine my cousins will be calling you as well. Yvonne with Info on a workshop near you, and Lilo for a request to see the show. What's interesting is that Ivan and Lila were on the outs, not even talking, and have been brought together by my car (and possibly by your concert). See the concert again and that's will be coming with Lila, I think. You have to give me your impression on the difference between them. I think their respective hairstyles give a big clue. As you probably guessed Yvonne's little lie about going to the show alone left me feeling disappointed and unsure of her whole ankle. I find those little unsolicited lies the worst of all. I'll admit I have lived with too many and hold too many throughout the years that these little ones are truly annoying and colors my perception and future interactions with the prevaricator (or fibber); that sounds better. Got to go. It is 2 AM London time and I have received both of your emails. You're right my email was staggering! I do have a lot of time on my hands. I need a damn hobby. I have to re-read your reply email in order to carry forth from where we left off.—D

GOOD MORNING: Did you know Celia Cruz died 2 to 3 weeks ago? I meant to mention it before. I assume Carlito may have played with her. I got to see her perform last year and loved her energy And love of her fans. How funny is it that I took my mom to a cancer society sponsored makeover party this evening as she was so at a loss putting on make up exclamation you know I was a little help to her (truly, the blind leading the blind). I was saddened by her reluctance to try and, less productive, no less than three times by me. Neither one of us ever played dress up as a girl. My mom looked amazing with some mascara and lipstick though. She couldn't do the eye make up shadow and liner which does take a deft If not experienced hand alas she had fun and met other women going through worse and looking worse. She was able to see the beauty in a woman who was completely bald and devoid of eyebrows knowing it could be her. All right, I am going to close this out, re-read your last email, go to bed and dream of hobbies so my emails don't stag are you in the future! Who am I to try to knock a man off of his feet?—Cheers, D

8/4/03:

London: since starting this email we have spoken and I could have taken an actual flight to London based on next months projected phone bill—LOL. I think the question I had about our conversation this morning has been answered—you went more into detail tonight. I am aware that in answering your questions, with attention to the scope of people you know,

I realize that is not ideal (and that you do not want to be relegated to any such anecdotal categories); somehow, I thought through this deflection you can see my viewpoint objectively. Maybe it works, possibly not. You also followed up with the question on whether I like to initiate a relationship. I said no quickly. I will temper that by saying I just don't want to have things dictated to me until I know with whom I am dealing. So it's not that I initiate, per se; but I go at my own pace within the context of the other persons initiative.—D

>>> ME: My initiative often is not rooted in romance. Now knowing somewhat your style, your deflection is certainly appreciated. The context of my initiative? Shit. You could end up barefoot and pregnant following my initiative LOL. Perhaps context dictates initiative? The trick is to keep the initiative alive with the unspoken reward of sincerity. I am not surprised

that your initiative is not rooted in romantic fantasy. Mine is—with one exception: it's got to pay off or I'm out.

Let me tell you, I cannot believe you have me on your couch and I couldn't turn the tables and get you to ask my questions about your schedule post August 10. Am I losing my touch or are you stubborn and willful—interesting. Incongruous to what I've said I feel towards my mother, I got the sense you were asking me about what I had written to get clarity on my thinking is that so? I am dragging a little today. No movie, I would fall asleep in the theater.—D

>>>ME: Yes, I enjoyed you being on my couch. I won't do you no harm. I am not stubborn, but I am extremely willful. It is all I have had to create my world; as I know it.

D: Great to talk to you today and to get your email I didn't expect your call at all and I had to try to catch your voice. You sounded like my first boyfriend, buddy. I had my first boyfriend this summer before my senior year of high school. My first sexual experience at the end of my freshman year in college. 17 still seems young for that. 10 year old seems Way too fast and slightly negligent on the part of the parents. But I have hotels that you countryfolk start a lot of things at an early age. All people do. Late bloomer?

>>> ME: Well, I sound like your first boyfriend; and you have the first name of the first girl I ever kissed. I'm sure in your viewpoint of child rearing you see several things that might ensure that a child walks straight, and narrow. I assure you my mom did all she could possibly do. Trust me, there's nothing she could've done to cease that curiosity.

D: So what are you going to do with the info on your granddad? Did you have to hire a lawyer to do research, or did you just have a friend look into it? I am a bit tired. I'll write more than a bit. I want to talk to you about my exposure to jazz and ask you more about your granddad, etc. It did feel strange to have you be confrontational with me on the subject. I will not presume to know a pinkies worth of what you know about Music let alone jazz.

We did DEF used it, but are you particularly sensitive on that subject? Is it hard to discern my tone in general or specific topics? My intention? How do I come across to you with regard to my respect of your talent and profession? Respond to that email, I suppose.

>>>ME: I want the information for general as well as specific purposes being the only Westray male down south I have to drive all the stuff

together. Besides, this man was a jazz musician. I don't have the convenience of looking left or right to a living male figure that is connected to me anyway. My patriarchal history is very important for my fortification. I have something resting on me and I accept the challenge. There is an equal amount of research to be done on my father. Your friend is doing it because she respects my work and is interested in my musical here having heard tell of the late great Joe Westray, my twin. I am the spitting image of Joe. His birthday is just days before mine.

D: I really didn't mean to snap. I was a little embarrassed.

MEL I wasn't sure of the semantics involved. I am not particularly sensitive, just particularly knowledgeable. I like the way you respond to my talent: Not overly complementary, artfully respectful, appreciative and insightful.

D: Did I get it right? It is a little difficult to discern your intention regarding certain subjects.

ME: If I were not me, it would be even more difficult. I think I do a pretty good job of deciphering your neutral tone. Whatever you know for certain, in any subject, I will respect. Hopefully, we can learn some things together. I like your mind. Forgot, need to buy a CD. This is when having particular friends in town comes in handy. They could run the errand for me. I'm feeling rather comfortable and don't want to put on outdoor clothes to go out.

D: So wait, did you open the door to the front desk woman and a young boy, but neck it? Doggone.

>>>You know it Yeehaw!

D: Oh yeah who knew when I was kidding you about changing your name That you have such a tradition in heritage associated with it. My bad. You think I can implement a great movement to revive Latin in place of slang?

>>>You can do this boo. You can do it. Looking forward to seeing you sometime soon.—Ron

D: I am getting off the phone with you when the second pregnant pause happens in our phone conversation. Otherwise, I end up visiting with you for hours. Just get back on line all right and I won't have to make any such decisions. With a cursory glance I was trying to find an emoticon that would jive with that last statement. But no such luck. It is less time consuming getting to know you on email. I was tired or should I say my usual morning demeanor returned when I got to work. The conversations

I think will pay for them self. What do you think? I too will splurge on something worthwhile for the time. Thanks for splurging on me a little.

Take a sigh. I got your message about the CDs. I would love to complete this mission for you. Oddly I am not located near any popular record stores. I can run the errand but it will cost me several pounds to round-trip this transaction. What's the priority level? Is ordering online and option? Is this a test? LOL I have two more days here. Let me know.

★ ★ ★

>>>Yes sweetie it was indeed a pleasure to see those plans through especially for you and yours.

D: Why? You don't even know me. Why is it especially for me?

>>>Well let's just say I feel like you are good people. How much information do you think it takes to know a person? Can you actually know someone? The propositions seems remarkably similar dealer to see how many licks to reach the end of a 20 question the answer being solely based on the experience of the licker? Oh yeah, what did I mean in my last letter about let me not digress? I was referring to the sexual tension at the time: Raw sensitivity? Can you dig it?—Pun intended … lol. One of the last things you said to me this morning makes me wonder if you said what you wanted to say or if there was more. You know the whole don't try to be the mirror about it if you are interested and know that I don't want to be in any of your pre-existing male categories. I am not sure if you just wanted to make sure you had that on the record or if it did come out of the context of our previous topic in that conversation. That previous topic was about certain bandmates and my perception of them in my perception of their perceptions.

So I am not sure if there was more of a connection to that or if you just wanted to see what you did and were searching for the clearest possible manner in which to say it. After all, you don't really know much about my behind. No pun (well, a little pun intended). Do you subscribe to the school of doubt that says men and women cannot be platonic friends and that there is some sexual tension that needs to be address?—D

>>> In light of the view you have provided two angles I guess I was a little influenced by both.

My motive was to make a statement to you. Perhaps some part was sparked by the examples you mentioned. I just wanted to be clear as not to get tangled in any pre-existing web designs (pun intended) No I don't know your behind. It's not so important. What that sounds risky you say? No, I just figured that what I experience, though influenced from behind (the past) I couldn't risk that one. That is all the reference I need. It's up to all of us to direct our futures. If the same things continue to inhibit you and your relationships, it is either because you cannot control your destiny or that you wish to be impeded—which is usually for one reason: fear of the unknown.

I think that some relationships should be platonic. I also think that some relationship should not be platonic. I further believe that it is up to the parties involved to know which they have, and act without adieu. I am an in love the moment romantic. If it works, I'm there; if not, I'm gone.—R

Now that I have digested what you have said I do stand by my words that I don't like to play games. In regard to men, I have been told that I take longer than expected to make up my mind.

I do shy away from being in the midst of palpable relationship. I like the energy of flirtation, but I don't want the expectation of follow through. I do, however initiate spending time together to get to know more about someone, but I do so in a more neutral manner. I think people rush to act on the chemistry and after that subsides burns out your left with someone you really don't want to share a drink let alone a full day with. And then again, there are the trust issues I have with the general population.—D

>>>How does that lack of trust manifest itself with you? We both don't play games. This can make us or break us? Well, I guess if there's no game playing, we should be cool. It always seems to boil down to a question of who's pace is being followed. The woman: cool, cautious, affected from behind, etc. The man: desirous yet cooly aware of old patterns. Sound a little like the same person right? Shower away from palpable chemistry is a conscious decision. Succumbing to affection is organic. Expectation is definitely a downer. I don't have any expectations, but I do like surprises LOL. I can be neutral, if that's what you want. I realize you are not speaking directly to me in your previous paragraph, but I want to address it anyway.

Yes, I can be as neutral as you need for as long as you desire. The question is at the end of your probation, will I still have the passion that underlay the beginning; if I don't, is it my fault or the natural result of the relationship? For once I would just like a relationship that just functions off of itself.

Whether or not the sex whatever stars in the beginning, middle or the end: two single parts which only need the other half to operate smoothly and accurately in real time.—Ron

Anyway back to your point, I understand it. I have heard it most of my adult life. Though I don't trust, I will gamble on trusting in romance.

When I am disappointed, I simply sharpen my tools for the next go-round. I am not easily jaded. Now that you share where you were in Paris, it is no wonder I felt very comfortable talking with you then. Subconsciously and then consciously, I sensed that your initial-lust had subsided; and it put me, immediately, at ease. Being quite comfortable with that I have to be honest, reading your first email did make me say, "Oops"—it made me pause. You sensed it, I'm sure. I know now we were both asking ourselves where did that come from?—when I called you in June, and when you sent me that first email. I have certainly learned a little lesson in how sensitive you are to energy.—D

>>>I'm glad it timed out right. Yeah your call and my letter, that's real.

Let's just keep it really real. OK?

Perhaps we can find a uniqueness in our interaction.

I prefer it that way.—Ron

D: thought you would be in Paris already. Well at the hotel at least. Yeah you can consider this email a filler flowers. Not a carnation but more like a bouquet of pockets with a single rolls. I am not sure of the preceding email is the rolls in the budget or shall I wait to name another email, yet to come, that such rolls. Even though you're burning an extra year or two opening up multiple emails from me, I figure, I will give you a little flight after this drought of mine. Hey do your best to have a high energy evening. I'm sure both Deidre and I are sending you great energy to you on the bandstand today. I'll speak to you soon!—D

D: Ron, what's doing with you? Will you forgive me for being selfish? While I was feeling sorry for myself knowing I wouldn't see a Siberian possum for a bit I retreated to dealing with the Monday night and forgot about being gracious and giving. I like to think of myself as such, so I snapped out of it and made a deposit in your mailbox. Can I tell you it's hearing and seeing your email tag name in June, it still tickles me to this day. Ironic that I will miss your more frequent rumination while you're in my favorite, thus far, country, Italy. Now that you mention feeling a bit detached from the group or particular nights, I suppose that's a very real feeling and happens more than I would've ever thought. Just like you want to pick up on the energy of a Roman audience, I can imagine picking up on subversive and diverted into Jesus when you were trying to put forth a somewhat integrated energy as a group. Wow! That must be hell tough, especially day in and day out with the same group. I do think people can sense when you're on a high (a non-chemical or non plant-based high ... lol) I can imagine it does get inextricably mixed into the majesty and dignity of your art. Looking within helps and may provide the answer or just reinforce the answer you already know.

As far as looking within when it comes to my mom, I thought I have forgiving her. But I am painfully aware that either I have not, or I am still in need of a sincere apology. What do you do when you want an apology from someone who cannot or refuses to give you one? I know you are to give yourself what you could not get from your loved ones. I should just accept the fact that I will not get one, and deal with what it is. What I usually do is don't deal with that person. I cut people out of my life as deftly as a surgeon.

The quandary is I don't want to cut my mother out of my life, again. That is not the kind of daughter I want to be. However, I am faced with a mother who doesn't know how to be open or honest or loving, in the least. She is stifled with fear and resentment. I have asked questions in order to find out the source of why and who she is. The most solid answer I've gotten is, "I don't know; and no I have never thought of that."

The crazy thing is that I still ask the questions. How the hell do you deal with and love a family member that is a functioning drunk or coke-head? They're going to drink and snort. Tough love? I am not that skilled yet. I am not sure I want to be. At least not in the sense that I will give tough love to help the abuser. I would give tough love to help and shield myself. Yes, you are right, I have grown very tough skinned as a result of all of this; but that just really belies all the raw sensitivity below the surface. I feel you on the trust issue you have. But that is what is most important to me. I know I have to open up my ability to trust and to trust myself. All right, I will talk with you soon. I got a pick up my mom and take her to her first chemo-therapy session in less than eight hours.—D

ME: Hey how are you gorgeous.

Yes I have a net for catching up with the erroneous. I'm pretty good on paper, eh? I'm better in person. The letter writing with you is fine. As I have been wanting for someone with whom I could communicate on a level. You have invigorating my pen. Thanks. Sardegna was a blast. I stayed on the beach for most of the day prior to sound check. Needed you there—so much.

The salt water was very healing. The gig to follow was a drag. I guess I was a little worn out; it, almost seemed that everyone knew I had an invigorating day; and that they did their best to see that it didn't shine too bright the following night—not calling any names. I felt strangely opposed to the band that night. It was very strange. Not that I hadn't felt this way before. It was the most intense that evening. But enough of that. All problems are internal, right? Thank you for your honesty regarding your relationship with your mother. I can imagine that you have become pretty tough skinned as a result of your history with her. Is forgiveness and option here? What is her story? Have you gone within to see what made her the way she is?—Ron

D: Your email did catch me off guard and sent me back on my real haunches. So I apologize for the delay. Lest I be one of those women that spurns a brother when he shows initiative, honesty, spontaneity and some vulnerability. My brother needs no outside impetus to retreat to a hardened shell of guarded and apathetic behavior towards women. I did enjoy our conversation, I needed to engage with someone and it was nice getting to know a little about you. This is the second time you have rescued me in this manner rescue seem strong, but when I was in France for three weeks, I was so thrilled to see familiar faces and speak fluently in my native tongue in my last five days that I was dreaming about seeing Homey's megawatt smile in person. That's when we actually spoke beyond pleasantries on the bandstand do you got a little bandstand or stage? And you seemed to exhibit a sensitivity and awareness that extend it beyond yourself. So you were flushed out a little bit more to me.

As for your note, I'll do you do reference one of my favorite lines, to love and be loved in return. I do appreciate the honesty of the lust that you let sleep through your message as you can tell from our conversation I am pragmatic, so I am appreciate your honesty. I am a romantic as well, so, I really do appreciate the end result, that being the expression in the form of an immediate note. In regards to my pragmatism, I'd like to know what it is and then if I choose to see things as I want to, that's my choice. At least, I do know what years and have the option of dealing from that realistic perspective. Most Minnesota women deal with things as they wish they were. I think that goes for most people regardless of gender. My philosophy is give me the truth and if I want to play for letting me play myself, don't play me for a fool. I run across men that are so concerned about not hurting the feelings that they think I have. I had no idea of this latent lusting. The majority of the time I am not aware of others' perception of me.

So I don't know if you will take my response to why I called you as the truth or wonder if I am playing naïve, but the truth is this: I did call you to get info on the step test July to her days in Paris. I remembered you played with excepted in New Orleans last April. I was at the jazz fest saw John, David and spoke to W but didn't get a chance to say hello to you or Merlin. By the way, I absolutely love his energy and small. Years ago, I played a post concert coed pick up basketball with him, and I have liked him ever cents. Knowing he's a merry family man makes me feel so free and expressing my admiration of him and reveling in the glow of the smile and hugs. Funny, if I had not asked the hotel operator to try you, I would have sat down to eat at the same restaurant as Ted and his girl. It would've been great to meet her. So I did call you hoping to facilitate the fantasy I have of my girl Deidre singing with W and his band ...

I have to admit, I am glad you recognized my name, as my only descriptor I had to jog your memory was the fact that I look like your ex. He just told me that 20 minutes before I called you. So it was the mention of your name and the recall of our Parisian conversation that made me feel fully comfortable calling you out of the blue. Let me know if I have left you puzzled or reticent. Let me know if I love any question on acid or any of the services on addressed. I do think you picked up a piece of my personality. Outgoing and friendly yet reserved and sometimes I'll stare. You're right, there are aspects to another dimension yeah express. Alas I am sure we will talk soon. Stay cool.—D

★ ★ ★

Critique the Critic

I let this "square" off easy. To me, this blurb represents the general—condescending—nature of the critic.

CRITIC: What *are* the values and philosophy of jazz?
ME: self-preservation, and the expression of a positive ideal.
CRITIC: Or in other terms, what makes jazz such a special music?
ME: at this junction in history, the resilience [of the art form] alone is enough to be honored and admired. the hope that's in the music is the idea.
CRITIC: Feel free to develop any topic you want, these are just guidelines.

ME: i'll leave the developing to you, but i will finish my thought on my style (we were interrupted midstream at last opportunity). I was alluding to my like of Trane, when you added that, "Well, you don't sound like Trane." I then stated that the context determined my approach, and that some time (another context) you might find me sounding similar in approach to John. I must, for sake of clarity, state that it is not my intention to emulate any one musician's sound or style per se. I am impacted by John's style, from a "tour de force" standpoint (as is everyone).

BTW: concerning the "do you have a band" question: In keeping with jazz tradition, I lead bands on the basis of availability. I am always preparing myself for opportunities, far and wide. Composition has progressed alongside my development on the trombone.

★ ★ ★

Y. came over twice from Japan this year. She came to Harlem in March. I recall she turned 21 on my futon, in her birthday suit, as we watched the US-Iraq invasion during one of many afterglows; and she was in South Carolina for the prior Christmas holidays.

I will never forget you. Thank you for good memory. If you come back to Japan, tell me your visit. I want to see you. You said to me that I was special to you. You were special to me, too.
I'm your baby forever. Goodbye—Y.

Chapter 32

Gigs

With the Jazz at Lincoln Center Orchestra:

Theatre Antique/Jazz a Vienne, Vienne, France.

Auditorium Stravinsky, Montreux, Switzerland.

Testaccio Village Festival, Rome, Italy.

Teatro Monumento G. Dannuzio, Pescara, Italy.

Pinede Gould, Antibes, France.

Bridgewater Hall, Manchester, England.

Horrogate Festival Yokshire, England.

Royal Albert Hall/BBC Proms, London, England.

Jazz in Marciac (25th Anniversary), Marciac, France.

James Miller Auditorium, Kalamazoo, MI.

Symphony Center, Chicago, IL.

Oscar Mayer Theatre, Madison, WI.

Paramount Theater, Austin, TX.

Cowan Fine Arts Center, Tyler, TX.

The Centrum, Spring, TX.

Laurie Auditorium, San Antonio, TX.

Bass Performance Hall, Fort Worth, TX.

Tulsa Performing Arts Center, Tulsa, OK.

Bennett Auditorium, Hattiesburg, MS.

Curtis M. Phillips Center, Gainesville, FL.

Atlanta Symphony Hall, Atlanta, GA.

Rutherford Spindale Auditorium, Spindale, NC.

Verizon Hall, Philadelphia, PA.

Eisenhower Auditorium, University Park, PA.
Kleinhans Music Hall, Buffalo, NY.
Calvin Theater/Iron Horse Ent. Group, Northampton, MA.
Symphony Hall, Boston, MA.
Kennedy Center for the Performing Arts, Washington, DC.
New Jersey Performing Arts Center, Newark, NJ.
Weis Center for the Performing Arts, Lewisburg, PA.
Joseph Meyerhoff Symphony Hall, Baltimore, MD.
EC Glass Civic Auditorium, Lynchburg, VA.
Tilles Center, Brookville, NY.
Historic Battery Park, New York, NY.
Prospect Park Bandshell, Brooklyn, NY.
Midsummer's Night Swing, New York, NY.
City Hall Plaza, Mt. Vernon, NY.
Alice Tully Hall, Lincoln Center, New York, NY.
Staller Center for the Arts Stony Brook, NY.
Bailey Hall, Ithaca, NY.
Stanley Theatre, Utica, NY.
Spaulding Auditorium, Hanover, NH.
Merril Auditorium, Portland, ME.
Maine Center for the Arts, Orono, ME.
The Music Hall, Portsmouth, NH.
Hitomi Memorial Hall, Tokyo, Japan.
Suntory Hall, Tokyo, Japan.
Minato Mirai Hall, Yokohama, Japan.
Sumida Triphony, Tokyo, Japan.
Symphony Hall, Osaka, Japan.
Hamamatsu Concert Hall, Hamamatsu, Japan.
Toin Memorial Hall, Yokohama, Japan.
Orchard Hall, Tokyo, Japan.
Morioka Shimin Bunka Hall, Morioka, Japan.
Utsunomiya Shimin Hall, Utsunomiya, Japan.
Hatsukaichi Bunka Hall, HiR.ima, Japan.
Seoul Arts Center, Seoul, Korea.

National Concert Hall, Tapei, Taiwan.
Petronas Center, Kuala Lumpur, Malaysia.
The Esplanade, Singapore.
Blaisdell Hall, Honolulu, Hawaii.

Ron Westray w/Wynton Marsalis, The Koger Center, Columbia, SC.

* * *

Edwin came to South Carolina to paint me and Mom's house around this time: Beau was with us about 13 days; he reports eating oatmeal every morning and listening to James Brown 24/7. Mom reports that he later called to, in a joking manner, tell her these words: "I ain't scared of you, Mrs. Momma."

Met Beau's niece, D.P., around this time, too. I liked her. She was ghetto. After she'd spent a week with me in South Carolina prior to, I was too harsh in some random conversation, per usual, and that was that. The year started off out in San Fran with D.X. She treated me to dinner at the Farralon on New Year's Eve, before retreating back to her place for dessert. Saw K.I. during this time as well as W.

Reconnected with A.M. from college. Also met A.B. this year; she booked me at the Apollo.

* * *

Hula-Hooping versus Chauvinism

One fine dusk, a fair and timely young lady chose to practice her chosen art of hula-hooping in a nearby park below my fourth story window. The gate of opportunity is ever-expanding, while the gate of sacrifice contracts. This calls for a timely decision. The exercise started in an upright and erect stance followed by the successful gyration of the light weight, plastic, circular tube of about three feet in diameter: Having gained momentum, a choreographed joined of the hands allowed gravity to have its effect on the hula-hoop, sending it in a descending and spiral motion down the girl's body. As she responded to the physical forces controlling the hula-hoop, she has just been acted upon by the hula-hoop. The hoop wins and hits the ground.

Then, in multiple motions, the round-plastic-circular thing was rotated around her neck at very fast revolution, achieving a smooth, intriguing and evocative motion of the neck and the pelvis. Having realized the potential of her coordination, she shifted by such a degree as to force the tube down the right shoulder at a forty-five degree angle, arriving in the vicinity of the stomach, igniting a ferocious thrust of the lower back and mid-section. This motion ensured that the hula-hoop would never, never, never stop.

At the height of ocular delight and her physical excitement, three young men had also observed and encouraged this rite of hooping from afar, but at ground level. The middle of the three was the first to "step." And in an aggressive fashion he insisted that she instantly reproduce the same intriguing dance they had observed and interrupted.

The young lady was stammered by the demand. After a gentle, and wise, refusal, the middleman thrust his jacket to the ground and challenged the young woman to a hula-hooping duel. The young lady kindly offered her hula-hoop to the middleman, who with little finesse and even less interest, proceeded to parody the gyration the young lady had so naturally achieved. The spectacle resembled that of a man chained by the legs and hands, while being tugged forward by his crotch, in small increments. Having thoroughly emasculated himself by performing a mock and inferior sexual rite, middleman manned himself upright and, of all things, offered his male counterparts a try. They savvily declined. In a defeated fashion, middleman handed the hula-hoop back in and stormed off without a word (yeah baby). The two guys that had formerly stayed behind now approached in order to shake the hand of the young woman, one by one.

Again alone, and now with more vigor than before, the young lady resumed her practice. Practice makes perfect and she's going to get results.

★ ★ ★

1600 Penn Ave

One calm summer day, while perusing through the Madison room, in the residence at 1600 Pennsylvania Avenue, I noticed a painting that seemed out of texture in such a highly ornamented environment. The room was filled with artifacts from the Madison era. The uniformed official announced this and other facts as we, the visiting jazz musicians, prepared to perform for the president, seated among his bodyguards and a host of political and social luminaries, you dig?

Because of sheer quality, the furniture in this room seemed right in time. There was a mantle above one of two fireplaces. On this mantle rested a clock, which, by all appearances, served President Madison. I was surprised and happy to perceive that it was still ticking and that it had better time than my guess. Curiously, the clock had lost many vital implements, but was still alive and in time. This spoke quality. Dozens of oil paintings, representing various administrations, ringed the circular-shaped room.

For me, it was still backstage. Feeling a little silly, I walked in circles trying to absorb and accept the meaning of heritage and the origins of wealth. What made it so prevalent in some and so void in others. Pacing, these questions danced in my mind. Though I had visited the White House during the Clinton administration, today seemed like a first time (I suppose it would be like that anytime you entered the White House, as a civilian).

I stopped to smell the roses many times before exiting the Madison Room. Next door was the Adams Room. In this room was a gigantic vase of roses that signaled out to me as if I had an exoskeleton, wings and antennae. I immediately left the white roses and headed for these reds. The fragrance snuggled therein was the strongest I had ever smelled.

I lingered awhile, and though there were many people around, no one else stopped to smell the roses. (I'm no Dr. Phil.)

Then, I left the Adams Room and wandered back into the Madison, careful not to stray too far from the group. This time I looked a little higher than before. Over the second mantle was an unframed oil painting of a purple mountain. I stood in shock, trying to appreciate some imbedded value inside the painting. I did not discover the meaning until sometime later.

Ah, the mountain, it turns out, coincides with a certain verse in an American national anthem. This information was somewhat reassuring, but the painting still reminded me of a thrift-store find. I quivered a bit. Is it possible that the inhabitants of the White House could not discern quality as it relates to context? Sure, you see it all the time with the powerful and affluent—no taste. Not in the White House. Oh, yes. I started to poke a little fun at the painting with my constituents in jazz humor, which is refined sarcasm.

Having opened the subject, I further discovered that it was a Georgia O'Keefe, given to former first lady Hillary Clinton as a gift. I will not comment any further on the gift, but Hillary always wins (well, not in '08 … or '16 … lol).

I found this out too: Shortly after the Clinton era, The President and Mrs. Clinton were criticized and later reprimanded about the amount of White House property they left the premises with. Asked to return some of the "personal gifts," Hillary returned this painting, and that's how it ended up there.

Laura Bush must really like it. It will be better placed at The Ranch in Crawford.

★ ★ ★

"Westray is the first musician to ever be appointed 'musical director' while still a member of the ensemble."

The Lincoln Center Jazz Orchestra with Wynton Marsalis, demonstrating their dedication to the great music of jazz, took on one of the great masterpieces of jazz—the music of Charles Mingus. *Don't Be Afraid … The Music of Charles Mingus* features six compositions by the legendary bassist and composer. LCJO trombonist Ron Westray arranged the music and directed the ensemble for the 2002 concert at Alice Tully Hall, and the subsequent recording, in 2005, which was produced by Delfeayo Marsalis.

Chapter 31

Gigs

With Wynton Marsalis and the Jazz at Lincoln Center Orchestra:

Campbell Hall, Santa Barbara, CA.
Cal Poly Theater, San Luis Obispo, CA.
Cerritos Center, Cerritos, CA.
Wilshire Ebell Theater, Los Angeles, CA.
Escondido Concert Hal, Escondido, CA.
Centennial Hall, Tuscon, AZ.
Boettcher Concert Hall, Denver, CO.
Folly Theatre, Kansas City, MO.
Stephens Auditorium, Ames, IA.
Hancher Auditorium, Iowa City, IA.
Memorial Chapel, Appleton, WI.
Gallagher Bluedom PAC, Cedar Falls, IA.
Marcus Center for the Performing Arts, Milwaukee, WI.
West Side Theater, Gary, IN.
Playhouse Square, Cleveland, OH.
Hill Auditorium, Ann Arbor, MI.
Bridgewater Hall, Manchester, England.
New Castle City Hall, New Castle, England.
Cambridge Corn Exchange, Cambridge, England.
Barbican Theatre, London, England.
Dome Corn Exchange, Brighton, England.
Poole Arts Center, Poole, England.
Leicester De Montfort Hall, Leicester, England.
Cultural and Congress Centre, Lucerne, Switzerland.

Auditorium di Milan, Milan, Italy.
Teatro Medica Palace, Bologna, Italy.
Tonhalle, Dussedorf, Germany.
Festplelhaus Baden-Baden, Baden-Baden, Germany.
Musikhalle, Hamburg, Germany.
Philharmonic Im Gasteig, Munich, Germany.
Philharmonic, Berlin, Germany.
Alte Opera, Frankfort, Germany.
Midland Center for the Arts, Midland, MI.
The Pavilion, Highland Park, IL.
Fraze Pavilion, Kettering, OH.
St. Patrick's County Park, South Bend, IN.
Mann Center for the Performing Arts, Philadelphia, PA.
Wolftrap Farm Oark, Vienna, VA.
Garden State Cultural Arts, Holmdel, NJ.
Syracuse Jazz Festival, Syracuse, NY.
Palace Theater, Albany.
MDC Hatchshell, Boston, MA.
Southham Hall @ National Arts Center, Ottawa, Ontario-Canada.
Hummingbird Center, Toronto, Ontario-Canada.
Chautauqua Amphitheater, Chautauqua, NY.
Eastman Theater, Rochester, NY.
Wilfrid Pelletier, Montreal, Quebec, Canada.
Planting Fields Arboretum, New York, NY.
Polideportivo de MendizorR.a, Vitoria, Spain.
Hollywood Bowl, Los Angeles, CA.
Benaroya Hall, Seattle, WA.
Elismore Theater, Salem, OR.
Van Duzer Theater, Arcata, CA.
Sacramento Community Theater, Sacramento, CA.
Masonic Auditorium, San Francisco, CA.
Lyons Stage, Monterey, CA.

For when He new experiences finds, He says, "Behold, a friend."

—Mom, 2001

Chapter 30

Gigs

Ron Westray Ensemble: Fort Tryon Summer Jazz Series, New York, NY.

With Wynton Marsalis and The JALC Orchestra:

CD Café Jazz Club, Beijing, China.

Shanghai Theater Center, Shanghai, China.

Xing Hai Concert Hall, Guangzhou, China.

Spray Farm Winery, Melbourne, Australia.

The Royal Theater, Canberra, Australia.

Convention Centre, Brisbane, Australia.

Sydney Opera House, Sydney, Australia.

Queens Wharf Event Centre, Wellington, New Zealand.

ASB Theatre, Auckland, New Zealand.

Sun Yat Sen Memorial Hall, Taipei, Taiwan.

Festival Hall, Osaka, Japan.

Orchard Hall, Tokyo, Japan.

Neal S. Blaisdell Center, Honolulu, Hawaii.

Mass MOCA, North Adams, MA.

Cocoanut Grove Ballroom, Santa Cruz, CA.

Pauley Ballroom, UC Berkeley, Berkeley, CA.

Stanford University, Stanford, CA.

Cerritos, Center, Cerritos, CA.

Artemus Ham Hall, Las Vegas, NV.

Symphony Hall, Pheonix, AZ.

Lied Center U. Kansas, Lawrence, KS.

Northrup Auditorium, Minneapolis, MN.

Navy Pier, Chicago, IL.
EMU Convocation Center, Ypsilanti, MI.
Johnston Hall, Moravian College, Bethlehem, PA.
Symphony Hall, Boston, MA.
Peppin Auditorium, Middlebury College, Middlebury, VT.
James L. Knight Center, Miami, FL.
Mahaffey Theater, St. Petersburg, FL.
Thalia Mara Hall, Jackson, MS.
Jones Hall, Houston, TX.
Bass Concert Hall, Fort Worth, TX.
Powell Symphony Hall, St Louis, MO.
Wexner Performance Space, Columbus, OH.
Roseland Ballroom, New York, NY.
Chautauqua Auditorium, Boulder, CO.
Jazz Aspen, Snowmass, Aspen, CO.
Hollywood Bowl, Los Angeles, CA.
Lobero Theater, Santa Barbara, CA.
Silver Legacy Resort and Casino, Reno, NV.
Britt Festival, Jacksonville, OR.
Schnitzer Hall, Portland, OR.
Benaroya Hall, Seattle, WA.
Orpheum Theater, Vancouver, British Columbia.
Shubert Performing Arts Center, New Haven, CT.
Wolftrap, Vienna, VA.
Liberty State Park, Jersey City, NJ.
Jazz a Vienne, Vienne, France.
Zelt Festival, Freiburg, Germany.
VS Swingt Festival, Villingen, Germany.
Jazz Open Festival, Stutgart, Germany.
North Sea Jazz Festival, Den Haag, Netherlands.
Estival Jazz Lugano, Lugano, Switzerland.
Umbria Jazz Festival, Perugia, Italy.
Schlesweig-Holstein, Schlesweig-Holstein, Germany.
Prague Jazz Festival, Prague, Czech Republic.

Weiner Konzethaus, Vienna, Austria.

Kleines Festpielhaus, Saltzburg, Austria.

Opernhaus Zurich, Zurich, Switzerland.

Teatro Municipal, Sao Paulo, Brazil.

Teatro Gran Rex, Buenos Aires, Argentina.

Symphony Hall, Birmingham, England.

I was writing for the band now. Swing Dance Tour of 2000: "Mr. Personality," "Maybe Later," and "You Are Out Of Sight.

Chapter 29

Gigs

With the Jazz at Lincoln Center Orchestra:

St. Petersburg, Russia.
The Kremlin, Moscow, Russia.
Vienna Opera House, Vienna, Austria.
Vitoria Jazz Festival, Vitoria, Spain.
Copenhagen Jazz Festival, Copenhagen, Denmark.
North Sea Jazz Festival, The Hague, Holland.
Ottawa Int. Jazz Festiva, Ottawa, Ontario, Canada.
Tanglewood Festival, Lennox, MA.
Prague Jazz Festival, Prague, Czech Republic.
Alice Tully Hall, Lincoln Center, New York, NY.
Iowa CCC, Fort Dodge, IA.
Orpheum Theater, Minneapolis, MN.
Demmer Recital Hall, Ripon, WI.
Orchestra Hall, Detroit, MI.
Clowes Memorial Hall, Indianapolis, IN.
Grinnell College, Grinnel, IA.
Hoyt Sherman Place, Des Moines, IA.
Boulder Theater, Boulder, CO.
Luther Burbank Center, Santa Rosa, CA.
Bimbo's Club, San Francisco, CA.
Freeborn Hall, Davis, CA.
Harmon Hall, San Luis Obispo, CA.
Luckman Center, Los Angeles, CA.

Ballroom at The Hilton, Salt Lake City, UT.

Schnitzer Hall, Portland, OR.

Civic Auditorium, Santa Cruz, CA.

Luther Burbank Center, Santa Rosa, CA.

Memorial Auditorium, Stanford, CA.

Masonic Auditorium, San Francisco, CA.

San Luis Obispo PAC, San Luis Obispo, CA.

Cerritos Center, Cerritos, CA.

Royce Hall, Los Angeles, CA.

McCallum Theater, Palm Desert, CA.

Centennial Hall, Tuscon, AZ.

Ardrey Auditorium, Flagstaff, AZ.

Boettcher Concert Hall, Denver, CO.

Popejoy Hall, Albuquerque, New Mexico.

Chavez Theater, El Paso, TX.

Meyerson Symphony Hall, Dallas, TX.

Bass Concert Hall, UT Austin, Austin, TX.

Hancher Auditorium, Iowa City, IA.

Orchestra Hall, Chicago, IL.

Folly Theater, Kansas City, MO.

Stephen's Auditorium, Ames, IA.

Powell Symphony Hall, St. Louis, MO.

Emens Auditorium, Muncie, IN.

Mershon Auditorium, Columbus, OH.

Hill Auditorium, Ann Arbor, MI.

Playhouse Square, Cleveland, OH.

Kennedy Center, Washington, DC.

Bailey Center, Ithaca, NY.

Symphony Hall, Boston, MA.

Avery Fischer Hall, Lincoln Center, New York, NY.

Maxcy Hall Sports Complex, Potsdam, NY.

Corning Center, Corning, NY.

Tilles Center, Greenvale, NY.

McCarter Theatre, Princeton NJ.

Meyerhoff Symphony Hall, Baltimore, MD.

New Jersey Performing Arts Center, Newark, NJ.

La Villette Jazz Festival, Paris, France.

Symphony Hall, Birmingham, England.

Barbican Theater, London, England.

Fines Arts Center, Amherst, MA.

Troy Savings Bank, Troy, NY.

Merrill Auditorium, Portland, ME.

★ ★ ★

Running by Scared

I'm so scared of people's plans.
"run something by me," as they say
I always consider what might be our business?
It usually turns out to be yours.
This time I'll see?
What you gonna run by me?

The Deck—
You almost fell off the one Mr. Middleton built for me out of scratch.
Deliberately outside of the ___, placing your bif behind on the "rail" of rob's "bannister."
When I considered that you knew the law—suits and torts and courts—I asked your big ass off of that rail, and again, returned to my well placed incoherent state—Oh you thought?
Man … hell! … I don't know what to call you …
but let me say this …
That was a multi-level deck of client cards you played …
Don't even think again how glad you were to see me …
I'm gladder that I come.
Gladder, as Real is the Word … but only for the soul.

Part of the Art:
LET IT BE REAL (Porgy and Bess)

Coconut, I got to keep you.
I Love You Coconut—and I got to keep you.

Coconut, you be the only one who trust me.
You know why?

★ ★ ★

On The Rim

Actually, it's the Rim.
The Rim is just for the Women & (small) Children
stop, no, no—The rim man.
Ladies and Men don't need no rim, nowhere.
On the car? That's fine.

My man, my main, main …
Had I resisted coming to Your party under a simple umbrella—
I should would have heard it—
but my interpretation of it—
as they say?—
Not real.
Cause Real is The word—but only in the Soul.
(Yes God is Real, for I can feel him in my soul)

We're never far from our past—
Anything may trigger the past in us …
But, how will you escape?
Do you wish to?
Don't leave it before now
go on first to survive the you
Then, see for yourself that ain't nobody really occupied with your thing.

Sister Pie … sometimes you wonder …

You both lookin' at me sweaty, stink
Grease, grime and other work stuff—
work hair, head-rag/slide ins—
Miles on bare feet in the same spot
Keep lookin' …
Soon you'll wonder why a nice mans comes to call on sister pie
even like that!

Don't you ever wonder?
Well, should you think about it …
The name [sister pie] is like a pair of wooden shoes from Japan
You'll know who you're with.

⋆ ⋆ ⋆

Serendipity ME

Serendipity is not akin to shopping—the sales
The sales will have been gone by years when she acquires.
Perhaps, never now, than, then—but always.
You've seen it, but just didn't want for the feeling.

Gotta go now—
Got something to change around … and listen here …
I do curse, some.
I use to boast that I didn't
And then, I heard in my minds eye, my grandmother,
with a trembling lip [and jaw] full of Bull of the Woods tobacco and a heat burned neck,
calling me …
"Gin Yann—come hear you little shit." [Annie Ree]

But, I say to you—
Ron—
come now my son.
V.—
how are you my dear?

⋆ ⋆ ⋆

Holy who you are, Hallelujah.
Thank you for your highest Praise and
Happy A to Z.
Happy To, For, From …
Word?… Holy who you are

Mrs. Z: The Sincere Apology in a Lifetime
And … if my wordz, over the years you have known me, have, in any way, placed any personal failure upon you … Speak Now …

Now, that I may, for the first time ever, sincerely apologize for the offense of my words—
especially in the area of the aforesaid—my words causing you personal defeat and/or harm.
... Then I take it that all is well, as i have spoken to you, Sincerely.
I love you with no comparison to the way the all wise God loves you ... cause, people?
I have never considered dying for either one of you.
I'll die to you—even from you
But, for you?
Love, remember God loves you the most.
I Love You cause I've Grown Accustomed to you ... and I love doing ...
and laughing and talking with you.
You may say I love these things (you don't have to be sick either)
I Love You, but, so far, I haven't considered laying down my own life for you.

Now, if it wasn't for God—The Lord
I couldn't have told truths.
Think on life and living prayerfully—Thinking Thanks, always.
To God Be the Glory for the things He has done above all I could ask.
Then, [God] turned around and let me be myself again today.
I am richly blessed @ 60, and I'll wait on Those of you who are not yet 60.
Won't be long for any of you.

Chapter 28

Gigs

Upper Manhattan Jump w/ Frederick Renz and the Early Music Ensemble, Fort Tryon Park Summer Jazz Series, NYC.

The Ron Westray Ensemble featuring Brian Blade, The Izzy Bar, New York, NY.

Frederick Renz and The Early Music Ensemble, New York, NY.

The Jason Lindner Big Band, Smalls, New York, NY.

Spike Wilner Quartet, Smalls, New York, NY.

Grant Stewart Quartet, Smalls, New York, NY.

The Jazz at Lincoln Center Orchestra:

El San Juan Hotel, Carolina, Puerto Rico.

Centro de Bellas Artes, San Juan, Puerto Rico.

Teatro Alpha Real, Sao Paulo, Brazil.

Flynn Theatre, Burlington, VT.

The Calvin Theater, North Hampton, MA.

Midsummer's Night Swing, Lincoln Center, New York, NY.

Rossiya Hall, Moscow, Russia.

Lucerna the Great Hall, Prague, Czech Republic.

Filharmonia Harodowa, Warsaw, Poland.

Gewandhaus zu Leipzig, Leipzig, Germany.

Kolner Philharmonie, Cologne, Germany.

Philharmonie, Munich, Germany.

Victoria Hall, Geneva, Switzerland.

Stadtcasino, Basel, Switzerland.

Theater Champs Elysees, Paris, France.

Sala Verdi del Conservatorio, Milan, Italy.

Paulau de la Musica, Barcelona, Spain.

Auditorio de Zaragoza, Zaragoza, Spain.
Palacio de Congresso, Madrid, Spain.
Teatro de la Maestra, Sevilla, Spain.
New Jersey Performing Arts Center, Newark, NJ.
Blumenthal Performing Arts Center, Charlotte, NC.
Emory University, Atlanta, GA.
Tennessee Theater, Knoxville, TN.
Ryman Auditorium, Nashville, TN.
Germantown Performing Arts Center, Memphis, TN.
Thomasville Cultural Center, Thomasville, GA.
Center for the Performing Arts, Gainesville, FL.
Van Wezel Peforming Arts Center, Sarasota, FL.
Coral Springs City Center, Coral Springs, FL.
Woolsley Hall, New Haven, CT.
Dorothy Chandler Pavilion, Los Angeles, CA.
Ardrey Auditorium, Flagstaff, AZ.
Masonic Auditorium, San Francisco, CA.
Warner Theater, Washington, DC.
Symphony Hall, Bos.
Ford Centre for the Performing Arts, Toronto.

★ ★ ★

Although I don't see you as much as I'd like you are often on my mind and always in my heart. I cherish the memory of the good times we knew and look forward to the day when we see each other. And I know the joy of your presence will warm my world just as the thought of you now warms my heart.

—MC

★ ★ ★

From MC

Hey baby! I actually wrote this letter on the seventh but I had a little trouble getting it to print out on our computer. Here is my hand written version I know you are probably already back from tour so I apologize that this letter wasn't waiting for you as I indicated it would be.

3/7/98:

It's raining and once again you've infiltrated my thoughts I guess somethings never change (*smile*). Your Valentine's Day card was very sweet in fact you made my day. I hope your visit to Seattle as well as the other places your tour took you to war pleasant the coincidence I spoke of in our phone conversation is true although this isn't the letter I had begun writing before you called I decided to just start over because I wound up telling you everything I had written it is still so easy to talk to you. Everything with me is fine. H. and I finally moved yay and our new place is real cool. It is in the middle of Georgia Tech's campus so it's very convenient and close to everything. I could walk to the Ying-Yang café if I wanted to. Hopefully you'll get a chance to visit soon.

Music is going great! I'm getting a lot of original material written. And record it. So far I have two songs that I know I am going to use on my demo. I also have a voice teacher that is really good. Her name is Keira and she works with a lot of artists from some of the major labels here, LA face, so so DEF, etc. Ron this woman has worked me like you wouldn't believe. In one of my earlier sessions I almost fainted trying to keep up with the exercises she has me doing exclamation she also has me taking herbs and has asked that I not drink or eat any dairy products. Dairy supposedly builds up mucus in a nasal cavity, and blocks your true self from coming out. Have you ever heard of that? I'll take the herbs Ron, but I don't know about the dairy thing. I got to have my pineapple shake and butter pecan ice cream every once in a while! anyway, I've been with her for about three months now and I can tell a slight difference in my sound already. Songs that used to be hard to sing or not so hard anymore. I figure by the summer I'll be giving Chaka Khan a rough for her money. Now I'm really getting pissed at myself, ha?

Work is still fine which I guess is a blessing because a lot of people hate what they have to do to make a living. My boss has been on me about graduate school so I've been thinking about that a lot lately. Other than that nothing is going on. I still think about you from time to time sometimes it's a song that I hear, or a funny phrase someone says that reminds me of you. Rainy days especially serve as a reminder. I guess things turned out between us to wait they were supposed to. I am just glad that we still find joy in sane and being even though we aren't together anymore. I know I've said that before, but hell its my letter. So I can be redundant. I'm going to get out of here for now, I hope you enjoyed the card as well as the factorial dose of southern exposure I include figured you could use a little up there in New York. Till we meet again—MC

★ ★ ★

Nearly catching me in the gut, accidentally, O. shoots himself in the hand the day before the gig in my hometown of Columbia, South Carolina, while showing off his .25 MAB. I guess he forgot it had a bullet in the chamber. Admittedly, I had shot the weapon earlier in the day, at his urging. But it wasn't my weapon, and I didn't own an automatic yet. Debate me on this, but if he understood the weapon, he should have cleared the chamber upon my handing it back and before sticking it back down his pants like a thug, eating dinner with it there and later retrieving it, in close quarters, to demonstrate how … POWLWOWL!!!

The police showed up because I had checked him into the emergency room with my insurance credentials. Another team of officers reported to my mother's home to let her know that I had been shot. My mom later reported to me that one of her visitors at the time emphatically denied this information stating that "Officer, that's not possible. I just saw Ron Westray!" I guess I had, for a time, achieved an almost "Lazarus-like" status (if you get my drift). This claim finally came through, and I paid it. Later, the guys and I laughed and laughed. This could have easily been "cried and died."

I remember, years later, bringing it up, in jest, around J., who was there (in close proximity of the renegade bullet); he said, "That's over, man." He was right.

I never talked about it again until now.

★ ★ ★

To Be a Rogue

Affords you the opportunity to leap over artistic struggle claiming the rewards of those who searched the way to define their experience. The cost is simple: you must stay ever on the run—through history, backwards or forward. You must mask the lack of true experience and feeling.

That much potential [fiction] fails precisely at this point: through the [writer's] refusal (often through provincialism or lack of courage or lack of opportunism) to

achieve a vision of life and resourcefulness of craft commiserate with the complexity of the actual situation.

—Ralph Ellison

Practice

Perhaps in the swift change of American society, in which the meaning of one's origins are so quickly lost, one of the chief purposes of living with music lies in its ability to give us an orientation of ourselves in time. Music is memory. Music is memory.

★ ★ ★

Is it who I am or how I am? Is it what I said or how I said it? Why do I address guys in the band the way I do? Why have I taken an aggressive stance? Has the environment been selected for chaos? Why do circumstances reverse to reflect me as flawed or weak?

Tricky

Oh Vicky played a mean old stick when tricky picked.
He turned into a dick and accused Ol Noble trick of being a prick.
Now everybody knows that he's the band bitch.
'Cause Tricky always scratching when he gets tha 'itch.
To weak opinion the band replied, "Yeah!"; in this coward-moment they all became him.
Ole tricky done been hurt before but not like this day in Milano.
Trying while lying? Can't rely in [ya] 'cause you Jivin' while Smilin

—Tray

There exists a fundamental breakdown between me and all members of the organization of which I am a part. I have contributed to the best of my ability above and beyond the call of duty, and I feel that my efforts have proven beneficial to the band. In addition to bringing a respectable amount of zeal to the mission, I have treated my fellow band members with kind words, consideration and respect. Over the years I have gotten less back then I have given—congeniality encouragement and so on. These are some of the tangible things. There exists a host of things unseen, yet relevant, that, as you might suspect, I have experienced. I have, in my eagerness to be, desired from this organization that which was never offered—and that is not part of its present mission. That is, to be a star—*in* it. I have been pulled and tugged at so subliminally, yet consistently, in the midst of, or as a result of, my confidence and willingness to "step up."

My tolerance started from the first day I ever rehearsed, and it lasted for seven years, through an unexpected nephew, a bitter grandmother, physical and mental breakdowns close to home, failed engagements, a failed-nightclub and a $12,000 loss. Later, I realize that it was time to get real. Stick your chest out in front of that piercing arrow called jealousy. Like tearing the carcass off fresh road kill, I have been stripped of all the honor I brought to this organization; the dignity and pride I have exemplified has been reduced to this proclamation: "Because you are the biggest asshole in the whole band, ask anybody."

I will admit that my armor has been rattled. My responses have deteriorated to that of a child. This disposition has come at the end of a not-so-easy journey with a pack of laughing hyenas. The joke is self-esteem, and you're it. Right now, I am treating the bite with venom.

That is enough defending myself. It's not necessary at this point. I have been alienated. They have won. I have been transformed. My punishment has been served. I have temporarily lost my honor, and that I try to uphold. I haven't lost my self-esteem (but maybe a little self-respect). It hurts to admit that; but at my worst, it's not as bad as things I have seen. I have to continue steadfast on my mission to inspire. They never wanted my inspiration. I was to share in their limitations not present options of higher possibilities. I succumbed to this for some years recently. Now, it's consume or be consumed. My meals aren't going down so well. I have not sought out victims. I have simply presented a hidden range of my personality to these men who have waited for my downfall. The caliber of the individuals, excepting the leader, is very weak. I am weary. At this point I am losing not gaining. Boss would say that it's what you make of it. I say you need people who want to help you make something of yourself. This is not available in this band. It is older men versus younger men versus slightly younger men. It has been impossible to assert my true potential. I hate being deceived and targeted. I have had to narrow it down to the financial comfort and experience the gig is affording me. There is one negative side: I feel complacent.

I must be free. I must collaborate with other musicians. No more fake-assed men, who, in their gruffness, don't want to promote success, leadership or pride in others. I've had to absorb the darts tossed by those in my own circle of acquaintances. Isn't that likely? I find that some musicians cannot detect something that is soulful; but things involving a show of general technique astounds them. I feel as though I've gotten lazy with success (such a little amount at that). Right now, the idea of having my horn at my mouth four hours a day, every day, is lost between being a prominent trombone at JALC, a master's degree candidate (and a lover of women). I feel as if my focus is gone sometimes, and I'm practicing the same things over and over, or else I'm going back patching up some basic rudimentary shit that I slopped over in school. The bottom line is that this is bullsh*t—and if I'm going to be the great trombone player I am, I need to lose the contemplation and just go shed.

Later

The melodies aren't running as rapidly through my head right now. I think I'm stifling my inspiration by being myopic with the process. But, I can hear, and I know what sounds appropriate. I was not raised in a fashion that led me to believe that everyone is out here to get me. I was raised in a very caring environment. Am I naïve? Do I observe the important and not just the general? Vice versa? If a man does not blatantly disrespect my personal integrity, then I can only observe him. I don't feel I have petty issues about how I should be treated. I'm not being paid enough. Most of the cats who complained about the pay for the tour are still being paid the same thing for other gigs. To be successful is a give-and-take. You have to know when to make yourself known and when to just chill and keep swinging. I'm not going to do anything I don't want to do—nothing.

⋆ ⋆ ⋆

Alas, I finally reached a state of depression. I don't know whether to be embarrassed based on the fact that my faith and Christian belief should lift me above that or to accept my human weakness and try still to rise above it. I'm not satisfied with my playing, and I'm in the midst of men who appear much more talented than me. I have strengths that they don't, but I don't know what it is. I feel ignored. Maybe I'm projecting some type of aura that turns people off. Maybe because they can't really figure me out they rather not be bothered. I feel that there is a conscious effort to make me feel inferior because of my experience; and my musicianship is being questioned. None of this is helping me a bit. I've really got to come out this quick. I felt so uninspired tonight I'm not getting any feedback from my fellow musicians. Maybe I'm not playing enough for them. I realize that I should not be playing for them, but for me. I am embarrassed to be affected by these factors.

Now, some chick of J.'s is at the bus serving food. Everyone (and their mom) have been called to have some food except me. Should I force myself into their space and conversation and hope that they will allow me some food? Should I sit here like everyone else did before they were summoned? I was finally addressed as "Mr. Westray," in regard to having some food. I've actually thought about quitting, but I can't do anything else. I really wouldn't be happy doing anything. I'm not happy—most all with myself as a musician. I am finding out each day how much I know about myself and music. It's time to refuel. If I don't, no one will care. I'll just be another sad, out-of-work musician. The knowledge I have acquired has brought me to this point.

God is in charge of my evolution as a man and as a musician. Did I miss some inspiration on one of those nights when I was in bed? Should I have been sitting at my piano receiving? I have received no musical inspiration from being in bed? I realize I should make a change in the way that I perceive sex and women. I wonder just how tied into my sense of personal success is my morality? I feel very mixed up right now. Who can I talk to? (other than to touch this parchment with a touch of the blues). Sometimes, I feel unnoticed other than by the God that created me.

⋆ ⋆ ⋆

Memory versus Action

Things past, affect this present moment—every action has a reaction—
Things long-remembered—some forgotten—lingering like a lost love.
Wandering: Like a dancing gypsy,
I am misguided by all these things.
Looking back, I can think of many things that make my present me.
I can see the sum total of that which I have already allowed myself to become,
and those things that I have not allowed myself to become.
Some things I did not become are good (like a prisoner in America's industrial prison complex). Some things I did not become are questionable: like drug and alcohol-free.
Build up. Tear down—you know?
Great for me that time shall transform me anew—forged of experience. I am.

⋆ ⋆ ⋆

Desire versus Rationale

Is it desire or rationale that forces you to approach a girl and make her yours in a night? Having learned that it won't work like that for my type of guy, I believe in one-night love affairs. Unfortunately I'm not the type of guy who can share for nothing. Do I really want to know who they are? Should I remain abstinent aside from the women who have already bitten? There are three still around willing to share any intimacy with me. I've been a swinger since the age of 10. I guess I've gotten my share. The road is dry this time around. It's mostly by choice. I can't fake it. My rap is dead now. Doing is based on memory and action—memory withstanding.

There are always causes and effects to your everyday disposition and dress. Long days of thinking lead me to believe in a condition called love. This condition forces me to constantly evaluate the self-love of love versus the despising by men of your truest self—which is it? What would cause me to take common interactions and construe them as divisive? Or is it ego and selfishness versus selflessness? Or selfishness versus selfishness?

Whichever, it sure does cause one to aspire to greater heights of expression—like writing. Unlike some, my life is tied, by choice, to music; but my satisfaction is at an all-time low. Of course, this has stirred my aspiration as a writer. I no longer see the opportunity or the effect of expression in Western Music. I have basically reduced my goals through oppression, suppression, ignorance and lack of deduction or whatever. Today, make your own history.

Amid the codification of my personal experience, perhaps *some* recognition belies the pen.

Because, as a musician, I have only existed in a world of predators—seldom preying.

If you stop caring enough to fight, defeat is imminent; but to argue is to be less than sure. If I can learn to write, maybe *there* is freedom. There are no time limits because the written word is time—if we can learn to correct faulty penmanship. There's also the idea of time and patience as virtues of long suffering. This becomes the primary condition of a working life. Superiors are quick to say the choice is yours; it's not quite that simple. All problems are internal; and so many things hurt inside; but I Am.

* * *

3/24/98:

Dear Ronald,

This letter comes by way of a need to express stuff they have been very pressing and close to my heart. It comes out of respect for who you are and the friendship or bond we have established one that I value greatly. I have a need to express to you all that I am currently thinking and feeling. Spring is here. The things of winter I did and now it is time for new life. Having gotten beyond the pains of my accident, I have and have had nothing but time to think of my future. I see so many things for myself. It only gets better. More importantly it will only be better by the active steps I take to ensure the outcome of what I ultimately desire.

For most, this all directly relates to you. Ronald, I thoroughly enjoy the time I spent with you. I enjoy walking the city smelling the crest era, holding hands with you. I enjoyed holding onto and being held at nights by you. I missed your kisses, your hands, your touch. While I enjoy these many pleasantries, I equally enjoyed the conversation we had the night before you left. It left an indelible impression on my mind. As I have been pondering the direction of our relationship and that last conversation, I would like to conclude that I am no longer insecure about who I am to you. I know that you love me, and I know that you know that I love you. I am very much in love with you and have no desires for anyone else.

After the conversation, you seemingly put any insecurities to rest. Unfortunately, whereas I am no longer feeling insecure, I am also finding that I am no longer feeling for the direction of this relationship anymore. I remember in the conversations that you stated that perhaps I was not happy. And that calculation you were correct. I am not happy with the thought that we possibly will not have a future together. But on a more positive note, I must say that I am happy and knowing that I love you. I know that the love I have for you is unlike any I have not. I have never experienced loving a person where I fall asleep and rise the next day with thoughts of him.

Honestly, although I have discussed marriage with others in the past, you are the first that I have ever envisioned myself with, the first I have your vision as a husband, partner and father of my children. This is truly a first for me but perhaps not the last. Ronald please know that I respect your integrity, Your intentions and your outlook on your future. I am a firm believer in knowing that what one wants, preparing for you, I am being sure before proceeding.

I never want to be a part of making someone do something that his heart does not lead up to do. Especially when he revolves around decisions concerning me. And knowing your convictions, I must honestly say that I don't see myself waiting around for you to come around. I don't see myself going to the motions of marriage with someone to whom I am not married. This truly bothers me spiritually and emotionally. I have no regrets about where I have been with you, Ron, all I have done has been out of love and wanting to be that much closer to you. I know that you know this. But sadly enough, this doesn't erase the hurt that I feel when I consider a future with you.

Perhaps we are once again on two different pages. Because we are both very determined in our positions, I don't see much choice in the directions we will take. I know that you express contentment and where we were at this point, but it really isn't fair, to me. Furthermore, my unhappiness and continue it will only increase with the intensity of my emotions. I love you with all my heart. There is no hiding it. I am not looking for a replacement. I am not even looking to date others. That has never been my thing. If you would like, I would still like to see you. You are very close to me. Honestly, I don't think I will be spending any less of time at your place anymore. I don't want to put myself in anymore compromising positions. These decisions hurt a lot now, even thinking about them as I am typing. But I know in the long run it will prove to be what is best. Ronald, I honestly believe that this is best. If we hang on any longer we will only become better. We know each other too well to simply continue dating like this. We both deserve to feel at peace and to be happy in our affairs. You don't need ultimatums and I don't need handouts. I need to be happy and I can't prolong this union anymore.

There are no apologies and regrets. We both have bright futures ahead of us. Spring is here and we should keep moving forward.

I'll always love you—L.

Chapter 27

Gigs

The Jason Lindner Big Band, Smalls, New York, NY.

The Village Vanguard, Bone Structure w/ Wycliffe Gordon.

With the Jazz at Lincoln Center Orchestra:

Orchestra Hall, Chicago, IL.

Mershon Auditorium, Columbus, OH.

Hancher Auditorium, Iowa City, IA.

Bass Concert Hall, UT Austin, Austin, TX.

Powell Symphony Hall, St. Louis, MO.

Auditorium PIO IX, Rome, Italy.

Via Della Conciliazone, Rome, Italy.

Teato Carlo Felice, Genoa, Italy.

Teatro Communale, Genoa, Italy.

Teatro Municipal, Piacenza, Italy.

Teatro Comunale, Modena, Italy.

Teatro Carlo Felice, Modena, Italy.

Concertgebouw, Amsterdam, Netherlands.

Wiener Konzerthaus, Vienna, Austria.

Konzerthaus, Vienna, Austria.

⋆ Espace Lumiere, Paris, France ⋆

Banilieus Blues Festival, Paris, France.

Barbican Theater, London, England.

Fox Theater, Atlanta, GA.

Dreyfus Hall, W. Palm Beach, FL.

Mahalia Jackson Theater, New Orleans, LA.

Michigan Theater, Ann Arbor, MI.

Swasey Chapel, Granville, OH.

E.J. Thomas Performing Arts Center, Akron, OH.

Oscar Mayer Theater, Madison, WI.

Macomb Center for the Performing Arts, Macomb, WI.

Millet Hall, Oxford, OH.

Memorial Hall, Chapel Hill, NC.

Farthing Auditorium, Boone, NC.

Center for the Arts, Atlanta, GA.

UGA Performing and Visual Arts Center, Athens, GA.

McCarter Theater, Princetown, NJ.

Schaeffer Auditorioum, Kutztown, PA.

Fulton Theater, Pittsburgh, PA.

Fisher Auditorioum, Indiana, PA.

Bucknell College, Lewisberg, PA.

Bermuda Arts Festival, Bermuda.

State Theater, Portland, ME.

Quick Center for the Performing Arts, Fairfield, CT.

Alice Tully Hall, Lincoln Center, New York, NY.

* First major falling-out between me and L. as a dating couple. Having sponsored a trip to Paris, I didn't appreciate the coy bullshit in front of my boys (accompanied by moodiness during other occasions)—after all, we were conquering much on the road—much less toting some unappreciative, American chick around Paris. But, as she had stated, she had been to Paris once before as a kid. Oh, I see.

* * *

As I said, this was our first major parting. As usual, L. didn't feel that she had done anything wrong and that it's just my temper. This would remain the pattern for years to come. I would not see or speak to L. again until my move to Harlem several months later.

During this hiatus, I was probably dating the most women I have ever dated at one time. Most all were home girls. M.C. and I hearkened all the way back to middle school and high school, though we never dated back then. Now, we were really intimate. V.G. and I met in the third grade. After school, one day, I gave her her first kiss. I was issuing far more than kisses now.

AP, who will always be my favorite, I had known from church since we were young. We made a bond to do what we were doing forever. She lasted about 13 years before she needed more than that.

There was also A.C. who had been a vocalist in the Jazz Band with me back in college. We connected well after we graduated, however. She was in between home, NYC and, ultimately, the open seas as a cruise ship performer. When a man says favorite, he means the one that will attempt all of his (harmless) fantasies, without rancor. *I should have married that one*, I often say. I needed more expansion. She was too close to home, and I was only a third of the way into a 15-year world-touring career. Notwithstanding A.C. I continued to see this group of home girls, intermittently, during times of stress up until age 40. Looking back, my problem was that I didn't realize, many times, girls felt about me the same way I felt about them.

I always felt vulnerable making that initial move. My numbers could have been much higher.

I am still like that. I don't like to pursue. I found this place of equitable expression of interest. Because of this, and in relationship to the amount of "attempts" John Q. Public will, generally, endure, my numbers remain, comparably, conservative. Overall, I feel like the women I have interfaced with (and shall interface with) are the women for me.

I can report a noticeable decline in interested eye contact. So, the game is even harder now.

*You know my numbers are down, right? It f*cks w/ your karma, and chicks know. I am into chicks who are into me, or at least who pretend to be into me until some bull shit comes up. There are women that can tell you that I am as loyal as to them as they are to me.*

★ ★ ★

3/18/97:

My dearest Ronald,

This is just a little note to let you know that some things never change. You are constantly on my mind … I immensely enjoyed my first-time experience of Paris. One that I spent with you! Only regret is that you and I didn't have the kind of quiet, intimate time alone that Paris are forced to lovers. Ronald, do you know this: I love you, and the thought of being without you makes me more in love with you. I care deeply about you. Many men come with bits and parts of packages. You are a four pack, it's beyond repair, one that I've grown to love and cherish and accept, with hopes of gaining mutual acceptance.

I love you in the fullest capacity of who you are and all that you bring to our relationship. I haven't looked any further because I found all the fulfillment I need in you. I do love you and I am in love with only you. And saying so, I might not always express my love towards you at the time or in the way that makes you happy is. Ultimately you and I singularly, should be happy. I want you to be happy with me. But if I don't afford you happiness, you should have all that you deserve. Ron, never doubt my love, and in-loveness or fidelity toward you. It is and has been only you. May you always have the best.

Always in love—L.

⋆ ⋆ ⋆

Best Move for the Money

I moved to Harlem, New York, around this time.

During this time I was a member of Bobby Short's entourage; I also met Z. She remains one of the most sophisticated women I have ever met. I hate I messed it up: I lied one weekend about L. coming to town. It happened to be her birthday weekend. You can't do that kinda of stuff to older women.

I learned the hard way. Looking back, she was in her sexual prime; and retrospect is some bullshit. She was ten years my senior, but very attractive and a professor of English and comparative literature. Though I suspect she would have started bossing me around.

Chapter 26

Gigs

The Village Vanguard, Bone Structure w/ Wycliffe Gordon.

Blues Alley w/ The Marcus Printup Quintet, Washington, DC.

Recording and Touring, The Marcus Roberts Ensemble w/ The Orchestra of St. Lukes.

* * *

Second date with L. in Washington, DC.
The Henley Hotel is where I made second base.
Third base and Home plate followed during this year.

* * *

He Tales and She Tails

He could kick my ass. He had an older brother.
He could kick his ass. He had an older brother.
He could kick my ass. He had an older brother.

He was wild.
I wouldn't wan't to fight him
He had already turned her out

I had it for scraps
'Remember that Sat. in the shed?
She already had a 13 year ole boy friend

I was 10.
She was my first

She had him, but would go on to prefer him over him (the other one)
I wish I could have hit it when we were just kids
He caught her in her prime
She went on to have a baby for him
He got killed by a car

She will always be my first love
You got raped later
I'm sorry
I remember when she was young and tender
She use to call once she got married
What's that?—payback?
She had a big butt.

She was smart from the start
She met him. He slapped her sad
He nearly killed her. He turned them both out

She was nice
She had the most beautiful butt in the world
I was too young to give it a twirl
I would have tried
She's still fine

I met her
It was on
She was a little older and a little wiser
HE was hitting it, too
I won.

He took some fruit
Her brother wanted his life.
She threatened to end it all.
Her first—My fifth
I bolted.

He called her dorm.
She screamed in the phone with fear and loathing.
I wanted the same thing.

She was of Oriental descent.
Couldn't access it
Odyssey

There she was.
Her sister already had a baby already.
Was it hers?

She could get high as gas—prices!
Then give up that round at Le Chevette
She was perfect for me.
He was still tapping it.
I won.

He never saw her again after the hotel incident.
That was it.

He took a piece of fruit at Aunties.
She was so fine and mellow.
He bolted.

She had a baby for him.
He took her.
He lost.

Ah, P.A. with the big head

She was the bomb.
He really liked her style
You so ghetto—girl
He passed you down to me.
Sweet and plump—with that little lisp
Saw you years later in Harlem—
you had a little girl with Autism and an old man story
Whew, wee had a ball.
The sliding door at your moms was so quiet.

She was discovering herself before mom gets home.
I was number twelve, or so, that day.
Thank you.

She was a freak.

She was younger
He would come home
What's up bruh?—Ain't nothin

She rolled her eyes in disgust.
You know you want him.
You didn't look so tired.

She always seemed uncomfortable.
She was the same.
She calls to this day.

She was so good.
HE checked in later that night—a school night
Glad the fire would not ignite
Her brothers were insane.
I heard what they did when he got you pregnant.
Could've been—He

She gave him her crabs.
She lived in a trailer in city limits.
She was always in those dingy, white-jeans.
He followed you home one night.
She gave him the claps.
3 days later—go see the doctor.

He never scored on Prom Night.
She had five minutes.
He made the most of it

★ ★ ★

I met K. this year, too. I met her in church. Granny introduced us. Greenview Baptist Church is home church. My dad was a founding member of the church, and his name is engraved into the cornerstone of the building, alongside the other founding deacons. This didn't bode well that year I showed up after Prom Night, in my tuxedo, with two other friends, who had not been to church in a long time. My grandmother, who was mother usher, quickly escorted me and my friends up to the balcony, where we were less likely to be seen by the congregation and more likely to be seen by our peers, who still pick at me to this day.

There are so many things for them to pick at me about: *Is your Momma still mean, Tray?* I think that's the most popular one. Off of that is "jail bird" because I went to the holding cell, downtown, the night before the first day of high school, after blabbing off too much at the skating rink security guard. My new Levis could not shield me from that one.

But then there was also "bird man" because of the garbage bag full of starlings, robins, doves and other assorted birds I was apt to hunt and kill during the cold months, all executed in jeans and penny loafers (with the pennies).

My mom said to me one time, "If you aren't writing, yet, something's wrong."
That statement always echoes in my mind.

The voices say ain't nothin to say … it's just what it is …

Oh secret thought of all those writing, and those that have not yet written—
but will
Bless the stroke of these keys—that I may gather my account—so small in the
context of all.

★ ★ ★

Just a few minutes ago I entered Walgreens, as I have many times. The lil' clerk girl, woman or whatever thought she had me pegged just because I had on a British racing cap, a sport coat over a Guyabera, some old jeans and some Reeboks to boot … the prep in me, you know. She thought I was a vagabond. So, she tells ol' boy to go check out aisle 13, because "that man" just went over there. I didn't hear that part, but "ol' boy" gave it away by asking me from 20 feet away, "How are you doing today, sir?"

I simply, like an old man, stopped reading the active-ingredients column, twisted my body contrary to natural movement and looked at him silently as he approached—my posture said "you couldn't be serious."

The clerk kept on walking, right past me (seemingly never even expecting a reply). The question was never real in the first place. This kind of thing is a recurring theme in my life … I guess the little boyhood thieveries punish your karma when you enter stores (even when you are a grown man with an ex-wife and kids). Once, a girlfriend told me that I carry an air of suspicion about me … but once again, I think she was trying to mess with my head.

See, my mother is a special case too. I really get a lot from her in the way of successful lawlessness. In listening to her childhood stories, I realized that she was one of those kids at ease with the death of things. She lost her father at age three or so and has never met any of his family to this day. So she was the bad-assed little girl who would come by and stone your chickens to death. On another given day she might have busted several of your field pies just for the hell of it. I had that as a child. This is anger. I don't have to hire a psychiatrist to tell me that. My mother recognized this in me. Strangely, she didn't go out of her way to suppress it. She even supported my neighborhood "hunting" expeditions. I was the best shot in the neighborhood. I could shoot pears off of trees by the stem, if that was the one you wanted, and an occasional plum. I could discern the difference in a squirrel's ear and the leading edge of a pinecone's tip at 100 feet. I still can, thank the good lord. For these reasons, I excelled at the hunt. And no matter how many dead robins, doves and squirrels I bagged and brought home to show, she would say that's great, Ron-Ron. She knew I was nuts. But imagine making me suppress that.

One day and many dead animals later, my mother explained to me that the killing of animals was wrong if you did not eat them as food. So let the grills begin! The next weekend she had her good friend Mr. Sherrod come by and show me how to skin small game and how to dress small birds for cooking. Mr. Sherrod was a retired brick mason and ex-military guy. Looking back, when I think of him, I think of Jack Nicholson; he had that ornery but intoxicating old vibe. He was old enough to be my mother's grandfather. As a matter of fact when my mother was a child she grew up right next door to Mr. Sherrod's then-young family. By the time my mother was in high school Mr. Sherrod had her pegged as hot-to-trot.

By the time she was in college, she would hang out with Mr. Sherrod like any grownup needing a sponsor at the bootleg house. By the way, we still live in the same neighborhood—it's Greenview/Farrow Hills, United States. Yeah, I loved that dirty old man. So did so many others.

That's who showed me how to fish, too, Mr. Sherrod. One time I broke my leg and was restricted to a cast for half a year. Oh, how I wanted to go fishing though. This saint of a man took a young boy, with little experience and a broken leg in cast, fishing? The spot that I wanted to fish was one where I had fished before. The fishing hole rested down a ravine and off to the side of the secondary highway running atop. In some sort of damming process, this hole received water from the lake on the other side of the highway—Lake Elizabeth, I think. You could fish the hole from the surrounding banks. The really good fishing was on the other side of the deep well, where the cemented floor of the tiny dam spread out with slime and about two inches of water streamed off the edge into the well.

But to access that spot you had to scale the lower wall, which formed one side of the bridge above. There was a cement ledge that you couldn't even see about two feet under the murky water. It protruded out about eight inches. Being a brick mason, Mr. Sherrod was very strong and understood the construction behind the bridge's walls. Noticing that I was disappointed at not being able to get to the good spot, Mr. Sherrod took his time, hoisted me up onto his back like I was a kid, not a 12-year-old, and scaled that wall with me on his back until we reached the other side. The risk was immense. Like I said, Mom was a fox.

Decades later, when I was married, Mr. Sherrod was old but still gardening in his front yard. I hadn't seen him in decades. I had grown up now. Having heard tell that I was married, what he asked me was startling. In a semi-joking way, he asked, after so many years in between, "So, have you cheated on your wife yet?" We both burst into laughter. In retrospect, that was just like the fishing trip. Both times he was saying to me, "always be a man." That was the generation he represented.

I got it. I have never struggled with my sexuality. There was early exploring and pumping as they call it, but it was all in preparation for girls. In the South, we took shit to the extreme in between meeting up with fast enough girls. I'm not ashamed to admit this having heard similar tales from other now-grown men not struggling with sexuality issues. No one asked me about my sexuality, right? Well it seems that that's the underlying question in dating. Have you ever been bi-curious? Well, when I was a child I thought as a child, but when I became a man I wanted women … and before that.

That's another thing Dad passed on, along with music—that non-exclusive yearning for love or "in love with love" as my mother used to diagnose it. So it's pretty much all about sex these days, which was the proposition from as early as I can recall. Even that is by serendipity, it seems more than ever.

Momma got a lot of music in her too, even though she doesn't play an instrument … Boy, can she hear. My mother is the best listener in the world. If you say it, she hears what you are saying; so do I. She hears deeply into the meaning of things. She also is a great talker.

Another important mentor for me was Bernard "Pete" Wilson: I grew up around his car garage, tinkering and learning about tools and thugs and hustles. This interaction came at a curious and important time for me. Pete was slick enough not to cross any lines while "babysitting." Hell, the shop was the spot. I learned, quietly. Pete's friendship was crucial to the family, especially since these were the moped-motorcycle years for my sister and for me. Mom would always buy in pairs, starting with mini bikes, then mopeds, then a dirt bike for me. After I destroyed my dirt bike (which I earned through doing chores for one year), Mom told me she would never repair it. She never did. I lost interest in bikes until high school some years later, when Rob let me ride his Honda 450 custom.

★ ★ ★

7/22/96:

Dear Miss Everything,

This letter comes at a time of much jubilation for me, as the woman I have loved for some time now is about to love me. This is perhaps one of the greatest feelings I have ever experienced. The things I think the things I do the things I want to be clear on the places I go I'll have her in mind. She is mine, wish she is. She is jazz, she is Swing. In Love am I. Oh great love that men speak of. Pleasure to make your acquaintance. We've never met before, but I've heard great things. Will we see These things? When? Where? How often? I feel your power, oh great love that man speak of. The woman I love loves eternity. You can hear it in her sultry voice you can see it in her landing eyes. They live for a man that loves like her. Her character is French and gentle, his patient, caring, waiting for admission, submission to the idea of what is inevitable. They are in love, they are one adult. This scares her, for she is once again. This scares him, for he is responsible for being certain about his intent. He loves her unconditionally. She receives and reciprocates. At long last, they are in love. If he is, subside. His intent is sure in certain. She knows now. Thank you for love. This will be the last time they love.

You, L., are mine, Miss Everything. God bless our love. Let's go! Eternally yours—Westray

★ ★ ★

12/19/96:

Of Love and the Truth

L., so our little spat was silly, and unnecessarily abrupt. The conversation was not totally irrelevant; it was fueled by some basic issues that have always been prevalent in this relationship. I do love you, L. Never question that. I have done too much in this relationship, and it is actually backfiring on me in these ways:

the character that I exemplify quite possibly makes you feel insecure about your position in this relationship; the financial or monetary provisions I make for us when we're together (not that they are mandatory or naturally assume, rather they are performed on a matter of choice a result of the type of man I am) may also contribute to a feeling of insecurity (or feeling of non-contribution). Perhaps our professional disparities may be causing these feelings of insecurity. I say these things because I have thought about them a great deal. More than twice you have asked me, where do *you* fit? What do you bring to this relationship? It is in examining the statements that I came up with these three possible reasons.

In regard to the first possible reason, I have become the kind of man I am out of choice and experience if I decide to be there for a woman, I am there all the way. I only know one way to treat a woman—that is, with dignity, provisions and respect. I have quite possibly done too much in this regard. And you tried to warn me about doing too much, too soon, for you. In trying to win you over, it seems that I have done just that. I notice your frustration when I place you in less than a power position. Is it wrong for a real man to say, "Don't worry about that darling. I will handle it."

By comparing me to someone else, or blatantly disregarding who I think I am, I feel that you are trying to undervalue me. By doing so, perhaps you gain more of a sense of who you are. I have expanded a lot of karmic and spiritual energy into this relationship. Why are you still around? I'm around for many reasons: if I have to bow out it must be settled with you having a full understanding of why I must. I am fueled by some mad optimism about you becoming a different person. I have seen effort toward a more positive interaction following a conflict. But, it doesn't take long for it to wear off; and we are right back where we *are*. You might even say something like "one day you're going to look up and I'm going to have someone else who treats me like I want to be treated." How's that? Frankly, you have not created enough security to play with statements like that, me-love. Because you have never seem fully satisfied (with your self) in this relationship, I must take those types of statements seriously. You have not turned out to be everything I hoped for; but I would never pit a past, or future, relationship against the hope I have in us. We both know that we are very good picks for anyone looking.

The giving has been partly because of choice and partly because I need to see you delighted.

I saw you as one who could be given the best I had to offer. I think that you are frustrated sometimes financially, occupationally, geographically, or any adverb that may be used to describe the intermittent desolation of this love-affair. I only asked to be treated with respect and to be acknowledged for the man I am. You don't have to follow orders or any of that. Further, I will continue to progress in my field because that is what I am here to do. I value what you are achieving in your career. In many ways I feel responsible for some small portion of your recent successes. I was busting my chops for many years and many hours to prepare my place in the world of music. I have been focused for a long time. I recall encouraging you to focus. I knew where you were in your career after meeting you, and I know where you want to go. We are miles apart. Miles that I hope will be bridged by love and respect for differences. Are you willing to be my audience as you build a late [ballet] career? I believe that everything I am mentioning manifests in our relationship in some way. I was not attracted to your professional position. I was attracted to your zeal and interest and for your love of God.

Perhaps you need someone who does not bring this much love to the table. You fear that I am trying to define your identity through myself. I am not here to control or dominate you. I am here to protect you—and to allow you to protect me. That is all I have ever really wanted.

You believe that I am a nice guy with good intentions. This man wants a woman with opinions, and get up and go. This man needs a woman who exalts him. The weird thing is that I think that you do appreciate who I am but you try to diminish the full splendor of it as to not feel inferior within the relationship. I need you, too. Just as you are. If you cannot *build* me we will not work. We will only continue to clash. I can't expend anymore energy with no payoff. If we can't work together we will not worry. You must rid yourself of this fear of me trying to control you. What is that anyway? Has someone done that to you? By now we should've been able to choreograph a successful duet. I think your possibilities are limitless. I could appreciate the same faith from you. As I love you, I also am tired. Which of my opinions have been to your detriment? The New Year is just around the corner. We must make changes. Even married couples retreat. I trust and pray that you will except my invitation to join me at the cabin at BlairsVille

—Auld Lang Syne, Ron

* * *

4/8/96:

I Want to Talk About ...

Rather than destroy certain things, I figured I would just return them. Do with them as you like. Actually, I figured you might enjoy some of the photos for yourself. April 8 12:57 AM round, in an attempt to sort out my feelings and deal with the herd I'm experiencing, I need to write you this letter. After our conversation on Tuesday, I vowed, to myself, to never speak to you again. The person the other night was not the man I grew to love. The harshness and coldness with which you treated me made me feel as if I were just one of your sluts, or perhaps a whore you were dealing with—someone whom you never had feelings for. I never thought that you, with the love, respect and tenderness you once expressed for me, could become so calloused; and I'm concerned about many things that I assumed were genuine. In realizing all the occurrences, and the comments concerning my so called lack of affection (and I'm sure the influence of your Mom telling you that you were doing too much for me and that the relationship wasn't really what you were making it out to be). You became bitter and just as hurt about things as I was.

Of course, though, I could be wrong. But in wanting so strongly to believe that the love and the attention you expressed towards me was pure. I can only conclude that you were hurt—and in expressing your hurt, you did not say so—so as to protect your own feelings. Ronald, all of that is fine; and it is okay that we all express ourselves differently. These differences have also discouraged me.

In all honesty, I am having an extremely difficult time, dealing with, and expressing, this departure you felt to be mutual—though obviously one of which I have no choice. I love you and I'm still very much in love with you. I'm lonely without you, and it hurts to feel as if you don't care. Is that true? You simply just don't care anymore? I don't understand how week ago you loved me and wanted to spend the rest of your life with me. Then, after a disagreement, you just turned every emotion off? Was this, were we a game? Were you just caught up in a moment of passion—how you felt inside of me? Who was I to you? Did I mean anything to you or am I just another? I didn't want to trust another, but I let go and trusted you, Ron, I literally open myself up to you the way that I would never to another, because I trusted you. I trusted your words—who you said you were—who you said I was to you. I just did what you said you wanted to do with me—what you wanted to make work with me. I trusted that guy.

I wanted the same things. I always asked, "Are you sure that this is what you want?" You were always sure. Were these just words of broken promises? You promised to protect me—that you knew what you wanted—that I was who and what you wanted. Did you really know? Were you sure? I was. Ronald, I wish that you knew me—and knew that I was what you really want.

I haven't changed from when we met. I am, naturally, a very giving, and affectionate, person. Even people that don't know me sense this in my essence after being around me for a little while. There's nothing that I wouldn't do to please you (if you really wanted it). So what happened? Was I uninformed? What of myself did I not give?

All I wanted was to give my love, myself, to one person—to you, but I wanted to know, trust, you. I wanted to be sure that you would be what you said you would—and be there—like you said you would. I needed time. You couldn't wait. Ronald, as I look back, I have learned a lot of things. Now I'm asking you a lot of questions. I remember how elated you were when I finally agreed to be yours. You were in love with me and you lavished in the possibilities. Your love for me was greater than I knew. I did care deeply for you—and for how you felt. Though I cared deeply for you, I wanted to assure you that what I feel for you was genuine, and I expressed that my reasons for not being in sync with you were because we didn't know each other well. I needed time to accustom myself, familiarize, myself with you—and your ways. I wanted to be with you (otherwise I would not even venture). Honestly, we did not know each other well. That conversation always made you less than hopeful. That shot your confidence. As your liaisons and travel excursions continued to grow, my desire and comfort around you grew. I feel that we were progressing towards a somewhat better understanding of each other and each other's feelings.

Still, I needed time. I needed peace. I needed the pace to flow, slower; still, you couldn't wait. You felt that maybe it really wasn't what you thought it to be. Maybe you were trying to make it into something that, did not, and, will never exist. After affirming basic things we both felt to be true, you proposed to me. Elated, I excepted; I later reneged. I was afraid. I knew I wanted you. I was afraid because it all seems so sudden; and I felt it too soon to sacrifice all the freedoms I had just attained. I, still, needed more time. Throughout all the frustrations, I wanted you to, always, know that I wanted you—and to be with you. That never changed. Even your good friend said it takes at least two months of waking every day to the same woman to really get to know her. Didn't we deserve a longer time to work out issues in our relationship? I have expressed over and over I love you. I am in love with only you. But I still wanted to know more of you. What were you so afraid of? Did that request have no validity? It's funny, though. You were afraid to tell me about Amsterdam because you didn't know how I would react. You didn't know that about me. And all I've been asking for is time with you. Time to be your friend and you be mine. Time to be affectionate with you. Time for you to hear me breathe, and know that I feel as I do. Time for you to understand me; though I might become antsy when I'm tired, I would never disrespect you. I just want to go home and cuddle up next to you—make love to you. I want time to wear the lingerie you buy me—Time to just laugh and enjoy touching your hands, sharing a kiss with you. I adored you; and I wanted to be with you—if you trusted me and would let me. Would you want to be with me, or affectionate with me, if I constantly complained that you didn't do, or act, as I wish? I understand that there is give-and-take; but imagine how I feel. I just want time to breathe in the relationship—time for you to see me and love me. I loved you. But you couldn't wait. Maybe you just didn't believe it would ever happen. Guess what, ron? I fell deeply in love with someone; that, someone, was you. When and how? I don't know; but I got there—and it is a real place. Where are you now? I got to where you tried so hard to push me (because you were afraid I would never get there) It's deeper than I ever thought it would be. That's why it hurts to let go. Where are you now? I am afraid. I am here; and you have left me alone. You always said to me, "Others said they would be here; but where are they?" Where are you, now? Maybe you are just like them.

Maybe you, too, thought that you knew what you wanted, but didn't have the patience to let it become what it so naturally would've become. Maybe *you* were afraid. Why? You didn't trust me—believe in me—though I tried, so hard, to assure you? None has seen what my love has to yield. After all is finished, they all return, too late, only realizing that my love was deep; ours could have been everlasting. I love you. I am in love with you. I want you to want me. Have you ever wondered why I don't complain? Not everything about you is perfect, either.

But, at the core, I trust you. I trust your love for me and I love and accept you for who you are. When you are, you will be who you are. I respect you; and I only want to be with you.

Now, my heart is broken and the only one who can relate to me *is* you. Nobody else understands. Sometimes I wonder if you know how I'm feeling? Do you care? I wake up every morning—feeling cold and empty, knowing that the biggest part of my life no longer cares about me.

Is this how I have made *you* to feel? Have I hurt you? Why must you hurt me this way? Why would you be so cold and turn me away? All I wanted was to be with you? Sometimes I feel so angry. I can't help feeling that your mother has such a great impact in your life? Even in your relationship. Sometimes I feel as if she is the actual fuel that has made you put out the fire of our love. I feel as if she sees how strong your love is for me and is possibly afraid that she is losing you. I see the she has influence over the way you think, almost disallowing you to, feel, and deal, as you wish. I'm torn apart; because, I can't seem to get to you. I tried to bare all to you; and we disagree. It seems as if your frustrations and feeling, that this is not natural, is reinforced by your Mom's views. It's almost as if you are living your true love and feelings for me, *through* the way *she* feels about *how* you feel. Love hurts. It takes time. Some of the best things, in life, are the things that take time: work, desire, will and perseverance.

Your Mom doesn't know how I feel about you—how in love I am with you—how I feel without you. All she sees and hears is what you say (based upon what I feel to be, or have been, a somewhat impatient approach towards something strong and genuine, needing time). That being said, if she really understood, maybe she will be saying, "You two still have yet to know each other." That comes with time—and being around each other more. You can't invalidate that. Maybe the truth is that the distance scared you. Maybe you just wanted an instant relationship; you and I clicked instantly. Maybe you really didn't want to work or wait. The reality is that we are apart now; yet, we *were*. The other reality is that time allowed me to fall in love with you. Whether you want to believe it or not, Ron, I saw you. I understood you. I saw that you were afraid (afraid that if I didn't fall in love, fast enough, when you thought I should have, because you were there, that I would never). When it didn't happen the way you thought it should, you believed that it wasn't what it was meant to be (and would never be) You still tried to push things. I feel I love when I naturally should have. I was going to. For the first time, I know what it feels like to be in love—to have my trust violated. I know what it feels like to be angry because your love is misunderstood. I know what it feels like to love a man, so—that, career doesn't matter. You just want to get on with your life with him. I know why couples say leave the family out of it. I know what it feels like to go to bed crying and to wake up the next day crying. At first, I thought I won't cry. He obviously doesn't love me like you used to. But to cry and feel what I feel is only natural. My heart is broken. I would be foolish not to let it out. I wonder if you know what love is?—in love—really loving someone.

You've broken so many other hearts, maybe I was a fool to trust you. That way was so natural to you. It hurts so much. Many days, I don't even know what to say.

I want to say I don't ever want to see you or hear your name again; but, in my heart, I long for that void to be filled. I'm afraid to love you again. The way I feel, I never felt before. I wanted you to be the only one. I trusted you. I, always, wanted to be where you were. I wanted to lie down and wake up in your arms. You were all I saw—all I wanted. You didn't understand my love. Yet, I don't want any one else to possess it. Why am revealing these things to you? You, obviously, don't care. It's too late. But I've never been with another man before; and I miss you. I was a little nervous standing, bare, before each other. It was so new to me But you made me feel so comfortable; and so I went even deeper with you. You have a part of me that I can never have back. Half of me is gone; you have it. Ron, though I know, or believe, that is too late, I say these things so that you know who I am—and was. It means so much to be understood. I don't think you really understand me (or what you meant to me). You became my life and I wanted a life with you. I wanted so much to understand and be understood. I wanted to have time for you (and with you). I love you. I can't just simply turn it off. The way you treated me on the phone hurt me. Deep in my heart, I know I meant more to you. I thought we had something real. I thought we could say what we needed to say and it would be respected. I thought you respected my feelings. When I would said that if I didn't make you happy, you should find what does, that was not to send you on your way. You did express that I was who you wanted. I loved, and still love, you. Why would I ever want to send you away? Conversely, I wanted to see you happy with the way I was. Nonetheless, you left.

The reality could be, simply, that I did not make you happy; and you're feelings for me ceased. But I did not deserve to be treated so badly. What I did not say: I still can't seem to understand what happened. Am I the only one hurting? I feel sick and alone. I've never felt this way before. I don't know how you feel. You will probably never tell me. I loved you. I was in love with you. I was happy with you; and you made me laugh. I wanted to know all of you. I was happy with the prospect of anything (as long as it was with you). I was ready and willing to spend the rest of my life pleasing you; and now I miss you. Ron, I wish that I could have made you happy and that you could have been happy with me. I hope you find a love that doesn't scare you; and that you remain true to that love. Take time to allow time. Be careful.

P.S. I'm still here for you. I miss hearing you call me darling.

—Avec amour, L.

★ ★ ★

The beginning of this year was all MC. We had attended high school together but never even looked at each other romantically until now. I was still in love w/ L. but she was in DC and I was still doing my thing in SC. MC and I just clicked. We had the same sexual appetite. L. was still holding out—1950s style, believe that? MC wasn't. We kicked it the rest of the year up to the fall when L. gave in. Of course, this sent me reeling, and I broke up with all the girlfriends and asked L. to marry me. L. had the presence of mind to decline the offer. She knew I just didn't want to risk losing what I had just gained. That wasn't enough reason to get hitched. I pretended that she was wrong … She was right. Well, I was heartbroken and had dumped everybody. Sh*t!

* * *

"Wycliffe just told her the same thing and you said they are still getting married …" When you said that in the parking lot of Sandy's I wanted to laugh! Looks like the reality of your decision to jet is making a result of some pretty desperate and sophomoric tactics. Ha.

Let me spell it out for you. How she interprets her relationship has nothing to do with the way I handle mine. Since it is a comparison you want, how about this: like her I am capable of forgiving. We are all human, does without forgiveness love and life can't exist. But I can't forgive you; because you feel you've done nothing wrong. Disrespect: you don't define disrespect the way I do. You think sleeping with other women outside of your intimate relationship with a woman you are in love with is not disrespectful. You use the theory of necessity as justification for this. You dismissed my reaction as typical. You explained that I couldn't recall a time when you disrespected me to my face. So, the fuck fest, behind my back, doesn't count? I guess everyone is entitled to even the most ridiculous of opinions.

Ron, the fact is, you are very much aware of how I value our intimacy; yet, you get your groove on anyway. *That* is disrespect. Trying to convince me that it isn't only makes it worse. My temple is precious, and sacred, to me. The Ron I shared it with was indeed a privileged man. It was just one way to show how much I loved you. And because I loved you, mixed with the fact that you sexually satisfy me completely, I allowed only you to access it—promising it to you exclusively. You would not promise me the same because I wasn't your fiancée or your wife but I accepted that as your reason. It turns out the real reason you wouldn't say it is because you knew you couldn't hold out. So why say you can when you can't? It was true when you said, "Just because someone says they didn't, doesn't mean they won't." I think if someone can say they won't cheat, and can understand that if they did it would be catastrophic, then they would have the morality to not want to sleep around. You feel me?

Our definitions of necessity don't coincide, either. It is true that for most people sexual stimulation is a necessity. In layman's terms: you could have masturbated until you got home—like I've masturbated for you. That's respect—not mere loyalty (as you described my holding out for you as). I wonder if the women you were with view the intimate moments that they share with you as just a necessity? I wonder how Ron would deal with the his lover screwing other men because she needed it right then? Oh, I'm sorry, I keep forgetting that this issue is supposed to be separate from the real reason you left. I'll try to stay on track.

So what's up with you? How is Ron doing? According to you, you've been trying to figure out if your decision to end things was a bit hasty. You say you miss me, hanging out with, talking to, looking at, making love to, etc. And you've been coming clean, showing me your whole self. You are alleviating guilt with this brutal honesty of yours, in hopes that I'll at least respect the fact that you told me the truth, even if it hurts. We differ too much with this respect thing, so no. I don't respect that you're telling me the truth. Besides, you lied before you decided to be truthful, guess that, just got you.

What's up with me? How is M.C. doing? I'll tell you: these past few months I have, how would you put it, reached deep into my womanhood and did a lot of thinking. Do you know what I saw? I saw a clock that read, "It's time to grow." I have set some goals that should help me do just that. I am at peace, I have new focuses and I don't think a soulmate is one of them, then again it was when I bumped into you. So I'll just say that the next time I pursue a relationship, I'll at least know more about what he doesn't want. I don't want to be third to music, family, or anything else. I tried it, learned to like it, and trusted you completely. But it wasn't enough for you. You decided you weren't giving me what you need and you left. My next relationship will have to take precedence in both of our heads and hearts. If not, someone is going to get dropped as if they were heavy baggage, just like you did me.

I also don't want a man that can't see that sleeping around outside of our intimate relationship is disrespectful to me. I knew you felt this way a long time ago. But I really believed that you would never do anything intentionally to hurt me, so I stayed with you.

I became so secure in this belief that I really felt you wouldn't sleep with another, regardless of the fact that you couldn't say you wouldn't. The next man I make my intimacy exclusive to will define disrespect the same way I do.

Ron, I think in your own little way, you are saying that you want me back. If I'm wrong, please excuse my arrogance. But if I'm right, notice there is a difference between missing me and wanting me. Wanting me means wanting to accept the responsibilities of a commitment to me. You know this, so I think in reality you only miss me. I understand, right, cause I'd miss me too. And yes I miss you. So much that sometimes I have to fight tears. I missed our late-night phone conversations we share. I missed a kiss that led to the many slow and wet fires we lighted. I miss anxiously waiting for dozens of people to get off the airplane, then finally seeing your handsome and smiling face. But acting on what we miss won't be tied to a few things between us, because that's all you have time for. What we had was too strong to sink to this.

I guess I need to find a way to bring this letter to a close. In love one should never say never, so I won't say we'll never be together again. I will say this though: the man I just told you I don't want to be with is the only one you know how to be. If I am wrong, prove it to yourself, not me. Because this letter is not a request that you change for me. I wrote it because everything in it needed to be said. Perhaps you'll find it resourceful when you present your next relationship. I still love you. And like a true friend, I am still here for you even though you've hurt me. Surround yourself with your friends right now, Ron. They will help you get through this valuable lesson you are learning for the first time in your life: How to heal a broken heart.

—MC

Chapter 25

4/25/95:

It is cloudy …

And he sits in a darkened room—Black as night or onyx or the stormy night—or a cat. Alone and sad, Lady Day is his only refuge. He lights a candle, and watches the equalizer lights pierce the darkness and blink in syncopation with her voice. Hours pass as he thinks, wishes, longs.

It is cloudy and windy …

And there's a knock at the door. Is it her? He anxiously moves through the obscureness and opens the door. There she is—standing, shivering, wet from the rain and from her tears. She closes the door behind her, and as he is about to say "I'm sorry" she holds his attempt hostage; her kiss is the weapon. They stand in the middle of the darkness, tasting each other's lips, probing each other's tongues and licking each other's wounds that anger's horrible words left earlier that day.

It is cloudy, windy and raining …

And her kisses grow harder and wilder, as if she's losing him. He brushes her wet hair away from her face for more, holding and squeezing her so hard it affects the rate of her breathing. His clothes vanish, she touches and caresses, reading his body like braille. It reads: keep me. She gently pushes him backward and he collapses in the same chair he sat so despondent in just minutes before. Like the branch of an oak tree his piece is up right, strong, steel, and timeless; and she sees it even in the darkness. He reaches for her but is certainly paralyzed as he watches her untie her belt of the blood-red garment that conceals her naked body. It drops to the floor in slow motion. He stares hypnotically at the peach-toned black-woman—examining her every curve, angle, and contour. She glows like mercury in the darkness. The light from the candle reveals hunger and regret in her eyes; but a sultry glance speaks to mischief.

It is cloudy, windy, raining and thundering …

And she creeps over to the coffee table and carefully removes the crystal bowl of fruit siting there—all except for one, thick, stiff, ripe banana. He watches as her virtual-movie begins. Staring at him constantly, she stretches out on the table; and as if she were performing magic; her hands give the banana life. It finds her pleasure points, her sensitive spots, her come-commencers. It pokes and scrapes her erect nipples; it slowly, but relentlessly, prods her open-mouth. It rolls and tumbles down her sweaty mid section towards the rapids; at last taking a dramatic plunge into her waterfall, she moans as it swims inside of her, rocking slowly and hard, back-and-forth through her waters—so hard it sheds it's peel. The heat from her temple melts the ripe fruit matter that lay within the banana's outer-skin.

Thick and white, the banana smears itself all around the doorway to her temple and she breathes harder as its cool temperature reacts to the heat in her hothouse.

It is cloudy, windy, rainy, thundering and lightning …

He manages to free himself from her spell; that had kept him motionless in his chair. His hands multiply; they are everywhere—poling, pinching, rubbing, tugging and positioning his prey. His sucks her breasts like a hungry infant—and her neck like a vampire being summoned by a full moon. Her hair wet and dangling in straight strands like that of a wild creature, entangles his fingers. Every cell of her body is screaming for more; and her perceptive partner senses it. He sets her legs up like two arches as his mouths finds its way down the rapids. His tongue paddles through the banana remains—eating, sucking and licking. She fears losing control—and attempts to inch her way up the table; he snatches her back to the leading edge of the table, and selfishly satisfies his hunger for her. She trembles and shakes all over—and over—waddling in the orgasmic-fluids at the base of the table. The beast is unleashed.

It is cloudy, windy and raining, thundering and lightning and hailing …

And he snatches her tiny physique from the coffee table—pinning her around just long enough for her to see the storm's fury through the window; and then he creates a fury of his own—bending her over fast and hard, gripping her hips like a steer, he sticks it in rough—then tender. He moans as his oak-tree is watered. He closes his eyes, and pushes in until it reaches her belly button from inside. She is crying yet pleading for more. The dance continues—pushing, bending, thrusting, contorting, reaching, bucking, sticking, screaming, probing—simultaneously—until they reach ecstasy—crashing, burning.

My, my—weatherman says it's supposed to rain again this week.

—MC

★ ★ ★

Geminis are polyamorous. I made a painstaking effort at not revealing any of these written thoughts to him into several conversations we had while he was in St. Louis. Mainly because I figured I'd get angry and f*ck up the design I had intended for discussing them with him, but more importantly because I did not want any of his actions to be influenced by my doubts. He asked me on day two of his trip was I mad about anything pertaining to his visit to St. Louis. I stated that if I was, it was it because I feel deceived. I told him I would know exactly how I felt about his trip by the time he returned. I think I got it all: Why am I mad? Why don't I like this damn trip?

One: because his mentioning the trip was the first time a deer in the headlights; not catching the word St. Louis the first time indicates naïveté on my part.

Or does it indicate my confidence in others. An alarm shouldn't have to sound off in my head when I hear the man supposedly worthy of my love say that he is going to the city where his ex-girlfriend lives. Besides, in the event something develops that could have been foreseen, the truth has a way of manifesting itself—as it always does.

Two: because he is even there. This Negro has willingly put himself in a private atmosphere for several days with the woman who he is, admittedly, still attracted to—and has had many intimate moments with. Regardless of confidence in what I bring to the table, or the fact that he told me he was going, or what his feelings are for me, the feelings cannot be avoided.

Three: I may never know the true answer to the question of whether or not he was with her while he was there. Forget the bachelor-bachelorette thing; we chose to identify ourselves *as*, and the thought of him making love to another woman irks me. I asked would he consider his sleeping with another an act of disrespect? His reply: "You would first of all have to know that I slept with someone else." What the f*ck does that mean? If he says yes when I asked, he's damn sure telling the truth, but if he says no, it may not be true. Trust has little to do with it. He knows that if I ever feel as if I've been intentionally and continually disrespected, I'm out. As much as I will miss him.

He's not answering my calls, and he, obviously, can't make any. Then, there were hushed tones in his voice the one time when he did call. On the nights he didn't call, he offered his *not being able to* as a reason. Truth is, he chose not to. Well, why? Or perhaps he felt calling me from this woman's house would've been disrespectful to her? Was he just too busy doing things, like when he's doing music? On another note, if she supposedly knows he's involved with someone in South Carolina, she might feel the same. Or maybe he went to end things in a respectful, face-to-face manner. In spite of my dislike for some of his methods, I must accept them. And when he finds himself in St. Louis, again, it is not wrong for me to assume that he will no longer need to visit her or stay with her? In the event that he wants to, I'll get a telephone number, at least?

Baby, please excuse the disorganization; but my thoughts of you really are. These words are what I thought from Monday through Friday about your trip. I thought it would be fair for them to have a chance to marinate with you for a little while. I'll see you later today.

—MC

★ ★ ★

When I arrived home from graduate school in '94, Rob was sill living in the addition on the property and still helping Mom out farmhand style in the black burbs. It had been 10 long years of service for Rob on the lane. The romantic vision he had imagined for himself (and Mom) hadn't quite turned out as he'd hoped. Rob was my most consistent role model, to whom I owe most of my knowledge of building things, repairing things and inventing things.

Rob also let me ride his Honda 400 custom when I was in high school. For that, I am eternally grateful. All Rob wanted me to learn was how to ask another man may you use his property.

When I returned from Illinois, Rob and Mom were at odds. Mom was accusing Rob of having gotten junky and lazy. Rob insisted that Mom had no compassion for the load he bore helping out. "Help out where?" Mom replied angrily, "This place was standing when you got here, and it's gone be here when you march you ass back across the street to Mrs. Davis [Rob's mother]. She right there! You know how I don't play."

I needed to raise a little hell myself and show off a few new vocabulary words from school. Rob and I fell out during this period. Rob could've kicked my ass. Instead, he let me be. My interaction at this time with Rob was the most aggressive I had been man-to-man. It was almost as if Mom set it up just for me. It was a rite of passage to see Rob's departure through to the end. This is also the year I got together with L. Though we met in '94, we did not communicate for one year after meeting.

I had assumed Rob's duties around the house. I replaced the bathroom at Mom's. I could not imagine my future. I had been on the road (fresh out of grad school) for less than a year. I was still based in SC and had opened, and shut, the doors on my first (and only) jazz club, The Wooden Flute. In between being on the road with W, I opened the club on Main Street in Cola, South Carolina. I spent all my discretionary income, this year, paying rent and so on on a jazz club in a southern city. I was hoping to bring some of the culture that I was experiencing on the road back to my hometown which desperately needed it.

Lots had changed for L., and my random call while in DC was a refreshing surprise. The time was fall and we met at my hotel, talked and caught up on things. After this visit I sent her a letter simply stating, "I enjoyed laughing and talking and being with you." I copped that line from some sh★t my Mom hipped me to from her and Dad's days of wine and roses. After all, that was how I felt. Her father had died in the past year, and she was receptive to the idea of something new. So I invited L. down to South Carolina for the first time in September of '95 for the grand opening of TWF. The visit and the opening went well. L. was at the first concert at the club. It was the Marcus Roberts Trio. I was in love with L. and had a vision of our future already drawn out in my mind, though I was not ready for commitment. This contradiction would plague our relationship for years to come. Later, Boss came down south. I turned the house three times, breaking even, and I left the jazz club business.

Chapter 24

With the Jazz at Lincoln Center Orchestra:

Kirkland Fine Arts Center, Decatur, MI.

Pabst Theater, Milwaukee, WI.

Hancher Auditorium, Iowa City, IA.

Fine Arts Center, La Crosse, WI.

Main Hall, Decorah, IA.

Leid Center, Lincoln, NE.

Opera House, Seattle, WA.

Laxon Hall, Chico, CA.

Luther Burbank Center, Santa Rosa, CA.

Memorial Auditorium, Palo Alto, CA.

Zellerbach Hall, Berkeley, CA.

Wiltern Theater, Los Angeles, CA.

Centennial Hall, Tuscon, AZ.

Kent Concert Hall, Logan, UT.

Marriot Center, Provo, UT.

Bushnell Memorial Hall, Hartford, CT.

Symphony Hall, Boston, MA.

Monroe C.C. Theater, Rochester, NY.

Center for the Arts, Buffalo, NY.

Garther Auditorium, Cleveland, OH.

Orchestra Hall, Chicago, IL.

Memorial Chapel, Appleton, WI.

Ordway Music Hall, St. Paul, MN.

Hill Auditorium, Ann Arbor, MI.

Veterans Auditorium, Providence, RI.

Berlee Theater, Boston, MA.
Grand Opera House, Wilmington, DE.
McCarter Theater, Princeton, NJ.
Avery Fischer Hall, Lincoln Center, New York, NY.
Le Villette Jazz Festival, Paris, France.
Vienna Jazz Festival, Vienna, Austria.
JVC Jazz Festival, Torino, Italy.
Istanbul Jazz festival, Istanbul, Turkey.*
Kongsberg Jazz Festival, Kongsberg, Norway.
Vitoria Jazz Festival, Vitoria, Spain.
Vienne Jazz Festival, Vienne, France.
Capitol Radio Festival, London, England.
Munich Jazz Festival, Munich, Germany.
Antibes Festival, Antibes, France.
Salon Festival, Salon, France.
Pori Jazz Festival, Pori, Finland.
Norton Center, Danville, KY.
Mershon Auditorium, Columbus, OH.
Great Hall, East Lansing, MI.
Phi Beta Kappa Hall, Williamsburg, VA.**
Singletary Center for the Performing Arts, Lexington, KY.
Orchestra Hall, Detroit, MI.
Edmand Memorial Chapel, Wheaton, IL.
Royce Auditorium, Grand Rapids, MI.
Carnegie Hall Jazz Orchestra w/ Jon Faddis, New York, NY.
w/ Wynton Marsalis and The JALC Orchestra:
Merle Ruskin Theater, Chicago, IL.
Hill Auditorium, Ann Arbor, MI.
Orchestra Hall, Detroit, MI.
Garther Auditorium, Cleveland, OH.
Mershon Auditorium, Columbus, OH.
Kennedy Center, Washington, DC.
McCarter, Theater, Princeton, NJ.
Georgia Tech Theater, Atlanta, GA.

Wilson Concert Hall, Glassboro, NJ.

Broughal Auditorium, Bethlehem, PA.

Kresge Auditorium, Interlochen, MI.

Cincinnati Zoo Amphitheater, Cincinnati, OH.

Denver Botanic Gardens, Denver, CO.

Washington Park Zoo Amphitheater, Portland, OR.

Britt Pavilion, Jacksonville, OR.

Eisenhower Auditorium, University Park, PA.

Bennedum Hall, Pittsburg, PA.

F.M. Kirby Center, Wilkes-Barr, PA.

City Hall Auditorium, Portland, ME.

Symphony Hall, Boston, MA.

Tilles Center, Brookville, NY.

Chandler Center, Chandler, AZ.

Pantages Theater, Tacoma, WA.

Community Center Theater, David, CA.

Royce Hall, Los Angeles, CA.

Zellerbach Hall, Berkeley, CA.

Madison Civic Center, Madison, WI.

Ordway Music Hall, St. Paul, MN.

Weidner Center for the Arts, Greenbay, WI.

Center for Faith & Life, Decorah, IA.

Hancher Auditorium, Iowa City, IA.

Elliot Hall of Music, W. Lafayette, IN.

Jasper Civic Auditorium, Jasper, IN.

⋆Got picked up by a rover and robbed at a little bar in Istanbul; wrote a song titled "Esoteric Advent (Turkish Coffee)" for Atlantic Records.

⋆⋆First date w/ L. (though we met one year earlier).

She shunned me for a whole year, and I reached out again.

⋆ ⋆ ⋆

Broke off relationship with A.M. Not happy and not sad, just relieved. I thought she might pull me down and show no real interest in my development or the longevity of a musician. She was cute, country and a great lover. She deserves an intelligent, country guy. I'm not him.

Today was chill. I wrote a little; but I did not practice as much as I would have liked to. This has been the rule, not the exception, lately. I rearranged *Time Alone* in preparation for the Atlantic Records demo I promised Yves.

I was advised not to worry about this annoyance from the guy sitting next to me. I defined it as an imitation of quality in the midst of personal defeat, innate inferiority—the denial of one's caliber (or the lack thereof). Worse is the fact that it is amplified through instigation (higher authorities). I guess this sort of thing starts with my personal preparation and motives. It's not that I think I'm perfect. It's just that I am seeking perfection. Anytime I am bullshitting is free time I give myself. It seems that I have allowed a lot of that lately just to get along.

Perhaps it is my proud disposition and or choice of dress? It's never anything like that, right? Not the way you dress, man. Who cares? Right? There's no time for bitterness. There's work to be done.

★ ★ ★

Life, Love and Happy-Sad Time

It's eleven o'clock post meridian in the South, the end of a day.
As for me, a certain melancholy resides in my soul.
Music, imbedded that could not escape, today.
Tomorrow is different.
It is every artist's right to lack inspiration.
In the same way, it is the artist's gift to draw inspiration from things seemingly commonplace.
These days when thoughts of unrequited love make you smile and sigh.
These days when art flees as the squirrel, gathering no moss.
Thy trap of creation hath failed
Unborn inspiration, promised inspiration, unborn love, promised love …
The only light I see resides in tomorrow's idea …
Creative zeal? Ideas? Love found? Perhaps not?Less than today?
This is how we learn the value of things … lack thereof.
How great to consider—
How terrible is this artful day without inspiration?
It is the artist's right to lack inspiration.
The horn beckons. I cannot respond
The pen calls. I do not come.
Even the squirrel hath avoided my path.
God is having my attention today.

Others will call it something else.
I will not.
I owe all my day to the lord.
It is all the lord's.
Ah, sweet melancholy,
The smell of things past—
Does love really conquer all?
Does being alone produce a lack of vulnerability, even to love?
One chooses to be lonely; does he not? Love chooses; does it really?
Ah, sweet life rhythm—
Art and love are fleeting things
Chase them if you wish. You never catch up.
In your finished hour, the love bird still sings o'er yo head.
Let us continue in art, through love, in life, in bliss, with and without inspiration.
Today has gone. Tomorrow is unknown.
What doth it bring? That's what makes it interesting.

Chapter 23

Having mingled with the Wynton Marsalis Septet for one night on stage back in 1991, I had gone on to join Marcus Robert's band and completed my undergraduate degree in 1992. While home in South Carolina during the Christmas holidays, preceding the second semester of grad school in 1993, WME (Wynton Marsalis Enterprises) called my mom. W. wanted me to join his band for a flagship performance with Peter Martins and The New York City Ballet (a piece he had been commissioned to compose named *Jump: 6 1/2 Syncopated Movements*).

I accepted, and I could not have been more excited. Unbeknownst to me, this band would eventually morph into the Jazz at Lincoln Center Orchestra—a group I would be in for the next twelve years.

* * *

1/28/93:

I don't know how to begin this letter, I just know I need to write it. Right now I'm sitting in my bed trying to figure out how and why I allow myself to be hurt once again. I do realize now that there wasn't much I could do to avoid the situation. But somehow I'm still very angry at myself. I haven't done much of anything since the dreadful day I called your hotel room and Tonya answered. Ever since, I've run it over and over in my mind. The conversation we had on the phone. One thing that seems to hurt me the most is the fact that you generally did not want to stop seeing either one of us. It was quite evident to me that, had I not called you, I would still think I had something special with what I thought was a special guy. I don't know if I should hate you for hurting me or thank you for teaching me a lesson well learned! It seems as though the moment I felt we were the closest is the moment I found out you weren't that close to me at all.

I find myself thinking back to when you went to New York in June and you came home and I went to Savannah or vice versa. I was on my monthly and you really made me feel special with that speech about how much you cared and the fact that you knew nothing was going to happen. (Nothing needed to happen because you have been with her all week.) I said, thinking how much of a gentleman you were. Ron, you know you said you did not tell me because you did not want to blow any chance of us getting together. So now I find a part of that hard to believe. It seems as though you never had any intention on being with one person. Maybe we were not engaged but you know how I felt about being with you and the agreement we made. Just because you did not give me a ring has nothing to do with the verbal commitment we made. I think I am most hurt by the fact that I allowed you to come in to my life, only to stab me in the heart.

Right now you really don't know just how much you have hurt me. I don't even think I can convey it to you in this letter, or at all. My view of a serious relationship and your view now seems to be opposite of each other.

The connection I thought we had now dangles in the air like a broken power line. I thought we had so much in common and that we were so compatible. I don't know if I've ever been so wrong about something in all my life. People seem to have so many questions.

You are there and you don't have to deal with family and friends wondering why you and I can no longer talk. I thought I could sit back here in my room and go through this by myself but it doesn't seem possible. My eyes are red, my head is thumping and everyone that stops by or calls wants to know what is wrong and when will I be seeing you again. I don't know if I can forgive or forget how in one moment you destroy the one thing that I was counting on to work for me. I have my entire heart and soul into this. At one time we were very good friends but you destroyed it all in one fatal blow.

I hope you can go on in life, and everything works out. I can tell you that I don't hold grudges and eventually this, just like all tragic events in my life, will be behind me. I'm going to close the slider, but I must tell you before I go, if there was any doubt in your mind ever about how I feel about you, Ron, please note I love you with all my heart. I would have gone anywhere with you. You wll always be in my heart and mind. Please take very good care of yourself. With all my love. I hope this makes some sense. Please excuse all mistakes.

—AM

★ ★ ★

Of Musician, of Man

11/16/93, 2:13 a.m.

This is the first sentence in the memoirs of Ronald Kenneth Westray Junior. I've been trying to get around to writing down my thoughts for some time now, and I'm just getting around to it. So I guess this is when it's supposed to start. I greet you at age 23 as a Christian, as a man, and as a musician—yes, musician (like my father and his father). They would be proud today for what I have accomplished at such a young age.

I owe all of my successes to God and God working through one little lady:Virginia Bush Westray (by far the strongest and wisest woman I know). The idea for these memoirs were born by her (realizing that most great musicians have one). Mom showed me how to be a man, and how to be a musician, before any of my mentors. She is truly amazing and full of spirit. At this point, in my life, I understand her. She's Arapaho, you know … lol? I'm a trombonist by nature. I even look like a trombonist. I flow like the trombone. *My trombone and I are as one.*

I am jazz. It's natural. I have my bachelors degree in music; and I'm about to complete my masters degree. This very moment I'm in Charleston, Illinois, at Eastern Illinois University. It's a real hick town and the people are lost in space, but it's an experience I need. I think every jazz musician goes through that phase when he wants to appear as diligent as John Coltrane.

It helps you develop. At this point I must honor my own diligence. That's the true test. I shall earn the right to hold my head up and swing.

It's funny how when you are a serious musician your very happiness and overall just position shifts as a result of how much you are accomplishing.

I can go from feeling very good to feeling very down and discouraged (most times due to a specific musical scenario I wasn't pleased with). For instance, now, I feel good because I just finished practicing my horn and learning another Monk solo. My emotions are made of music.

Sometimes I let the fact that these cats at EIU don't patronize get to me. I know I'm playing the baddest shit around here; its likely they're in a state of denial. Or maybe it's a white/black thing? Numerator/Denominator, you know? Sometimes it gets to me. Mom says I should not let myself get discouraged if I'm not accomplishing some personal goals, but instead, to let the spirit direct what I want to do, or not do, on a given day. I find when I do relax in this I have great days mentally, spiritually and musically. There was a point when I had to teach myself how to be diligent. I practiced every day for no less than four hours. Now, I am dedicated and persistent. I have to balance this with having a life, too.

Sometimes I feel as if I'm forcing myself to practice or write music. I don't like the thought that I would ever have to force myself to do either. I pose the question to my mother, whether or not she thought that since I had actualized some of my goals in music, that I was not as diligent and hard working? She, very seriously, doubted that. I do too. Like she said, if I'm not practicing as much, the spirit's trying to catch my attention and lead me in other directions. Spirit-led, I feel a sense of direction and accomplishment. I'm in my formative stage. I know I have to finish learning how to play the horn first; then, there's learning this in all-twelve-keys and that in all-twelve-keys.

There is no question about what has to be done. Getting to the next level and making a musical statement is my ultimate goal. I'm not saying I haven't been able to do a little of that; but it's an evolution. I thank God for everything he's done for me.

★ ★ ★

To Speak of Swing

A precious metal that speaks at command translating feelings through the wind, of man expressing emotion through a universal language wisdom and experience with a hint of anguish—telling the history of America, the oppression of the people, the conviction of men, past, and the foresight of men, present.

Oh—serious musician and his horn.

I'm not hearing anything tonight. I won't force it. I will thank God. Thank you God for everything. Today was a good day. I got a good bit done musically. Consequently, I feel OK about things. I also had a great holiday. A.M. was here, and we had a great time.

Chapter 22

Gigs

World touring with George Wein's Jazz Futures II:

Hampton Jazz Festival, Hampton, VA.

Scullers Jazz Club, Boston, MA.

JVC Jazz Fest, New York, NY.

The Kennedy Center, Washington, DC.

The Regatta Bar, Boston, MA.

Fat Tuesdays Jazz Club, New York, NY.

The Bebop Bar, San Sebastian, Spain.

Jazz a Vienne, Vienne, France.

JVC Jazz Festival, Paris, France.

Nice Jazz Festival, Nice, France.

JVC Jazz Festival, Stuttgart, Germany.

The Smithsonian Jazz Orchestra, National Performances, US.

During this time I travelled internationally, for the first time, as a young, touring musician. I remember meeting Grover Washington Jr. in the hotel where all the musicians stayed (Nice, France).

I met this Algerian babe at the bar. She would be my first (s)experience with a non-American woman. All the right parts were in place and working—well; and begin! She followed me all over Europe, and even called my Mom's house looking for me when the tour was over. Mom still picks at me about that: "'Is Ronald there?'" she will say, mimicking a quasi-foreign accent, from time to time.

* * *

9/19/92:

A.M.,

I hope this letter finds you as sexy and enticing as the last time I saw you. I'm sure it has. I would like to say again that I am enjoying the time we are spending together. It sure is a great experience getting to know you better. The more I learn about you, the more I want of you. Coming out of a stale relationship and being with you is refreshing. I hope I can make up for any deficits incurred in your previous relationship as well. It seems that we have the symptoms of the start of something very special. I am and have always been very attracted to you, and being this close makes me very happy. I hope the feelings are mutual. My chemistry for you is strong and genuine. I see only the best happening between us, and I hope you have placed the same positive actualization in your consciousness so that it may manifest.

I know this letter is pretty mushy but it's how I feel. I don't think anything I said has been rushed, because I have thought about most of it for longer than you may know, and you know what they say? "Falling in love is wonderful" … So they say.

—Ron

Chapter 21

Gig

Marcus Roberts Ensemble, National Performances, US (first professional gig).

* * *

Greenstreets

Around 1991, Wynton Marsalis brought his septet to a club called Greenstreets in my hometown of Columbia, South Carolina. I was the jazz hotshot on the campus of SCSU, so I wanted to meet Wynton and his band—especially Wycliffe Gordon, the trombonist, some years my senior.

After observing the first set of music, I approached the bandstand at intermission. Wynton came to the edge of the stage, and I shook his hand and introduced myself.

ME: Hi, Mr. Marsalis. I'm Ron Westray, and I'm a jazz trombonist.
W: Where yo' horn at?
ME: It's in my car outside.
W: Go get yo' horn!

This was my moment of truth, where preparation collides with opportunity. I scurried out to my car, retrieved my horn and *ran* back into the nightclub. I was then invited to the backstage area while the band was still on break. The first cat I met was Wycliffe Gordon. We talked about trombone mouthpieces and the HBCU band traditions, including the frat we are both part of (Kappa Kappa Psi, National Honorary Band Fraternity). Next, Wycliffe asked me to play something for him. I started playing Charlie Parker's "Donna Lee," a song noted for its tour de force quality. The rest of the band, including Wynton, peeked around the corner in astonishment of such a young musician playing such a complex song—on, of all instruments, the trombone (an instrument not generally regarded for its utility). By this time, Wycliffe had joined in with me, and we were playing in tandem as if we had been playing together our entire musical life.

After that, Wynton invited me to join the band for a song or two during the second set. The audience was filled with my friends, my colleagues and even my family (my sister had bought the tickets for both of us). When the audience saw me walk onto the stage with the band, they exploded, as if they, also, knew that I had been working toward this moment most of my life. Well, I killed it, and I ended up playing the entire second set with the ensemble.

Afterwards, Wynton said, "Hey, the J-Master [Marcus Roberts] is coming to this club next week. We are going to tell him about you. Make sure you come and meet him."

So I did. Rinse and repeat, the crowd goes wild, and I report back to campus as a musical hero. Having gotten a taste of the big leagues, I practiced with more fervor than ever before. One weekend at the very end of a conversation with my mother regarding such things as coming home to do laundry and such, she said, "Oh, by the way, Marcus Roberts called? He wants you to join his band for rehearsals in Florida." I almost leapt through the phone. I could not believe what I was hearing. This was the equivalent of making the first-round jazz draft.

I flew to Tallahassee, Florida, where I met Marcus's first band: Nicholas Payton on trumpet, Herb Harris on tenor sax, Scotty Barnhart and Marcus Printup on trumpets, Brian Blade on drums and Chris Thomas on bass. Later the band would include cats such as Adonis Rose on drums and Roland Guerin on the bass. I went on to rehearse and tour with Marcus for the remainder of my undergraduate career—graduating with my BA in music performance, on time, in 1992.

As they say, the rest is history.

★ ★ ★

Mom's Compassion

Mom said she'd recently had a dream in which she reports that a person called in distress saying, "Ginger help, I'm suffocating," at which time she reports yelling back through the phone saying, "Well, save your breath!"

Certain nights when my mother felt the vibe was ripe, she would say, "Come on kids, let's take a walk around the neighborhood." Mom's hunches were, normally, spot on. Either someone was being arrested up the street, or there was a husband with his wife in the headlock or various other wrestling moves of the time. Or simply Po-Boy, the grown-up child of a man, masturbating toward the street at the front door of the little hut of a house he lived in. Po-Boy, turns out, went to school with my half uncle, Uncle Bubba. Charlie Neal's his name (my Granny Neal's last husband). She has outlived them both and is still talking shit about both of them; Leroy Leman Bush, my maternal grandfather, and Charlie Neal, Sr., father of my mom's half brother. So he went to school with Po- Boy. Word has it that Po-Boy got messed up in the war or something. You could depend on him standing there at any given time, dusk or otherwise, wagging his bird at the highway. It was a community tradition you might say.

You might say that this tradition of surprise explorations was a part of our family code. Well, the tradition would mellow for a season: One fine, summer dusk, Mom suggested that we walk to Granny's house since it was still light out. I was about 14 by now, and the walk there seemed to pass without notice. I have no memories of the walk there.

We made it to Granny's house in a short time. After all, she lived in GreenView and we in FarrowHills. One, the older black community with streets all named after biblical characters, and one the younger, married, black professionals and their children. The two communities blend without pause geographically, but the generational ramifications were as solid as a speed bump. Once there, we sat with Granny in the way we still do. Greenview Baptist Church sits right up the street from Granny Neal's house, on Isaac. She is mother usher and lives on Luke. The street that runs to the church from her home is Abraham St. She has to be able to get to the church in time to see it all. Believe me, she sees it all. Still does. Granny had been retired from the mental-health department of South Carolina for some time now, and the church had always been her life and was now more so than ever. As if in a news broadcast, we would sit and listen for at least one hour, all of Granny's latest church news:

"Yeah the reverend is seeing Mrs. Smiley on the side, and that boy of his wears jeans to church sitting there looking all high and stuff … Ron, you don't mess with none of them drugs, do you son?"

"No, Granny," I said.

"Good. That stuff's bad for you."

(Granny had been off cigarettes for about five years but still chewed snuff. She finally kicked that too, later, after seeing a hypnotist. Granny Neal was at once progressive and ancient. I love that.)

"And here come his wife with a fur on sitting there looking all pious, and the reverend standin' up there sweating like that. I asked him, "reverend are you all right, you seem to be stayin' in the office til right up to time to preach, and then you come out here sweatin' and stuff.'"

"Mrs. Neal, you ought to stop pickin' at me, you know I get caught up in the Word."

"I told him, 'You need to cool down.' Don't you know, we found liquor in his office cabinet? Yeeeah," she said in a low gravely voice like that of a nomadic monk. "And … we heard he got fired from his salesman job at the Stivers-Lincoln Mercury Dealership. Yeaaah!" she bellowed again. "He propositioned a woman customer and she sued the whole dealership and got a free car out of the deal. We gone get rid of him soon. Oh yeah! We think he on drugs too. He's preachin' man though, I tell you!" she said with confidence, shaking her head vigorously from side to side.

"Ron go get me one of them pies out the freezer. Not the ones on the left though, them's for the reverend's 5th anniversary at the church. We got the Zion Canaan Singers comin' and ev'rything!"

By the time this story was done, it was dark and time to head home. Granny offered to drive us home, but Mom and I were still feeling adventurous. "We just gone take it on in, Granny."

"Well, Ginyann"—that's short for Ginger Ann, short for Virginia Ann (Bush, my mother's maiden name)—"don't forget that pillow I stitched for you," Granny said. "Ron, run round there and grab that off the back porch for your momma son."

After retrieving the pillow were on our way out the front door. Leaving Granny Neal's was always a bit more elongated than it had to be. Granny seemed to always have one more thing to say or for you to do. But Mamma was the best at just leaving. After all, Mom had already escaped from Jennie Ree's (short for Jennie Ree Neal, long for Granny Neal … the one and only); and, the night was young …

By this time, it was quite dark, and we were heading home on foot. "Momma, Granny Neal sure is somethin' aint' she?" I said maturely.

"Hmm, you think you know, you don't even know who you dealin' with son." Ma said, matter of factly.

"I think I will wear my new Nikes to school tomorrow."

Continuing our walk back home, both Mom and I saw across the street the shadow of a burly man. Seconds later we both heard the huge shadowy figure say, "Heeey Baaaby," with a lust that spooked both of us. Mom said, "I'm not your baby," and we kept walking, assuming more of a trot. The encounter was weird, but we kept our cool. Home wasn't too far ahead now. About 20 yards beyond the foul remark, at the intersection of Easter Street and David St, the very linking point between Greenview and Farrow Hills, Ma and I noticed that the character from earlier had crossed the street and was coming up behind us at a noticeably faster pace.

Before we could react to the seemingly inevitable assault, in a sobbing, angry growl, the assailant bellowed, "AARWRUHHAHR!!! Bitch! I should have killed you when I had the chance!" Time stood still as we heard the deluded and plodding footsteps of our very real assailant closing in. Momma said, "Run, boy!" Then, with no regard to my fate, Mom disappeared into thin air, running faster than I had ever assumed was possible. We still laugh about it to this day.

She still reminds me that when it gets right down to it, she's gonna look out for Ginger. I understand that. After all, I had on numerous occasions, and at the inconvenience of many an adult party, proven how fast I was. And I had all the stitches to prove it. I had beaten James Jones at the 50-yard dash on field day when I was in the fourth grade. I was 14 now. However, for these and other unknown reasons, Mom left my ass in the dust!

We must have sprinted about four city blocks (that's about four or five front yards in the South). I could only sense the sound of my mother's flittering feet. And like a fleeing child-slave, I followed the rhythm instinctively. Seconds later, we ended up in one of the front yards—the parents of one of my sister's girlfriends, Carol Smith, as it turned out. Mom was in the hedges.

I rang out like a child, "MA?"

"Shut up, boy!" she said sharply but quietly (like Harriet Tubman calming a nervous comrade before having to shoot them dead).

Then, in complete silence, we soberly awaited the confrontation with the mad shadow of a man in the front yard of our neighbors. Many minutes passed, many thoughts passed and in some time we realized that we had, simply, outrun him. We finally made it to the side door of the house and rang the doorbell with utmost covertness. After a pregnant pause, and much to their bewilderment, Mr. and Mrs. Smith answered the door. "Yes?" they asked simultaneously. Momma whispered, "It's Mrs. Westray and Ron-Ron. Please let us in? We are being chased by someone."

Carol awoke and meandered into the kitchen. Then came Roger, Carol's younger brother. It was like waking up the Bear Family or something. They let us in and, at their kitchen table, in conference style, we explained to the Smiths in vivid and panting detail what had just occurred. They believed us, and Mr. Smith gave us a ride home after fully ensuring that we were in our right minds and that we were physically okay. The would've-been-wannabe-killer had failed at his, seemingly, first attempt. We never talked about that night with the Smiths again.

Chapter 20

I've been out of university for approximately three to four weeks after my sophomore year—in which time I've managed to total my car and get 11 stitches in my hand. My first band director, Al McClain, is so pissed at me. Now he doesn't think I'm serious. That hurts a little. I wouldn't say that this summer is getting off to a flourishing start. I was a little discouraged with these misfortunes taking place one after another, but I know that God has a greater plan ahead as my mother likes to say; and I believe he does. Therefore, I have decided to go ahead with plan A, which is to get myself in my thoughts, my music and just overall a quest for knowledge. I try to spend a minimum four hours on my trombone each day, on my quest to total proficiency. Some days I go almost five hours straight. I want to make history on the trombone.

My first priority is staying close to God; respecting my mother and making her happy comes next; and third is completing my degrees. I have a lot of respect for art; and I want acknowledgment. I must practice. End of session.

Back to the shed: People think I'm talented. I have a long way to go. I have chosen music, and I plan to be all that I can—at the least, a damned good trombonist. Because, after all, the greatest form of revenge is SUCCESS!

Appendix

The Lives and Deaths of Joe Westray and Ron Westray, Sr.

Joe Westray (June 1, 1913–July 9, 1980)

Joe Westray was a guitarist, bandleader, nightclub owner and president of the Local 471 musicians union for 10 years. A prominent figure in Pittsburgh's jazz scene, he owned and rented all kinds of residential and commercial properties—plus several trucks to handle a hauling contract with a big food chain warehouse. In his memoir *Dirt Street*, Hosea Taylor explains his time with Westray's band in 1946–47. He describes Joe as a very aggressive and forceful man who was somewhat affluent—a "wealthy businessman who probably was the first Negro bandleader in modern Pittsburgh to make it, money-wise."

Joe Westray was probably more entrepreneur than musician and a great model for other ambitious black men. Westray's band, "one of the three hottest Negro jazz and dance bands in the city of Pittsburgh at that time," was contrasted with Will Hitchcock's Big Dream Band and Walt Harper's group. In fact, Walt Harper credits Joe with teaching him many angles of the music business.

Westray was guitarist George Benson's longtime teacher. His most famous sidemen were Erroll Garner and Ahmad Jamal. At 14 years of age, saxophonist Stanley Turrentine joined Westray's band, playing gigs in the immediate region.

A graduate of Carnegie Institute of Technology (now Carnegie-Mellon University), Westray also played the Electra-harp, a kind of electric pedal steel guitar manufactured by Gibson. He was "a top arranger" who wrote a huge amount of work for singers and other artists—in addition to scoring for his own band. In 1962, upon retiring from active playing, Joe devoted more time and energy to business matters but took up the Hammond (B3/C3) Organ.

Westray Plaza was located on 913–917 Lincoln Avenue in East Liberty, in the Lincoln-Lemington-Belmar neighborhood—it was his most-remembered business venture, housing a skating rink and a dance hall.

At his July 12, 1980, memorial service at Shiloh Community Baptist Church, the pall bearers were prominent local musicians: LeRoy Brown, Nelson Harrison, Walt Harper, Honey Boy Minor, Thay Whiteley and Fred Pryor. It was a testimony of his significance to the Pittsburgh music community.

★ ★ ★

Pittsburgh's Hottest Spots

From left, Coleman Richardson on alto sax, William "Wimpy" Mosbey on trumpet, James "Honey Boy" Minor on drums, Joe Westray (behind Minor) on guitar, George "Ghost" Howell on bass and Erroll Garner on piano.

★ ★ ★

Ronald Kenneth Westray, Sr.

My father was born in Pittsburg, Pennsylvania, in 1944 to Vernal Barnette and Joseph Westray. He joined the military after high school (a time period that included issues of juvenile delinquency as well as doo-wop under the street posts).

Dad was based in Fort Jackson, South Carolina, while being trained as a military paramedic. Meanwhile, my mother, Virginia Ann Bush (who is from Columbia, the capitol), was attending Allen University in order to become a teacher. When dad came out of the army, he sought employment as an EMT in Columbia and also formed a band to continue singing, which was his real passion.

He was found dead when I was 5 years old. There was foul play suspected; but the case remains cold. I always felt that he was poisoned by some method, became disoriented and ended up in the pond where he was ultimately found. LSD was big during those years, and it would have taken only one "tab" in a drink to send him to his maker. Dad had also dabbled in local politics in the South and had made a statement regarding a local politician. He was found dead shortly after that.

I remember my father clearly. I remember his voice, him combing my hair as I cried and him dropping me off at kindergarten and swabbing the sides of my mouth with his thumb and his saliva. In fact, the first smells I remember is dad's coffee-laden saliva and that delicate blend of Pine-Sol and Clorox that greeted you at the entrance of V.V. Reid Kindergarten in Greenview.

I remember the comforting flavor of chocolate milk at lunchtime and the smell of what I now recognize as lemon verbena, emanating from the huge, freshly changed trash bag hanging out of a nearby canister. V.V. Reid was a clean place.

I also remember the sobering rhythm my classmates would sing to any underdog of the moment: *Ny-ny-neh boo-boo, stick-yo head in doo-doo.* (This sentiment still rings true when expecting or needing moral support from people.)

My babysitter was Mrs. Carrie Brown. She was a very old, black woman that looked like an even older white woman. Mrs. Brown had thick, gray hair that streamed all the way down her back when loose. She wore her hair in a bun most times, though. She was an evangelist. She had the heart of an angel and was the epitome of southern. She and Mom were real close, especially after Dad passed. Later on, when I was in college, Mrs. Brown was dying, and I had the pleasure of watching Mom wash her down, using a porcelain basin next to her bed (the method of her time). Mrs. Brown was still very present as she urged me to continue to do well and to pray and trust the Lord. Her hair was down that day. Mrs. Brown died during my next semester. The one thing that sticks out is the smell of those recycled jelly jars all the kids drank from: Though cleaned, they smelled like rain upon hitting the dry southern soil combined with an essence of Gerber baby food past. I remember Dad's "cover band" rehearsing at the house and Mom hosting the band members. I remember being backstage at local performances.

Dad and I took a trip to the naval base in North Carolina a few weeks before his demise. That's one of the last memories I have of him. I still have pictures of our trip that day. Needless to say, I grew up with everyone telling me what a handsome young man I was, and how much I resembled my father. The Westray men have very strong features. Some say I look more like Joe than I do my dad. Actually, I look like both of them because they look alike. I also look like my mother. That's because her father, Leroy Bush, looks a lot like my father. I once called this to my mother's attention. She had never considered it. I believe this is why Mom chose Dad, without even knowing it. After all, Leroy Bush died when Mom was only 3 years old. Mom remembers sitting on her father's lap on the porch and staring at him as he sang "Hey! Ba-Ba-Re-Bop" to her.

Neither my father nor grandfather lived to see me become a musician. I like to think that they already knew I was.

★ ★ ★

The Police Report

This police report became public information over a decade ago; one of my father's colleagues in the EMT field, Stuart Platt, forwarded it to me. You might say it was a life-changing revelation as the facts had only been articulated in bits and pieces by my mother through the years. Community rumors had haunted our family for decades about Dad's untimely and mysterious death, including that my mother had him "knocked off." It was consoling to finally read a technical report such as this. Dad's death is still a cold case.

SOUTH CAROLINA LAW ENFORCEMENT DIVISION

MARK SANFORD, Governor

REGINALD I. LLOYD, Director

April 17, 2008

To: Mark Goudelock

Lexington County EMS

From: Mary Perry

FOIA/Subpoena Compliance Coordinator

Re: SLED Case#: 76-264

Ronald Kenneth Westray

Please find enclosed the summary reports concerning SLED's investigation into the death of Mr. Ronald Westray, Sr. As of this date, the case remains unsolved. If you have any questions, or if I can be of service to you in the future, please do not hesitate to contact me.

SOUTH CAROLINA LAW ENFORCEMENT DIVISION

JAMES B. EDWARDS, Governor

J. Preston Strom, Chief

March 9, 1976

★ ★ ★

To: Chief J, P. Strom SLED CASE 11

From: Lieutenant C, Laney Talbert, Jr.

PLACE: Fairfield County

RE: Ronald Kenneth Westray

On February 21. 1976, an all points bulletin was sent statewide which reported Ronald Westray as missing. After receiving this report from Deputy Sheriff Taylor, which was made to the Richland County Sheriff's Department. Captain Laverne with the Richland County Sheriff's Office contacted Lieutenant Fender at SLED and Lieutenant Fender called me and told me to contact Captain Laverne at the Richland County Sheriff's Department, and he would give all of the details this car that was found in Fairfield County.

On the morning of February 23 1976, I went to the Richland County Department and talked with Captain Laverne. He informed me that Investigator Jack Hensell was assigned to this missing person case, and under the circumstances, they needed help with this case. Investigator Hensell and myself went to the home of Ronald Westray with his wife Virginia. Mrs. Westray was not at home at this time. Virginia Westray's mother, Mrs. Jennie Neal, told us that Ronald had acting very strangely in the last couple of weeks. She told us also that he had received the Holy Ghost in the Church of the Apostolic Faith of Jesus Christ. She said that on Friday night before he was reported missing on Saturday, she and Virginia had tried to reason with him, but he got upset and pushed both of them during the discussion that they were having.

Mrs. Neal said that Ronald had become involved with this religion to the point that he believed God was speaking directly to him and that he must follow God's word. She further said that Ronald was a supervisor at the Carolina Ambulance Service and taught classes in rescue all over the state.

★ ★ ★

Emergency Run

With no seat belt, I'm in the jump seat, siting high above the road in a vehicle with no hood in front and with the engine under the floorboard between Ron Westray and me. It's a little after 8 on a Saturday night. Ron is making a u-turn and wheeling the ambulance back across the Broad River Road Bridge back to where we just came from. I'm being bounced up and down and State photographer Ed Tilley is hanging on in the back of the ambulance to a wheeled stretcher that isn't tied down. Ron turns up a dirt and gravel road, spots a parked car with four people in it, and says, "we'd better ask directions" I roll down the window and call, "Can you please tell us how to get to Broad River Terrace?" Until it comes out of my mouth, I don't realize that this address has not registered with me. All that's been flashing in my head is that we're on our way to Signal 15—a gunshot wound! The boy in the back seat of the car seems to be passed out.

The two in the front seat can't agree on the directions, so we roll on, twisting winding streets in a subdivision and reading street signs that don't help until we see two teenaged girls. They gave us directions, Ron nods, another u-turn, back through winding streets and across the road and we're wheeling up to an apartment complex. Crowds of people and cars surrounded the other ambulance, which was already there. In at the front door where there is a bullet hole in the left surround window.

Tilley, with his cameras dripping from his neck says to a cop, "What happened here" Answer, "Shoot out at the OK Corral."

Officers are loading guns and talking in the room off to the right. I turn left and follow the blood on the floor, still bright red. The EMT and a doctor from the Richland Memorial Hospital emergency room have already started the I.V. J. S grins and wraps the victim's arm. Nurse Janet Chanson, holding the I.V. grimaces at me about the blood on her, otherwise, white pantsuit. A young cop with a peach fuzz mustache chases Tilley out.

On the stretcher, the middle-aged patient keeps repeating, "I want to give my billfold to my mother before we go." Bernard Simmons, the doctor, keeps telling him he has to keep it for identification purposes. It's finally settled when the guy gets his mother to take the money out and return the billfold to his pocket. The aged mother sits at a Formica kitchen table at the rear of the room, her hands, nervously, plucking at the pile of blood-soaked bath towels on the table, muttering, "He shouldn't ought to have done it."

EMTs wheel the stretcher towards the door, Janet keeping pace with the I.V. held aloft. I grab the emergency drug bag and stack it in the ambulance while the team of EMT's Robert Smith and Jim Cowan load the guy in the back. Ron drives us back to Richland Memorial Hospital as the backup unit. He's a nice-looking guy with a mustache and "five or six years with CAS. He's also an EMT instructor and says he does public relations for the company, as well. He talks about what great guys are in the Advanced Paramedic Training Course (the ones we are following that evening). "But we lost one of the really great ones to an industry because it pays a lot better. And a lot of guys were medics in the military come out and go north where the pay is better."

Ron spent two-and-a-half years, of his four years in the Army, in Vietnam. She said that when Ronald left home on Saturday, right after Wayne Vistal, Ron's employer, had arrived, Ron stated that he would be back in a few minutes and then never returned home. Investigator Hensell and myself interviewed MR. Wayne Vistal, Ronald Westray's employer. Mr. Vistal stated that, "Westray had been acting like was at the point of a nervous break down." Westray had become very religiously involved, stating that he had been chosen to do God's work and that he (Westray) could do no wrong, because God told him what to do and to try to baptize everybody on the job.

Mr Vistal stated that he was going to talk Westray about this situation Saturday at Westray's home. He also said that, usually, Westray was a very reliable person, very intelligent, and very industrious and had been teaching first aid and Emergency Medical Technician courses to all the rescue squads in the area and that he was active in the Midland Alcohol and Drug Rehabilitation Program and the MCAA (Midland Community Action Agency).

I also interview the secretary of the Midlands Concerned Citizens group, who is Mrs. Billie Joe Roberts. She informed me that Westray had come to her on her job and asked her to be the secretary for this Concerned Citizens group that he was founding. She quit her job as secretary to a medical equipment company and went to work for Ronald Westray. She set up the press conference when Ronald Westray got on television and blasted Dewey Duckett, the director of MCAA. Westray stated in this press conference on television that Mr. Duckett was lax in his method of operations and was not running the organization the way it should be run and that if they wanted Westray to run the operation that he would gladly volunteer for the job and that he would run it right.

On the morning of February 23rd, 1976, Westray's automobile was located abandoned in Fairfield County on Highway 215 near McCrory Liston High School (Liston Lane is where Ronald lived, BTW) and Salem Cross Roads.

I went to Fairfield county and met with Deputy Sheriff James Taylor at the abandoned automobile. This Oldsmobile had bucket seats (swivel type). The driver's seat was swiveled around, facing the door. From observing through the glass, there was a black Bible on the other front seat and some papers on the back floorboard. I called SLED headquarters and asked that one of the fingerprint technicians be sent to prices this car. Agent Ira Parnell came to the scene. We used a coat hanger to unlock the door. The entire automobile was dusted for fingerprints inside and outside with non-conclusive results. Westray's address book was found four feet from the car, opposite the left front wheel, by Chris Feaster, nine years old.

Keith Lewis, City Police and Fire Dispatcher in Winnsboro was at the SOC station on Highway 215. He said he saw Ronald Westray pass the SOC station on Saturday, Feb. 21st 1976 at approx. 3:15 pm, headed north. He said he waved to him but that he did not wave back. He told us that he knew Westray personally because Westray taught him in an Emergency Medical Technician course in Fairfield County. While headed north on 215, Odis Feaster and Willie Crompton saw Westray's Oldsmobile parked at about 4 pm on Sat. at a picnic area (the same general vicinity where this car was later found abandoned).

Deputy Sheriff James Taylor of the Fairfield County Sheriff's Department said that when he came by there late Sat. afternoon, he noticed the car at this picnic area.

He says he didn't pay particular attention to it. He also noticed it was still there on Sunday afternoon. When he saw the car was still there on Monday morning, he thought that he'd better check on it to try to find whom the owner is. This car is a 1974 black Oldsmobile Cutlass "S" with a gold stripe down the trunk with a white vinyl top, bearing S.C. 1976 license plate number LBT 351.

Deputy Sheriff Taylor and myself called Sheriff Montgomery on the County radio and asked him to come to this automobile. When Sheriff Montgomery arrived at the automobile, I told him I though it would be a good idea to get the Fairfield County Rescue squad and search the woods in the immediate area of the car. While we were waiting on the rescue squad to arrive, Carolina Ambulance Service had about six or seven men at this location. After all, Ronny was one of them. When the rescue squad got there, these men from Carolina Ambulance joined in with them and searched the woods, paying particular attention to the woods on the same side of the road where the car was found abandoned, producing nothing. Then it was decided to search the woods on the other side of the road, which produced nothing, at this time.

On Wednesday, Feb. 25th, 1976, Westray's wallet was found across the road from the car along the edge of the woods. His clothes were found about 50 yards into the woods from his wallet. These clothing items consisted of a pair of dark green pants, a green, flowered shirt, an undershirt, a pair of undershorts, a pair of socks, a pair of brown, low-cut dress boots, a pair of dark, rimmed glasses and a pair of gold metal, rimmed glasses. I photographed the wallet and the clothes and picked both the wallet and all the clothes up and put them in the trunk of my car.

About 100 yards from where his clothes were found was small pond, approximately a half acre in size. We got the Fairfield County Rescue Squad back in the scene. They drug the pond thoroughly, but recovered nothing.

The next morning, February 26, 1976, Chief Strom called me in his office and asked what I thought of calling the Columbia Fire Department Rescue team in on the case and let them search this pond, because they have much better search equipment than a volunteer rescue squad like Fairfield Rescue would have. I told him I thought this was a good idea.

As a result of this, the Columbia Fire Dept. Rescue squad was called in after I conferred with the Fairfield County Sheriff's Dept. on the matter. At 2:20 on Thursday afternoon, the Columbia Fire Department Rescue Team found Ronald Westray's body in the pond on the northeast side, about three feet from the shore in about six feet of water. Agent Ira Parnell came back to the scene. He and I both took photographs. The Columbia Fire Department put Westray's body in a vinyl bag, zipped it up and the Asst. Coroner Joe Silvia, who is of the Fairfield County Rescue Squad, was present along with other members of the Fairfield Squad when the rescue team from the Columbia Fire Dept. found the body. Asst. Coroner Silvia told me that he could handle the situation but would prefer to have the Coroner there as well. We contacted Coroner Pope, and he arrived on the scene at approx. 4 pm. Coroner Poe got in touch with McCutchen's funeral home in Winnsboro and had them to bring a hearse to the scene.

The body was placed in the hearse, and M. C. Williams, the driver, and Deputy Sheriff J. W. Brice of the Fairfield County Sheriff's Department left Fairfield County for the Medical University of South Carolina in Charleston, who had previously been alerted and was expecting the body in order that the autopsy might be performed. Dr. Brissey at the Medical University performed the autopsy on the body of Westray.

From the location of the car, the wallet, the clothes and the pond, which is almost in a straight line, it would give a person the idea that Westray was trying to leave a trail. Enclosed in this report are a copy of the Richland County Sheriff's Department offense report, the RCSD runaway and missing person's verification report, and a copy of the all points bulletin sent statewide, a copy of the pages of the address book that was found, a photograph of Westray, and the drawing of a map of the area that I drew showing the position of the car, the position of the wallet, the clothes, the pond, and the place in the pond where Westray's body was found.

March 9, 1976,

This case is still being investigated. Further progress reports will follow.

Respectfully submitted,

C. Laney Talbert, Jr. Lieutenant

SLED

* * *

To: Chief JP Strom

From: Lieutenant C. Laney Talbert, Jr.

RE: Ronald Westray (CHARACTER 13)

Lieutenant Sam Frierson was assigned to assist Lieutenant Laney Talbert and Agent McKinley Weaver on Thursday, March 11, 1976, in the case involving the death of Ronald K. Westray.

We met with James Venable, who is an investigator out the office of Jack Mcguinn, the Attorney representing the Westray family, on March 15 1976. Aspects of this case were discussed by the aforementioned.

On this date, statements were taken from Wayne Vestal and Henry Petit. Wayne Vestal is the manager of the Carolina Ambulance Service and Henry Petit is the assistant Manager of the same, the place where Ron Westray was employed. MR. Vestal stated that he met Ronald Westray in July of 1968 when Ron Westray applied for employment with the Carolina Ambulance Service.

Mr. Vestal stated that Ron Westray was hired and served as a shift manager and later as public relations and training director.

According to Mr. Vestal, Ron was a good worker and there was no unusual behavior on Ron Westray's part until Friday, February 13, 1976, when according to Mr. Vestal, Ron Westray came and told him that he, Westray, was going to hold a news conference about the problems at the Midlands Community Action Agency. The next unusual behavior noticed by Mr. Vestal was on Monday, Feb. 16 1976 at the news conference. Vestal stated that Ron was normally a soft-spoken, quiet person, but during the news conference, Ron Westray's voice was very high pitched and sounded radical. According to Vestal, it was during this time period that Ronald Westray responded to a call at the Blue Cross/Blue Shield office on Alpine Road at which time he encountered a patient who supposedly was having a seizure. Vestal stated that it was reported to him that Ron Westray stood in front of the patient saying, "I rebuke you, Satan, in the name of Jesus Christ."

Vestal stated that on Saturday, Feb. 21,1976, at approx. 1:46, Ron Westray's mother called the ambulance service and stated that she had talked with Ron over the phone and that Ron had hung up on her and she wanted someone to go out and do something about the incident. Mr. Vestal stated that when he received this information about Ron's unusual behavior he, in turn, called Virginia Westray to see if he could help. Vestal stated that he asked Virginia Westray if she thought it would do any good for him to come by and talk to Ron. She said yes. Vestal stated that he did go to Ron's house. Vestal stated that upon entering the house, Ron was siting in a chair next to a door and looked as if he was reading the Bible. Vestal stated that after exchanging cordialities, Ron stood up and stated that he had to go up the street to meet someone and he left. Vestal stated that in discussing Ron's behavior with Ginger Westray, she agreed that Ron had been working too hard.

Vestal further stated that he felt that he should give Ron two weeks vacation to see if this would help the problem. Vestal stated that he left word for Ron to call him. This was the last time he saw Ron Westray alive.

Henry A. Petit was interviewed by these investigators on March 15, 1976. He stated that he first met Ronald Westray in 1968 and that he starting noticing Ron's change in behavior at the time of the press conference Ron held concerning the Midlands Community Action Agency. Mr. Petit also stated, basically, the same as Mr. Vestal concerning the incident at the Blue Cross /Blue Shield bldg. Mr. Petit also stated that he continued to see the change in Ron's behavior.

Petit stated that he'd overheard a telephone conversation on Friday, Feb. 20, 2976, between Ron and his wife, Ginger, and that during the conversation there was a very unusual type of laughing. Mr. Petit also stated that he was familiar with the call that Ron Westray's mother had made to the ambulance service on Feb. 21, 1976. Petit stated that on Mon. Feb. 20, 1976 he received the news that Ron Westray's car had been found on Highway 215 in Fairfield county, and that he and Wayne Vestal drove up there. Petit corroborated that on Tuesday Carolina Ambulance offered their assistance to the Fairfield County Sheriff's Department in trying to locate Ronald Westray.

* * *

Virginia Westray, wife of Ronald Westray was interviewed, along with Vernal Barnette, mother of Ronald Westray, on March 16, 1976. They gave statements at this time concerning Ronald Westray's behavior prior to and on the day he left home, Feb. 21, 1976.

Virginia Westray's statement is so in depth and detailed that these agents are only able to highlight portions of it in the report:

- In her statement Virginia Westray tells of when she first met Ron and of Ron's "rededicating" of his life, his baptism.
- She explains Ron's involvement in the mannequin repair business.
- Mrs. Westray explained in her statement the night in December when Ron openly confessed his love for Diane Green at their house in front of Bennie Williams and Diane Green. She tells of an argument at this time in front of Bennie Williams.
- She tells about Ron's involvement in the MCAA controversy and about the ensuing change in behavior. She goes on to discuss Ron's constant persistence in trying to persuade her to "rededicate" her life and stated that Ron said that he was going to be "caught up in the twinkling of an eye" and that his time was near.
- She stated that on Saturday, Feb 21, 1976 the last day she saw Ron alive, Ron was up extremely early, 7 am, and that he was already dressed when she awoke.

That morning Ron said that he was going to help people and preach the word of God and if it was God's will, he would be back. That same morning, Ron said, "It's time and I am going to be caught up in the rapture." Ron left the house for the second time around 1 pm, around the same time Wayne Vestal came by that day.

- After Ron did not come home that night, Mrs. Westray went to the Sheriff's office and reported him missing. She notified Attorney Thomas Broadwater on the morning that Ron's car was found and she and Thomas Broadwater went to where the car was. Attorney Broadwater referred her to Attorney Jack McGuinn because she was not satisfied with the investigation. This is how she met James Venable, who is Jac McGuinn's private investigator.
- Mrs. Westray was upset and did not understand Ron's taking Beverly Fisher to the Slender Now meeting, upon investigator Venable's findings. She explained, however, that God had told him to take Beverly to the meeting.
- Virginia Westray said that Ron Westray told her on Feb. 16, 1976 that he had seen the kingdom of God in a ray of light. Virginia went on to state that from Feb. 16, 1976 until Feb. 21, 1976, Ron was a changed individual: irrational, insensitive, no appetite, unpredictable statements and a creepy laugh.
- Mrs. Barnette's statement reflects on a conversation that she had with Ron on Saturday, Feb. 21.

★ ★ ★

Interviewed on March 16, 1976 was Frank Northrup who was, at one time, a member of Ron Westray's band named Big Fun. Mr. Northrup explained that he had not seen Ronny since the early part of Feb. 1976.

Frank stated that he never saw Ron Westray take any hard drugs besides marijuana, but that Ron had smoked marijuana in the past. Northrup talked to people who stated that Ronny had been acting strange. But Northrup emphasized that Ronny could be hyper-acting sometimes, anyway. He did say, however, that he had seen a change in Ronny.

★ ★ ★

On March 17, 1976 these agents went to the scene where Ron Westray's body was found (a pond area located off of Highway 215 in Fairfield County in the Jenkinsville section). Accompanying these agents were Forensic personnel, Lieutenant M.N. Cate and Agent Ira Parnell. These investigators interviewed Don Johnson on March 18, 1976.

Johnson's statement reflected that he had known Ron for seven to eight years and had played in several of his bands. The names of the bands were as follows: The Sounds of Soul, Big Fun and Sound Track.

Ron stayed with the last band, Sound Track until he, "got religion," according to Mr. Johnson. Don Johnson went on to state that the Lord had told (Westray) to stop singing rhythm and blues and he was going to form an ensemble to sing spiritual music so that he could use his musical abilities to serve the lord.

According to Johnson, on Saturday, Feb. 21, 1976, Ron Westray came by the Richland Memorial Hospital where Johnson works and talked to him about getting baptized. Ron Westray told him that he (Johnson) needed the Holy Ghost in order to get to heaven and that we were living in the last days. Johnson told Westray that he had already been christened in a Methodist Church. Westray was insistent that he (Johnson) go with him. Westray told him that he (Westray) had to go get his daughter baptized that day, but that he could not find a preacher and had to baptize her himself.

He then told Johnson that he was moving a little too fast and that the Lord wanted him to slow down some. Johnson states that they talked a little longer and finally Westray left. Donald Johnson states that this was the last time he saw Westray.

* * *

Virginia Westray, Mrs. Barnette and Augustus Stone, half-brother of Ron Westray, were interviwed at SLED Headquarters on March 19, 1976.

These investigators played a recording for them of the telephone conversation between Mrs. Barnette and the dispatcher at the Carolina Ambulance Service that took plce on Saturday, Feb. 21, 1976. This recorded conversation was provided by Carolina Ambulance Service. In this conversation, Mrs. Barnette called from Pittsburg, Penn to the Carolina Ambulance Service in Columbia, SC.

The Recording reflected that she (Barnette) had received a call early that morning from Mrs. Neal (Virginia's mother). Mrs. Neal told her that Ronny was acting very strange and that she should call and talk with him.

Mrs. Barnette told the Carolina Dispatcher that she had, in fact, called and talked with Ron and that Ron told her that Jesus was coming and he was going back in rapture. Ron told her that no one could help him, and that he was going to be caught up into heaven in the twinkling of an eye. Mrs. Barnette requested some qualified person to go out and check on the situation.

* * *

These Agents accompanied by Agent Hugh Hunn and Lieutenant Tate, met wtth Dr. R. M.

Brissie, Assistant Medical Examiner, employed by the Medical University of South Carolina who conducted the autopsy on Ronald Westray. This meeting took place on March 22, 1976.

Also at this meeting was Dr. Edward H. Burn, Acting Superintendent at Crafts Farrow Department of Mental Health in Psychiatry, Chief of Professional Services and Chief of Court Services. These Agents furnished Dr. Burn with background information (according to persons interviewed concerning Ronald Westray's behavior prior to his disappearance).

After the discussion with Dr. Burn and Dr. Brissie, Dr. Burn indicated that he would forward a report based on the information furnished him by the investigating officers. Dr. Brissie was asked if the investigating Agents could collect Ronald Westray's clothing that was found in the woods Off of Highway 21 (which had been forwarded to the Medical University of South Carolina). He stated that the clothing (Westray's) had been destroyed as per policy initiated by Dr. Joel Sexton, Chief Medical Examiner, Department of Pathology, South Carolina Medical University. Dr. Brissie was asked to furnish these agents with a letter of explanation describing the policy as to why the clothing was disposed of.

At this meeting, Dr. Brissie furnished these agents with a copy of a report indicating the types of tests that were performed on Ronald Westray to determine the presence of LSD in the stomach contents of Ronald Westray. The report (which was provided by Dr. Brissie) is signed by Dr. Richard H. Gadsen (Professor of Biochemistry and Laboratory Medicine).

* * *

These agents then interviewed Diane Green, former girlfriend of Ronald Westray, on March 23, 1976. In her statement, Diane Greene stated that she met Ron back in 1974 and they started dating shortly thereafter. She explained that her relationship with Ron was very intimate. She, at one time, had been assisting Ron with his mannequin repair business. She admitted being present at Ron's home in December 1975, along with Virginia Westray and Bennie Williams when Ron Westray openly stated, in front of Virginia Westray that he had been having an affair with Diane. According to Diane Green, Ron said that he was trying to get everything out because of his change in religion.

After this December night, Ron Westray became more involved with religion and started acting very strange. She admitted seeing Ron three, or four, more times after that. Ron came to her house around 11 or 11:30 am on Feb. 21, 1976, and he did not seem very well. Ron appeared, to her, to be under the influence of drugs. His eyes appeared very heavy and weak. He asked her to meet him that evening at 6 at the Capital Cabana; however, she did not. She later learned that Ron's body had been found.

* * *

These agents accompanied SLED divers to the pond area on March 24, 1976 to search for physical evidence that might aid in the investigation. The diver's report reflects the conditions of the floor of the pond and also indicates that even an experienced swimmer would have had difficulty exiting the pond.

Also discussed was the temperature of the water. It was learned by the Agents from Chief Meteorologist at the Columbia Airport, that the high on February 21, 1976 was 80 degrees F., and that, usually, water is much less than this temperature. Agent James McClary, who participated in the diving, furnished the Agents with a cold-water exposure chart. This chart came out of the Diver's Navigation Manual by Jack E. Glatt.

★ ★ ★

Agents interviewed Mrs. Billie Joe Roberts on March 25 1976. Mrs. Roberts stated that she met Ronald Westray on Feb. 13, 1976 at her place of employment at Counts Rescue Equipment in Ballentine, South Carolina. Westray had come by to pick up some parts he needed from the company pertaining to the Carolina Ambulance Service.

Apparently, there was a discussion between Westray and Mrs. Roberts concerning the MCAA. Westray wanted to set up a press conference to discuss some improprieties at MCAA. Mrs. Roberts told Westray that she was familiar with the press and that she could arrange such a press conference. Mrs. Roberts' boss, David Counts, became upset with her for talking with Ron Westray on the phone so much that day. She attended the press conference that day on Feb. 16th, 1976. That was he last time she saw Ronald Westray. In talking with Mrs. Roberts, she described Westray as a humanitarian.

★ ★ ★

These Agents interviewed Beverly Fischer, a friend of Ron Westray's on March 25, 1976. Beverly Fischer was a secretary to Ron at Carolina Ambulance Service.

In her statement, Mrs. Fischer, indicated that on Saturday, Feb. 21, 1976, at approx. 11 or 11:30 Ron Westray came by her house and tried to force his religious beliefs on her. She said that she told Ron where she stood on religion and he quit. She said she never knew Ron to drink or smoke. She said that Ron did take her to a Slender Now meeting, which is a weight watcher's program and told her that the Lord told him to take her with him.

The "Slender Now" meeting was prior to Feb. 21. Beverly Fischer continued that when she heard that Ron was missing, she thought it was a religious conviction and that he may have been called by God.

★ ★ ★

These Agents interviewed Carl Edwards on March 25, 1976. He stated that he met Ron around 1963, when they were dating the same girl. Carl Edwards believed that Westray may have gotten the information the he (Edwards) had been employed with the Governor's office from Beverly Fischer. Ron Westray called to arrange a meeting with him. This call took place on or about Monday or Tuesday, Feb 16th or 17th. The call indicated that Ron Westray wanted to see the Governor. Edwards went by Carolina Ambulance Service to see Ron Westray. Westray told him of his new found religious convictions and that he (Westray) was concerned about the MCAA. Edwards told Westray that he should sit down and talk with Dewey Duckett, who, at the time, was the Chairman of the MCAA. Edwards never saw Westray after that.

* * *

These Agents interviewed Mr. HG. L. Roy Jones, Director of the Mid Carolina Council on Alcoholism on March 29, 1976. Mr. Jones knew Ron Westray through his work.

Mr. Jones told these Agents that Ron Westray was having some financial problems and he referred Westray to Mr. Warner Wells, Branch Manager of the First Citizen's Bank. He said he also referred him (Westray) to the Consumer Counseling Service in the United Way Bldg.

* * *

These agents interviewed Mr. Paul Nelson who works at the Carolina Ambulance Service on March 30, 1976. He was also a friend of Ronald Westray. Mr. Nelson stated that when he first started working for the CAS that Ron Westray trained him in the procedures of the Ambulance Service. He often talked with Ron about music and religion, but that the religious discussions were not in great depth.

According to Nelson, days before, he (Westray) started talking heavily about getting a job at the MCAA. During the week prior to Ron Westray's disappearance, Westray changed all of a sudden and seemed very reserved and worried. Westray told Nelson that he (Westray) had been moving too fast lately and he had better wait on the Lord because if he moved too fast the devil would get into him and take control.

Nelson remembered seeing Westray on the morning of Feb. 21st, 1976 and Ron seemed to be his old self again.

* * *

These Agents interviewed Donald Keith Lewis on March 1976, who had told officers, in the preliminary stages of this investigation, that he had seen Ronald on Feb. 21, 1976, on Highway 215 and he was driving his (Westray's) Oldsmobile. Lewis is a dispatcher for the Winnsboro Police Department and also a fireman. Lewis knew Westray because Westray taught him EMT at Fairfield Tech during Feb, March and Apr. of 1975. He had known Westray for about two years. Lewis used to be a Fairfield ambulance driver and used to see Westray often at Richland Memorial Hospital.

Lewis saw Westray on Saturday, Feb 21 on Highway 215 in front of the SOC station. Lewis and his wife were headed south towards Columbia and Ronny was headed north. According to Lewis, Westray was alone in the car. It was around 3:20 pm. When Lewis saw Westray, he was driving along at about 40 to 45 mph and he was slumped down in the seat.

Lewis remembers that Westray looked, while driving, at a black woman that was walking along the road. Lewis and his wife drove to Columbia and attended a movie.

About 10:30 pm Lewis and his wife drove back North on Highway 215. They both noticed Westray's Oldsmobile parked just below McCrory Liston High School, but just assumed he'd met someone and parked, perhaps. Lewis did not think anymore about it until Monday, Feb. 23rd, when he received a radio request from Sergeant James Taylor for a license check on the Oldsmobile. Lewis told Taylor he knew whom the car belonged to. Taylor told him to run the check anyway. He did, and it came back registered to Ronald Westray. Taylor asked Lewis to call and try to locate the owner.

Lewis knew that Westray worked for CAS, so he called the RCSD via radio. RCSD said the already had a missing person's report and asked him for his (Lewis) name. The name of Jim Cowan, who instructed a class along with Ronny at Fairfield Tech was obtained from Lewis, along with the following names: Marilyn Pierce, Judith Bouknight, and Raymond Louis Coad. Lewis, along with these other three persons, was in the class at Fairfield Tech taught by Ronny and Jim. It was learned that Marilyn Pierce, a white female, was friendly with either Westray or Cowan. Since there was hearsay information that Ronny was supposedly having and affair with a white woman from the Winnsboro area, these Agents thought it necessary to interview Mrs. Bouknight and Mrs. Pierce since they were the only white females enrolled in this class.

★ ★ ★

These Agents interviewed Warren Grant, a friend of Westray's who works for WOLO TV, on April 1, 1976. Warren Grant explained that he had lunch with Ronald Westray on Feb. 13, 1976, at the Elite Restaurant and that Ron wanted help setting up a press conference. Westray told him that he had some info that Dewey Duckett was not doing right by the black people or the white people at the MCAA.

Grant again saw Westray at Richardson Cleaners on Farrow Road and Westray told him that he (Westray) was going to hold another press conference (Westray had held one press conference prior to this day with the help of Billie Joe Roberts). Grant saw Westray on the 19th of Feb. 1976 and Westray was a changed individual. Grant did not believe that Westray drank alcohol, but he did "chain-smoke" cigarettes, somewhat.

Grant heard Westray mention that he had travelled to the Jenkinsville area a lot. Grant told these Agents that he did not see Ron Westray after Feb 19th, 1976.

★ ★ ★

These Agents interviewed James Harold Cowan, III, who is employed at the CAS, on April 1, 1976. Cowan told these writers that he assisted in the teaching of an emergency medical tech course at Fairfield Tech.

Cowan states that is was he who dated Marilyn Pierce and had taken her to a community fair at Fort Jackson. Mrs. Pierce is separated from her husband. Cowan knew Ronny played in a band, and that the band, on a number of occasions, played in the Jenkinsville area during the weekend.

★ ★ ★

It was learned from Agent Hugh Munn from SLED that a subject by the name of Mike Reeves who is the manager for The Modern Realty Company, and lives near Mr. Munn, might have some information pertaining to this investigation.

Mr. Reeves was interviewed on April 2, 1976, by Mr. Munn, at SLED headquarters. Mr. Reeves stated that he knew Mr. Westray pleasantly, but that they were not close friends. The last time Reeves saw Westray was two weeks prior to Westray's disappearance. They ran into each other at the Kmart in Dentsville and Westray had another man with him.

They had general conversation about Ron deciding not to play rock and roll anymore.

★ ★ ★

These Agents interviewed Marilyn Pierce on April 8, 1976, and she stated that she did not know Ron Westray well. She only knew him as an instructor and according to Mrs. Pierce, Ron Westray conducted himself in a business like manner. Mrs. Pierce did state that she had dated Jim Cowan and that they were very close friends. The last time Mrs. Pierce saw or heard from Ron was in May of 1975 at the completion of the EMT Course.

★ ★ ★

These Agents interviewed Phyllis Graham on April 8, 1976. Miss Graham stated that she first met Ron Westray in August of 1974. She dated him up until August of 1975 when she found out that he was married with children. She did not see Ron Westray again until Friday, Feb. 20, 1976 when he called her at work to talk to her about his religious change. During this conversation, Westray told her that he was not planning on going home that night because his wife had her gay, male colleagues at the home. She did not see or hear from Ron Westray again. She later learned that Ron Westray was missing.

★ ★ ★

Bennie Williams, one-time close friend of Westray's, was interviewed on April 6, 1976 by Lieutenant Talbert and made arrangements to meet with the investigating Agents on April 8, 1976. Bennie Williams was interviewed, at SLED headquarters, on April 8, 1976, by the investigating Agents.

Williams stated that he met Ron Westray while he was in a band named Sound Track. He knew Ron Westray for approx. one year up until his disappearance. Bennie Williams began playing in Sound Track with Ron Westray and they became close friends. Mr. Williams worked for a short time with Westray in Westray's Mannequin Repair business. He made a trip with Ronny to Pittsburg, Penn., to buy an organ from Ron's father (Joe Westray), to use in the band.

According to Williams, Ron Westray dated Diane Green, who, later worked with the mannequin repair business. In December 1975, Williams had the occasion to be in Ron Westray's home, along with Diane Greene and Virginia Westray, where Ron Westray openly confessed to having an affair with Diane Greene. Williams admitted that he and Virginia had an argument that night concerning Ron. The argument was about Virginia not understanding Ron's behavior.

Ron Westray appeared to Williams like salvation had hit him, and asked all of the people present (Diane Greene, Bennie Williams and Mrs. Westray) to get down on their knees and pray with him. Williams continues that Ron Westray had stated that he'd "seen the mountain-top," that he saw himself up in the robes, preaching the word and a chorus singing. Everytime he would ask Virginia a question she would say, "Buke the Devil, Buke the Devil, Ronny." Ron went to bed sometime later, but he and Diane stayed on at the Westrays until the early hours of the Morning.

A short time later, after that December night, he and Ron fell out. Williams believed that the reason for their fall out was Virginia. Sometime later, Williams was sitting on the corner by Washington Carver Village waiting on the bus when Ron drove up. Ron asked Bennie and several others to go to with him to the Town and Tourist Motel to a press conference about the MCAA and Dewey Duckett. Bennie Williams was the only one to accept the invitation. Williams told the Agents that the speech that Ron gave that day did not seem like his own words. After that day, Williams did not see Ron anymore. Bennie Williams admitted that he had smoked marijuana with Westray before, particularly on the drive back from Pittsburg. That was the only involvement with drugs that Williams knew Ron Westray had.

Your investigators have not discovered anything in the statements furnished by people or any physical evidence available at the time of this writing that would indicate a homicide. This inquiry is being placed on cold case status unless further evidence is develops or is discovered.

Respectfully submitted,

C. Laney Talbert, Jr. Lieutenant

Sam H. Frierson, JR. Lieutenant

McKinley Weaver, Agent

SLED

★ ★ ★

James B Edwards, Governor

April 18, 1977

Mrs. Virginia Ann Bush-Westray

445 Liston Lane

Columbia, South Carolina

Dear Mrs. Westray:

I am in receipt of your letter of April 15, and I want to let you know how sorry I am to know of its contents. I certainly want to apologize to you and your children for any part that the State may have played. I am reviewing the findings of the investigation in this case and would appreciate you calling my office so that I may discuss this with you. My deepest sympathy goes out to you and your children and I want you to know this. Your husband certainly exercised great courage and for that we can all be proud. I will look forward to seeing you personally.

With deepest sympathy,

James B. Edwards

JBE:sb (Governor, SC)

* * *

A few weeks after Dad's death, Mom presented us with a letter she'd composed while in the hospital recovering. At the end of the letter, Mom suggests to my sister and me how we might proceed along the "other pages" of Dad's future, unlived.

Your Daddy … Was a Good Man

March 30, 1976

To: V. Westray and Ronald Kenneth Westray, Jr.

From: Your Mommy, Virginia Westray—whom God has spared through this grace to be with you still … Daddy, he took (Daddy was prepared. We must prepare).

This is a memory capsule for the two of you. It does not and could not contain all of the eleven years your father and I were together. When you are older and I am older still than my present 32 years—then I shall talk with you further about your father, my husband. For today, let me deal with our now past.

Daddy was born in Pittsburgh, Pennsylvania, on Dec. 18, 1944. He attended the public schools there and upon graduation he left home for the U.S. Army. I met him while he was at Fort Jackson, SC, and I was at Allen University.

We met on his birthday in '64 while attending the Joe Simon show at a local nightclub. At this time, we both loved to dance. We met, we danced, we dated the remainder of December—all of January—all of February—and ... on March 13, 1965, we married.

We lived in a small, three-room apartment off of Farrow Road for only three months, because Daddy was sent to Korea for a thirteen-month tour. I moved back home awaiting his return. When Daddy returned, we moved into a small house I'd secured. I graduated from college and we lived at 117 Paul Street, in Greenview, for two years. In 1967, Monique was born, and we moved to 445 Liston Lane when Monique was only three months old.

Daddy, at this time, was employed by the American Red Cross Blood Center as a Blood Custodian. Soon, daddy became a bit tired of this job's stagnant routine and he applied for a job at Carolina Ambulance as an Emergency Medical Technician. He was highly prepared for this position, having been a medical corpsman during his military career. In 1968, Daddy's resume was accepted at C.A. (Carolina Ambulance). Later, he would rise from E.M.T. to Director of Public Relations and Training. This position he held diligently.

In 1970, Ronald K. Westray, Jr., was born. Daddy was very proud of a son, since we had already been blessed with a little girl.

Daddy worked always for perfection. He belonged to many organizations and his way of relaxing was through reading and song writing. Your daddy could really sing—I mean, he could "turn a club out" when he wanted to. He and his groups were very popular. The very last group he sang with was called The Ron Westray Ensemble. He left this band in Dec. of 1975 to rededicate his life to Jesus Christ. He lived only two months after making this decision. However, these two mos. were the highlight of your daddy's life ... a life soon to end. We all were unaware.

One example of his soaring spirit is reflected in a speech he gave on 2/16/76 (one week before he was last seen alive). He spent the week preceding his disappearance and death on T.V., on radio, and in his person always mindful to acknowledge God. The last cause your daddy fought for was the "cleaning up" of the Midlands Community Action Agency ... a cause which would, perhaps, contribute to the loss of his earthly life. When you read the speech, you must think as I am thinking—that he must have been destroyed for what they thought he knew and would tell. Your daddy seemed troubled to me from 2/16/76 [to] 2/21/76. He acted troubled. He prayed and he cried and he read his bible fervently.

On 2/21/76, your daddy—my husband—left home at about 1:30, telling us he would return shortly. He never returned. He was first missing for six horrible days, before his body was found in a pond off of Highway 215 in Jenkinsville. Your daddy was buried on March 11, 1976, which is Ash Wednesday. This was a meaningful coincidence, don't you think?

Soon, March 13, 1976, arrived. With Daddy buried only three days, it was a hard anniversary to bear.

The other pages now will be for the two of you to remember Daddy the way he was at the zoo & at Carowinds—just being Daddy with his two favorite people.

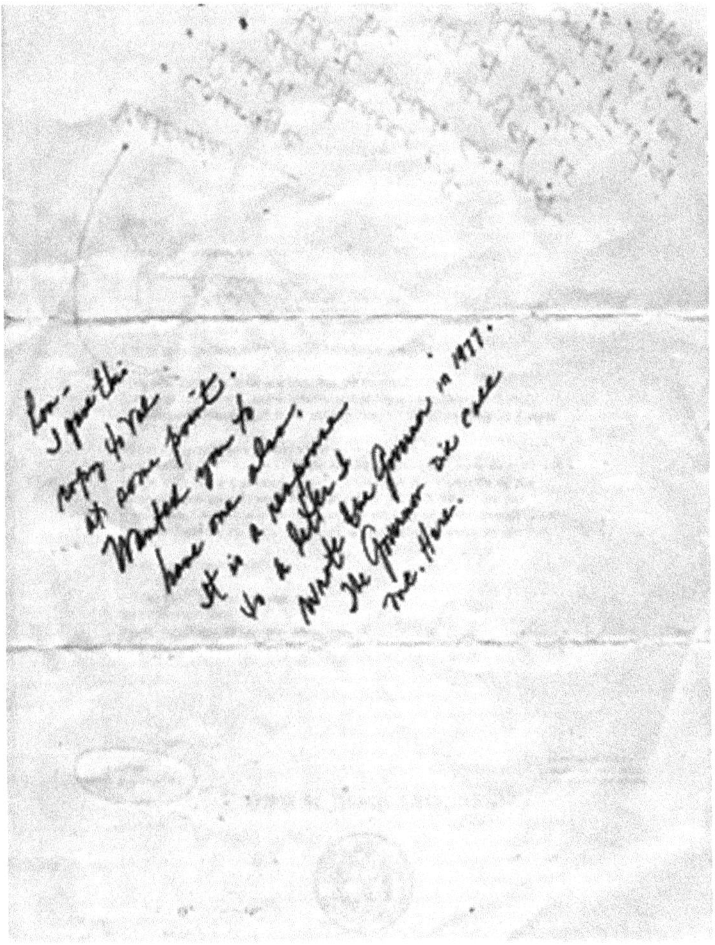
Lon—
I gave this
copy to Vel
at some point.
Wanted you to
have one also.
It is a response
to a letter I
wrote the Governor in 1977.
The Governor did call
me. Hone.

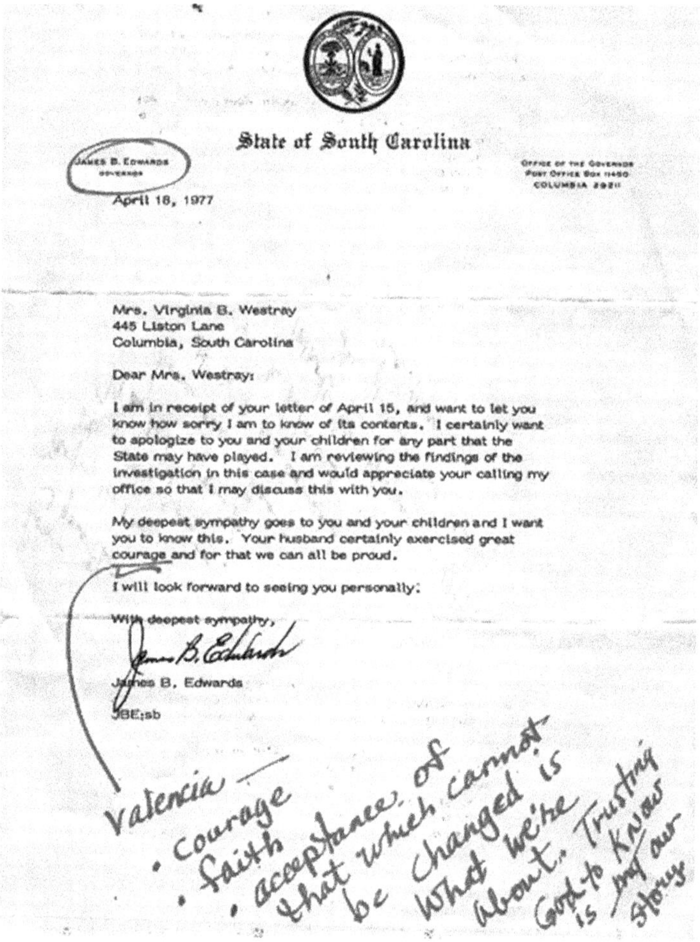

State of South Carolina

JAMES B. EDWARDS
GOVERNOR

OFFICE OF THE GOVERNOR
POST OFFICE BOX 11450
COLUMBIA 29211

April 18, 1977

Mrs. Virginia B. Westray
445 Liston Lane
Columbia, South Carolina

Dear Mrs. Westray:

I am in receipt of your letter of April 15, and want to let you know how sorry I am to know of its contents. I certainly want to apologize to you and your children for any part that the State may have played. I am reviewing the findings of the investigation in this case and would appreciate your calling my office so that I may discuss this with you.

My deepest sympathy goes to you and your children and I want you to know this. Your husband certainly exercised great courage and for that we can all be proud.

I will look forward to seeing you personally.

With deepest sympathy,

James B. Edwards

James B. Edwards

JBE:sb

Valencia
• courage
• faith
• acceptance of that which cannot be changed is what we're about. Trusting God to know is ~~my~~ our Story

Well, Dad was right. He was caught up in the blinking of an eye. I remember watching him get in the car that Saturday. I was 5½ years old.

Dad is buried here, the Gates of Heaven cemetery. It is located near where he was found. Dad and Mom are up ahead, to the left. The plot right next to Dad waited 42 years for Mom. We purchased it just days before her funeral in 2018.

My Dear Daughter in May 13, 2007
The Lord. May Our Heavenly Father
Yahweh Bless and keep you always in His care. I thank
you for the Nice package you
sent me some time ago. I am
late in writing to let you know
how much I appreciate everything
that is in that package Aspirin,
The Hair oil, the oil for the skin
well I thank Our Heavenly father for all
of the things that was in the Package.
May. Yahshua (Jesus) give you many
Blessings for your Kindness to me
and other older People. I will give
Thanks always for you In Yahshua
(Jesus) Name. I Know I am late
in sending you my Thanks.
But Better late than Never as the
Old Saying is (smile) Yahweh Bless
you always is my prayer
Hall Lee Yah! I love you
P.S. Augusta send a love to Mother Burnette
his wife Juanita also
Derrick and

Your Daddy
..... was a good man.

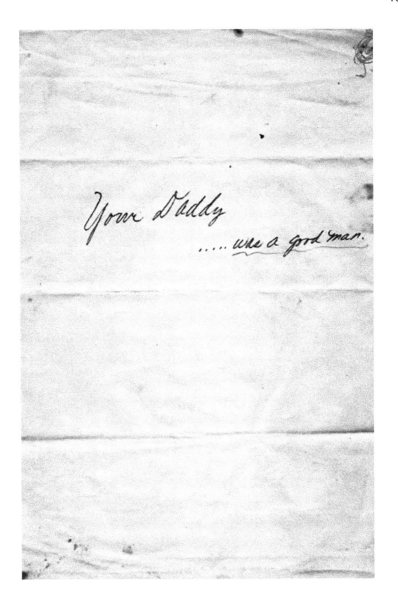

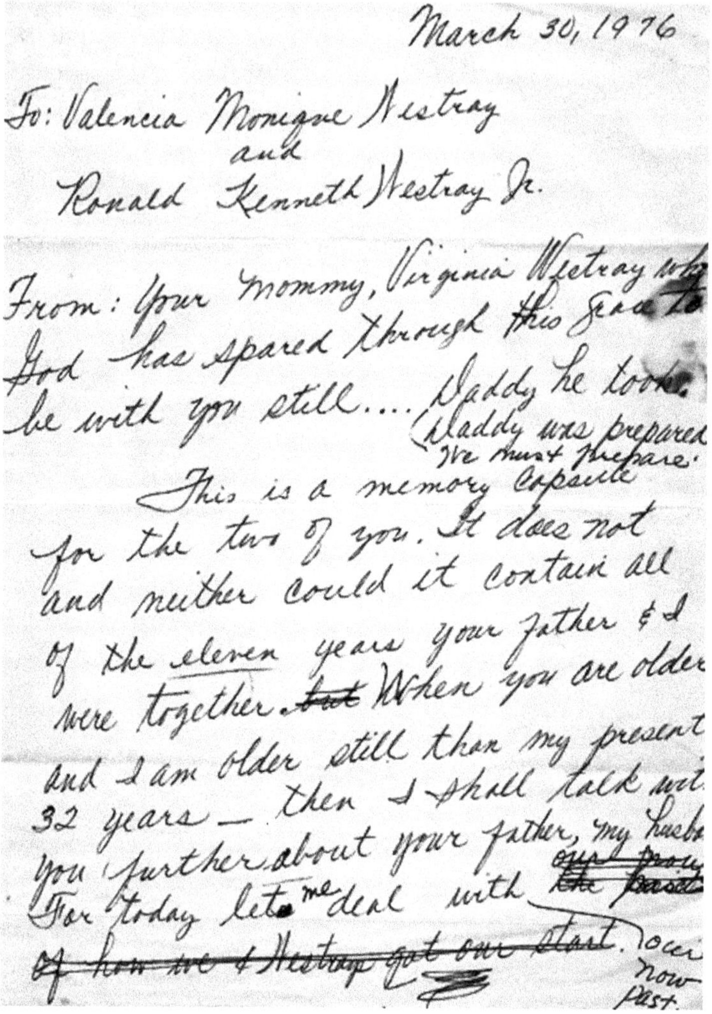

March 30, 1976

To: Valencia Monique Westray
and
Ronald Kenneth Westray Jr.

From: Your mommy, Virginia Westray who God has spared through his grace to be with you still.... Daddy he took. Daddy was prepared We must prepare.

This is a memory capsule for the two of you. It does not and neither could it contain all of the ~~eleven~~ years your father & I were together. ~~but~~ When you are older and I am older still than my present 32 years — then I shall talk with you further about your father, my husband. For today let me deal with ~~our prov~~ ~~the past~~ ~~of how we & Westray got our start~~. our now past.

Daddy was born in Pittsburgh Pennsylva
on Dec. 18, 1944. He attended the public
schools there and upon graduation he
left home for the U.S. Army. I met
him while he was at Fort Jackson S.C.
and I was at Allen University. We met on
his birthday 12/18/64 while attending the Jo
Simon Show at a local night Club. At the
time we both loved to dance. We met, we
danced, we dated the remainder of Decemb
all of January – all of February – and.... on
March 13, 1965 we were married. We lived
in a small 3 room apartment off of Fare
Road for only 3 months because daddy was
sent to Korea for a 13 months tour.
I moved back home awaiting his retu
When daddy returned... we moved in a small house I graduated from
college and we lived at 117 Paul Street

in Greenview for 2 years. In 1967 Monique
was born and we moved to 445 Liston
Lane when Monique was only 3 months old.
Daddy at this time was employed by th
American Red Cross Blood Center as a Blo
Custodian. Soon daddy became a bit tired of
this job's stagnant routine and he ap
for a job at Carolina Ambulance
Emergency Medical Technician. He was highl
prepared for this position having been
a medical corpsman during his militar
Career. In 1968 Daddys resume was accepted ~~went~~ to C.A.E. at Carolina Am ~~and he~~
Larry Lowery rose from ~~[illegible]~~ E.M.T. to Director of Public Relations
and Training. This position he held dilig
In 1970 Ronald L. Westray Jr. was born
Daddy was very proud of a son since w
had already been blessed with a little gir
Daddy worked always for perfections. He
belonged to many organizations and his way
of relaxing was through ~~his many band~~ reading and song writing

Your daddy could really sing... I mean he
could "turn a club out" when he wanted to.
He and his groups were very popular. The
very last group he sang with was called
The Ron Westray Ensemble. He left this
band in Dec. of 1975 to rededicate his
life to Jesus Christ. He lived only 2 mo
after making this decision. However, th
2 mos were the highlight of your dad
life..... A life soon to end. We all we
unaware. One example of his soaring
spirit is reflected in a speech he gave
on 2/16/76. (One week before he
was last seen alive. He spent the week
preceding his disappearance and death on T
on Radio, and in his person always mindful
to acknowledge God. The last cause your dad
fought for was the "cleaning up" of the
Midlands Community Action Agency..... a cause wh
would ~~h~~ & perhaps contribute to the loss of his

earthly life. When you read the speech, you must
think as I am thinking — that he must have been
destroyed for what they thought he knew and would
tell. Your daddy seemed troubled to me from
2/16/76 — 2/21/76. He acted troubled — He pray[illegible]
and he cried and he read his bible ferv[illegible]

On 2/21/76 your daddy — my husban[illegible]
left home at about 1:30 telling us he [illegible]
return shortly. He never returned. He was
first missing for 6 horrible days — before
his body was found in a pond off of
Highway 215 in Jenkinsville.

Your daddy was buried on March [illegible] 1976
which is a Jewish ASH WEDNESDAY Holiday for mourners. This
was a meaningful coincidence don't you think?
Soon March 13, 1976 arrived with daddy
buried on 3 days it was a hard Anniversar[illegible]
to bear. The other pages now will be for
the two of you to remember daddy the way
he was at the zoo at Carowinds. Just
being daddy with his two favorite peop[illegible]

Closing (Framework)

The *wagon-wheel effect* is an optical illusion in which a spoked wheel appears to rotate differently from its true rotation. *Stroboscopic* conditions ensure that the visibility of a rotating wheel is broken into a series of brief episodes in which its motion is either absent (in the case of movie cameras) or minimal (in the case of strobe-lights), interrupted by longer episodes of invisibility. It is customary to call the former episodes *frames*. The wheel can appear to rotate more slowly than the true rotation, it can appear stationary or it can appear to rotate in the opposite direction from the true rotation. This last form of the effect is sometimes called the reverse-rotation-effect. Continuous illumination allows for truer observation. In order to be understood, I have attempted to shed light on the many frames of my life and times.

CPSIA information can be obtained
at www.ICGtesting.com
Printed in the USA
LVHW020149300921
699079LV00007B/23/J

9 781839 980398